This Honorable Court

THIS HONORABLE COURT

A History of the United States Supreme Court

by

Leo Pfeffer

BEACON PRESS BOSTON

Library of Congress catalogue card number: 65-13536
Published simultaneously in Canada by Saunders of Toronto, Ltd.

Printed in the United States of America

TO

DR. MAX SCHAY

Contents

This Honorable Court

chapter one

A Most Ingenious Paradox

For as long as there have been public schools in the United States, countless numbers of children have been accustomed to start the school day by reciting a prayer or listening to a teacher or pupil read a few verses from the Bible. In thousands of schools all over the nation, when classes resumed after the summer recess of 1963, the school day began without recitation of a prayer or a reading from the Bible. Those public school principals who thought it appropriate to inform the children of the reason for the change, told them that in June the United States Supreme Court had declared that public school Bible reading and prayer recitation were unconstitutional and must be stopped.

In 1894, the Congress of the United States enacted, as it had done on previous occasions, an income tax law, and millions of Americans painfully but dutifully prepared income tax returns and mailed them in to the government with check enclosed. Suddenly, on May 21, 1895, all these Americans stopped mailing tax returns and checks to the government, not to resume this unpleasant duty for almost twenty years. The reason? On May 20, 1895, the Supreme Court had declared the income tax law unconstitutional.

Our Supreme Court is not quite a unique institution; a few countries (Australia, for example) have liked what it has been doing and have established similar Supreme Courts for themselves. But nowhere else can anything like it be found. If the Parliament of Great Britain were to enact a law imposing an income tax upon Englishmen or requiring teachers to lead their children in prayer, it is inconceivable that any court in Britain would dare to consider whether Parliament had the power to do what it did, much less to decide that it had no such power.

Nor do the publicized decisions handed down by the Supreme Court resemble the kind of decisions one would generally expect from a court of law. To the average American, a court is a forum that decides controversies between individuals, such as claims for damages arising out of an automobile accident or a suit to collect for goods sold and delivered, or criminal proceedings ranging from homicide to passing a red light. The Supreme Court, being principally a court of appeals, would not be expected to hear witnesses and hold jury trials. But like the appeal courts of the states, one would expect it to hear appeals from jury and other lower court trials and to reverse those decisions that it finds to have been erroneous.

The Supreme Court does not consider itself a tribunal whose purpose it is to correct the mistaken judgments of lower courts. It will not take an appeal simply because the lower court's decision may have been erroneous. To a disappointed litigant it may appear to be shocking that —as he is told by his lawyer—though the law is definitely on his side and the lower court made an egregious error of law in deciding against him, nevertheless he must pay money he really does not owe or may not receive money legally due him simply because the Supreme Court will not bother itself to right an obvious miscarriage of justice. Where a criminal case is involved the sense of shock will be even greater. The fact that an innocent man can go to jail or even to the death chamber is not of itself sufficient reason for the Supreme Court to accept an appeal. In the 1920's few non-lawyers could understand why the Supreme Court would not consider an appeal in the Sacco–Vanzetti case and permitted the execution of two persons who millions of Americans believed were innocent of the crime of which they were convicted. While the Sacco–Vanzetti case arose in a state (Massachusetts) court, it is equally true that the Supreme Court will not intervene in a federal case, whether civil or criminal, merely because the lower court may have decided the case wrongly.

This does not mean that a litigant in a federal lower court has no recourse if the judge decides a case incorrectly. In our American judicial system every litigant generally has at least one right of appeal. In the states he appeals either to an intermediate appellate court or directly to the state supreme court. In the federal system he appeals to the circuit court of appeals. But if any of these courts decides the case incorrectly, that fact is not of itself sufficient to invoke the jurisdiction of the United States Supreme Court.

The reason for this is a simple, practical one. One Supreme Court, consisting of nine men, could not possibly undertake to correct the errors that might be contained in the innumerable decisions of the numerous state supreme and federal circuit courts. There is just no practical alternative to allowing the decisions of these courts to stand in well over 95 per cent of the cases they handle. This is not nearly as bad as it may at first glance seem. There must be an end to litigation at some point, and even if the Supreme Court accepted every appeal brought before it, the loser in every case would be assured by his lawyer that the Supreme Court was wrong but that there simply was no higher tribunal to which an appeal could be taken.

Efforts are made to bring only a minute fraction of decided cases before the Supreme Court and of these the Court accepts only a small fraction to hear and decide. Unlike state supreme courts, the United States Supreme Court, for all practical purposes, is master of its own calendar; that is, it is not required to hear any appeal it does not wish to hear. The cases that the Court does agree to hear and decide are those of great public importance, cases which directly or indirectly affect large segments of the population. A decision that Congress may or may not enact an income tax or compulsory military service law, or that a state may or may not set up separate public school systems for whites and Negroes, or that prayers may not be recited in public schools, obviously affects millions of Americans. While not all or perhaps not even most of the Court's decisions affect so many persons directly, the Court will rarely take a case unless the principle at issue is of great public importance. The numerous Jehovah's Witnesses cases, for example, directly affected only a tiny religious sect; but the principles of freedom of religion and speech formulated in those decisions concerned the whole American nation.

The majority of Supreme Court decisions are not what are generally called constitutional law decisions. They are decisions in which the Court interprets the numerous laws Congress enacts in a variety of fields—tax laws, copyright laws, bankruptcy statutes, maritime laws, labor relations acts, and a host of similar enactments of Congress. These decisions are generally technical; they are rarely reported outside of trade journals or legal publications. Yet dull, specialized and technical as they may be, they are important to the American public generally.

Take one illustration. Every American adult male knows that it costs but one dollar to look sharp, feel sharp and be sharp, and for that same dollar you may also get not only a safety razor but six double-edged blades and a neat carrying case. This great luxury is purchasable at such a low price only because the patents on safety razors have expired and manufacturers are free to enter into the competitive market on equal terms. Before the patents expired, the price of a safety razor alone was generally not less than five dollars. There is nothing more dull, technical and completely non-understandable to the layman than a decision under the patent law, but millions of American consumers may be affected in their pocketbooks by how a particular patent law case is decided by the Supreme Court. (A patent is issued only for inventions or improvements that are "novel," i.e., original. When Fuller was Chief Justice, towards the end of the nineteenth century, the Court had to decide on the "novelty" of a patent for a triangular piece of cloth to be sewn in the crotch of men's underwear for reinforcement. "Not a man in the Court," the Chief Justice said, "but had seen his mother sew that kind of a patch in his drawers." Needless to say, the patent was thrown out, and commercially made reinforcements could thereafter be purchased at a considerably lower price.)

It is in hearing and deciding cases under federal statutes that the Supreme Court acts most like one would expect a court of law to act. The high courts of the states act that way and so too do the high courts of foreign countries. But decisions such as these are almost never reported on the front pages of the general press and do not often find their way even into the back pages. When the average American today thinks of the Supreme Court it is in terms of decisions outlawing racial segregation in the public schools or declaring unconstitutional gerrymandering in favor of rural over urban and suburban voters, just as his father in the 1930's thought of it in terms of decisions nullifying the NRA and other legislative efforts of the New Deal, his grandfather in the 1890's in terms of decisions outlawing federal income tax laws, and his great-grandfather in the ante-bellum days in terms of the Dred Scott decision.

These are the Court's constitutional law decisions. They are the most dramatic of the Court's actions, the ones in which it invokes the superior authority of the Constitution to check action by Congress, the President or the states. The uniqueness of the Supreme Court as a judicial tribunal is to be found in these decisions, and lies in the fact that in other countries (except the few that emulate us) decisions such as these are not made by the judicial arm but by the political arms of the government. In other countries it is the cabinet and the parliament, not the courts, that decide with finality questions regarding election districts or the rights and burdens of political dissenters or racial and religious minorities. In the United States, on the other hand, as early as 1832, de Tocqueville noted that practically every political question sooner or later becomes a judicial question.

The truth of the matter is that when the Supreme Court decides constitutional questions such as these it is not really a court of law at all, at least not in the usually accepted sense. It uses all the forms and trappings of a court of law and on the surface its decisions look like those usually handed down by conventional law courts. But if form is brushed aside and a square look is taken at the reality of the situation, the conclusion is inescapable that in these cases the Court acts not as a judicial but as a political organ of government. In short, it is supreme, but it is not really a court.

Generally it is assumed that when, after considerable debate, both houses of the federal or a state legislature pass a measure and the President or the governor signs it, the debate is over and we have a law. But, in reality, the legislative process is not at an end and the debate is not over. It may, and frequently does, simply shift to another building. From the legislative chambers the proposal went to the White House or the Executive Mansion of the governor. Now it comes to the marble palace occupied by the Supreme Court. It is only after a majority of the Court agrees that there ought to be a law that it can be said with reasonable finality that there is one. If the first two decisions, by the legislative and the executive, that there ought to be a law are political decisions—and who would deny that they are?—is it unfair to say that the third is likewise political? What is there to distinguish the first two steps from the third? (Before 1937 the Court's power to declare laws unconstitutional was generally exercised only in cases affecting business or property interests, and rarely in those involving civil or personal rights. Since 1937 the converse has been true, but the question is the same in both types of cases.)

The conventional answer is that only the Court passes on the constitutionality of a law. But the members of the legislatures, federal and state, and the President and the governors, no less than the members of the Supreme Court, all take an oath to support the Constitution. Unless we are prepared to charge them with deliberately violating their solemn oaths, we must assume that before voting for the measure or signing it they had considered its constitutionality and had in good faith reached the conclusion that it was constitutional. How is that different from what the Supreme Court does?

Another conventional answer is that the legislature and the executive are concerned with the measure's wisdom whereas the Court is concerned only with its constitutionality. But the difference between constitutionality and unconstitutionality is a difference in degree, just as is the difference between wisdom and unwisdom. An unwise law may not for that reason alone be unconstitutional, but a very unwise law is. Unreasonable or arbitrary laws, the judges say, are unconstitutional; but "unreasonable" and "arbitrary" are simply legalistic jargon for very unwise, and what to a majority of the Court may be very unwise may be profoundly sagacious to a majority of Congress or of a state legislature. There is nothing wise or unwise but a majority vote makes it so.

True, a legislator, federal or state, will vote against a bill and the President or governor will veto it if he thinks it unwise, while a member of the Supreme Court will vote against it only if he thinks it very unwise, or very, very unwise. But a member of Congress has only a one five-hundred-and-thirty-fifth negative vote, while a member of the Court has a one-ninth negative vote, so it is not unreasonable that a more stringent standard should be in operation when the member of the Court casts his negative vote. The President does have a 100 per cent negative vote; but his exercise of it can be overruled by two-thirds of Congress, while the negative vote of the Court majority can be overruled, at least theoretically, only by the slow, tortuous and rare process of constitutional amendment.

If one could examine the consequences of the Supreme Court constitutional law decisions divorced from the rather cumbersome judicial machinery that grinds out the decisions, the conclusion appears inescapable that these decisions are part of a single political-legislative process along with the decisions of the legislatures and of the executives. To the non-lawyer there would appear to be little difference whether the required judicial approval of an act of the legislature is considered an independent step or the third step in a three-step process, the first two of which are the enactment by the legislature and approval by the President or governor.

Aside from their practical consequences, evidence of the political nature of Supreme Court decisions with a constitutional background can be found in the style and language of the decisions themselves. The average opinion of a state court in a commercial or property law case is written with a legalistic style that repels the non-lawyer, to whom it is generally completely unintelligible, as it often is to a lawyer who does not specialize in the field of law involved in the case. The Supreme Court's constitutional law opinions, on the other hand, are quite readable and understandable to the layman. They read like political essays rather than legal documents. They are often reprinted in whole or substantial part in the New York *Times* and there is hardly a book of readings in political science used in college which does not contain large portions of such opinions.

Two decisions, both highly controversial, will suffice to illustrate this point. In 1951, in the case of *Dennis* v. *United States,* the Court upheld the conviction under the Smith Act of the top leaders of the Communist party in the United States. Justice Clark, who had been Attorney-General when the prosecution was begun, disqualified himself. The remaining eight judges voted six to two that the Smith Act was constitutional but they needed five separate opinions to state their views. This itself is an indication that the Court's constitutional law decisions are in a class different from the conventional decisions of a court of law. Almost never in a case involving commercial law or real property does one find such fragmentation of reasoning among the judges.

The difference is even more clearly indicated by the substance of the five opinions. Of those in support of the convictions, Jackson's may be taken as illustrative. To him the Communist party was not to be equated with the traditional American radical parties for whose protection the freedom of speech guarantee was placed in the Bill of Rights. The Communist party, he said, is realistically a state within a state, an authoritarian dictatorship within a republic. It demands constitutional freedoms for itself but not for its members, to whom it simultaneously denies freedom to dissent, to debate and to deviate from the party line. Therefore, he said, traditional guarantees of freedom of speech and of association are not applicable and do not prevent prosecution of the leaders for unlawful conspiracy, as "there is no constitutional right to 'gang up' on the Government."

Justice Douglas' opinion is illustrative of the reasoning of the dissenting Justices. (The other was Black.) To Douglas there was no authority given by the Constitution to distinguish among different types of unorthodox movements and political heresies; the guarantees of freedom of speech and of association protect them all equally. Only if there is a clear and present danger that the government will be overthrown unless preventative action is taken may these freedoms be impaired. As for that, while "Communism on the world scene is no bogeyman, Communism as a political faction or party in this country plainly is." Douglas expressed doubt "that there is a village, let alone a city or county or state which the Communists could carry."

The second decision was the 1954 case of *Brown* v. *Board of Education*, in which the Court, this time unanimously, overruled an 1896 decision and held that compulsory racial segregation in the public schools is unconstitutional. The reason was that the Fourteenth Amendment requires the states to treat all persons equally, and segregation by law has a detrimental psychological and educational affect on Negro children by creating in them a sense of inferiority which affects their motivation to learn and retards their educational and mental development.

For our purpose it is not material whether Jackson or Douglas was right, or perhaps more right, in respect to the threat of American Communism to our republic, or whether the 1896 or the 1954 Court correctly evaluated the effects of racial segregation. My point is that judgments such as these are not the type that the conventional court of law is called upon to make. Realistically they are not legal judgments but political or political-sociological judgments. When the Supreme Court makes judgments such as these it is not simply deciding a controversy between the two litigants before it but it is shaping the nature of American political, moral, economic and cultural patterns in a radically different way than the ordinary court does when it decides a question of business or property law. In a realistic sense the Supreme Court is legislating or at least participating in the legislative process.

THE COURT AS LEGISLATOR

Strange as it is for a court of law to engage in acts of legislation, even stranger is the way in which it engages in these legislative acts. Until some fifty years ago, it used exclusively judicial instruments; more recently it has availed itself also, although still secondarily, of legislative instruments. When a court is faced with a question of law it ordinarily seeks the answer to it in earlier decisions in which the same or an analogous question was presented. Unless the legislature has intervened to abrogate or modify the decision in the earlier cases, the court will generally give the same answer as was given before. The layman calls this following precedent; to the judge or lawyer it is also known as *stare decisis*. One of the criticisms leveled against the Supreme Court in recent years is that it has too often disregarded precedent. Even if this criticism is valid, *stare decisis* is still the principal instrument employed in deciding constitutional as well as non-constitutional cases. True enough, earlier precedents are overruled by the Supreme Court in constitutional cases more often than they are overruled by it and other courts in non-constitutional cases. Yet even in constitutional cases, following precedent is the rule and overruling it the exception. And when the Court does overrule precedent, it usually recognizes an obligation to justify its action in its opinion.

Legislation's approach is diametrically opposed to that of judicial action and *stare decisis*. The theory of judicial action is that the court does not make law but simply announces what the law is; legislation, of course, makes law. The rationale of *stare decisis* is that the status quo is good and should be continued. The rationale of legislation is that a change is needed; if the quo is to remain in status what is called for is legislative inaction.

The legislature engages in the legislative process by enacting laws, the Court by vetoing (i.e., declaring unconstitutional) and interpreting them. The former method is the more dramatic and has led the Court into most of its public controversies. In recent years the Court has perhaps more often employed interpretation. This is an ancient tool used by courts ever since legislatures began to take part in the making of laws. Theoretically, when a court interprets a statute it seeks to find out what the legislature intended when it enacted the statute, and when the court finds the intent it applies it to the controversy before it. But in most cases the legislature had never contemplated the particular problem before the court and therefore never had any intent with respect to it. In such a case, what the court really does is to try to decide what the legislators would have intended if they had thought about the problem.

In major political, economic and social Supreme Court cases, the power to interpret the acts of Congress can be an extremely effective instrument, almost as effective as vetoing a law by declaring it unconstitutional. In 1951 the Court upheld the conviction of the top echelon of American Communists for violation of the Smith Act. Six years later, in *Yates* v. *United States,* it set aside the conviction of lower echelon Communists for violating the same act. The act had not been repealed or modified by Congress in the interim, and the Court did not declare it unconstitutional in 1957. The Court simply interpreted it in such a way as to require reversal of the convictions.

Even more significant, perhaps, is the decision in *Pennsylvania* v. *Nelson.* Here the Court interpreted the Smith Act and the Internal Security Act as indicating an intent on the part of Congress to preempt the entire field of anti-subversion legislation and prohibit state legislatures from enacting little Smith Acts and little Internal Security Acts for their particular states. One can read the debates in Congress that attended the enactment of these laws with the utmost care without finding in them an expressed or even clearly implied intent on the part of Congress to prohibit the states from enacting anti-subversion laws. The Smith Act had been passed in 1940; the Internal Security Act in 1950. In both years fear and hatred of Communism were at peak levels in the United States. It is a fair guess that if on either occasion the question had been squarely put to Congress, very few of its members would have consented to the proposition that by enacting the law they were barring the states from adopting similar laws. What in fact the Court did in the Nelson case was itself to enact a law, which it read into the federal laws, that the states may not enact statutes seeking to punish or prevent subversion against the federal government. (The fact that in the Nelson case the Supreme Court of Pennsylvania had come to the same conclusion does not affect this conclusion.)

As a practical matter it often makes little difference whether the Supreme Court declares a particular law unconstitutional or interprets it in such a way as to deprive it of its vital force. Of course, in the case of invalidation for unconstitutionality, the only way to overcome the decision is the slow and difficult process of amending the Constitution; whereas an interpretation not desired by Congress can be vitiated by enacting a law in which the contrary intent of Congress is clearly stated. Yet the force of legislative inertia is so potent and the power of even minority legislators to block enactment of laws so strong that even

Court interpretations disliked by the majority of Congress are not easily dislodged. In any event, the fact that Congress can override a particular Court interpretation does not negate the Court's participation in the legislative process any more than the power of Congress to override a Presidential veto negates the President's participation in the legislative process.

THE COURT AND CONTROVERSY

Early in April of 1952, after lengthy but futile negotiations between the United Steelworkers of America and the steel industry, the union announced that it would go out on strike within five days, thus shutting down every major steel plant in the country. At that time the United States was engaged in the small but bitter Korean conflict and President Truman believed that a steel shutdown would seriously impair our nation's efforts in the conflict and jeopardize national defense. Accordingly, on April 8th, a few hours before the strike was to begin, Truman issued an order "seizing" the mills, that is, directing Secretary of Commerce Sawyer to take possession of and operate the mills. Sawyer immediately issued an order declaring himself in control of the mills throughout the country and appointing the presidents of the various companies to be his managers and to continue operating the mills as theretofore, but now as agents for the government rather than for the stockholders.

The steelworker who clocked in on the morning of April 9th could detect no difference; everything was as it had been. The only indication of a change was a notice posted in the plant that the mill was now in the possession of the federal government. If the worker did not observe the notice and had not read the morning paper he would not have had the slightest idea that there had been any change. Nevertheless, the union was satisfied and called off the strike. The barons of the industry, however, were not, and went into court to get an injunction against Secretary of Commerce Sawyer. By a vote of six to three, the Supreme Court ruled that Truman had no right to seize the mills and ordered Sawyer to get out. Harry Truman, one of the fightingest of Presidents, meekly accepted the decision, and the mills went back to the stockholders.

In 1954 the Supreme Court handed down a decision declaring racial segregation in the public schools unconstitutional. In this short decision the Court sounded the death knell for patterns of culture and life to which the South was passionately committed. On what many in the South were to call "black Monday" in May of 1954, nine men in black robes declared that black equals white and, even more remarkably, imposed by law a social revolution upon a great portion of the country.

The details of this event must be left for a later chapter. What is relevant here is that the decision brought down upon the Court a torrent of abuse and criticism from almost all the political leaders of the South. Senator James O. Eastland of Mississippi denounced the Court as "the greatest single threat to our Constitution." The General Assembly of Georgia adopted a resolution demanding the impeachment of the members of the Court who had participated in the racial segregation decision, on the ground, among others, that they sought "by judicial decrees to carry out communist policies." On a somewhat more dignified level some nineteen senators and seventy-seven representatives, all from the South, joined in a "Declaration of Principles," strongly condemning the decision and almost as strongly the Court that announced it.

Beginning in 1955 the Court handed down a number of decisions which, according to many within and without Congress, seriously hampered, if they did not completely frustrate, the efforts of the government to protect the nation from internal subversion. One decision effectively curbed the previously almost unlimited power of Congressional investigating committees to jail uncooperative witnesses. Another emasculated the Smith Act under which the leading American Communists had been sent to the federal penitentiary. A third denied to the army the right to grant less than honorable discharges to persons whose pre-induction statements and associations were suspect. Others placed substantial obstacles in the way of the government's efforts to remove suspected subversives from the civil service, deny them passports to travel abroad, obtain their criminal conviction without opening up confidential FBI files for inspection by their lawyers, or deport them for their membership in the Communist party.

Here again the details of these cases must be left for later in this volume. Here it is enough for our purpose to note that these decisions aroused against the Court the ire of the most vigorous and articulate anti-Communists in Congress, particularly Senator Eastland and Congressman Frances E. Walter, chairmen of the Senate and the House committees concerned with internal security.

Nor did the Court content itself with impeding the federal government's war on internal subversion; it was no less diligent in restraining the states' individual crusades against Communism. Among the decisions handed down during the second half of the 1950-1960 decade were those which refused to allow the states to deny an ex-Communist a license to practice law, restricted their power to remove "Fifth Amendment Communists" from state civil service, hampered their efforts to withhold tax exemption benefits from suspected subversives, curbed the activities of their legislative investigating committees, and, perhaps most serious, denied to the states the power to enact laws punishing subversion against the United States. It need hardly be remarked that these decisions too brought upon the Court the wrath of militant defenders of Americanism. The most restrained and dignified, and for that reason perhaps the most devastating, condemnation visited upon the Court was a resolution signed by thirty-six of the chief judges of the state supreme courts deploring what they considered an unjustifiable disregard of states' rights by the United States Supreme Court.

In March, 1962 the Court, in a decision (*Baker* v. *Carr*) likely to prove perhaps as historic as the Brown decision, ruled that legislative malapportionment, under which rural areas in the states have disproportionate power in both state legislatures and in the Congress, would be declared unconstitutional. The effect of this decision is almost certain to increase the importance of the urban vote compared to the rural vote.

In June of 1962, the Court ruled that public schools could not constitutionally open their sessions with the recitation of a prayer.

Thus, in a period of ten years the Court told the President that he could not seize the steel mills, though he deemed the seizure necessary for national defense, Congress that it could not do what it considered essential to protect the nation from subversion, the southern states that they could not enforce the laws they enacted to preserve their customs and way of life, the northern states that they could not take the measures which to them were necessary to meet the threat of domestic Communism, the farmers that their political power would be drastically curtailed, and the public schools that they could not pray.

It should surprise no one that decisions such as these caused considerable discontent in influential circles, nor that bills were introduced in Congress aimed at curbing the Supreme Court. In 1958, for example, a host of such measures were introduced. One bill would have simply deprived the Court of power to reverse decisions in cases involving Congressional committees, the federal loyalty program, state anti-subversion statutes, and other actions by states in the field of anti-subversion, including refusal to admit a suspected subversive to the bar. Another would have removed the binding effect on state and lower federal courts of Supreme Court decisions which ignore legal precedent and are based on "considerations other than legal." (In the Brown case the Court cited writings of social scientists on the harmful effects of segregation.)

Other bills proposed less devious means to meet the danger of decisions that disregarded precedent and were based on considerations other than legal. Early in February, 1959 a group of about two dozen men and women, representing the "Christian Nationalist Crusade," entered the office of the clerk of the House of Representatives in Washington and left a petition, said to be fifteen hundred feet long, which was headed "Impeach Warren." The petition, carrying names from all over the nation, read:

> Whereas certain members of the Supreme Court of the United States, have, in our opinion, violated their oath by substituting legislation decisions [sic] for legal precedent, and whereas their decisions, if enforced, will tend to destroy law enforcement agencies, Congressional investigation of treason and subversion, and whereas their unprecedented and unconstitutional decisions are designed to destroy the sovereignty of the several states, we the undersigned respectfully petition the Congress of the United States to begin impeachment proceedings.

Although this proposal was echoed in the early 1960's by Robert Welch and his John Birch Society, this later effort, too, came to naught. (One passionate Birchite felt that impeachment was too lenient a punishment for so heinous a traitor and suggested that Warren ought to be shot.) Other unsuccessful bills introduced into Congress during the same period include one that sought to amend the Constitution to require previous service upon some court as prerequisite to appointment to the Supreme Court (Warren had no previous judicial experience before he became Chief Justice) or to require the President to consult the American Bar Association before making an appointment. Other measures would have limited the term of Supreme Court Justices to twelve, ten and even four years, and still others would have allowed Congress or even only the Senate to overrule decisions by the Supreme Court.

These and a score of similar measures evidenced a widespread dissatisfaction with the Court and its decisions. But it would be a mistake to assume that this dissatisfaction was a temporary or unprecedented consequence of the segregation and civil liberties decisions of the Warren Court. Actually it represented a chronic condition. Almost from its birth, the Court has been the subject of continuing criticism and of demands for limitations on its jurisdiction and powers. For example, the decade of 1820-1830—by no means the stormiest in the Court's history—saw the introduction of a multitude of proposals aimed at curbing the Court and curtailing its powers. Jefferson proposed that the tenure of the Justices be limited to six years. Senator Richard Johnson of Kentucky introduced a resolution to allow the Senate to overrule Supreme Court decisions in constitutional cases. Another proposal would have declared that the Court had no power to pass on the constitutionality of acts of Congress, while another would have permitted the Court to exercise the power but only by vote of five of the seven judges. Finally, one would have "packed" the Court by providing for three additional judges. Every decade, before and after the 1820's, saw serious consideration given to these and similar proposals.

All this is to be expected. Throughout its life the Court has exercised political power; no one has yet been able to do this without making enemies, and the more important and effective one is in doing it, the more enemies one makes. The role of the Supreme Court in politics has been important and effective, and it is not surprising therefore that it has made many enemies, who likewise have played important and effective roles on the American political scene.

What is surprising and indeed paradoxical is that the Court has escaped the consequences that elsewhere inevitably befall those who make important and influential enemies in politics. The Court has miraculously come through practically unscathed, at least until now, from the heated controversies which have surrounded it almost from the day of its birth in 1789. Specific decisions of the Court have been nullified by amendments to the Constitution (although far more often by the action of the Court itself in overruling them). On rare occasions the jurisdiction of the Court has been temporarily curtailed, and one amendment has been adopted which permanently withdrew from the Court the power to hear and decide suits against any state which does not wish to be sued. But these are comparatively minor and peripheral restrictions on the

Court's power. (Instead of suing the state, one sues its governor or other state official who acts unconstitutionally.) The organizational integrity of the Court has not been touched by any act of Congress nor by any constitutional amendment. No member of the Court has ever been removed from it other than by death, voluntary resignation or retirement. The size of the Court, fixed by Congress, has fluctuated between six and ten, but has so long now been nine that it is safe to predict that it will remain at that figure for many years to come.

NOT BY MIGHT

When the Court ruled that Truman's seizure of the steel mills was unconstitutional, he, in a very uncharacteristic manner, turned the mills back to their officers and boards of directors. When, beginning with 1954, the Court sharply bridled, if in fact it did not cripple, Congress' campaign against domestic Communism and subversion, Congress fulminated and protested, but it accepted the restraints. When, during the same period, the Court played even greater havoc with the states' similar campaigns, they too obeyed. And finally, when in 1954 the Court handed down a death sentence against the South's passionately held social system of racial segregation, the South protested loud and long, but slowly and painfully began to resign itself to its fate and accept Negro children at least in token numbers in its public schools and Negro adults in its trains and buses.

But suppose Truman had refused to comply with the decision and had ordered his Secretary of Commerce to retain control of the mills. And suppose Congress and the states had gone on their way in investigating subversion and punishing subversives, and the South had simply ignored the Brown decision and continued to exclude Negro children from schools attended by whites. What, in each case, could the court by itself have done? The answer is, simply, nothing. Secretary Sawyer could have remained in technical possession of the steel mills; Congressional and state legislative committees could have continued questioning suspected subversives and federal and state police officials could have thrown recalcitrant witnesses into jail, and Negro children could have been kept in Negro schools.

The President of the United States is commander-in-chief of the armed forces and obviously this affords him an instrument of enormous power to effect his will. Congress is the only agency of the federal government that can levy taxes and appropriate funds and this control of the purse strings—as any federal department head can testify—likewise constitutes an instrument of great effectiveness for carrying out its desires. The states control their own revenues and maintain strong police forces. The Supreme Court has none of these instruments of power, neither army, nor treasury nor (except for a few aged and primarily traditional bailiffs) police force. To paraphrase the word of the Lord unto Zerubabel, it is not by might, nor by power but by its spirit that the Court prevails.

Here, then, we are faced with a three-fold paradox. First, a high judicial tribunal, operating within judicial customs and using judicial instruments, exercises important political and legislative functions. Second, in doing so it makes many enemies in highly important and influential circles, and yet escapes any effective attack upon its status or its powers. Third, all other agencies of government, federal and state, accept these political and legislative decisions even though the judicial tribunal has absolutely no weapon in its arsenal that could be employed to compel compliance on the part of anyone.

Where lies the answer to this triple paradox? Where does one find the solution for the riddle of a court that exercises political power not possessed by any other tribunal in the world and yet has no means whatever at its disposal to defend that power if it were seriously challenged? How does it come about that the Court, which throughout its troubled and contentious life has continually made enemies among the most influential segments of the nation, nevertheless enjoys a prestige and occupies a status reminiscent of the High Priesthood of ancient Israel, which too was the keeper of the Holy Covenant?

The answer, I suggest, is to be found in the biography, or life history of the Court. This book is such a biography. It will seek to examine the meat upon which the Court has fed that it has grown so great. For it is clear that the Court is not a static but a dynamic institution; it is radically different than it was in the days of John Jay, its first Chief Justice, or even in the days of John Marshall, its greatest Chief Justice; and in all probability, a half-century hence it will be radically different than it is today.

As I have indicated, although the Court uses the jargon, patterns and rituals of a judicial tribunal, its influence upon the evolution of the American system has been basically in its role as a political rather than judicial institution. Whether or not so intended by the fathers of the Constitution, it has become in fact a third branch of the political government, exercising vast powers and influencing our political, social and economic society.

It follows therefore that the life history of the Court cannot be studied in a vacuum but must be examined against the political, social and economic background which gave rise to its major decisions and which in turn was vitally affected by these decisions. At the same time, due consideration must be given to the influence upon the Court's evolution of the titans inside and outside the Court (Jefferson, Marshall, Jackson, Holmes, Franklin Roosevelt, Warren, etc.) and of their titanic struggles. Only thus can a fair, balanced, reasonably realistic picture of the Court be achieved, and an answer be sought to the most ingenious triple paradox that is our Supreme Court.

chapter two

Court of Humble Birth

Under the Constitution, in order to be elected to the House of Representatives one must be a citizen of the United States, and have been such for at least seven years, must be twenty-five years of age or older, and must be a resident of the state from which he is elected. For appointment to the Supreme Court, even the Chief Justiceship, no qualifications are imposed by the Constitution; neither as to age, nor as to citizenship, nor as to residence in the United States.

Not only does the Constitution neglect to specify the qualifications of the Chief Justice of the United States, it does not even expressly provide that there shall be one. The only reference in the Constitution to a Chief Justice is found in the section dealing with impeachments. There it is stated that when the Senate is conducting the trial in an impeachment of the President, the Chief Justice is to preside (presumably, because the regular presiding officer, the Vice-President, would not be disinterested inasmuch as he would succeed to the Presidency if the President were found guilty). Nowhere, however, is it specifically stated that there shall be a Chief Justice or what his or his Associates' qualifications should be.

The most probable, if surprising, explanation is the relative unimportance of the Supreme Court in the governmental scheme evolved by the men who assembled at Philadelphia in 1787. This is doubly surprising in view of the fact that most of these men were lawyers and would therefore be presumed not to underestimate the importance of their profession. Yet if we examine the amount of space devoted to the Supreme Court in the Constitution, and the amount of debate on the subject in the Constitutional Convention, the conclusion is inescapable that the Court was of relatively minor importance in the minds of the fathers of the Constitution.

In the text of the Constitution published by the Library of Congress in 1952, Article I, which deals with Congress, takes up 232 lines of print; Article II, which deals with the President, covers 98 lines; Article III, which concerns itself with the entire judiciary—Supreme and lower federal courts—takes up only 37 lines of print. The debates in the

Convention tell the same story. Little attention was paid to the Supreme Court, and much of the debate that did concern the Court resulted in minimizing substantially the important role that the Court might have been accorded by the framers of the Constitution. There was a good deal of discussion on a proposal that the Court should share with the President the power to veto acts of Congress before they were to become law. Had the proposal been accepted, the Court would have become an explicit participant in the legislative process. In such case, it may be assumed that considerable more attention would have been paid to the make-up of the Court. The proposal, however, failed of adoption and relatively little further attention was paid to the Court by the makers of the Constitution.

"The judicial power of the United States," the fathers of the Constitution simply said, "shall be vested in one Supreme Court, and in such inferior Courts as the Congress may from time to time ordain and establish." There was no discussion in the Convention nor provision in the Constitution as to the qualifications of the Chief Justice or his Associate Justices, nor as to how many Associates there should be. Congress has therefore assumed that it has the power to decide how many men make a Supreme Court, and has fixed the number in varying amounts from as low as six (including the Chief Justice) to as high as ten, with nine being the number it appears finally to have agreed upon as the Court's permanent size—subject to an ever-present temptation toward court-packing.

There was some discussion in the Convention as to how members of the Court were to be appointed. On one extreme were those who urged that the power be vested exclusively in the President; at the other were those who favored selection by Congress. Madison favored a compromise under which the selection would be made by the Senate. (Nobody was radical enough to suggest that the Justices might be elected by the people.) The final solution was a compromise between Madison's view and that of those who favored appointment by the President: the President would nominate judges but the nominations would have to be approved by the Senate.

The amount of compensation the judges were to receive was also the subject of some discussion. The members of the Convention feared that by controlling the salaries of judges Congress might effectively control their decisions. To avoid this it was speedily decided that while Congress would be authorized to fix the salaries, it would not be permitted to reduce such salaries in respect to any judge in office at the time, so that the reduction would affect only judges appointed after that time. It was also suggested that since a carrot can be as effective as a stick, Congress should not be allowed to raise salaries in respect to sitting judges. It was pointed out, however, that inflation was an ever-present possibility and a salary fixed at one time might well be inadequate years later. The suggestion that this possibility could be met by measuring the judges' salaries not in terms of dollars but of some stable commodity such as wheat was discarded as impracticable. The Convention ended up by forbidding Congress to reduce salaries of sitting judges but permitting salary increases.

Finally, some consideration was given to the question of how long judges should serve. The proposal of a few members of the Convention that the judges should be removable by the President on request of Congress, was received with coolness. James Wilson of Pennsylvania, shortly to become a member of the first Supreme Court, argued against it on the ground that the independence of the judges would be seriously impaired thereby. The debate was short; only Connecticut voted for the proposal. All the other states agreed that they should "hold their office during good behavior," i.e., for life unless removed by impeachment proceedings.

With the exception of the discussion regarding the suggested veto power of the Court, this was practically the sum total of the consideration given by the Convention to the Supreme Court. All in all, it was not very much. Charles Warren, the leading historian of the Supreme Court, found astonishing the slight discussion devoted to the judiciary article reported in Madison's Notes on the Convention. The most probable explanation for this paucity of concern seems to me to be the relative unimportance of the Court in the minds of the delegates to the Convention. This, of course, is inference. What can be said with reasonable certainty is that nothing said by the delegates to the Convention indicates that any of them anticipated the tremendous role in American political history that the Court was destined to play.

Nor was the amount of consideration given by the Convention to the Court's jurisdiction and powers in any way commensurate with the controversies which their exercise evoked in later years. The subject was not neglected, but it does not appear to have aroused extended or passionate debate. The Constitutional Convention might well have broken up over insoluble differences as to the powers of Congress and the selection of its members (i.e., proportionately to population or equally among the states) or over the slave trade; it was not likely that it would have broken up over the powers of the Supreme Court.

The authority of the Supreme Court to nullify as unconstitutional acts of Congress and the states has throughout its history been the major source of its power to influence the political, economic and social patterns of the nation. The assertion and exercise of that authority has been by far the chief source of the controversy that has characterized the Court's history. It is this authority which makes the Supreme Court supreme. In view of such importance, one would expect considerable debate on the subject in the Convention. Surprisingly, there was practically none. There was nothing in the meager discussions on the subject to indicate that the remarkably foresighted fathers anticipated either its future importance or the controversy it would engender. Nor does the sparse discussion shed much light on the subject. It can hardly be said to be conclusive. Remarks were made indicating that some of the delegates were of the opinion that courts had such power. There were also remarks indicating that a few were of a contrary opinion. But all the remarks were purely incidental to some other contested issue. At no time was the basic issue the subject of debate. The Constitution itself is completely silent on the question; there is nothing in it which can fairly be said clearly to imply the existence of a power in the federal courts to declare laws of Congress, or even of the states, unconstitutional.

It is extremely doubtful that the omission of an express reference was motivated by a belief that the people would not approve the Constitution if it specifically authorized judicial nullification of unconstitutional laws. Perhaps in part the explanation for that omission and the paucity of debate is to be found in the assumption that the existence of the power was so widespread and so well known that it could be taken for granted and therefore did not need to be expressly stated. It is more likely, however, that the principal reason is that the framers of the Constitution simply did not consider the matter very important.

THE COURT'S DOMAIN

With the exception of the provision that the Chief Justice shall preside when the Senate acts upon an impeachment of the President (in Article I), all references to the federal judiciary and its powers are in Article III. What were the specific powers—or, more accurately, over what types of cases was the Court given jurisdiction by the fathers of the Constitution? They were the following:

1. Cases affecting ambassadors and other foreign diplomatic officers. This means that if a hot-tempered ambassador from a Latin American country punches another ambassador in the nose, the latter, if he so desires, can sue the former in the Supreme Court. However, since ambassadors rarely punch each other in the nose or seek redress by a suit for damages if they do, this has proved to be the least exercised of all the powers of the Supreme Court. As a matter of fact, there is not a single instance in the entire history of the Court in which a suit between ambassadors was brought directly to the Supreme Court.

2. Suits between states. Boundary disputes between states are by no means uncommon, and the Court has been required to pass judgment on these disputes. States quarrel with each other also over such questions as the diversion or the contamination of rivers which flow from one state to another. But suits between states have represented only a small and hardly significant proportion of the Court's business during the years and none of them has ever given rise to serious controversy on a nationwide scale.

3. Suits between a state and citizens of another state. This language would seem to authorize a suit in the federal courts (and, indeed, in the Supreme Court) against one state by a citizen of another state, and so, as we shall shortly see, it was to be interpreted by the Supreme Court.

4. Appeals in cases of maritime or admiralty jurisdiction, that is those arising on the high seas or on navigable rivers that extend beyond the borders of a single state.

5. Appeals in cases in which the United States is a party. This includes all federal criminal trials.

6. Appeals in suits between citizens of different states and between citizens and aliens. The purpose of this provision was to insure an im-

partial tribunal and protect out-of-state litigants from the consequences of local prejudices.

7. Appeals in cases arising under the Constitution. This has proved to be the most controversial of all the Court's fields of power. It is this short phrase which is the Court's warrant for nullifying the acts of the President, the Congress, state governors, legislatures and courts which it deems inconsistent with the Constitution.

8. Appeals in cases arising under federal laws. Interpreting and applying federal laws has constituted the major business of the Supreme Court.

9. Appeals in cases arising under treaties made by the United States.

STORM OVER THE CONSTITUTION

The makers of the Constitution did not anticipate either the importance the judiciary article would have in the political and economic evolution of the nation or the controversy it would arouse. Its importance unfolded gradually over the years; but its controversial nature appeared immediately. No sooner had the product of the deliberations at Philadelphia been made public than a storm of protest and condemnation broke out.

Opposition was not limited to the judiciary article; it extended to the whole Constitution. The fathers had expected some difficulty in securing ratification, and had accordingly provided that the Constitution should take effect when approved by ratifying conventions in but two-thirds of the states—a provision for the dismemberment and overthrow of the existing government by unlawful means. But even so limited, approval was difficult to achieve. The conflict was bitter. In the Pennsylvania legislature, opponents of the Constitution sought to delay action by leaving their seats to break a quorum and thus prevent election of delegates to the state ratifying convention. Thereupon a Federalist mob invaded their lodgings and dragged them through the streets back to the assembly room, where the legislature proceeded to fix an early date for election of delegates to the ratifying convention. In New York City Alexander Hamilton and John Jay sought to quiet an aroused demonstration of workingmen against the Constitution. During the fracas a stone was hurled at Jay striking him on the head. He fell to the

ground unconscious, but he recovered and lived to see the Constitution ratified and himself appointed the first Chief Justice.

While the opposition to the Constitution was based on many of its provisions, it must have surprised the framers that no provision was subjected to more severe condemnation and subjected to greater fears and apprehension than the article on the judiciary. But in respect to the role that specifically the Supreme Court was destined to play in American history, the public was as unsuspecting as the fathers of the Constitution. Astonishingly little public attention was given to the question of the power of the Supreme Court to declare acts either of Congress or of the states unconstitutional. The assertion was made by Hamilton in several of *The Federalist* papers that although there was not "a syllable" in the Constitution that directly empowered the Court to invalidate laws on the ground that they were unconstitutional, nevertheless this power must be implied from the very nature of the government that the Constitution sought to set up. *The Federalist* articles, however, were published only in connection with the New York ratification campaign, which took place after the requisite nine states had already ratified the Constitution and thus had made it legally effective. Moreover, *The Federalist* articles in which this assertion was made did not appear until the very end of the series; it was first made and explained in number seventy-eight of a total of eighty-five articles.

All in all, there is little evidence to indicate that more than a small percentage of the people of the United States that participated in any way in the ratification of the Constitution gave any thought to the question of whether or not the Supreme Court would have power to declare laws unconstitutional. This is not what concerned them; what they were troubled about was principally the relationship of the lower federal courts to existing state tribunals. In the press, the public meetings, the state legislatures and the ratifying conventions the principal subject of criticism and condemnation was not the Supreme Court but the lower federal courts. The burden of the criticism was that federal courts would ultimately displace the local state courts.

In the Virginia ratifying convention the argument in defense of the judiciary article was assigned by the Federalists to John Marshall, then a young but brilliant lawyer from the backwoods. Marshall scoffed at the claim that the federal courts would supplant the state tribunals. On the contrary, the federal courts would make the state courts more efficient by relieving them of part of their burden. The "law's delay," which Shakespeare's Hamlet complained of in the early seventeenth century, is with us today, as every practicing lawyer well knows, and was likewise with the generation of 1787. The reason for it then, as it is today and as it probably was in Shakespeare's day, was the overcrowded condition of the courts' dockets. This deplorable situation, said Marshall, would be alleviated by the Constitution. "Does not every gentleman know," he asked rhetorically, "that the causes in our courts are more numerous than they can decide? Look at the dockets. You will find them crowded with suits which the life of man will not see determined. If some of these suits be carried to other courts, will it be wrong? They will still have business enough."

Actually, the popular opposition to the proposed federal judiciary was not in the main motivated by any parochial desire to protect the state courts from foreign competition. The people's fears were based upon more practical considerations. Throughout the states, legislatures had enacted laws aimed at lightening the burden of the lower economic classes, the debtors, workingmen and small farmers. Among these were laws restricting the enforcement of debts and foreclosure of mortgages, requiring creditors to accept as legal tender the cheap paper money issued by the states, and confiscating for the benefit of the general public large tracts of land formerly owned by residents of Britain or Americans remaining loyal to Britain during the Revolution. The state courts had to a greater or lesser extent accepted and given effect to these laws. Local tribunals have always been more sensitive and responsive to popular feelings than centralized courts. The people generally, being mostly in the lower economic classes, were fearful that the distant federal courts, manned by persons appointed by the President to serve for life, would be less sympathetic to their plight and more hostile to the state legislatures' efforts to alleviate it. Perhaps most important was the fact that while the judiciary article of the Constitution guaranteed trial by jury in criminal cases, it omitted such guarantee in respect to civil cases, thus giving suits for the collection of debts a much greater chance of success.

In the Constitutional Convention it was generally taken for granted that there had to be a Supreme Court and there was no need to justify the provision creating such a court. The same was true in the state ratifying conventions. There was little articulated opposition to the creation of a Supreme Court. The burden of the opposition was to its powers and jurisdiction. What concerned the opponents most was the provision which gave the Court jurisdiction to decide suits between a state and citizens of another state. This meant obviously that any person could hale any of the states to the bar of justice in the Supreme Court. This, said the anti-Federalists, was unthinkable; it was an indefensible assault upon the sovereignty of the states.

Opposition to the idea that the Supreme Court could compel a state to answer to a complaint by a private person residing in another state was strong and widespread. (The intensity of the opposition will become apparent when we relate the case of *Chisholm* v. *Georgia* in the next chapter.) The defenders of the Constitution vigorously denied that any such idea existed in the minds of the framers. The only purpose of the provision, they pleaded, was to enable a state to sue a private person; but never the reverse.

There were many things in the Constitution (the judiciary article was but one) that the anti-Federalists did not like. But what they liked least was not the presence of something but the absence of something. The Constitution contained no bill of rights and this omission was by far its most vulnerable point. Scant consideration had been given in the Constitutional Convention to the inclusion of a bill of rights. George Mason, author of the Virginia Bill of Rights—the progenitor of all bills of rights in the United States, state and federal—urged at the Convention that the proposed constitution be prefaced by a declaration of the rights of the people. The delegates, however, were interested in restraining, not protecting, the rights of the people. The debate was short; a vote was taken, and not a single state could muster majority in support of Mason's motion. Here, too, the fifty-five fathers were singularly lacking in foresight in failing to anticipate the popular reaction to the omission.

The reaction was widespread, strong and vocal. In state after state ratification was strenuously opposed because of the omission of a bill of rights. In Virginia, George Mason, Richard Henry Lee and the revered Patrick Henry led the opposition. It was a betrayal, said Henry in the Virginia ratification convention, of the spirit of the Revolution to accept a constitution without a bill of rights; such action was unworthy of free men. In Massachusetts, the opposition was led by the Revolutionary patriot Sam Adams, as venerated by the common people there as Henry was in Virginia. Writing to Richard Henry Lee he lamented that "the

Seeds of Aristocracy began to spring even before the Conclusion of our Struggle for the natural Rights of Men."

In vain was the argument of Hamilton, Jay, and other champions of the Constitution that a bill of rights was not necessary, since the national government had in any case no power to abridge the natural rights of Americans. True enough, said Oliver Ellsworth, the Constitution does not guarantee freedom of the press; but neither does it guarantee freedom "of matrimony or of burial of the dead. It is enough that Congress has no power to prohibit either." But a guarantee by inference did not satisfy popular demand. Jefferson undoubtedly reflected public opinion when he wrote from France, where he was serving as minister, "that a bill of rights is what the people are entitled against every government on earth, general or particular, and what no just government should refuse, or rest on inference."

There were insinuations and even outright charges that the omission of a bill of rights was being used simply as a smoke screen by those whose economic interests impelled them to oppose any constitution and any strong central government. A Federalist pamphlet widely distributed in Maryland hinted broadly that the prohibition of paper money probably united more opponents of the Constitution than any demand for a bill of rights. Who said, the pamphlet demanded, that the Constitution did not declare any rights? "It provides that no man shall suffer by ex post facto laws or bills of attainder. It declares that gold and silver only shall be a tender for specied debts; and that no law shall impair the obligation of a contract."

All this was in vain. In almost every state ratification convention amendments were proposed to add to the Constitution guarantees of rights and liberties. It was quite clear that unless drastic action were taken the Constitution was doomed. And so the Federalist leaders solemnly promised that when ratification would be completed, a bill of rights would be added to the Constitution by amendment. It was this promise that finally swung the balance, by a very narrow margin, and gave America a new constitution and a central government.

THE PROMISE REDEEMED

The Federalists were true to their word. The first Congress under the new Constitution assembled in April, 1789. Almost immediately

Madison, who had been elected to the House of Representatives, began to press for the redemption of the pledge that had made the new government possible. The Federalists controlled the Congress and thus had it within their power to treat the ratification campaign promises with the same forgetfulness with which so many other campaign promises were destined to be treated. A number of Federalist leaders in Congress did in fact urge that as there were so many other important matters to be taken up, amendments for a bill of rights should be postponed for consideration at some later time. Madison persisted; the Congress, he said, was pledged as a matter of good faith to act on the proposed amendments and delay would give rise to grave suspicions.

The debates went on through the summer, but by the end of September both Houses agreed upon a bill of rights, largely the work of Madison, which was submitted to the states for ratification. Some two years later the requisite number of states had registered their approval and the Bill of Rights, constituting the first ten amendments, became part of the Constitution.

In brief, the First Amendment forbade Congress to enact laws establishing religion or prohibiting its free exercise, or to abridge freedom of speech, press, assembly and petition. The Second guaranteed the right to bear arms, a provision which achieved sudden prominence on the assassination of President Kennedy. The Third prohibited the quartering of soldiers in private homes in peacetime without the consent of the owners. The Fourth forbade unreasonable searches and seizures. The Fifth guaranteed prosecution of felonies by indictment, barred double jeopardy, compulsory self-incrimination, deprivation of life, liberty or property without due process of law, and the taking of private property for public use without just compensation. The Sixth guaranteed a speedy, impartial, public and local jury trial in all criminal prosecutions and guaranteed the rights of compulsory process to obtain witnesses and of assistance of counsel. The Seventh provided for jury trials in civil actions, and the Eighth prohibited excessive bail, excessive fines, and cruel and unusual punishments. The Ninth provided that rights not specifically enumerated should not therefore be deemed denied, and the Tenth that powers not expressly delegated to the federal government are retained by the states and the people.

Madison pressed for a bill of rights after his election to Congress principally because he felt that good faith demanded that the pledges that were made in the ratification campaigns should be honored. Its value, he felt, could only be modest. In respect to abuses by the government, he wrote to Jefferson, a bill of rights would "be a good ground for an appeal to the sense of the community." In respect to action by tyrannical majorities, liberties solemnly declared in the national charter "acquire by degrees the character of fundamental maxims and as they become incorporated with the national sentiment, counteract the impulses of interest and passion." However, he added almost as an afterthought that if a bill of rights were adopted, "independent tribunals of justice will consider themselves in a peculiar manner the guardians of those rights."

Thus Madison relied primarily on the moral effect of a declaration of rights. In this respect he appears to have reflected the general appraisal of even the warm advocates of a bill of rights. In the debates on inclusion of a bill of rights, both within the Constitutional Convention and during the ratification campaign, little attention seems to have been given to the part that the courts would play in enforcing the rights. Undoubtedly, there was a general assumption that the courts would be involved, but principal reliance appears to have been placed on the moral effect of a declaration. The Federalists in the Convention failed completely to anticipate the role the Supreme Court was destined to play in the protection of property rights, and the anti-Federalists outside the Convention failed equally to anticipate the role it was to play in the protection of personal rights.

THE FOUNDATION IS LAID

The first Congress established the foundations not only of American constitutional liberties but also of the Supreme Court, which a century and a half later was to become the chief protector of these liberties. The pattern of the federal judicial system set in the Judiciary Act of 1789, though changed in detail during the years, is still in effect today. The act was the work principally of Oliver Ellsworth of Connecticut, with assistance from William Paterson of New Jersey, both members of the Senate and both later to become members of the Supreme Court.

The act set up a three-level system. At the bottom were the thirteen district courts, one for each state. These courts were to have original jurisdiction of all suits that under the Constitution could be brought in the federal courts, with the exception of some that could be brought directly to the Supreme Court.

On the top level was the Supreme Court, to consist of a Chief Justice and five Associate Justices. This court was to have final jurisdiction in all appeals from cases which originated in the federal district courts. It was also to have jurisdiction in appeals from decisions of the highest state courts in cases involving some provisions of the federal Constitution or an act of Congress.

Most important for our study was the famous (to constitutional lawyers) section 25 of the Judiciary Act. The section is written in that technical, legalistic jargon which is like a foreign language to the non-lawyer and is often puzzling even to the trained lawyer. It seems to say that the Supreme Court has the power to declare unconstitutional any law enacted either by Congress or a state; and so it has been interpreted by courts and constitutional lawyers. But it does not really say it; rather it implies or assumes it. What it says is that if a state court should hold that a particular federal law passed by Congress is unconstitutional, or that a particular state law is constitutional, then in either case the decision can be appealed to the Supreme Court, which can affirm or reverse it. Constitutional lawyers are agreed that what the framers of section 25 intended by this was that the Supreme Court should have full power to declare laws either of Congress or of state legislatures to be unconstitutional and void.

If that is what they meant, why did they not say so? Even lawyers, if they make a particular effort, can write clearly and understandably. Why did Ellsworth and Paterson beat around the bush and imply through the use of obscure language what they could have said simply and directly? Perhaps they were afraid of the public reaction; and this is the explanation that has been given by some historians of the Court. But on closer examination this explanation does not supply an adequate answer. The Federalists, who devised a system of checks and balances to make difficult the passage of any legislation by Congress, would have no objection to an additional check in the form of a judicial veto by the Supreme Court. As for the anti-Federalists, they would have no objection to a judicial veto on the not-to-be-trusted federal legislature, and in fact the anti-Federalists in Congress did support this provision of section 25.

The reason that Ellsworth, Paterson and the other Federalists in

Congress implied rather than stated that the Supreme Court had power to invalidate statutes is, I think, that they assumed that this power was inherent in the Court because of the very nature of the government formed at Philadelphia. Not Congress but the Constitution conferred the power upon the Court. (This is what Hamilton had said in *The Federalist*, and what Marshall was to say a decade and a half later in *Marbury* v. *Madison.*) All Congress was doing was spelling out the manner in which the Court was to exercise its inherent power. Hence, there was no need or occasion to declare that the power existed; indeed, such a declaration might imply a doubt that it really did exist.

In addition to the thirteen district courts and the Supreme Court, provision was made for three circuit courts. Each of these was to consist of two judges of the Supreme Court and one district court judge, although any two of the three constituted a quorum. The circuit courts were to hear appeals from the district courts just as the Supreme Court was to hear appeals from the circuit courts. In addition, the circuit courts had jurisdiction to conduct trials in many civil and criminal cases, so that the circuit court was at the same time a court of appellate and of original jurisdiction. It was service on the circuit courts by Supreme Court Justices that was to give the Supreme Court considerable trouble. But more of that later.

chapter three

An Inauspicious Beginning

THE FIRST CHIEF JUSTICE

George Washington was elected by all the people, but his heart belonged to the Federalists. He was greatly influenced by Hamilton, whose yearning for the aristocratic, perhaps even royal, way of life he shared. When he became President he ceased shaking hands with people, and instead acknowledged salutations by a formal bow. At Presidential receptions he wore a black velvet suit with gold buckles and yellow gloves; his hair was powdered, he carried a cocked hat with an ostrich plume, and he wore a sword in a white leather scabbard. The more radical of the anti-Federalists charged him with conducting himself as a king.

Washington shared also, though to a somewhat lesser degree, Hamilton's distrust of the common people. In Massachusetts in 1786, an ex-soldier of the Revolutionary War, Daniel Shays, led a populist movement of agrarians and debtors who sought to scale down the state debts, eliminate the special privileges enjoyed by property, issue paper money and in general ease the position of the indebted classes, the farmers and the town workers. The movement led to armed insurrection which, though speedily crushed, greatly alarmed the upper classes. Washington was thoroughly frightened and intensified his efforts towards the establishment of a stronger national government which would be able effectively to suppress such radicals as Shays and his followers.

When, therefore, this new national government came into being and Washington, as its first President, was called upon to appoint the officials who were to administer it and carry out its objectives, it was inevitable that he should appoint only those who were committed to that government and its objectives. There was no room in his administration for such anti-nationalists and radicals as Patrick Henry, Luther Martin, George Mason or Sam Adams. Even Jefferson, whom Washington designated Secretary of State, was not completely an exception. He supported the Constitution, and was shortly to save the Union by influencing the southern members of Congress to vote for assumption of the revolutionary obligations at their face (rather than depreciated market) value after Hamilton warned him that the northern, creditor states were prepared to secede if this were not done.

There were no exceptions in the judicial department. Appointees to the federal judgeships created under the Judiciary Act of 1789 were sought exclusively from among those who had helped draft the Constitution, or had supported it in state conventions or ratifying campaigns. This was not motivated by any desire to pack the courts, nor was it the result of any conspiracy on the part of the Federalists especially to control the judiciary as a brake upon the legislatures, federal and state. To suggest this is to ascribe to the judiciary an importance it did not then possess in the eyes of Washington and his associates. Washington appointed Federalists to practically all offices because he wanted to appoint the best people, and for him the best people were Federalists.

It was therefore in the ranks of the leading Federalists that Washington looked for his Chief Justice. After considering several prospects he chose John Jay of New York. Jay was then acting as Secretary of Foreign Affairs under the Confederation, and Washington offered him his choice of retaining that position in the new government or of accepting the Chief Justiceship. While Jay was making up his mind one cynic wrote that the "Keeper of the Tower is waiting to see which salary is best, that of Lord Chief Justice or Secretary of State." Some ten years later, a leading anti-Federalist pamphleteer wrote that, "If Washington wanted to corrupt the American judges, he could not have taken a more decisive step than by the appointment of Jay."

Both charges were false. Jay's personal wealth and earning capacity made it improbable that the difference of five hundred dollars annually in the salaries of the two offices would determine his choice. His personal incorruptibility is attested by the fact that on one occasion during the Revolutionary War he pledged his individual responsibility to secure a loan from Spain to the Continental Congress and on another urged that the city of New York be destroyed even though this scorched earth policy would have wiped out most of his own wealth. Nevertheless, these charges against him, unfounded as they were, are understandable; his entire career and his character made him anathema to the lower classes and their anti-Federalist leaders.

Unlike the humbly-born Hamilton, who aspired to aristocracy, Jay, like Washington, was born in it. His father was a wealthy merchant who owned considerable real property, and Jay's inherited estate was greatly augmented by his marriage into the baronial Livingston family. In 1768, at the age of twenty-three, he was admitted to the bar and soon developed a successful legal practice. Elected to the First Continental Congress in 1775, he opposed separation from Great Britain, but once the decision was made, became unreservedly loyal to the cause of independence. In 1777 he became chairman of the committee which drafted the first constitution for the state of New York. In this capacity he succeeded in obtaining the inclusion of a stringent provision imposing property qualifications for voting, thus giving practical effect to his favorite and oft-repeated maxim that "those who own the country ought to govern it." It was unfortunate but undeniable, he believed, that "the wise and the good never form the majority of any large society," and must always strive against the "never ceasing union of the wicked and the weak."

Shortly after the New York constitution was adopted, Jay became the first chief judge of that state. He served for less than two years and resigned to return to the Continental Congress. In 1778 he became president of the Congress and three years later was appointed to a delegation of five to negotiate a treaty of peace with Great Britain. The negotiations proved highly successful, and Jay and his associates returned with a treaty far more favorable to the United States than Congress had dared to expect. In 1784 he became Secretary for Foreign Affairs, a position he held until he accepted appointment as Chief Justice five years later.

Although Jay was not a member of the Constitutional Convention, he fought valiantly in New York for ratification. Along with Hamilton and Madison he participated in the writing of *The Federalist* papers. He wrote only five of the eighty-five papers, yet his prestige was considerably greater than that of either Hamilton or Madison so that his contribution to the ultimately successful effort was not limited by the small amount of his writings. Besides *The Federalist* papers he published *An Address to the People of New York*, and spoke often in defense of the Constitution, on one occasion, as we have seen, almost losing his life in a near riot. In the New York ratification convention he ably assisted

Hamilton in winning approval through shrewd engineering tactics, notwithstanding the fact that the majority of New York citizens were probably opposed to ratification.

By birth, breeding and belief, Jay epitomized what Washington deemed to be the ideal statesman. His judicial experience was comparatively slight, but his brilliance, competence and personal integrity were not open to serious challenge. With his talents and background it is surprising that he did not make a great Chief Justice and that when he finally succeeded in ridding himself of the office six years after he took it, he left the Court not substantially advanced in its evolution toward the position of importance it occupies today. This may be explained perhaps by his apparent dislike for his job, perhaps by his forbidding personality and his personal vanity. Whatever the reason, Jay's career as Chief Justice is most fittingly described as undistinguished.

THE FIRST JUSTICES

In appointing the members of the Supreme Court, as in performing any other function of the Presidency, Washington had no precedent to follow. And whatever he did established precedent; his decision to limit his own term of office to eight years established a precedent that has been broken only once, a breach which resulted in a constitutional amendment designed to avoid repetition. So too, in appointing to the Supreme Court persons of his own general political philosophy he established a precedent which in later times, when political philosophies found expression in organized political parties, resulted in the usual practice of appointments to the Court from the ranks of the President's party. There have been deviations from this practice, but these have been infrequent.

In another aspect of his appointments to the Supreme Court Washington established a precedent that has been generally adhered to by his successors. As he sought political uniformity, so conversely did he seek geographic diversity. He chose the six Justices so that the North and South would be equally represented on the Court. Three of the Justices he appointed came from the North (New York, Massachusetts and Pennsylvania), and three from the South (Virginia, North Carolina and South Carolina). Much may be said for and against this practice, but it recognizes realistically that the Supreme Court is part of the political life of the nation.

From Pennsylvania Washington chose James Wilson. Jay had the Chief Justiceship thrust upon him; Wilson vainly sought it. He did what is generally done by law school graduates seeking positions with law firms, but is simply not done by persons striving for high judicial office: he sent Washington a formal letter of application for the position of Chief Justice, stopping short only of listing his qualifications and experience. ("Shall I," he asked, "enumerate reasons in justification of my high pretensions? I have not yet employed my pen in my own praise.")

Despite Wilson's modesty, he turned out to be the most able member of the original Court and influenced it far more than did Chief Justice Jay. A highly successful Pennsylvania attorney, he was elected to the Continental Congress and became an able theorist and eloquent advocate of the revolutionary cause. He was one of the few persons (there were five others) who signed both the Declaration of Independence and the Constitution. In the Constitutional Convention he was a proponent of a strong national government and along with Gouverneur Morris wrote the final draft of the Constitution. In the Convention he favored election of the President and of the senators by the people directly rather than by an electoral college and by the state legislatures, and in general was the most democratic-minded of the Federalists. This seems quite surprising in view of the fact that during the Revolution he had acquired the reputation of being tainted with the spirit of high aristocracy and had been mobbed by a band of patriots. Although Wilson did not share the Convention leaders' distrust of the people, Washington thought very highly of him, and placed his nephew, Bushrod Washington (later himself a member of the Supreme Court), in Wilson's office to learn the law.

An ironic aspect of Wilson's somewhat checkered career was his authorship of the provision in the Constitution that no state shall pass any "law impairing the obligation of contracts." The purpose of this clause was to protect the creditor classes from the confiscatory designs of the debtors who controlled the state legislatures, primarily through compelling acceptance of depreciated paper as legal tender.

Then and for some years later Wilson was a member and legal protector of the creditor class. As director of the Bank of North America he succeeded in having its charter restored after the Pennsylvania legislature repealed it on the ground that it "hath been found to be injurious to the welfare of this State." He was heavily involved in land speculation (even after his appointment to the Supreme Court) including the notorious Yazoo lands fraud case, which was to become the subject of an important Supreme Court decision. The various speculations collapsed and he spent the last two years of his life evading arrest and imprisonment for nonpayment of his debts. (To evade arrest in Pennsylvania he found it necessary to exchange circuit duty with a fellow Justice from North Carolina.)

From South Carolina Washington appointed John Rutledge, an aspirant for the Chief Justiceship who, unlike Wilson, allowed his friends to press his claim. When Washington passed him up in favor of Jay, Rutledge became somewhat disgruntled but was prevailed upon to accept an Associate Justiceship. During the Revolution he was elected governor of South Carolina but resigned because the state constitution, which he deemed too democratic, was adopted over his veto. The new constitution limited the office of governor to persons owning plantations of at least ten thousand pounds currency, "clear of debt," and Rutledge, upon his re-election after his resignation, was able to qualify under that provision. In 1782 he became a judge of the state supreme court and in 1787 a delegate to the Constitutional Convention.

Rutledge remained on the Supreme Court for two years, during which he did not attend a single session of the Court. The reason for this was that it had practically no work to do during this period, and Rutledge, who lived further away from New York and Philadelphia where the first sessions of Court were held than did any of the other Justices, found no reason to take long and arduous trips merely to manifest his presence. In 1791 Rutledge resigned from the United States Supreme Court to become chief justice of his state supreme court, a step almost inconceivable today. This sheds considerable light on the measure of importance which the Supreme Court held in the eyes of its own members during its infancy.

William Cushing was Massachusett's representative on the first Supreme Court bench. His father and grandfather before him had been royal judges and he himself became the first chief justice of the Massachusetts supreme judicial court under its constitution of 1780. In that capacity he was involved in many of the cases against debtors which gave rise to Shays' insurrection, and he was particularly detested by the insurrectionists. Nevertheless, he was a person of conviction and courage. He was the only member of the Massachusetts royal court to cast his lot with the revolutionists. When his court was surrounded by Shays' followers during the disturbances accompanying legal collection of debts, he steadfastly refused to allow "mob rule" to influence his decisions. Moreover, he handed down an important decision to the effect that the clause "All men are born free and equal" in the Massachusetts constitution was not merely a pious platitude but had the legal effect of abolishing slavery throughout the state.

From Virginia Washington's first choice was George Wythe, but Wythe preferred to remain a state court judge. Washington's second choice was John Blair, a personal friend who had served in the Virginia state courts and had been a member of the federal Constitutional Convention. Like Wilson, he was to engage heavily in speculation while on the bench, but his speculations proved successful and he was able to amass a small fortune by the time he resigned from the Court after six years of service.

For the sixth seat on the bench Washington chose Robert Harrison of Maryland. Five days after he was confirmed, however, he was chosen Chancellor of Maryland and he returned his commission to the President so that he could accept the state judicial post. In his place, Washington selected James Iredell of North Carolina. Iredell had been leader of the Federalists in North Carolina and had succeeded in pushing through ratification of the Constitution. For this he expected to be rewarded by Washington in the form of a federal district court judgeship, but to his pleasant surprise Harrison's withdrawal resulted in his being offered the vacancy on the Supreme Court. Iredell was the youngest man on the bench, being only thirty-eight at the time of his appointment.

These, then, were the first Supreme Court Justices. All were Federalists, committed to a strong national government. All had participated either in the drafting of the Constitution or in the campaign for its ratification. All were members or representatives of the propertied, creditor classes, and all believed that the purpose of government was to protect the rights of property against the covetous depredations of the lower classes.

AN INAUSPICIOUS BEGINNING

On February 1, 1790, the first Monday of the month, Chief Justice Jay appeared at the Royal Exchange Building at the foot of Broad Street in New York, then the national capital, ready to do business. Contemporary newspapers reported that the courtroom was "uncommonly crowded" with federal, state and city officials who came to witness what was expected to be an impressive opening ceremony. Unfortunately, besides Jay, only Justices Cushing and Wilson were present; none of the southern Justices showed up. Lacking a quorum the Court could conduct no business. The clerk of the Court did dutifully enter minutes of the proceedings (or lack thereof), but being from Massachusetts, where the highest court was called the "Supreme Judicial Court," he absent-mindedly began the minutes with the words, "In the Supreme Judicial Court of the United States," so that the very first line of the official minutes of the United States Supreme Court contains a glaring error. All in all it was an inauspicious first day.

The next day Justice Blair arrived from Virginia and a quorum was finally present. The court crier, in a ritual that has remained unchanged, announced that the Court was in session and ready to do business. ("Oyez! Oyez! All persons having business before the honorable, the Supreme Court of the United States, are admonished to draw near and give their attention, for the Court is now sitting. God save the United States and this Honorable Court!") The court crier sat back and waited for something to happen. So did the Chief Justice and the three Associate Justices. But nothing happened. Justice Blair might just as well have stayed home. The Court was open for business but it had no business to do, and so it simply adjourned for the day. The same thing happened the next day, and the day after that, and daily after that until February 10th. The only business the Court had to perform was to license a few attorneys to practice before it when their cases would be appealed to the Supreme Court.

The most controversial issue facing the Court and the one most talked of by the public was the attire the Justices should wear while on the bench. The aristocratic Hamilton characteristically favored the elegant gowns and wigs worn by the English judiciary, while the republican Jefferson opposed all needless official attire. If the Justices felt that they had to wear judicial robes, Jefferson would go along with that. But, he implored, "for Heaven's sake, discard the monstrous wig which makes the English judges look like rats peeping through bunches of oakum!" The Justices compromised by adopting the robe and discarding the wig—all, that is, except Cushing; this scion of a line of English judges could not bring himself to forego the wig, and persisted in wearing it for many years to the mingled excitement, amusement and displeasure of the public.

After ten days of no business, the Court called a halt to the term and adjourned for six months. In August of 1790 it re-assembled, but again it had nothing to do. This time it sat for only two days and declared the term over. The same thing happened again in February of 1791, in August of that year and in February of 1792. It was fully three years before the Court had any real business to take care of.

This delay in getting started was to be expected. After all, the Court was intended primarily to be an appellate tribunal, and naturally it would have to wait until cases went through the lower courts, federal and state. But, reasonable as the delay was, it nevertheless indicated that in its early years the Court was hardly an institution of major importance in the government designed at the Constitutional Convention, an outcome probably not unexpected by most of the members of that Convention. Like its first day, the Court's first years were quite inauspicious.

THE BURDEN OF THE CIRCUITS

Though the Supreme Court had nothing to do, the Justices were not unoccupied. The Judiciary Act of 1789 required them to serve as circuit court judges as well as Supreme Court Justices. The act divided the country into three geographic regions and two Justices were permanently assigned to each circuit, where, together with the local district judges, they were required to preside over court twice a year in each state. The method of travel was by carriage or, more often, horseback. In addition to riding circuit, the Justices were of course expected to come to the capital (first New York and then Philadelphia) twice a year to participate in the Supreme Court sessions. Quite justifiably, one of the Justices described his life as that of a "travelling postboy," and complained that "no Judge could conscientiously ride" his circuit

(North and South Carolina and Georgia) "and perform the other parts of his duty." For all this Justices received forty-five hundred dollars a year (the Chief Justice five hundred more), a sum which even by the standards of those days was hardly munificent.

The hardships suffered by the Justices finally caused them, in 1792, to join in a letter to the President setting forth their grievances ("we cannot reconcile ourselves to the idea of existing in exile from our families") and pleading for relief. The President turned the letter over to Congress, which more than six months later accorded only modest relief. All it would do was to provide that the circuit courts should thereafter consist of but one Supreme Court Justice and one district court judge. It also instituted a somewhat fairer system by providing that the Justices were to rotate among the circuits, distant and near, rather than as theretofore being permanently assigned to fixed circuits.

Despite its shortcomings and the hardships it imposed on the Justices, the early circuit court system contributed significantly to the development of the Supreme Court. The first important business transacted by the Justices of the Supreme Court and the first important decisions handed down by them were in the circuits. Before we consider these, mention should be made of Jay's unsuccessful and Rutledge's successful effort to escape from the Supreme Court.

Almost from the time he ascended the bench as its Chief Justice, Jay began to seek ways to get off it. He had been on the bench no more than two years before he began to feel that "the office of a Judge of the Supreme Court of the United States" is "intolerable, and therefore almost any other office of a suitable rank and emolument is preferable." Undoubtedly the burden of circuit court duty lessened considerably the attractiveness of being a Supreme Court Justice, but combined with it was the rather low esteem in which the general public held the federal judiciary.

In 1792 Jay felt that the office of governor of New York was one of "suitable rank and emolument," and made a determined effort to get elected to it. Apparently deeming even an unattractive bird in the hand worth holding until the more attractive bird in the bush could be captured, he did not resign as Chief Justice and while in office conducted a vigorous and bitter campaign against George Clinton, a fact that apparently aroused no serious criticism. (Today it would be astonishing that a Chief Justice of the United States should run for the governorship of any state, and shocking that he would do so without resigning his judicial office.) As events turned out, Jay's prudence was justified, for he failed to win the election and willy-nilly had to stay on as Chief Justice. The next year he again considered running for governor of New York but allowed himself to be dissuaded by Washington. It was not until 1794, after almost five long years as Chief Justice, that he finally received what appeared temporary relief, in the form of appointment as special ambassador to Britain that turned out to be permanent relief by reason of his election to the governorship of New York.

Rutledge was more fortunate. After serving a term of only two years, he was appointed chief justice of the South Carolina supreme court, and promptly resigned from the federal bench. Faced with the need to find a replacement from South Carolina, and recognizing that a "suitable" candidate might very well not be a willing one, Washington adopted the rather singular expedient of offering the office simultaneously in a joint letter to two prospects, Edward Rutledge, the retiring Justice's nephew, and Charles C. Pinckney, asking whether either of them would accept. The President might have found himself in an awkward position if both had answered in the affirmative, but he was more than spared this embarrassment of riches when both declined, preferring to remain where they were in the state legislature.

Unable to find a replacement in South Carolina, Washington turned to another southern state, Maryland, and promoted Thomas Johnson, a Federal district judge in that state. Johnson, then fifty-nine years old, did not relish the prospect of arduous journeys on circuit, but Washington prevailed upon him to accept the promotion by assuring him that Congress would afford relief by altering the circuit system. The relief that Congress did afford (requiring but one Supreme Court Justice on each circuit), however, proved inadequate and Johnson resigned after serving little more than a year.

To replace Johnson, Washington chose Senator William Paterson of New Jersey. Paterson was then (1793) forty-four years old and therefore better able to endure the rigors of circuit duty. Of a wealthy family (the Van Rensselaers), he was a staunch Federalist by association and conviction. He had been a member of the Constitutional Convention and later was elected to the Senate, where he became junior partner to Ellsworth in the drafting of the Judiciary Act of 1789.

It is interesting that this circumstance—the enactment of the Judiciary Act while Paterson was a member of the Senate—may well have rendered his appointment to the Court unconstitutional. It was the Judiciary Act which may be said to have created the office of Associate Justice (the Constitution does no more than state that there shall be a Supreme Court) and the Constitution provides that no member of either House of Congress may be appointed to an office created while he was a member of Congress. When this most unfortunate oversight was called to Washington's attention he sent a message of regret to the Senate in which he stated frankly that he considered the nomination "to have been null by the Constitution." Whether by reason of senatorial courtesy or disagreement with the President's interpretation of the Constitution, the Senate elected to overlook the oversight and allow Paterson to take his place on the bench.

THE CIRCUITS ANTICIPATE THE COURT'S DECISIONS AND TROUBLES

Like the Supreme Court, the circuits were slow in getting started, although, understandably, not quite as slow as the Supreme Court. When they did begin to decide cases, they anticipated some of the most important and controversial decisions the Supreme Court was later to hand down.

The first important decision handed down by a circuit court invalidated as unconstitutional a state statute whose purpose it was to afford some relief to a hard-pressed debtor from the demands of his creditors. In 1791 the legislature of Rhode Island, on the petition of a debtor, passed an act granting him a three-year extension to pay his debts and exempting him during that period from being imprisoned or having his property seized for non-payment of his debts. This, said a circuit court consisting of Jay and Cushing (together with a district court judge), the legislature may not do for it clearly violates the provision in the Constitution devised by their colleague Wilson that a state may make no law impairing the obligation of contracts. When a person borrows money he not only expressly contracts to repay it with interest at the end of the agreed period of time, but also implicitly contracts that if he does not do so the creditor shall have the right to avail himself of all the means the law allows for the collection of debts. A law which extends the time to pay the debt or postpones the availability of legal measures to collect it obviously impairs the obligations of the contract.

This decision did everything that the opponents of the Constitution feared. With one stone it severely wounded state sovereignty and the rights of the oppressed lower classes. The decision was handed down in June of 1792 and received widespread newspaper publicity, at least in the New England and Middle Atlantic states. Yet it appears to have aroused practically no opposition at all, even though only five years earlier an effort was made to impeach the judges of the Rhode Island supreme court for holding unconstitutional a statute requiring creditors to accept cheap paper money in payment of their debts.

Whatever the reasons for this strange silence, it very likely instilled a sense of courage and confidence in the Justices, for the next year the circuit court acted the same way upon a similar moratorium statute in Connecticut. Two years after this, in *Vanhorne's Lessee* v. *Dorrance*, Justice Paterson, sitting in the circuit court, advised a jury that a Pennsylvania statute seeking to settle a dispute between residents of Connecticut and of Pennsylvania to certain lands in Pennsylvania was unconstitutional and invalid. This case is considered by many to be a landmark, but apparently in large measure because it is assumed that the statute was invalidated as violating the United States Constitution. Actually, the act was declared void because it violated the Pennsylvania constitution. "The Constitution," said Paterson, "expressly declares that the right of acquiring, possessing and protecting property is natural, inherent and unalienable."

The opinion, however, shows quite clearly that Paterson was referring not to the federal but to the Pennsylvania constitution, although neither expressly declares any such thing. Yet, in a sense *Vanhorne's Lessee* v. *Dorrance* was a landmark case, for Paterson's reasoning and arguments leading to the conclusion that "Whatever may be the case in other countries, yet there can be no doubt that every act of the Legislature repugnant to the Constitution is absolutely void," were exactly those used by Marshall eight years later to arrive at the same conclusion in the historic case of *Marbury* v. *Madison.*

In these cases the circuit courts declared unconstitutional laws enacted by state legislatures. But they also declared unconstitutional and void an act passed by the Congress of the United States—this ten years before Marshall was to do the same thing in *Marbury* v. *Madison.*

In 1792 Congress passed a law that disabled and invalid soldiers and sailors should receive pensions but that their claims should first be passed on in the circuit courts. The decision of a circuit court could be reviewed by the Secretary of War, who could modify or set aside any particular award made by it. When, during the same year, a claim under this statute was brought before the circuit court in New York, Jay and Cushing declared that the law was unconstitutional since, under the separation of powers made in the Constitution, judges could not be required to perform non-judicial duties. The law contemplated that the act of passing on the claims was to be non-judicial for it provided that appeals were to be made not to the Supreme Court but to the very unjudicial Secretary of War. However, out of humane considerations and to avoid unnecessary delay in providing needed aid to the unfortunate veterans, Jay and Cushing stated that they would pass on the claims in their individual, non-judicial capacities. The other Justices followed suit, with the exception of Wilson who refused to serve even in a private capacity.

One of these claims was filed by an ex-soldier named Hayburn, and when Wilson and Blair refused to proceed with it, the Attorney-General of the United States appealed to the Supreme Court, in effect asking the same five judges to pass upon their own decision. Hayburn's case was never decided by the Supreme Court because by the time a number of technical procedural difficulties were straightened out, Congress, in 1793, amended the law by repealing the provision for presenting claims to the circuit courts. However, in the following year the Justices, in their capacity as members of the Supreme Court, did pass on the validity of their non-judicial, private acts. To make a test case, the Secretary of War refused to pay the claim of one Yale Todd, whose claim had been approved by one of the Justices acting voluntarily as a commissioner. When the case came to the Justices in the Supreme Court they decided that what they themselves had done as commissioners in their individual capacities was invalid and void in the first place, and that therefore the Secretary of War did not have to pay Yale Todd's claim.

This decision brought a frustrating and completely unsatisfactory end to the whole sorry mess. But what is interesting and relevant to our chronicle of the trials and tribulations of the Supreme Court is the reaction that the decision of the circuit court in Hayburn's case aroused.

This was the first case in which a court held unconstitutional an act of Congress and the excitement it evoked was as conspicuous as the silence that greeted the circuit court decisions holding state statutes unconstitutional. The decision and the judges who handed it down were attacked and defended with equal vigor. For the first but far from last time in the history of the Supreme Court demands for impeachment of the Justices were made within and without Congress. Although the House of Representatives did direct an inquiry into the matter, nothing came of it, as nothing was to come of the equally strident cries for impeachment that were thereafter to follow in the wake of almost every highly controversial decision of the Supreme Court.

It is at first glance remarkable that the bitter opposition to the decision and the call for impeachment came from the Federalists, while its defense came from the anti-Federalists, who but ten years later would damn Marshall for daring to assert that the Supreme Court had the right to declare an act of Congress unconstitutional. On closer consideration, however, the reaction of both parties is not so remarkable. In 1793 the Federalists controlled Congress and did not relish the idea of their laws being nullified by anybody. To them Congress was the only real hope for keeping the untrustworthy state legislatures in check, and anything which weakened the powers of Congress necessarily gave aid and comfort to the enemies, actual and potential, who controlled the state legislatures.

Conversely, the anti-Federalists in 1793 welcomed any rein, even from the Federalist bench, on the aristocrats in Congress. Moreover, as the leading anti-Federalist paper of the period noted, if the judges could nullify the invalid pensioners' law, there was hope that at some appropriate future time they would be able to nullify the law establishing the hated national bank. For that reason, when Jay ran for governor of New York in 1792, he was attacked bitterly by the anti-Federalists on many grounds but was not criticised for his decisions holding the invalid pensioners' law unconstitutional. In 1803, of course, the situation was entirely different, and the anti-Federalists could clearly see the grave evil of allowing aristocratic, life-appointed judges to nullify the people's will expressed through their representatives in the national legislature.

THE COURT STARTS OFF ON THE WRONG FOOT

If one looks for symbolism in the Supreme Court's history it may be found in the fact that the first significant decision of the Court got it into trouble. That decision was in the case of *Chisholm* v. *Georgia.*

During the war Georgia (as had the other states) had confiscated the property of many of the Tories who lived in the state. After the war the Tories sought to get their property back, but rather than requesting it themselves, they had assigned their claims to other, less unpopular citizens. The ex-partner of one of these Tories claimed that his former associate owed him money on the partnership account and sought to get it paid out of the Tory's confiscated property. When the state of Georgia refused to accept or pay the claim, the partner (actually, his executor, as he himself had died), a resident and citizen of South Carolina, brought suit against the state of Georgia in the United States Supreme Court. Georgia indignantly protested that as a "sovereign" state she could not be haled into court and refused to defend the suit, claiming that the Supreme Court had no jurisdiction even to consider it. The question before the Court, therefore, was whether in those circumstances judgment by default could be rendered against Georgia as it would be if an ordinary defendant had refused to appear in court in answer to a summons and complaint duly served on him. Justice Iredell alone said no; the others said yes.

When ratification of the Constitution was before the people of the United States there were many cries of opposition because it apparently authorized the federal courts to allow just the type of suit brought by Mr. Chisholm against the state of Georgia. The very idea that a sovereign state could be made to answer before a federal tribunal was an insult to its dignity. Had the Federalist protagonists of the Constitution sought to justify such an action, the Constitution would have been doomed. Instead they uniformly and vigorously denied any such implication. In Number Eighty-one of *The Federalist* Hamilton dismissed the suggestion as ridiculous. Jay himself agreed, as did all the other Federalist leaders. Because the people were assured and relied upon the assurance that the Constitution did not authorize federal judges to compel a state to defend itself in court, they, reluctantly, ratified it. Now that the Constitution had safely reached its haven, the Justices of the Supreme Court in practically their very first case blandly treated their pre-ratification assurances as campaign promises are frequently treated; that is, they simply forgot about them. Could a breach of faith be more egregious?

This was the indignant reaction of not only the anti-Federalists but of many of the Federalists as well. And who can deny that it appears to be a quite natural and justifiable reaction. Yet, on closer examination the matter is not as black and white as it seems at first glance. The Court's task is to interpret and apply the Constitution, not the speeches or essays of its supporters. As Justice Felix Frankfurter said many years later in a similar situation, it was the Constitution, not the speeches, that was adopted. If a particular provision in the Constitution is unclear or ambiguous, it is entirely proper to consult the writings and speeches of the draftsmen to find out what was really meant by it. But where the provision itself is so clear as not to admit of two meanings, it might well make anarchy of constitutional law if the judges could disregard the plain meaning of the Constitution in favor of some contrary interpretation given in the course of the drafting or ratification of the document. We do not know how many people read *The Federalist* Number Eighty-one or heard the assurances given by Jay and his colleagues. We have the right to assume that every one who voted for ratification had read the Constitution and had a right to rely on its plain meaning.

Nor can there be any doubt that the meaning of the provision upon which the Court relied is plain and unambiguous. Section 2 of Article III provides that "The judicial power shall extend to all cases . . . between a State and citizens of another State." There is no more warrant for saying that this means only suits in which the state is a plaintiff suing a citizen of another state than to say that it means only the converse. Unless the purpose of language is to conceal rather than convey meaning, section 2 means exactly what it says: that the Supreme Court shall have jurisdiction in any suit in which a state is a party, whether a suit *by* it against citizens of another state or a suit *against* it by such citizens.

Nevertheless, to the anti-Federalists of 1793 the decision represented Federalism at its worst: breach of faith and of solemnly given assurances, wanton disregard of the independence and sovereignty of the states, and a decision in favor of the aristocratic Tories and against the common people. Even the Federalists could not unanimously support the decision, for its practical effects were not limited to the anti-Federalist southern states. The Federalist New England states, too, had confiscated Tory property during the Revolution and the announcement of the Court's decision was followed immediately by the bringing of suits to recover confiscated Tory property, not only against South Carolina and Virginia, but Massachusetts as well. A wholesale institution of such suits posed a threat of disaster to most of the states in view of the critical condition of their finances.

The reaction in Georgia was most violent. The first full scale decision handed down by the Supreme Court met with passionate defiance. Georgia made it expressly clear that it had no intention of complying with the decision or even recognizing that the Supreme Court had any moral, legal or constitutional right to have undertaken the case in the first place. The intensity of feeling is indicated by the passage in the Georgia House of Representatives of a bill which provided that any federal official who sought to enforce Mr. Chisholm's judgment should be declared "guilty of felony and shall suffer death, without benefit of clergy, by being hanged." The bill never became law; but this did not matter since no effort was made to collect the judgment.

This first defiance of the Court was successful. However, to prevent a repetition of the incident, Congress and the states took less dramatic though more permanently effective action. Congress speedily proposed and the states in due course approved what became the Eleventh Amendment, providing expressly and in language not subject to misinterpretation that the jurisdiction of federal courts did not extend to any suit against a state by a citizen of another state.

The amendment enabled the Court to get off the tiger it had so rashly mounted. After the amendment was adopted, the Court ruled that its effect was to deprive the Court of jurisdiction of all suits against a state by citizens of another state, whether they had been begun before or after the amendment was adopted. Since it was not likely that many of the other states would have treated judgments against them more hospitably than had Georgia, the institution of suits after the Chisholm decision presented the Court with the equally unpleasant alternatives of overruling that decision almost immediately after it was announced or seeing its rulings successfully defied by the other states as well. By declaring that the amendment swept all the pending cases from the Court's docket, the Court was saved from the necessity of making a choice.

JAY'S TREATY AND LIBERATION

One of the aspects of the Chisholm case that contributed to the anti-Federalists' fury was their belief that it represented an indication of the pro-British bias of the Federalist Court. The French Revolution had caused tremendous excitement in the United States; the Federalists condemned it and the anti-Federalists defended it. When the French Revolution was followed by the war beween Britain and France, the Federalists' sympathies went to Britain, the sympathies of the anti-Federalists, who were beginning to call themselves Republicans and to be called Jacobins and "Frenchmen" by their opponents, went to republican France. The net result of Jay's decision in the Chisholm case, had it been enforced, would have been to impoverish republican states for the benefit of British sympathizers and subjects.

Within two years the Republicans were to be even more convinced of Jay's feelings toward Britain. Loose ends of the late war remained to be tied. The United States had a number of grievances: the northwest frontier was still garrisoned by English troops in violation of the peace treaty of 1783; Britain refused to make compensation for slaves carried away by her army at the close of the Revolution; she refused to enter into any commercial treaty with the United States but on the contrary imposed restrictions on American commerce; worst of all, she violated not only the neutrality of the new nation but its pride and dignity in authorizing her navy to board American merchantmen on the high seas to search for contraband destined for France and to impress American seamen.

Washington decided to send Jay to England to negotiate a treaty for the settlement of these outstanding differences, and Jay, although expressing reluctance, accepted because of the importance of the mission. In order to carry out his mission, he was appointed a special ambassador, and the appointment had to be approved by the Senate. Jay's acceptance of the appointment without resigning from the Court seems quite inconsistent with his earlier reluctance to act as commissioner to pass on the pension claims of invalid veterans. When the Senate considered the appointment there was considerable opposition to it because of what was felt to be the impropriety of the dual service. At least some of the votes to confirm the nomination were cast with the expectation that Jay would resign from the Court upon his confirmation as ambassador. It soon became apparent that, as Madison wrote Jefferson, "such a resignation was no part of the arrangement," and that Jay had as yet no intention of resigning as Chief Justice.

It should be noted that others followed the precedent which Jay set. Jay's successor as Chief Justice, Oliver Ellsworth, while retaining his office of Chief Justice, accepted a mission from Washington's successor to negotiate a treaty with France. Ellsworth's successor, John Marshall, occupied the offices of Secretary of State and Chief Justice of the Supreme Court simultaneously for four weeks. About a hundred and fifty years after Jay set the precedent, Robert Jackson was to serve as chief prosecutor at the Nuremberg war crime trials without resigning from the Supreme Court, and even more recently, Chief Justice Earl Warren was to serve as head of a commission to investigate the assassination of President Kennedy.

Jay remained away for about a year. When he returned, the product of his endeavors shocked the nation. His lack of skill as a trader, or his personal vanity and susceptibility to flattery (which the British Prime Minister deemed his greatest vulnerability), or his pro-English bias, or a combination of all three had resulted in a treaty which the American people judged to be little better than a give-away. In fairness it should be pointed out that he had little to bargain with, that even the most skillful negotiator would have had difficulties and that he did secure the main object of his mission, the evacuation of the British from the northwest posts. In return, however, Jay had to make many concessions, including acquiescence in the British doctrine of contraband and the practice of impressment of sailors (both of which were opposed by the Federalist merchants of New England), the guarantee by the United States of the collection of debts due to British creditors (which infuriated the Republican debtor class), and omission of any provision for return of or compensation for the slaves carried off by British soldiers (which alienated the southern landed class and practically forced them into a not entirely happy alliance with the Republicans). It was only the prestige of Washington, the political skill of Hamilton and the spectre of Jacobinism that finally enabled the administration to squeeze through the necessary two-thirds majority for ratification in the Senate, and this only because the entire debate and vote were held in secret.

During the course of the nationwide controversy Jay was burned in effigy far and wide, and this obviously could have but unfavorable consequences to the prestige of the office of Chief Justice and of the Supreme Court as well. Nevertheless, Jay finally succeeded in winning election to the governorship of New York, and in June, 1795, the first Chief Justice moved from the Supreme Court to the governorship of a state. John Jay had finally achieved his liberation.

Jay's intention to accept the governorship was made known to the President several weeks before his resignation was formally presented. Whether at Washington's suggestion or on his own, however, this was not done until the Senate had adjourned. The effect of the delay was to require the President to make a recess appointment. Had the resignation been submitted earlier, Washington's nominee would have been voted upon by the Senate before it adjourned and would undoubtedly have been confirmed. As it was, the nominee was to serve temporarily until the Senate could act on his appointment when it reconvened six months later. Jay was criticized by his colleague Iredell on the ground that really worthwhile persons would not be willing to accept temporary appointments. But as it turned out, had the resignation not been delayed, the consequence may well have been that the nation and the Supreme Court would have had for their second Chief Justice a madman serving for life. The nation would have survived; it is less certain that the Court would have.

On learning of Jay's intention to resign, Washington sought to induce Hamilton to accept the position because he wanted one, who, like Jay, would not "be scared by popular clamor." Hamilton, however, declined, preferring to return to his law practice and New York politics. Before Washington had a chance to look around for a substitute, he received a letter of application for the position from none other than John Rutledge of South Carolina. Rutledge's action must have seemed strange. Just a few years earlier he had resigned from the Court to accept a judicial position in his own state, and during the period that he was a member of the Court he never once attended any of its sessions. Washington did not bother to delve into Rutledge's motives or the workings of his mind. He immediately sent Rutledge a letter telling him how delighted he was to grant the application, informing him that the Secretary of State had been instructed to make out a commission to Rutledge as Chief Justice, and requesting him to attend and preside at the next session of the Court to be held at the capital (Philadelphia) on the first Monday in August. The appointment was immediately made public, and although it came as a complete surprise to the people and disappointed some of Jay's colleagues on the bench who expected or hoped that the post would be filled by promotion within the Court, there was no reason to believe that there would have been any difficulty in obtaining approval from the Federalist Senate, had it then been in session.

Then strange things began to happen, stranger even than Rutledge's application for appointment. To appreciate them, it is necessary to keep the chronology of events in mind.

The Jay Treaty had been received by Washington in March, 1795. For three months the Federalist leaders debated among themselves what to do with that which even Hamilton in confidence called the "execrable" product of "an old woman." At the end of three months, they came to the conclusion that the treaty was a Federalist work that could not be disowned; there was no alternative but to push it through as secretly as possible. Accordingly, on June 8th the Senate met in extraordinary session and received the treaty. After eighteen days of secret debate, the Federalist leaders finally mustered the necessary two-thirds affirmative vote, ratified the treaty and adjourned (on June 26th), but not before it also voted that the document, like the debate, was to remain secret and not be published. Senator Stevens Thomas Mason of Virginia, however, refused to be bound by the agreement of the other gentlemen of the club, and turned his copy of the treaty over to Benjamin Bache, grandson of Benjamin Franklin and publisher of the Philadelphia *Aurora*, the leading Republican paper in the country.

On July 1 the text of the treaty was published in the *Aurora*. Also on July 1, Washington wrote to Rutledge informing him of his appointment to the Chief Justiceship. Although the commission itself did not arrive at South Carolina until July 24th, the letter of July 1 arrived considerably earlier, in all probability before arrival of the July 1 issue of the *Aurora* with the text of the treaty. In any event, by July 16 Rutledge undoubtedly had received Washington's letter and also knew of the contents of the Jay Treaty.

On July 16 Rutledge addressed a public meeting at St. Michael's Church in Charleston, South Carolina and delivered an impassioned harangue against the treaty. As reported in *The Federalist* papers, which would have no motive to paint the picture worse than it was, Rutledge insulted the President, declared that "he had rather the President would die (dearly as he loved him) than he should sign that treaty," insinuated that Jay and the Senate "were fools or knaves, duped by British sophistry or bribed by British gold," and were guilty of "prostituting the dearest rights of freemen and laying them at the foot of royalty." This, of course, was substantially what the people at large, or at least all but the staunchest Federalists, were saying all over the country. But they had not just been notified of their appointment to the nation's highest judicial office by a President who placed his immeasurable prestige behind the treaty, nor were they required to obtain the approval of that appointment by the same Senate that had ratified the treaty, however reluctantly.

The whole thing seemed senseless, but the explanation was to come later. When Rutledge received his commission making him Chief Justice of the United States, he was quite likely already insane. The tirade against Jay and the Senate at St. Michael's Church was the first public indication of insanity. Other actions and words indicated a progressive impairment of the mind, although a complete mental breakdown did not occur until somewhat later. It may have been, as suggested by one of his friends, that the cause was the death of his wife, which affected him so that "his mind was frequently so much deranged as to be in a great measure deprived of his sense."

After delivering himself of the denunciation of Jay, his treaty and the Senate that ratified it, Rutledge calmly sailed for Philadelphia to take up his duties as Chief Justice, blithely ignoring, or perhaps not aware of, the furor he had aroused. Washington was in a quandary; Rutledge had received the commission and was entitled to preside over the Court as a full-fledged Chief Justice until such time as the Senate acted on the appointment. Presumably, the commission could be withdrawn by the President, although there apparently was no precedent for this, but such action might be more embarrassing than letting matters run their course. Aside from the incident at the church, Rutledge's conduct seemed normal and the President trusted that the mental attack was an isolated one which would perhaps not recur. In any event, Washington did nothing and Rutledge arrived at Philadelphia in time to preside over the Court at its session which began on the first Monday of August, 1795.

Washington's judgment seemed to have been justified, for Rutledge presided with dignity and no untoward consequences. Only two decisions were handed down during the term and both involved the practice of privateering then being carried on by England and France. (Neutral vessels suspected of trading with the enemy were captured and brought into the port of the captor's country or to a neutral port where a prize court—generally a local consul—awarded the vessel to the captor if it decided that the vessel had in fact been engaged in contraband trade.) Neither of the decisions is of particular significance in this chronicle of the Court.

At the close of the August term Rutledge left Philadelphia to take up his circuit duties. When Congress convened in December, Washington let it be known that Rutledge's name would be sent to the Senate for approval. However, after short debate, the Senate rejected the nomination, thus bringing an end to Rutledge's brief term as Chief Justice. Perhaps the rejection accelerated his decline; within a few days thereafter he was reported to have attempted to drown himself, and his mental deterioration became increasingly rapid. More likely, it played no part in the decline and Rutledge would have become completely insane even if his appointment had been approved by the Senate. Since he did not die until 1800, it was fortunate that the nation was spared the painful experience of witnessing an insane man presiding over the Supreme Court and participating in its decisions. (The Constitution contains no provision for removal of a Supreme Court justice other than by impeachment for "treason, bribery or other high crimes and misdemeanors." Neither insanity nor, as the history of the Court was to show, senility comes within any of these categories.)

ELLSWORTH, CHASE AND NATIONAL SUPREMACY

On the Senate's rejection of the Rutledge nomination, Washington offered the Chief Justiceship to Patrick Henry. This would seem a surprising choice in view of Henry's early radicalism and his vigorous efforts to defeat ratification of the Constitution. But Henry had acquired wealth in his later years, and with it a conservatism which made him talk like and become attractive to the Federalists. (Later in 1796, Hamilton sent John Marshall to sound Henry out on running for the Presidency.) Henry was sixty years of age and felt himself too old to accept the office. Washington then promoted Justice Cushing and the Senate confirmed the appointment the day after it was made. But Cushing was even older than Henry; he was sixty-four and declined the appointment, although he did retain his membership in the Court for fourteen more years, until his death in 1810.

Next in point of seniority on the bench was Wilson, and if the post of Chief Justice was to be filled by promotion, his outstanding ability entitled him to it. However, Wilson had only recently been involved in the Yazoo land frauds (later to come before Marshall's Court), and the ensuing scandal may have been the reason for Washington's decision not to appoint him. Here again as in the case of Rutledge, the country was fortunate, for the spectacle of the Chief Justice of the United States skipping around the country to elude creditors and avoid imprisonment for debt would not have enhanced the prestige of the Court. Washington would have liked to appoint Iredell, but felt that he could not do this without humiliating Wilson, and accordingly decided to go outside the Court. His choice was Senator Oliver Ellsworth of Connecticut.

Ellsworth, the principal author of the Judiciary Act of 1789, had been a member of the supreme court of Connecticut. He was an extremely wealthy, right wing Federalist whose aristocratic bent is indicated by the fact that he was a member of a Congressional committee of three which unsuccessfully proposed that the President ought to be addressed as, "His Highness, the President of the United States and Protector of Their Liberties." Ellsworth's Federalist colleagues in the Senate quickly approved his appointment and he took office in time to preside over the February, 1796 term of the Court.

Another vacancy occurred about the same time through the resignation of Justice Blair. To succeed him Washington appointed Samuel Chase, chief judge of the Maryland general court, a signer of the Declaration of Independence, but now an ardent Federalist. Irascible, vain, overbearing, tyrannical, with an instinct for tumult and a faculty for arousing hostility, he was to prove a stormy petrel on the Court.

During this term the Court decided the case of *Ware* v. *Hylton,* in which for the first time it nullified a state statute held to be inconsistent with a treaty entered into by the United States. During the Revolution, Virginia, along with other states, confiscated all debts due to British subjects. The legislature passed a statute providing that all debts owed by Virginians to Englishmen should be paid into the state treasury and the debts would thereby be deemed paid in full and discharged. The treaty of 1783 between the United States and Britain ending the Revolutionary War provided, however, that "creditors on either side shall meet with no legal impediment to the recovery of the full value in sterling money of all bona fide debts heretofore contracted." Since the Constitution declares that the Constitution, laws and *treaties* of the United States shall be "the supreme law of the land . . . anything in the constitution or laws of any state to the contrary notwithstanding," the Supreme Court held that the treaty superseded the statute and that British creditors could collect their debts from the debtors in sterling (rather than depreciated paper) even though the debtors had already paid the debt to the Virginia treasury in accordance with the law. This seemed somewhat hard upon the poor debtors who had acted in good faith and were now being compelled to pay twice, so Chase suggested that it would be the honorable thing for the state of Virginia to compensate them for their loss, although it was really not required to do so. Another interesting aspect of the case was that one of the attorneys for the debtors was John Marshall, (the only time he argued before the Court he was in a few years to head) and he argued (unsuccessfully) in support of state sovereignty and against the treaty.

The principle that a treaty adopted by the United States supersedes state law is clearly indispensable if our nation is to be able to engage in international affairs. No country would be willing to negotiate with the United States if the negotiated and ratified treaty could be nullified by one or more of the fifty states. Such considerations, however, meant little to the hard pressed American debtors of English creditors, three-fourths of whom dwelt in the South. To them, the decision, coming on top of the Jay Treaty, was merely final proof that the Court was a tool of the Federalists to carry out their pro-British, pro-creditor class policies.

Two years later, in the case of *Calder* v. *Bull*, the Court indicated that a state law inconsistent with the Constitution would be set aside to the same extent as one inconsistent with a treaty. However, since the Court held that the particular state law challenged in the suit was not unconstitutional, the decision appears to have aroused no excitement, even among the anti-Federalists, perhaps because people do not get excited over the assertion of a power that is not exercised.

THE ALIEN AND SEDITION ACTS AND THE DEMISE OF THE FEDERALIST PARTY

The Jay Treaty had infuriated the people of France as much as it had the Americans. The French Directory, executive arm of the revolutionary government, was equally bitter at what it considered to be almost a British-American alliance under Washington's administration, and accordingly treated the United States with hostility and its representatives with disdain. John Adams, who sought to continue Washington's policy of avoiding actual involvement in the war between France and Britain, decided to send a diplomatic mission to France, as his predecessor had sent Jay to England. Learning from Washington's errors, he sent a three-man mission rather than a single ambassador. In order to satisfy the Republicans he appointed Elbridge Gerry, *persona grata* to them and to France; to keep Gerry out of mischief he appointed two staunch Federalists to accompany him, John Marshall and Charles C. Pinckney.

Completely underestimating American pride and nationalism, Talleyrand, the French foreign minister, treated the mission with open contempt. The mission arrived in Paris in October, 1797, and was kept cooling its heels for months without getting to see Talleyrand. The only persons they did get to talk to were three mysterious gentlemen who visited them after dark and informed them that a settlement with France could be arranged if the American government apologized for its past conduct, made a large (ten million dollar) loan to France and lined the pockets of Talleyrand and his associates with a handsome bribe (two hundred and fifty thousand dollars). After several months of fruitless effort to reach an understanding, Marshall and Pinckney departed for the United States, leaving Gerry behind to see what he could accomplish alone.

When Marshall landed at Philadelphia he found to his great surprise that he was a national hero. He was paraded through the city to the acclaim of multitudes as the man who dared stand up to the French. When Adams, in March of 1798, had received Marshall's letter recounting the treatment the mission had received in Paris, he immediately reported it to Congress. With a flair for the dramatic he identified the three mysterious gentlemen as Mr. X, Mr. Y and Mr. Z. All that the Federalists had lost by the Jay Treaty and more were recouped through the XYZ affair. Patriotic fervor was at its height. The toast, "Millions for defense but not one cent for tribute," was repeated a thousandfold through the land. In the election of 1798 the Federalists won their largest majorities. Preparations were made for war, although it was expected that France rather than the United States would be the one to declare war. (Later, when Talleyrand indicated that he had no intention of engaging in armed conflict with the United States and began to exhibit a desire towards reconciliation, Hamilton and his right wing Federalists traveled up and down the country crying, "War, War!" when there was no war. They never forgave Adams for not himself declaring war.)

During this period France and everything French were an abomination. The Republican party, which was long considered the pro-French faction, shared the hatred of the real patriots, and Jefferson, its head, was deemed by at least the Hamiltonian Federalists to be a traitor in the tradition of Benedict Arnold, even though he was Vice-President of the United States. The Reverend Timothy Dwight, president of Yale University, delivered a Fourth of July sermon in 1798 in which he asserted that Jeffersonian Republicanism meant nothing less than "our wives and daughters the victims of legal prostitution; soberly dishonored; speciously polluted . . . our sons become the disciples of Voltaire, and the dragoons of Marat." Republicans were called "Frenchmen" and "Jacobins," the latter term having much the same connotation and arousing the same passions as the term "Communist" in the days when Senator Joseph McCarthy dominated the American political scene. A Federalist writer urged his readers to treat Bache, the publisher of the Republican *Aurora*, "as we should a TURK, A JEW, A JACOBIN, OR A DOG."

Taking advantage of the temper of the times, the Federalists pushed through the Alien and Sedition Acts of 1798, and this turned out to be their greatest mistake. As Talleyrand had miscalculated the proud and patriotic spirit of the American people, the Federalist leaders miscalculated its commitment to freedom and liberty. The difference was only that while Talleyrand quickly realized his error and hastily and effectively made amends, the Federalists did not see the light, if they saw it at all, until disaster had struck.

The Alien Act was aimed at the troublesome foreigners who were coming into the country, not only from revolutionary France but from anti-British Ireland. Xenophobia and nationalism often appear to be siblings, if not twins, and the nationalist upsurge of 1798 looked with disfavor on all foreigners. The Naturalization Act of 1798 extended from five to fourteen years the length of residence in the United States necessary in order to acquire citizenship. The Alien Act authorized the President to direct the deportation of "all such aliens as he shall judge dangerous to the peace and safety of the United States, or shall have reasonable grounds to suspect are concerned with any treasonable or secret machinations against the government." The act provided that it was to be in effect only for two years, and during its duration no person was actually deported pursuant to its terms, although two shiploads of Frenchmen voluntarily left the country in fearful anticipation of its enforcement.

The Sedition Act, however, was enforced. It imposed fines and penalties against anyone who uttered or published false, scandalous, and malicious sentiments tending to bring the government of the United States or its officers into disrepute or to excite the hatred of the people. This act too was only to last two years, and compared to the anti-subversion acts of World War I and post-World War II periods, its terms and consequences were extremely mild. During the two years of its duration not more than twenty-five persons were arrested under it, fourteen indicted and ten convicted. The most severe sentence imposed was a fine of four hundred and fifty dollars and eighteen months imprisonment, which may be compared to the twenty year sentences upheld in *Abrams* v. *United States,* in the wake of World War I, or even the ten thousand dollar fine and five years imprisonment imposed in the Smith Act prosecutions after World War II.

Nevertheless, this first experiment on the liberties of a freedom loving people aroused tremendous anger and opposition. The prosecutions were declared to constitute a Federalist "reign of terror." The act was condemned far and wide as unconstitutional. The legislatures of Virginia and Kentucky adopted resolutions, drafted by Madison and Jefferson respectively, declaring not only that the law was unconstitutional but that as sovereign states they had the right to declare it unconstitutional. They called upon Congress to repeal the law and, equally without success, upon other states to join them in their resolutions. Virginia talked of secession and suggested that it had the right of "interposing" state authority between its unconstitutionally persecuted citizens and the federal government, a suggestion that would find its echo a century and a half later in the aftermath of the school segregation decision. Jefferson, almost alone, was serenely optimistic; he had supreme trust in the good judgment of the American people and was confident that the fever would soon pass, that America would recover its senses and that the net result would be to sweep the Federalists out of office, a confidence which proved to be justified to an extent even greater than Jefferson probably expected.

What enraged the people as much as anything else was the role played by the judiciary and particularly the Supreme Court Justices in the enforcement of the act. The Supreme Court itself never had occasion to pass on its constitutionality, but the individual Justices enforcing the act in the circuits left no doubt what the result would have been if the issue had ever been presented to the Court as a whole. Popular anger against the Justices was caused not so much by their upholding the constitutionality of the act or even their vigorous enforcement of it, as by the manner in which they conducted trials under it. In their charges to grand juries, in their conducting of trials and in their instruction to trial juries, they abandoned all pretense of impartiality and showed themselves to be intense Federalist partisans. "We have seen," said one Congressman, "judges who ought to be independent, converted into political partisans and like executive missionaries pronouncing political harangues through the United States."

None of the strictures against Adams and his administration for which publishers of Republican papers were indicted and punished exceeded in violence the denunciations heaped by the Federalists upon Rutledge after his St. Michael's Church speech, or upon Jefferson, who was as much Vice-President of the United States as Adams was President. But this fact did not deter Justices Cushing, Chase, Iredell and Bushrod Washington (the first President's nephew, appointed to the Court by Adams when Wilson found in death final liberation from his creditors). A Congressman who was indicted, on the basis of statements made in his circular letters to his constituents, after the grand jury received a charge from Iredell, asserted that it had become "a regular practice of the federal judges to make political discourses to the grand jurors throughout the United States. They have become a band of political preachers, instead of a sage body to administer the law." Cushing, in a charge to a grand jury in Virginia, portrayed the horrors of the French

Revolution and urged the jurymen to be on their guard against French wiles and "the plot against the rights of Nations and of mankind and against all religion, and virtue, order and decency." In his charges to trial juries, Paterson on at least two occasions practically instructed the jury to find the defendants guilty; he did this by telling them that they could find the defendants guilty of any of several crimes, without mentioning that they could also find the defendants not guilty of any crime.

But by far the worst offender was Justice Chase. Chase's reputation was somewhat tarnished when he came to the Court; as a member of Congress during the war he had been discovered profiteering by taking advantage of secret information concerning the commercial policies of Congress and as a result he had been dropped from the Maryland delegation. Perhaps because of this, Chase found it necessary to prove his patriotism by showing no softness to Jacobins. Certainly his temperament was such—even Federalist lawyers found him irascible and possessed of an uncontrollable temper—as seemed to fit him for the role, assigned to him by the Republicans, of the American "Bloody Jeffreys." Chase made himself a terror to all who came into his court as defendants, particularly in political cases. It was he who had the distinction of imposing the harshest sentence imposed under the Sedition Act. This occurred in a case in which the defendant withdrew his plea of not guilty and pleaded guilty, notwithstanding which Chase directed the prosecution to present its full case against him. Although the defendant manifested repentance and expressed regret for his seditious remarks, his refusal to name his associates (because, he said, "I shall lose all my friends") infuriated Chase and caused him to impose the heavy penalty.

It is possible that if Hamilton and his faction had succeeded in embroiling the United States in war with France all this would have been forgiven, and indeed the Federalist judges might have received the acclaim as national heroes that had been accorded Marshall on his return from Paris. But neither Adams nor Talleyrand wanted war. Nor for that matter did most Americans. The increased taxation necessitated by the preparations for a war was becoming a burden on American taxpayers. England, moreover, was not playing its cards shrewdly either; instead of relaxing tensions with the United States it intensified its practice of impressment of American seamen. The result was that in the elections of 1800 the Federalists were decisively defeated and swept out of the White House, the Senate and the House of Representatives. For another twelve years they struggled as a minority, controlling a few New England states, but the War of 1812 finally brought an end to the party.

THE MIDNIGHT JUDGES OF JOHN ADAMS

Under the Constitution as it read at that time, the new administration would not take office until the March fourth following the election. From the first Tuesday in November, 1800 until the fourth of March, 1801, the Federalists still controlled Congress and the Presidency, and in that period much could be done, particularly with the judiciary, whose members were appointed for life. Two weeks after Congress convened in December, the administration introduced a bill to revise the national judiciary. The Supreme Court was to be reduced, after the next vacancy, to five members, to prevent (said the Republicans) an appointment by Jefferson to the highest tribunal. (It was expected that Cushing, who was already senile, would shortly resign. Actually, he held out until his death a decade later.) To make the lot of the present Federalists on the Court easier, they were relieved of the onerous burden of sitting in circuit. To fill the gap, the act provided for the creation of ten new district and sixteen new circuit court judgeships. In addition, a large number of other offices were created, these too to be filled by deserving Federalists.

The Republicans in Congress vainly fought the bill; the Federalist Congress passed it and Adams signed it into law in February, 1801. It has often been charged that the Federalists anticipated the crucial role the judiciary would play in future affairs and that their court-packing program was designed to maintain Federalist control of the nation after they left the White House and the Congress. It is far more probable that they chose the judiciary simply because only that was available to them; had they been able to fill executive or legislative offices for life duration, they certainly would have preferred those. As the Republican *Aurora* remarked, the measure was "a bill providing sinecure places and pensions for thoroughgoing Federal partisans." The real role that was to be played by the judiciary was not to become apparent until after Marshall's term, and even then it would be the Supreme Court's rather than the lower courts' role that would be crucial. If the Federalists had really appreciated the Supreme Court's future role, they would have enlarged its membership, rather than cut it down, and added new Supreme Court Justices rather than circuit judges. The Federalists were merely acting on the proposition that to the vanquished belong such spoils as they can keep from the victors.

In any event, no sooner had the bill been signed than Adams began making appointments. As quickly as they were made they were rushed to the Senate for confirmation and then back to Adams' Secretary of State Marshall to fill out and sign commissions for the new appointees. Into the very night before Jefferson's inauguration Adams continued to nominate officers, including judges, the Senate to confirm them and Marshall to sign and seal the commissions. The victorious Republicans denounced Adams' appointees as "midnight judges." A report of an incident that was said to have occurred in Marshall's office received wide circulation. Levi Lincoln, Jefferson's incoming Attorney-General, strode into Marshall's room at midnight, holding Jefferson's watch in his hand. Dramatically pointing to the watch, Lincoln told Marshall that the fourth of March had arrived and bade him instantly to lay down his pen. Covered with humiliation, Marshall laid down the pen and left the room. The story is probably apocryphal, but at most it was only a slight exaggeration; Marshall kept signing and sealing commissions at least as late as nine o'clock in the evening of March third.

Marshall was acting as Secretary of State; but he was also Chief Justice of the Supreme Court. Ellsworth, broken in health, had resigned. Adams, without asking Jay's consent, reappointed him to the position he had earlier held. The ever caustic *Aurora* commented that: "John Jay after having thru decay of age become incompetent to discharge the duties of Governor, has been appointed to the sinecure of Chief Justice of the United States." (Actually, Jay was then only fifty-six and lived for twenty-eight years longer.) "That the office of Chief Justiceship is a sinecure," the *Aurora* continued, "needs no other evidence than that in one case the duties were discharged by one person [Jay] who resided at the same time in England, and by another [Ellsworth] during a year's residence in France."

Jay, however, declined the opportunity of returning to the position he had finally succeeded in quitting, and the Hamilton wing of the Federalist party then urged the promotion of Paterson. Adams, instead, without consulting Marshall or any other person, nominated him to the office. The appointment was greeted with apathy more than anything else. The Federalists in the Senate were hardly enthusiastic; one of the leading senators called the appointment a "wild freak." Moreover, they were a little resentful that Paterson had been slighted and for a short time the Hamiltonians even considered refusing to confirm, but with a little (one week's) delay they approved the appointment when it became clear that Adams would in no case appoint a Hamiltonian. The Republican politicians were in the main utterly indifferent; and the masses of both parties neither knew nor cared about Marshall's elevation. The truth of the matter is that after twelve years the Supreme Court and its Chief Justiceship were still not very important to the people of the United States.

chapter four

The Prudent Roar of John Marshall

A terrible blunder was committed by someone in 1800. In that year the capital was moved from Philadelphia to Washington. A beautiful mansion (later known as the White House) was provided for the President. A magnificent Capitol was prepared for the Congress. (As to be expected, the ever-carping Republicans complained that both were "much too extravagant, more so than any palace in Europe.") Then, to the horrified embarrassment of everyone, it was discovered that no provision at all had been made for the Supreme Court. The person or persons whose responsibility it was to look after these things had simply forgotten all about the Court. There was just no place to put the third branch of the Government.

What was to be done? The Court had removed itself from Philadelphia with the rest of the government, but, unlike them, when it arrived in Washington it found that it had no place to go. Whatever sense of desperation the Justices may have felt as the opening day of the term approached was apparently not shared by anyone else; or perhaps there were many more important things to be taken care of. It would have been terribly embarrassing to have had to postpone the opening day for lack of a place to transact business.

Fortunately this did not prove necessary. A fortnight before the scheduled opening day, the Commissioners of the District (who really had the responsibility for housing everybody other than the President and the Congress) diffidently wrote to Congress that, "As no house has been provided for the Judiciary of the United States, we hope the Supreme Court may be accommodated with a room in the Capitol to hold its sessions until further provisions shall be made, an arrangement which we would not presume to make without the approbation of Congress." Congress, let it be said to its credit, responded promptly. The very next day the Senate set aside a room for the Supreme Court of the United States. It was not much of a room, about twenty-four by thirty feet, not much larger than a good-sized living room. It had originally been assigned for use by the clerk of the Senate, and it is probable that he was not too happy about the deprivation. An ill-favored thing, perhaps, but it was the Court's own, and the Court was able to move into it in time to open the February, 1801 term on the scheduled first Monday of the month. As it turned out, the opening was postponed, through no fault of the District Commissioners, the Senate or its clerk. It simply happened that on the opening day only the elderly Cushing showed up. It was two days later that Chase and Bushrod Washington arrived, making up the quorum necessary to do business and to enable the new Chief Justice to take his oath of office. Moreover, the whole thing could have been postponed for another six months, since the Court had no decisions to hand down during the whole February term.

For eight years the Court continued to hold its sessions in the Senate clerk's office—it was 1809 before the unhappily displaced clerk got his room back. In that year Congress provided for the Court a larger room in the basement of the Capitol. When the Capitol was reconstructed after it was burned by the British in 1814, the room set aside for the Court was enlarged still further, but with the expanding activity and prestige of the Court, this too soon proved to be inadequate. In 1860, when new wings were added to the Capitol for the use of the Senate and the House, the Court inherited the Senate's former chamber. It was not until 1935 that the Supreme Court moved to its permanent home, a magnificent marble structure designed by Cass Gilbert, with a huge portico containing eight Corinthian columns and a sculptured pediment and a large, luxuriously decorated and draped courtroom.

So it happened that at the beginning of John Marshall's term as Chief Justice someone forgot about the Supreme Court. At his death thirty-four years later, one thing could be said with certainty: no one would ever again forget about the Supreme Court.

THE LAST OF THE FEDERALISTS

Marshall was the last of the Federalists. Long after Washington had died and Adams and Jay had left the political scene, long after Aaron Burr's bullet had killed Hamilton, Marshall continued to give concrete and meaningful effect to orthodox Federalist dogma. Adams had chosen far more wisely than he could have dreamed. Jefferson and his Republicans had successfully buried the Federalist party in the election of 1800, but Marshall survived the debacle. By the time he died

Federalism had become so firmly established as the way of life of the judiciary that it could not be dislodged for a century, and then only because a man with Jefferson's forcefulness and prestige was President, and the nation was struck by the greatest depression it had ever known.

Marshall, the oldest of fifteen children, was born in 1755 in the western, frontier region of Virginia. He was a distant relative, on his mother's side, of Thomas Jefferson, who was to become his chief adversary. In his childhood Marshall on a few occasions came in contact with Washington and developed an almost reverential relationship to him. Early in the War of Independence he enlisted in the armed forces and shared with his idol the rigors of the Valley Forge winter. In 1780 he attended a course of lectures in law at William and Mary College. A few years later he married and at the conclusion of the war began to practice law in Richmond. His background in legal studies was slight and throughout his long career he never undertook to improve it substantially; even as Chief Justice he could not except charitably be called one who was learned in the law. However, then as now, legal scholarship and success at law did not necessarily go together; he became more than moderately successful in his practice and in time one of the recognized leaders of the Virginia bar. He was an eloquent and effective advocate with a reputation for a keen sense of logic.

Like so many other young lawyers, he entered politics practically simultaneously with his admission to the bar. In 1782 he became a member of the Virginia legislature and served almost continuously until the adoption of the Constitution. In emulation of Washington, he was from the beginning Federalist in his feelings and thinking. Like all Federalists he was horrified by Shays' Rebellion and saw a strong, central government, with stringent restraints on the people and their local legislative bodies as the exclusive means of preventing a recurrence.

Naturally, he supported the Constitution and fought for its adoption, not so much because it augmented the powers of the national government as because it diminished the powers of the state governments. In his arguments in support of the Constitution he expressed the view that the courts had the right and duty to declare void and refuse to enforce any law contrary to the Constitution, but this principle he did not extend to the Bill of Rights. That, he felt, was "merely recommendatory." To give it the same efficacy as, for example, the provision barring laws impairing the obligation of contracts would be unfortunate for "many laws which are found convenient would be unconstitutional." This view of the relative importance of property and personal rights is perhaps understandable in the light of the fact that as his success in legal practice grew he reached the point where practically all his cases were in defense of property rights.

In 1793 he ventured into the arena of land speculation. With one of his brothers and two other men he formed a syndicate which purchased from the British heirs the remainder of the great Fairfax estate, consisting of over 160,000 acres of the best land in Virginia. During the war Virginia had enacted a law decreeing the confiscation of all lands held by British subjects, and although she had never prosecuted the forfeiture of the Fairfax estate, she was always threatening to do so. Thus, Marshall's major investment for many years occupied a highly precarious legal footing, a fact which influenced and strengthened his natural inclination towards the protection of property rights from predatory legislation.

As his financial success increased so too did his political stature. By 1795 he was the generally acknowledged leader of the Federalist party in Virginia. In that year Washington offered him the post of Attorney-General, but he declined that offer as well as the offer a year later of the post of minister to France. He did, however, vigorously defend the Jay Treaty in heavily Republican Virginia.

The most fortunate event in Marshall's life was probably his acceptance of appointment with Pinckney and Gerry to the mission to France that led to the XYZ affair. For this single year's employment he received twenty thousand dollars over and above his expenses, an amount three times his annual earnings at the bar. More important, Talleyrand's venality and miscalculation of American national pride, rather than any manifested diplomatic skill on Marshall's part, catapulted Marshall into the heights of popular esteem. This fact and the endorsement by the now quite conservative Patrick Henry enabled him to eke out a narrow victory in an election for representative in the spring of 1799. During the course of the campaign he was queried on the most exciting issue of the day, the Alien and Sedition Laws. His reply was that while he believed the laws to be constitutional, he did not believe them to be expedient and would oppose any effort to renew them on their imminent expiration.

In Congress Marshall showed himself to be a Federalist, but a moderate and independent one. When a resolution to repeal the Sedition Law was presented, he voted in its favor, the only Federalist to do so. On the other hand, when the election of 1800 resulted in an equal Electoral College vote for Jefferson and Aaron Burr (although every person in the United States knew that the people had voted for Jefferson for President and Burr for Vice-President), Marshall favored Burr but was finally prevailed upon by Hamilton to keep out of the contest. But Hamilton could not induce him to take an active part in preventing what would have been an outrageous and dishonest flouting of the will of the American people; unfriendly neutrality was as far as Marshall would go.

In May of 1800 the increasingly tense relations between Adams and the Hamilton wing of the Federalist party had reached the stage of actual breach. Hamilton began intriguing with a view to replacing Adams by another candidate in the Presidential election. Hamilton's men in the cabinet were parties to the intrigue. When Adams got wind of what was happening he summarily discharged first his Secretary of War and then his Secretary of State. In each case he offered the post to Marshall, who refused the first but was finally prevailed upon to accept the second. He remained as Secretary of State until March 4, 1801, when Adams went out of office.

This was the man who, five weeks earlier, was commissioned Chief Justice of the United States and who was to dominate the Supreme Court for thirty-four years and make of it a world never dreamed of by Washington, Hamilton, Jay, Ellsworth or any other of the Federalist fathers of the Constitution and the Court. Six years before Marshall took the oath of office, Jay had, in his own words, "left the bench perfectly convinced that under a system so defective it would not obtain the energy, weight and dignity which are essential to its affording due support to the national government, nor acquire the public confidence and respect which, as the last resort of the justice of the nation, it should possess." With exactly the same defective system the Court under Marshall was to achieve all and more than that which Jay said it could never achieve.

REPEAL AND RETURN TO RIDING CIRCUIT

"The Federalists," wrote Jefferson after his inauguration, "have retired into the Judiciary as a stronghold . . . and from that battery all the works of republicanism are to be beaten down and erased." To the extent that this was more than merely a battle cry for the repeal of the Judiciary Act of 1801, its applicability was limited to the lower federal courts. Even Jefferson did not expect that whatever beating down there would be would come from the Supreme Court and its new Chief Justice. As far as the Supreme Court was concerned, all the act creating the "midnight judges" did was to attempt to deprive Jefferson of the opportunity to appoint a Republican to the seat which Cushing was expected to vacate shortly, and to relieve the Justices of the burden of riding circuit, neither of which would substantially increase their capacity for erasing the works of republicanism. And even in respect to the multitude of new district and circuit court judges, what the Republicans objected to most was not that they would wreak more evil, but on the contrary that they would wreak neither evil nor good. The business of the federal courts, the Republicans charged, had decreased and there was not enough to keep the present judges busy. The crime the Federalists had committed was the wasteful squandering of public funds through the creation of a host of new sinecures.

The available evidence does not indicate that either Jefferson or his lieutenants deemed the repeal of the 1801 act a major or urgent mission of republicanism. Historians and biographers with pronounced Federalist biases have depicted the campaign to repeal the act as a conspiratorial assault upon the judiciary and its independence, with Jefferson playing the role of arch conspirator. Actually, there is little to indicate that in 1801 Jefferson considered the Supreme Court, the rest of the judiciary or the 1801 act a major concern other than as an incident of gross political patronage.

The Republican leaders in Congress indicated no sense of overriding urgency. It was not until almost a year after Jefferson's inauguration that a bill was introduced to repeal the 1801 act. It took an additional two months of what appeared to be endless debate before a final vote was taken and the bill passed both Houses, in each case by a strictly partisan vote, all Republicans voting for the repeal, and all Federalists against it.

The principal argument of the Republicans was that there was no need for the new judges. "Could it be necessary," rhetorically demanded their leader in the Senate, "to increase courts when suits were decreasing . . . to multiply judges, when their duties were diminishing?" In respect to circuit duty by Supreme Court Justices, which the 1801 act had abolished, this, the Republicans argued, was necessary so that the Justices should meet the common people and appreciate their needs and demands.

The Federalists' argument was that the repeal was an attack on the independence of the judiciary. "Governments," one of their leading spokesmen said, "are made to provide against the follies and vices of men." Their purpose is "to save the people from their most dangerous enemy; to save them from themselves." The fathers of the Constitution recognized also that within the government the most effective instrumentality for achieving this objective was the judiciary. They therefore insulated the judiciary from control by the other two departments of the government to insure its independence. They provided that the judges should serve for life and should not be removable except on impeachment for the commission of high crimes or misdemeanors. They went even further and provided that their salaries could not be reduced while they were in office. If the judges' offices could be abolished by repealing the law that created them, would this not be a simple means of frustrating the purpose of the Constitutional fathers; for what is to prevent Congress from repealing not only the 1801 act but the 1789 act as well, thus abolishing all judicial offices, and then immediately enacting a new law again establishing judicial offices, this time to be filled by Jefferson's Republican henchmen?

As a matter of logic, the cogency of this argument cannot be easily denied. Its fatal weakness lay in the fact that the Republicans had swept the election of 1800 and that there were more Republicans in Congress than there were Federalists. The two months of debate with all its logic did not swing a single vote in either House. Nor was the Federalists' argument any more persuasive to those outside Congress than to those within it. The great majority of the general public received repeal with enthusiasm. Even among the Federalist rank and file, the principal reaction was indifference.

The Federalist leaders took the controversy far more seriously than did either the Republicans or their own followers. During the course of the debate the Federalists in Congress on more than one occasion broadly hinted at armed resistance, and the Federalist leaders in New England talked openly of secession if repeal went through. These were the same Federalists who had established a constitution to elevate and enthrone nationalism and who had expressed horror at the threat of dissolution of the Union which but a few years earlier they had found implicit in the Virginia and Kentucky resolutions.

But out of the talk nothing came. The repeal bill was passed and signed by Jefferson. A Federalist paper declaimed: "Our Constitution is no more"; but the New England states did not secede. The "midnight judges" returned to their law offices (or, more accurately, stayed there, for they never did get to don their judicial robes). And the Supreme Court Justices went back to riding circuit, not to be relieved of this chore until a century later.

THE TEMPORARY ABOLITION OF THE SUPREME COURT

The repeal of the Act of 1801 was the occasion for the first full scale debate on the Supreme Court's power to declare unconstitutional a law passed by Congress. The matter had previously been referred to more or less casually in the Constitutional Convention. It had been expounded in *The Federalist* papers, alluded to in some of the state ratification conventions and defended by Justice Paterson on circuit in his charge to the jury in *Vanhorne's Lessee* v. *Dorrance*. But not until the bill to repeal the Act of 1801 was argued in Congress was the line drawn and real debate begun, a debate which even today has not been finally concluded.

The reason for this delay is not hard to discern. This was the first occasion in which there arose the possibility that a Federalist Supreme Court might invalidate a law enacted by a Republican Congress. The Federalists' major argument against the repeal bill was its alleged unconstitutionality, and during the course of the debate there was frequent reference to the probability if not certainty that it would be declared unconstitutional by the Supreme Court. (The arguments in support of the Court's power were all echoed two years later in Marshall's opinion in *Marbury* v. *Madison.*) The ablest case against the power was made in the Senate by John Breckenridge, who had introduced in the Kentucky legislature that state's resolution against the Sedition Law.

"I did not expect, sir," he said, "to find the doctrine of the power of the courts to annul the laws of Congress as unconstitutional so seriously insisted on. . . . I would now ask where they got that power, and who checks the courts when they violate the Constitution?" To assert that courts may annul legislation would give them "the absolute direction of the government . . . for to whom are they responsible?" Which clause in the Constitution grants to the judiciary the power to overthrow legislation? "Is it not extraordinary that if this high power was intended, it should nowhere appear? . . . Never were such high and transcendent powers in any Government (much less in one like ours, composed of powers especially given and defined) claimed or exercised by construction only."

"The Constitution," he continued, "intended a separation of the powers vested in the three great departments, giving to each exclusive authority on the subjects committed to it. . . . Those who made the laws are presumed to have an equal attachment to, and interest in the Constitution; are equally bound by oath to support it, and have an equal right to give a construction to it. . . . The construction of one department of the powers vested in it is of no higher authority than the construction of any other department."

The Republicans were convinced by the reasonableness of their own arguments but they decided to give reason time in which to make itself accepted and effective. The original Judiciary Act of 1789 had set up two terms of the Supreme Court each year, one in February and the other in August. The 1801 act changed the schedule to June and December. The repeal law did not itself disturb the changed schedule, but after it was adopted another bill was passed which provided for only one term of the Court yearly, that to take place in February. The last previous term of the Court had been held in December of 1801; under the new law, adopted in April, 1802, the next term would take place in February of 1803, or a period of fourteen months since the last term.

The purpose of the delay was to avoid a speedy decision by the Supreme Court on the constitutionality of the repeal law. The Republicans' objective was in part to allow the repeal to take full effect by the time the Court could pass on it, so that the Court would in effect be faced with a *fait-accompli*. But more important, their objective was also to allow public opinion to crystallize in support of the law. The Republicans were confident that the sympathies of the great majority of the people were with them, and they believed that public opinion was not without influence upon Supreme Court decisions.

The new law was denounced by the Federalists as vigorously as they had denounced the repeal act. It was, they charged, an abolition of the Court for fourteen months. If this be permissible, what is to prevent Congress from suspending the functions of the Court for ten or twenty years, or forever? If a temporary abolition of the Court is constitutional, there is no logical reason to assume that a permanent abolition would not be equally constitutional. A permanent abolition, they argued, is obviously unconstitutional; a temporary one is no less so.

It is interesting to speculate on what would have happened if, as some Federalists apparently expected, the Court had agreed with them that the suspension was unconstitutional and had convened in June, 1802, as if nothing had happened. Suppose, further, that at this June session the Court had indeed ruled that not only the suspension law but the repeal law as well was unconstitutional, and that every one of the "midnight judges" was legally in office, entitled to hold court, decide cases and collect his salary from the federal treasury. What then?

There is, of course, no way of knowing with certainty what would have happened; when two roads diverge in history, only one can be taken. It is highly probable, however, that the Court's decision would have received the same defiance from Jefferson and the Republicans that its decision in *Chisholm* v. *Georgia* had received from the state of Georgia. Debtors summoned before the "midnight judges" would not come; the judges' decisions would not be enforced by Jefferson's marshals, and the judges themselves would receive no salaries. There would be nothing that the Court could do about this, and such successful defiance might have spelled the death of the Court as a political institution in its infancy.

Marshall's contribution to the evolution of the Court may lie as much in the decisions that he did not make as in those that he did. Among the assets of mind and personality which enabled him to establish the Court as neither Jay nor Ellsworth was able, not the least was his prudence. Marshall was too prudent to present Jefferson and the Republicans with an all-out challenge at the height of their popularity and at the nadir of the Federalists'. After the repeal law was adopted, he had suggested to his associates that they should refuse to sit on circuit, but his associates refused to go along. Lacking their support to even this partial defiance (talk of impeachment of judges was already widespread), he decided to bide his time, and quietly advised Hamilton that the Federalist party should endure what could not be avoided and that the "midnight judges" should go home. For his part, Marshall did the same. He stayed at home and did not come to Washington to convene the Court until the second Monday in February, 1803, the day fixed by the Republican Congress.

MARBURY V. MADISON

But if there was danger in acting precipitately, so too was there in delaying action unduly. If the Jeffersonians' open challenge of the Court's power to annul acts of Congress went unanswered for any length of time, the conclusion might well be that the Court acquiesced in their denial of its power. Marshall may have preferred to wait until he had an opportunity to lift the prestige of the Court above the low level at which it was left by the administrations of Jay and Ellsworth and particularly by the sorry behavior of the Justices sitting in circuit on cases arising under the Alien and Sedition Laws, but the day of decision could not be long postponed. A means had to be found not only to assert the Court's claim of judicial supremacy, but to do so in a way that would not enable Jefferson to stultify the Court by defying its mandate and leaving the Court no practical means to vindicate its claim. It may be assumed that Marshall devoted a good deal of his thinking time to this problem between April, 1802, when the law suspending the Supreme Court's operations was adopted, and February, 1803, when the suspension expired and the Court returned to its business. By that time, he had found the answer. The case of *Marbury* v. *Madison* was presented to the Court almost as soon as it opened its doors; the decision in the case was announced by Marshall only two weeks later, indicating quite clearly that it had been the subject of considerable thought during his enforced leave of absence.

If constitutional lawyers and historians were polled to ascertain what they considered the single most important decision in the history of the Supreme Court, at least nine out of ten would unhesitatingly designate *Marbury* v. *Madison.* If their evaluation is correct, a mighty oak has grown out of a quite insignificant acorn; for as important as the decision in the case may have been, so unimportant was the specific law suit which gave rise to it.

On March 2, 1801, less than two days before the end of his term,

President Adams appointed forty-two Federalists as justices of the peace for the District of Columbia, each to serve for a period of five years. On March 3 the appointments were rushed to the Senate, which promptly confirmed them. They were then rushed back to the office of the Secretary of State (Marshall) who affixed the appropriate seal upon them and placed them on his desk for delivery to the appointees. In the rush of the final hours, however, Marshall forgot all about them. The office of justice of the peace was at the very bottom of the political pork barrel and it is quite understandable that Secretary of State-Chief Justice Marshall would have more important things to worry about at that stage of the Federalist control of the government. In any event, when Madison, Jefferson's Secretary of State, arrived at the office, the commissions were still on the desk, undelivered.

On instructions from Jefferson, Madison delivered twenty-five of the commissions to the appointees but withheld the remaining seventeen. It seems likely that, because of the insignificance of the office, Jefferson did not take the trouble to substitute deserving Republicans for the twenty-five undeserving Federalists and withheld the other seventeen commissions simply as an economy measure, believing that twenty-five justices of the peace for the District of Columbia were enough. Indeed, of the accepted twenty-five, five refused their commissions and of the rejected seventeen, only four bothered to go to court to get their jobs. Even these appear to have been motivated not by a genuine desire for the jobs but by a decision of the Federalist party, in whose behalf the four were probably acting, to frighten the Jeffersonians out of attempting to repeal the 1801 act. Of the four who decided or were prevailed on to sue, one was William Marbury, and the accident that his name was placed first in the legal papers resulted in his immortalization in the history of constitutional law.

The Anglo-American system of law, known as the common law system, had developed a legal remedy called mandamus. This was a procedure whereby a court commanded an unwilling public official to do an act which the law prescribed. For example, suppose an election official in the South were to refuse to count ballots cast by qualified Negro voters. A court could issue an order of mandamus against him commanding him to count Negroes' ballots equally with those of whites. If, having been served with the order, he still refused, he could be jailed for contempt of court. Of course, before the order could be issued he would have to have an opportunity to appear in court and explain ("show cause") why the order should not be issued, as for example because the Negroes had not passed the prescribed literacy test.

Section 13 of the Judiciary Act of 1789 provided that the Supreme Court should have power to issue writs of mandamus against "persons holding office under the authority of the United States." Accordingly, the lawyer for Mr. Marbury and his three fellow would-be justices of the peace applied to Marshall, as Chief Justice of the Supreme Court, for a writ directing Madison to show cause at the next term of the Court why an order should not be issued against him commanding him to deliver the signed and sealed commissions to the plaintiffs. As it turned out, the next term of the Court was delayed by Congress for more than a year, and in the ensuing period Marshall's writ to Jefferson's Secretary of State became the subject of heated controversy in Congress and in the press.

To Jefferson and the Republicans the issuance of the writ violated their ideas of the Constitutional principle of separation of powers. If the courts could direct the President or his cabinet officials in the performance of their executive duties, it would make the President subordinate to the judiciary, which the Constitution never intended. Logic might suggest that an act of Congress specifying at what times the Court should hold its sessions might likewise constitute an interference by one branch of the government in the constitutionally conferred domain of another, but logic was irrelevant. To the Jeffersonians the only thing that mattered was that the writ constituted an assault by a Federalist judiciary upon a Republican executive elected by a people which had but recently decisively expressed its lack of trust in the Federalist party.

The Federalists were confident that when the Court would resume its sessions it would issue the requested order of mandamus commanding Madison to deliver the commissions to Marbury and his colleagues. Had that occurred, there is hardly any reason to doubt that Jefferson would have directed Madison to ignore the command and Marshall's Court would have suffered the ignominy of a defiance it had no way of countering. More, it is almost as likely that had Marshall issued the mandamus he and his associates would have faced impeachment. Marshall's prudence avoided both consequences.

Madison did not bother to come to court to show cause why the order of mandamus should not be issued against him. The Court proceeded to hear the attorney for the plaintiffs, and less than two weeks later Marshall announced the Court's decision.

There are three questions, said Marshall, that the Court must decide: (1) Is Marbury entitled to his commission? (2) If so, does the law provide him with a remedy to obtain it? (3) If it does, is that remedy mandamus? The answer to the first question is obvious: of course he is entitled to the commission. It was signed, confirmed by the Senate, and duly sealed by the Secretary of State. The only reason he did not get it was the latter's oversight in not handing it over to him. Certainly, Mr. Marbury should not be deprived of his office simply because of the oversight of the Secretary of State or of any other governmental official in the performance of a purely ministerial or clerical act.

The answer to the second question is equally clear. The refusal of Jefferson and Madison to deliver to Mr. Marbury what belongs to him is a wrong, and under our system it is the duty of the courts to right such wrongs.

Up to this point Marbury appeared headed for victory and Marshall for disaster. But in the last act the tables were turned completely. Marbury had sought to obtain relief by a suit for mandamus in the Supreme Court. He (or his very competent lawyer) did this on the basis of the provision in the Judiciary Act of 1789 that empowered the Supreme Court to issue mandamus orders. But this provision, said Marshall, is unconstitutional. Article III of the Constitution states that the Supreme Court shall have original jurisdiction "in all cases affecting ambassadors, other public ministers and consuls, and those in which a state shall be a party." Marbury's suit is not included in any of these categories (Marbury was not an ambassador nor Madison a state) and therefore the Constitution did not intend the Supreme Court to have jurisdiction of it. Since the Constitution intended that the Court should have no jurisdiction except that which was expressly conferred upon it in the Constitution, the provision in the Judiciary Act of 1789 purporting to confer additional jurisdiction, as in mandamus, is unconstitutional.

The question remains whether the Court has the power to declare unconstitutional and refuse to give effect to an act of Congress. There can be only one answer to this. Unlike the British Parliament, the Congress of the United States has only such powers as are conferred upon it by the people through the Constitution. If the limits placed upon Congress in the Constitution could be disregarded there would be no point to a constitution at all, and there would be no difference between governments with limited and unlimited powers. Moreover, the elaborate method specified in the Constitution for amending it would be meaningless if Congress could amend simply by passing a law inconsistent with it. Since these conclusions are absurd, the only alternative conclusion is that a law inconsistent with the constitution is void and of no effect.

If this is so, must the judiciary nevertheless give it effect? Certainly not. The function of the judiciary is to apply the law, but when it is faced with two inconsistent laws, which shall it apply? Clearly, it must apply the superior one, and between a law of the Constitution and one of the Congress, the former is undeniably the superior one. The Constitution itself states that it shall be the supreme law of the land, and the judges take an oath to support it. If they were to enforce the statute and disregard the Constitution, they would be false to their oath and would elevate the act of Congress over the mandate of the Constitution.

The upshot of all this is that Marbury was legally entitled to his commission and the Federal courts would get it for him if he brought the right kind of suit. What the right kind was, Marshall did not say; all he said was that mandamus was not and therefore Marbury must go home empty-handed. The upshot too was that Marshall had lectured both Jefferson and Congress on the proper conduct for Presidents and Congresses and warned them both that if they did not behave they would at some future time be taken to task.

Marshall's opinion was a loud roar, but at the same time a very prudent one. He asserted the principle of judicial supremacy emphatically and unequivocally but in a way which left Jefferson with no practical means to challenge or defy the assertion. As a matter of fact, in another decision issued only six days later, the Court again avoided a showdown with Jefferson and Congress by upholding the constitutionality of the law repealing the 1801 act. As for the assertion of judicial supremacy in the Marbury decision itself, it aroused relatively little public excitement or criticism even in the Republican press.

Marshall has been extolled by constitutional lawyers and historians for his opinion in the Marbury case as perhaps no other human tribunal has been since Solomon disposed of rival claims to a newborn infant. One who examines the decision without any preconceptions may find this extreme praise difficult to understand. In the Marbury case Marshall did a number of things which, if done by lesser judges, would have subjected them to rather severe criticism by constitutional lawyers. For example, he decided that the Court had no jurisdiction over the case, yet he proceeded to decide that Madison was wrong and Marbury was right; when a court has no jurisdiction over a case it is generally not considered appropriate for it to express opinions on the rights and wrongs of the controversy. Again, he ruled that section 13 of the Judiciary Act of 1789 was unconstitutional; yet he himself had issued the rule to show cause against Madison under that very section of the act. Moreover, he held the section unconstitutional even though it had been drafted by Ellsworth, Marshall's predecessor as Chief Justice, and the Supreme Court itself had on three occasions earlier acted under the section without any intimation by anyone that it might be unconstitutional. The reasoning on which the holding of unconstitutionality was based was extremely weak and was practically to be discarded by Marshall himself eighteen years later in the case of *Cohens* v. *Virginia.*

So much for the deficiencies; what of the merits? Here, too, one can reasonably get the impression that both the importance of the case and Marshall's performance have been exaggerated. The Marbury decision was not the first one in which the Supreme Court had asserted the power to declare an act of Congress unconstitutional; it had done so in earlier cases. Of the arguments presented by Marshall in support of the power, not a single one was original. Every one had been presented previously in *The Federalist* papers, in Paterson's charge to the jury in *Vanhorne's Lessee* v. *Dorrance,* in the debates in Congress attending the repeal of the Act of 1801, and elsewhere. Having asserted the power, Marshall prudently refrained from exercising it; in fact, it was not exercised again until a half-century later in the Dred Scott case, and then with catastrophic consequences.

It may smack of heresy to suggest that *Marbury* v. *Madison* hardly evidences greatness in Marshall and that the decision itself is a considerably less important one than is generally asserted. One can even make a plausible case for the proposition that had it never existed neither the course of American history nor of constitutional law would have been materially altered, and that when later Courts were prepared to declare acts of Congress unconstitutional they would have had ample precedent to rely upon without reference to *Marbury* v. *Madison.* This is, of course, pure speculation; yet it is no less reasonable than the oft-repeated contrary assumption that had the principle of judicial supremacy not been asserted by Marshall in 1803, it would have probably been lost to the Court for all time. However, there is nothing great or important but historians make it so, and historians have made Marshall great and *Marbury* v. *Madison* important.

ABORTIVE IMPEACHMENT

On February 4, 1803, Jefferson sent a message to the House of Representatives suggesting the impeachment of John Pickering, a Federal district judge of New Hampshire. Pickering's conduct on the bench had been quite injudicious. In one case, for example, the government had seized a ship for violation of the revenue laws and Pickering had simply declined to hear any witnesses for the government. He summarily ordered the vessel returned to its master and refused to allow an appeal from his decree, all to the accompaniment of cursings and profanities. The reason for this strange behavior was that he was hopelessly insane and an incurable drunkard. Certainly such a judge should be removed from office, but the Constitution allows impeachment only for high crimes and misdemeanors, and Pickering's insanity, drunkardness and injudicious conduct could not be called high crimes or misdemeanors. Nevertheless, within two weeks after Pickering's trial was begun in the Senate, his conviction was voted and he was removed from the bench.

With this as precedent, the Republicans were prepared to go after bigger quarry. Pickering's conduct had been hardly more injudicious than Chase's. Chase had been imperious and bullying on and off the bench. He had engaged actively in the election campaign of 1800, barnstorming the country against Jefferson's election. He had used the device of charges to the grand jury as a means of delivering philippics against democracy, the Republicans and all their works. In one case he charged the grand jury that "the bulk of mankind are governed by their passions and not by reason. . . . The establishing of universal suffrage will take away all security for property and personal liberty . . . and our constitution will sink into a mobocracy, the worst of all popular governments." Blandly ignoring the Declaration of Independence, he condemned "the modern doctrines of our late reformers, that all men in a state of society are entitled to enjoy equal liberty and equal rights."

Such notions will bring on mischief which "will rapidly progress until peace and order, freedom and property shall be destroyed."

Chase's conduct in the Sedition Law trials had been ferocious; he was by far the most hated of the Federalist judges. In one case, apparently feeling that the prosecutor was not doing the best possible job, he took over the role of prosecutor in order to point up to the jury an item of evidence showing the defendant's criminal intent. By the time he got through with his charge to the jury, they were left with no doubt that he expected them to find the defendant guilty, which they promptly did.

On another occasion, Chase became infuriated on reading a Republican campaign pamphlet, *The Prospect Before Us*, undoubtedly intemperately critical of Adams, which called upon the readers to choose "between Adams, war and beggary, and Jefferson, peace and competency." Chase read the pamphlet in Baltimore and departed for Richmond, the residence of the impecunious author, one James Callender, determined to have him indicted and convicted. On the way he was informed that Callender had been arrested as a vagrant, and replied that it was a pity that they had not hanged the rascal. Then, after an indictment under the Sedition Law was issued and there was some delay in apprehending Callender, Chase expressed the fear that "we shall not be able to get the damned rascal in this court."

Chase did not trouble to conceal his intent to have Callender convicted. During the course of the trial he continually harassed Callender's attorneys (leading Virginia lawyers who had contributed their services) in their conduct of the defense. His interruptions became so frequent, that they could take it no longer; they folded their papers and walked out of the case, the second time in two months this had happened during a trial presided over by Chase. Left without attorneys, Callender did the best he could, but the result had been foreordained, and the presence of counsel would have made no difference. He was found guilty and Chase sentenced him to prison for nine months and imposed a fine of two hundred dollars.

The other case in which attorneys walked out because of Chase's conduct involved a sedition and treason indictment against one John Fries, a militia captain in Pennsylvania, who had led a mob in forcible resistance to the collection of federal taxes on farms. The trial opened in April, 1800, and as it began, Chase threw on the table three papers, saying they contained the opinion of the judges (District Judge Richard Peters was the other judge in the case) on the law of treason. One copy was for the prosecuting attorney, the second for defense counsel, and the third for the jury. Indignantly, Fries' lawyers stated that they had never before come upon a case in which the judge decided the law before hearing the arguments of counsel. They picked up their papers and walked out of the courtroom, although Chase pleaded with them to stay, stating that the only reason he had prepared the paper in advance was to save time. Fries was left without counsel, but Chase assured him that the judges themselves would personally see that justice was done so that he really did not need any lawyer. At the conclusion of the trial Fries was found guilty and Chase thereupon condemned him to be "hanged by the neck until dead," thus earning for himself the sobriquet, "the hanging judge." (Against the unanimous advice of his cabinet and to the dismay of the entire Hamiltonian wing of the Federalist party, Adams pardoned Fries.)

These were the acts of misconduct on the part of Chase that were the basis of the House resolution to impeach him, adopted on March 12, 1804, within an hour after Pickering was convicted by the Senate. The resolution threw a great fear into the hearts of all Federalist judges, Marshall no less than his colleagues. All the members of the Supreme Court were in the audience during Chase's trial, and it is quite likely that they helped direct the defense. In the course of the trial Marshall was called on to testify and even friendly eye-witnesses noted that he appeared badly frightened, answering the questions put to him with cunning rather than dignity and frankness.

The degree of his fear is indicated by the remarkable suggestion he made in a letter to Chase at the beginning of the proceedings. "I think," he said, "the modern doctrine of impeachment should yield to an appellate jurisdiction in the legislature. A reversal of those legal opinions deemed unsound by the legislature would certainly better comport with the mildness of our character than a removal of the judge who has rendered them unknowing of his fault." What Marshall was indicating was a willingness to agree to a deal under which Congress would be empowered to overrule any decision of the Supreme Court it did not like, so long as it did not impeach the Justices who rendered it. This letter was written less than a year after Marshall roared so loudly in *Marbury* v. *Madison* that without judicial supremacy over Congress the Constitution was meaningless and could not survive.

As it turned out, compromise was unnecessary. The basic issue in the impeachment was a simple one: what was meant by the term "high crimes and misdemeanors" for which a Justice of the Supreme Court could be impeached. To those who pressed for impeachment it meant in effect conduct which deprived him of the confidence of Congress and the people. To the opponents, it meant conduct for which the Justice could be indicted and tried in a criminal court. Chase's conduct as judge had undoubtedly been improper, but neither insolence of office nor error in judgment, no matter how gross, is an indictable crime. There were thirty-four Senators at the time, and although twenty-five were Republicans, more than the necessary two-thirds, not enough of them believed that Chase's conduct constituted high crimes or misdemeanors. The vote was taken after a trial of about a month. Only nineteen voted for conviction; twenty-three votes were necessary. Chase, who had participated in the work of the Court during the entire period of the proceedings, continued to do so until his death in 1811, six years later.

The Republican leaders were infuriated by the failure of the impeachment. One of them expressed his rage in language the substance of which would often be echoed in the future history of the Court: "Is it not absurd, ridiculous that there should be any class of men in society in any office that should be treated like gods, placed so far above the reach of censure and almost dignified with papal infallibility? It really seems as if the people were afraid to touch this golden calf they have formed —this talisman, the fancied charm which is to preserve us through every danger."

The abortive impeachment of Chase had a profound effect on the history of the Supreme Court. Its immediate consequence was to restore confidence to Marshall and to enable him to continue his task of making the Supreme Court a major instrument in shaping the political, economic and social patterns of the nation. In addition it assured future Justices of security of office if they avoided bribery and corruption. Impeachment, Jefferson correctly predicted, "will not be tried again," even though it appears that "we have no law but the will of the judge." On the other hand, the Justices have implicitly recognized that in order to retain the independence won by the failure of the impeachment of Chase, they must merit it. There have been no political impeachments since the Chase episode; but there also has been no repetition of the flagrant intervention by Supreme Court Justices in partisan politics or the unconcealed use of the Court as an arm of a political party. Both the impeachment of Chase and its failure have had a significantly salutary effect on the Court and on the nation.

chapter five

The Long and Troubled Reign of John Marshall

When Marshall announced the decision of the Supreme Court in *Marbury* v. *Madison* in 1803, every member of the Court was a Federalist appointed either by Washington or Adams. Eight years later, the Federalist contingent had been reduced to Marshall and Bushrod Washington; the remaining five (an additional Justice was provided by an act of Congress in 1807 to meet the needs of the expanding western frontier) were appointed by Jefferson and Madison. Bushrod Washington died in 1829, and for the remaining six years of Marshall's life, he was the only Justice on the bench who had been appointed by a Federalist President. From the time of the Marbury decision until 1835, ten Justices were appointed by Presidents who were Republicans, Democratic-Republicans or Democrats, as the same party was successively known.

In these circumstances one would expect that Marshall would find himself a lonely and isolated minority during the major part of his long judicial career. The exact reverse is far closer to the truth. For practically the entire thirty-four years that Marshall was Chief Justice he dominated the Court. With relatively few exceptions, the great decisions that were handed down during the first third of the nineteenth century reflected his voice and views. Democratic Presidents came and went; so too did their Democratic appointees to the bench; but the Federalism that Marshall had inherited from Hamilton remained. At times Marshall might find himself in the minority; on a rare occasion even Bushrod Washington would disagree with him. But overwhelmingly, decisions written and announced by Marshall and expressing his views would be concurred in by his colleagues, often to the surprise of the public and the dismay of the anti-Federalist Presidents who appointed them.

To say that Marshall dominated the Court as neither his predecessors nor his successors did is inadequate. Actually, it cannot truly be said that any Chief Justice except Marshall has ever dominated the

Court. At most a Chief Justice may have exerted more than his proportionate influence in the operation of the Court and the shaping of its decisions; Marshall's immediate successor, Roger B. Taney, did, and so too for a time did Charles Evans Hughes. But neither these nor any other Chief Justice dominated the Court and made of it almost a personal organ as Marshall did. For convenience, writers often refer to the Justices in office at a particular period by the name of the Chief Justice presiding during that period, as the Taft Court, the Vinson Court, the Warren Court, etc. But when one speaks of the Marshall Court it is not merely a matter of chronological convenience, but a reasonably accurate description of the nature of the Court.

Wherein lies the explanation for the long domination by a Federalist Chief Justice of a Court composed almost entirely of Justices appointed by Democratic Presidents at a time when the Federalist party was either moribund or dead? There is no single answer to this question. The explanation lies in Marshall himself, in his associates on the bench, the Presidents who appointed them, and in the nature of America's politico-economic development.

Unlike Jay, who did not want to be Chief Justice, Rutledge, who could not be, and Ellsworth, who was largely indifferent, Marshall very much wanted to be Chief Justice—so much so that at the critical moment of Chase's impeachment he was ready to trade judicial supremacy for his own continuation in office. He not only wanted to be Chief Justice, he was willing to exert the strenuous efforts needed to achieve success in his position. Also, he had the energy, talent and personality necessary for its achievement. Finally, he had confidence, as his predecessors did not, in the Court itself and in his ability to make of it a major factor in America's development.

Almost as soon as he became Chief Justice, Marshall began making changes in the procedures and operations of the Court that were greatly to enhance its prestige and effectiveness. Perhaps the most important was the substitution of a single opinion for separate opinions by the various Justices. Before Marshall came to the bench, the practice, following that of long standing in England, was for each member of the Court to write and announce an opinion in every case, even if they all agreed on the outcome. There was thus no single opinion of the Court, but simply a number of opinions of the Justices. Under the change instituted by Marshall, if all the Justices agreed on how a case should be decided, the Chief Justice would generally designate either himself or an associate to write a single opinion for all.

Marshall exerted every effort to avoid dissenting opinions, going even so far as on some occasions simply to disregard minority votes, and on other occasions to change his own vote if he could thereby achieve unanimity and thus a single opinion. It is easy to recognize that the prestige of the Court and of its decisions is greatly enhanced when it speaks with a single voice.

Marshall was able to achieve this reform by undertaking to write the Court's opinions himself, thus doing his associates' work for them. During his thirty-four years on the bench, he wrote about half the Court's opinions; a fair distribution of the work load would have assigned to him no more than one seventh. In 1820 Jefferson wrote to a friend: "The judiciary of the United States is the subtle corps of sappers and miners constantly working underground to undermine the foundations of our confederated fabric. . . . Having found from experience that impeachment is an impracticable thing, a mere scarecrow, they consider themselves secure for life; they sulk from responsibility. . . . An opinion is huddled up in conclave, perhaps by a majority of one, delivered as if unanimous, and with the silent acquiescence of lazy and timid associates, by a crafty chief judge who sophisticates the law to his mind by the turn of his own reasoning."

It was of the greatest good fortune to the Court that Marshall had not only the will and the energy to speak for it in its formative years, but that he also had the particular talent necessary. He was neither scholar nor philosopher; neither a profound nor a creative thinker. He made no truly original contributions to law or to political science. His writing was often repetitive and prolix. If one studied his opinions carefully one could find that at times his logic left much to be desired and that his premises were debatable. But he wrote in a style which made it almost heretical to look closely into his logic or his premises. Jefferson might call his reasoning sophistry, but to most others it was irrefutable. He stated assumptions as if they were self-evident truths and spelled out a conclusion from them as if no alternative line of reasoning could conceivably proceed from his premises. When he stated, as in *Marbury* v. *Madison,* that one proposition was "too plain to be contested." or, in the same case, that another was "an absurdity too gross to be insisted on," few have had the temerity to contest the one or insist on the other.

He was a master of majestic generalities, and although closer scrutiny might reveal that they were often really meaningless (example: "We must never forget that it is a *constitution* we are expounding"), his imperious tone discouraged closer scrutiny. Even today law professors, sophisticated and skeptical as most of them are, generally do not challenge the universally acclaimed beauty and splendor of the emperor's robe.

Marshall's great will, energy and talent were even more effective in securing for him the domination of the Court because of the apathy, inertia and mediocrity of most of his associates. William Johnson, Jefferson's appointee to the bench and one of the few Justices who was able to retain a measure of independence from Marshall, explained to Jefferson the Chief Justice's domination of the Court in the early years by pointing out that "Cushing was incompetent, Chase could not be got to think or write, Paterson was a slow man and willingly declined the trouble, and the other two judges (Marshall and Bushrod Washington) are commonly estimated as one judge." Often Marshall would conduct court with only three Justices present, and if one of them happened to be Bushrod Washington, Marshall had a built-in majority, which he did not hesitate to employ.

But the inadequacy of his associates is not the full explanation of Marshall's ability to override and dominate them. The key is in Marshall himself and in his personality and character. Coupled with his strong will, boundless energy and imperiousness in his writing, was his genuine modesty and, indeed, humility in his personal associations. His concepts were aristocratic but his conduct was democratic. He shrank from publicity and from published adulation. He paid no attention to his clothes or personal appearance. On one occasion when he was about to leave his quarters to ascend the bench (in circuit) he discovered to his dismay that he did not possess a wearable pair of breeches and was compelled to use his judicial robe to conceal his sartorial deficiency. On another occasion, while walking near a market in Richmond, a gentleman who did not recognize him offered him a small coin to carry a turkey which the gentleman had just purchased; Marshall, Chief Justice of the United States, accepted, and with the turkey under his arm trudged the streets behind his employer. This modesty, warm personality and genial good humor were especially effective because during Marshall's entire term on the bench, the Justices boarded together while they were in Washington, and therefore a spirit of camaraderie developed which made of the Court something of a club.

It is quite understandable, therefore, that when two openings in the Court came about in 1811 by the deaths of Chase and Cushing, Jefferson would write to Madison that, "It will be difficult to find a character of firmness enough to preserve his independence on the same bench with Marshall." It was, in fact, so difficult that Madison was unable to accomplish it. But then, Jefferson himself had been successful only in Johnson. Besides him, Jefferson had during his term of office appointed two other persons to the bench, Brockholst Livingston of New York and Thomas Todd of Kentucky, and both promptly disappeared into the shadow of Marshall. Madison's appointees were Gabriel Duval of Maryland and Joseph Story of Massachusetts. Duval became completely deaf, and was therefore unable to hear the argument of counsel or participate orally in the conferences of the Justices.

The appointment of Story was one of those many strokes of good fortune which, combined with Marshall's own talents, made of the Supreme Court what Jay and Ellsworth never dreamed it could become. Story was from a wealthy Boston family, raised in Salem and educated at Harvard. He wrote poetry, entered politics, served in Congress and in the Massachusetts legislature and, at the youthful age of thirty-two, was appointed to the Supreme Court. Although nominally a Republican, he early associated himself with the Federalist remnants to whose thinking his social and economic background naturally inclined him. Jefferson warned Madison of Story, calling him a "pseudo-republican," and Story actually was Madison's fourth choice. Because Cushing had come from New England, his replacement (following Washington's precedent) had to come from the same region. Levi Lincoln, Jefferson's Attorney-General, was offered the post but he declined because of his advanced age and defective eyesight. Madison then appointed Alexander Wolcott, Democratic political leader of Connecticut, but he was so notoriously mediocre in ability and dubious of character that the Senate could not swallow the appointment and rejected the nomination. Next Madison offered the post to John Quincy Adams, who, like Story, had deserted dying Federalism for Republican ascendancy. Adams, then ambassador to Russia, was quickly confirmed by the Senate, but he preferred to continue in his diplomatic post and refused the appointment. Finally, Madison nominated Story and the Senate, accepting as did everyone else but

Jefferson his avowals of loyalty to the Republican party and principles, confirmed the appointment.

Story was quickly and completely captured by (or, perhaps more accurately, surrendered to) Marshall. The relationship between them was somewhat like that between Boswell and Samuel Johnson, one not merely of deep affection but of hero worship. Story was able to supply Marshall with what the Chief Justice most lacked, scholarship. He was a prodigious scholar who during the course of his lifetime wrote a host of law books, including a three-volume work on constitutional law, which became a standard text for use in law schools and by judges in writing their opinions. Marshall is reputed to have on occasion handed to Story a draft of an opinion with the statement, "This is the law; now you find the precedents." This may be merely a legend, but it indicates vividly the invaluable service Story performed for Marshall.

MARSHALL AND JEFFERSON

Another stroke of good fortune that contributed to Marshall's success was Jefferson's decision not to serve beyond two terms. The contemporary conception of the relationship between Marshall and Jefferson is largely colored by the Federalist bias of Marshall's principal biographer, Albert J. Beveridge, and of the principal pre-1936 historians of the Court, Hampton L. Carson and Charles Warren. Beveridge, particularly, views the period of Jefferson's administration as a time of continuous conflict between a mean, vengeful President motivated by nothing but personal hatred of Marshall, and a noble Chief Justice whose only offense was an unsullied devotion to his country.

This portrayal of a titanic war between Marshall and Jefferson (from which the former emerged triumphant) elevates Marshall to a status of importance he did not then possess. Actually Marshall and the Court were of secondary significance in the administration of Jefferson. Marshall was more of an annoyance than a threat to Jefferson. He was undoubtedly angered by Marshall's assertion in *Marbury* v. *Madison* of the right to issue a command against a member of the President's cabinet, but Marshall prudently refrained from attempting to exercise the asserted right. After the abortive attempt to impeach Chase, Marshall gathered courage and during the trial of Aaron Burr for treason he did order the issuance of a subpoena directing Jefferson to appear at the trial with certain documents, but Jefferson simply ignored the subpoena and Marshall was too wise to seek to hold the President in contempt of court.

Jefferson, too, was enraged at the way Marshall conducted the Burr trial, which led to acquittal, but this was hardly a matter of major concern. Burr's duel with Hamilton, in which the latter was killed, had horrified the nation and brought an end to whatever future political career Burr might have otherwise had.

More serious were Marshall's rulings on the enforceability of the Embargo Act of 1807. This was a measure conceived by Jefferson in an effort to meet the depredations of American shipping in the course of the wars between Napoleon and Britain. The Act of 1807 forbade all international trade to and from American ports, and its purpose was to employ the instrument of economic boycott to induce England and France to respect America's right of trade as a neutral. Marshall's rulings in circuit hampered enforcement of the act, but no more so than the rulings of Jefferson's own appointees, Johnson and Livingston. Neither Marshall nor any other Justice nor the Court itself declared the act unconstitutional and the failure of the act resulted not from any of the rulings of the Justices but from its unpopularity and the strenuous resistance to it, particularly in New England. (The New England states asserted the unconstitutionality of the act and their right to declare it unconstitutional in exactly the same way that Virginia and Kentucky had made similar declarations ten years earlier in respect to the Sedition Act.)

The only major decision that Marshall issued during the eight years Jefferson was President was *Marbury* v. *Madison*, and that had no immediate practical significance. His career as Chief Justice really began in earnest after Jefferson retired from the Presidency and active political life. Jefferson's successors until the election of Andrew Jackson gave Marshall little trouble. Madison was of a pacific temperament and studiously avoided the type of controversy which Marshall relished. Monroe, by the time he became President, had lost much of his early radicalism, and John Quincy Adams, like Story, though nominally a Republican was a Federalist at heart.

Yet the real secret of Marshall's success was not his tireless will, his engaging personality, his superior intellect, his associates' inadequacies, or the character and personality of the Presidents whose administrations coincided with his. Marshall was triumphant and Jefferson failed because the former sailed with and the latter against the irresistible tide of American economic evolution. The invention of the steam engine and its successful application to manufacture and to transportation over land and water doomed Jefferson's romantic ideal of an agrarian democracy composed of small farmers, artisans and tradesmen. The industrial revolution was on the march and it had no room for the small, individual entrepreneur in agriculture, manufacture, trade or commerce. The natural resources of the country were unlimited and so too appeared to be the economic appetites of the rapidly rising capitalist class.

Jefferson's pacifistic Embargo Act was an almost Canutian effort to stay, in the interests of peace, American capitalist expansion. (Jefferson was as anxious to avoid war with England as he had earlier been to avoid war with France.) The New England states, despite all their talk of secession during the period of their resistance to the act, did not secede because they recognized that nationalism was on the march and that it was in the long run the natural ally of an expanding capitalist economy. Marshall had inherited from Hamilton an obsessive devotion to the rights of property, and he too recognized that notwithstanding temporary deviations, nationalism and a strong central government were the surest means of securing the rights of property. Jefferson's day was dying as Marshall's began to dawn.

With the failure of Chase's impeachment, thereby establishing security for Marshall and his colleagues, and with the retirement of Jefferson from active politics, Marshall was ready to make of the Supreme Court a highly valuable instrument in the evolution of America's rapidly expanding capitalist economy.

LAND SPECULATION, FRAUD AND THE SANCTITY OF CONTRACTS

During the first decade of Marshall's administration a case came up in which he showed how the Court could aid in the forward march of an expanding land capitalism toward its inevitable victory over a disappearing agrarian democracy. The case arose out of one of the most scandalous incidents in the history of land speculation and exploitation in the United States. During the winter of 1794-1795 a swarm of land speculators, representing four syndicates, descended on the state legislature at Augusta, the capital of Georgia. Their pockets were lined with gold and shares in the syndicates, and they indicated clearly that they were ready to distribute both where they would do the most good. Included in their midst was James Wilson, Justice of the United States Supreme Court, who had in his pockets no less than $25,000 in bank bills. At the end of the session the Georgia legislature had turned over to the four syndicates a tract of 35,000,000 acres of its western lands, known as the "Yazoo" lands, for the sum of $500,000. (Wilson ended up with at least 750,000 acres.)

Even while this was happening, the smell of bribery and corruption spread from the capital to every part of the state. The transaction was made particularly horrendous by the fact that the Yazoo lands were rich cotton-bearing fields, and Eli Whitney had just invented the cotton gin, which, it was even then recognized, would ultimately enthrone King Cotton. It later became known that with but a single exception every member of the legislature who voted for the law granting the lands had received shares of stock in one or the other of the purchasing companies.

The extent of the resulting fury on the part of the people of Georgia can be judged by the fact that the residents of Augusta marched on the capital determined to lynch the guilty legislators but were dissuaded only by the pleadings of the minority of the legislature who had argued and voted against the grants. In every town and village resolutions were adopted demanding that the granting law be rescinded. One of the United States senators from Georgia resigned from his office in order to run for election to the Georgia legislature so as to vote for any appropriate measure that might be offered to undo the evil. The Yazoo fraud was the sole issue in the ensuing campaign and with only two exceptions every man elected to the new legislature was pledged to rescind the grants.

The new legislature immediately passed a law which recited that the land sale act was unconstitutional, created a monopoly, dismembered the state of Georgia, betrayed the rights of man and had been founded on usurpation, corruption, fraud and collusion. The act was therefore declared null and void, all claims under it annulled, and all deeds and documents connected with the transaction physically expunged from the records. After the rescinding law was adopted, the members of the legislature assembled in front of the capital and there the evil law, removed from the archives, was burned in a bonfire ignited by the rays of the sun shining through a sun-glass (so that Nature herself might join in the purging) while the clerk of the House pronounced loudly: "God save the State! and long reserve her rights! And may every attempt to injure them perish as these corrupt acts now do!"

While these pyrotechnics were going on the land grabbers knew better than to wait around for developments. To prevent innocent purchasers from being sucked in, the repealing act contained a provision that its terms should be publicized throughout the nation. But it was too late; between the two sessions of the legislature the syndicates managed to dispose of all the land. The average price was fourteen cents an acre for land which cost the syndicate less than a penny and a half an acre. Most of the sales took place in New England and the Middle Atlantic states, and the purchasers varied from syndicates of wealthy speculators who took over large amounts (one sale to a Boston group covered eleven million acres) to small tradesmen who invested their life savings in what the promoters' prospectus described as extremely attractive opportunities for large profits. It is not likely that the large purchasers were unaware of the events that gave rise to the grants, but there were undoubtedly many small purchasers who acted innocently and did not learn of the bribery and corruption until after they had parted with their hard earned savings.

This occurred in 1796, but it was not until 1810 that the validity of the rescinding act came to the Supreme Court for adjudication in the case of *Fletcher v. Peck.* Mr. Peck had obtained a number of acres of Yazoo land and had sold them to Mr. Fletcher. The latter sued Mr. Peck to get his money back on the ground that because of the rescinding law Mr. Peck had no title to sell to Mr. Fletcher. Not so, said Mr. Peck; the rescinding law is unconstitutional and my title is therefore perfectly good. Thus the case came to the Supreme Court.

It was plain to see that it had all the earmarks of a feigned case, one in which both sides were really striving for the same result. (In boxing it would be called a "fixed fight.") Marshall, in his opinion for the majority of the Court, made no mention of this aspect, but Johnson, in his concurring opinion, could not refrain from indicating that he was troubled. "I have been very unwilling," he said, "to proceed to the decision of this cause at all. It appears to me to bear strong evidence on the face of it of being a mere feigned case. . . . My confidence, however, in the respectable gentlemen [they included John Quincy Adams and

Joseph Story] who have been engaged for the parties has induced me to abandon my scruples in the belief they would never consent to impose a mere feigned case upon this Court." Most everyone else, however, was not so trusting. Pointing out that both parties and all who stood behind them had vast amounts to lose if the Court found that the plaintiff was right and that Mr. Peck really did not have good title to the lands, a member of Congress remarked in a speech on the floor of the House that he "never did see a judge who had talents and ingenuity enough to overrule and defeat both parties and their attorneys and award judgment to the plaintiff contrary to their united efforts."

Mr. Fletcher, the plaintiff, was not disappointed; he lost his case. The outcome was hardly surprising in view of the fact that the argument of his attorney, Luther Martin, had all the appearances of being purely perfunctory. (Besides, Mr. Martin was so drunk that the Court had to adjourn to allow him to recover sufficient sobriety to complete his argument. Whether his intoxication resulted from a moral distaste for the job he was doing must be left to speculation.)

This was the first decision by the Supreme Court actually holding a state statute invalid under the United States Constitution, and the opinion was of course written by Marshall.

As in *Marbury* v. *Madison,* there was little that was original in Marshall's opinion. Fourteen years earlier, after Georgia adopted the rescinding law, the syndicates sought a legal opinion on its validity from Alexander Hamilton, then universally rated as one of the nation's leading lawyers. Hamilton's opinion was that the law was unconstitutional, and the reasons he gave were the same ones Marshall, who had undoubtedly read Hamilton's opinion, set forth in *Fletcher* v. *Peck.*

The claim, said Marshall, that the original granting law was invalid because it had been procured by fraud and corruption could not be entertained. The case before the Court was one between two private citizens; neither they nor the Court could look into the motives of the members of a state legislature, but must accept at face value the official acts of the legislature. If a court in a law suit between two private litigants were empowered to delve into the motives of legislators, no law would be safe. Moreover, how corrupt must it be shown that the legislature was before a court could set its act aside? Would it be sufficient if one legislator were bribed or would it be necessary to show that a majority had been corrupted? And would it matter if notwithstanding its tainted origin, the measure enjoyed the support of the people of the state? These and similar unanswerable questions would always arise if a court could go behind a law duly enacted by the legislature to question the motives of those who voted for it.

Moreover, Marshall continued, even if the original transaction was tainted with corruption, the corrupters were not before the Court. Mr. Peck and the hundreds of others who purchased acres from them must be assumed to have acted innocently and without knowledge of the fraud. Under well established principles of common law, one who pays good money for property acquired by the seller through fraud cannot be deprived of it if he did not know of the fraud.

This, however, was not sufficient to dispose of the case, as Marshall well recognized. At most it showed that the action of the second legislature was unfair and that it changed common law principles; but neither of these facts justifies a court in declaring a statute void. To adjudge the rescinding act void, Marshall had to find it unconstitutional. This he first sought to do by asserting that it was a violation of vested rights and of the underlying principles of society and government. What this meant was that the Court could declare a law unconstitutional if it violated general principles of natural justice and property rights, later to become known as the "higher law," even though no specific provision of the Constitution could be pointed to. Recognizing that this too was inadequate, Marshall turned to the contracts clause. The rescinding act, he said, impaired the obligations of contract, for the grant given by the legislature was a contract and an implied term of that contract, as of every grant, is that the grant is permanent and the grantor will not try to get it back by claiming that he really did not mean it.

The decision in *Fletcher* v. *Peck* was received by the general public with widespread displeasure. It seemed to place the seal of constitutional sanctity not merely on contracts but on fraud and corruption. It reinforced the popular belief that the Supreme Court was an instrument for the elevation of vested property rights over all other values of the community, including legislative honesty and integrity. Its practical effect in respect to the ownership of the Yazoo lands was none; the lands had earlier been ceded by Georgia to the United States. However, on the basis of the decision and some energetic lobbying, the speculators were able to get Congress to pass a bill appropriating five million dollars to compensate them for their losses.

MORE LAND AND COURT TROUBLE

Fletcher v. *Peck* concerned land speculations involving Justice Wilson. *Fairfax's Devisee* v. *Hunter's Lessee* and *Martin* v. *Hunter's Lessee* arose out of land speculations in which Marshall himself was involved. Before he became Chief Justice, Marshall and his brother headed a syndicate which bought valuable Virginia tobacco and timber land from one Denny Martin. The latter had inherited the land from his uncle, Lord Fairfax, who died in England in 1781. During the war, the state of Virginia had declared the land forfeited because Lord Fairfax was an enemy alien. In 1789 Virginia granted the land to one David Hunter, so that what the Marshall syndicate bought from Denny Martin was really only a law suit against Hunter. The litigation dragged on, and it was not until 1810 that the Virginia court of appeals issued a determinative decision in which it held that the forfeiture had been effective and that Hunter and other grantees from the state of Virginia, rather than the grantees from Denny Martin, were entitled to the land.

The Marshall syndicate, of which the Chief Justice's brother was the active head, appealed to the Supreme Court, the case being known as *Fairfax's Devisee* v. *Martin's Lessee*. After sitting on the case for a year, the Court (or more accurately three of the seven Justices, for Marshall, Washington and Todd did not participate in the decision and Johnson dissented), in an opinion by Story, reversed the Virginia court's decision and held that the Jay Treaty nullified the forfeiture and vested the land in Denny Martin and his grantees. The Court accordingly sent the case back to the Virginia court of appeals with the direction to enter judgment in favor of the Marshall syndicate.

This the Virginia court of appeals refused to do. The question was raised whether an appeal could rightfully have been taken to the Supreme Court in the first place. The Judiciary Act of 1789 provided that appeals could be taken to the Supreme Court from decisions of state courts which raised questions under the Constitution, laws or treaties of the federal government, and the power of the Court to consider such appeals had apparently been taken for granted. But the Virginia court of appeals unanimously decided that this provision of the Judiciary Act was unconstitutional. The national and state governments, the court said, are equal sovereignties independent of each other, and the Constitution was a compact between them. The United States Supreme Court could no more pass upon and reverse a decision of the Virginia court of appeals than the latter could a decision of Marshall's Court. Both courts are equally competent to interpret the Constitution, federal laws and treaties; neither is superior and neither can issue commands to the other.

The Marshall syndicate immediately appealed this decision to the Supreme Court. The second case, entitled *Martin* v. *Hunter's Lessee*, was decided in 1816, three years after the first one. Again Marshall abstained and Story announced the Court's decision, although Marshall had seen it in advance and it was generally assumed that while the voice was Story's the words were Marshall's. The Constitution, the opinion said, was not ordained by the states but by the people and when the Court acts pursuant to the Constitution it is exercising powers conferred by them; hence, it can rightfully issue mandates directed to the state courts. There is only one federal Constitution and unless there are to be a host of varying interpretations to be given to it, there must be one tribunal which can hand down an interpretation uniformly binding and applicable throughout the nation.

The logic of Story's argument was unanswerable within the framework of the government contemplated by the framers of the Constitution. But Story recognized that logic alone might not suffice and that if the Virginia court of appeals denied its jurisdiction in the first appeal, it was not likely now to repent and accept the second decision. Accordingly, instead of issuing its mandate in favor of the Marshall syndicate to the court of appeals, as required by usual procedure, it issued it to the Virginia district court which had originally decided in favor of the syndicate and had been reversed by the court of appeals.

This attack by the Supreme Court on states' rights was assailed by the Republicans not only in Virginia but throughout the nation. Story was condemned as a "renegade," and in retaliation for the decision the Republicans in Congress defeated a proposed increase in the salaries of the Justices. Story, complaining that by reason of the increase in the cost of living the Justices were "starving in splendid poverty," considered resigning from the bench, but finally decided against it.

The Marshall syndicate got their land, but Virginia was not yet ready to give up its struggle for states' rights and the protection of its courts against usurpation by Marshall and his associates. The issue again came to the Supreme Court in 1821 in the case of *Cohens* v. *Virginia.*

Pursuant to an act of Congress, the city of Washington organized a lottery. Cohens sold some tickets in Virginia and was arrested for violating the state's anti-lottery law. He appealed his conviction to the United States Supreme Court on the ground that the conviction violated his rights under the federal lottery law.

The state of Virginia indignantly refused to argue the conviction before the Supreme Court. It instructed its attorneys to argue only that the Court had no jurisdiction to pass on the appeal. If the Court should decide otherwise the attorneys were to pick up their papers and return to Richmond. Virginia's attorneys presented to the Court every argument that had been urged in *Martin* v. *Hunter's Lessee* and in addition an argument based on the Eleventh Amendment. The Martin case was a suit between private persons but the Cohens case, as all criminal prosecutions, was a suit in which the state was a party, and an appeal to the Supreme Court was in effect a suit against the state without its consent. The Eleventh Amendment had been passed because the people of the United States agreed with Georgia that neither Mr. Chisholm nor any other private person could sue it against its consent, and what was true of Chisholm and Georgia was no less true of Cohens and Virginia.

Since Marshall was not involved in lottery tickets as he had been in land speculation, it was not necessary for him to speak through Story, and he therefore reverted to his usual practice of announcing the Court's major decisions himself. This is not, he said, a case of an individual suing the state, but of the state prosecuting an individual, and the Eleventh Amendment has accordingly no relevance. As for the other arguments, he repeated and expanded upon what had been said in *Martin* v. *Hunter's Lessee*. However, the practical upshot of the case was that Cohens would still have to go to jail, because, said Marshall, a fair interpretation of the federal lottery law indicates that Congress did not intend that it should authorize the sale of tickets in states where lotteries were unlawful.

Though the decision had no practical effect on the conviction of Cohens, the assumption by Marshall's Court of the power to upset state criminal convictions infuriated Virginia. The attack on the Court was led by Spencer Roane, chief judge of the Virginia court of appeals and the man whom Jefferson would have named Chief Justice of the Supreme Court had Ellsworth deferred his resignation until Jefferson was inaugurated. Writing to the press under an assumed name (a customary practice of which *The Federalist* papers is an example), Roane declared that "A death blow has been aimed at the very existence of the states." The decision, he said, "can only be accounted for from that love of power which all history informs us infects and corrupts all who possess it, and from which even the eminent and upright Judges are not exempt." Radical measures were required. Section 25 of the Judiciary Act, upon which the Supreme Court based its claim to jurisdiction in the Martin and Cohens cases, should be repealed. And even this might not be enough. The state of Virginia should itself propose a constitutional amendment to curb if not to abolish the Court. "The career of the High Court," Roane asserted, "must be stopped or the liberties of our country are annihilated." (Actually, the Supreme Court's power to review and set aside criminal convictions of state courts has proved indispensable for the preservation of American liberties.)

Jefferson and Madison, both of whom had retired from active politics but enjoyed a status of revered elder statesmen to the Republican party, were sympathetic to Roane's general aims but were considerably more conservative. Madison pointed out realistically that after all the Court's power was less formidable than Congress.' Jefferson suggested that the way to meet the "difficult task of curbing the Judiciary in their enterprises on the Constitution," was by a "joint protestation of both Houses of Congress that the doctrines of the Judges in the case of Cohens . . . are contrary to the provisions of the Constitution of the United States." While Roane considered this much too tame, the Virginia legislature was apparently not prepared to go any further. Resolutions were introduced to carry out Roane's radical measures, but nothing came of them. The Court emerged from Virginia's revolt perhaps a little bloody but nevertheless unbowed.

Barely out of trouble in Virginia, the Court speedily fell back into it in neighboring Kentucky. As in *Fletcher* v. *Peck*, it was land trouble, and again it was Wilson's modest clause against impairing the obligations of contract that was the cause. Land titles and registrations in those days were in a primitive state, and many Kentucky frontiersmen settled on unoccupied land, believing it to be free, only to find later that a deed to it was held by some land speculator in Virginia or elsewhere in the East. In order to work out some equitable arrangement, the Kentucky legislature passed a law providing that if the squatter had acted innocently and in good faith, the title owner of the land could not evict him unless he were reimbursed for the buildings and other improvements he had placed on the land during his squatting. A Virginia citizen brought an eviction suit in the federal district court of Kentucky against a Kentucky squatter, who demanded reimbursement for his improvements.

The case reached the Supreme Court in 1821 and the Court, in an opinion by Story (Marshall did not participate in the case) declared the statute unconstitutional. Henry Clay, on behalf of the state of Kentucky, petitioned the Court for a rehearing, pointing out that the alleged squatter, Biddle, did not even bother to have his attorney appear on the original argument so that the case was decided with only one side being heard. (Clay did not say so, but the implication that this was a feigned case was quite clear.) The Court granted the application for reargument, and Clay presented the state's position that the law was constitutional.

It was not until 1823 that the Court handed down its second, final decision in *Green* v. *Biddle*. In the interim Kentucky witnessed as violent an attack on the Supreme Court as Virginia had during the course of the Martin and Cohens cases. (This time Virginia was noticeably subdued; most of the absentee owners of the Kentucky lands were Virginians or northern speculators who had bought their titles from Virginians.) The leader of the attack was Kentucky's Senator Richard M. Johnson, later to be Vice-President of the United States. Bushrod Washington now delivered the opinion of the Court—or, more accurately, three-sevenths of the Court, for Marshall, Todd and Livingston had been prevented by indisposition or illness from participating in the case, and Johnson dissented. The Court stood its ground, and the decision was the same.

Washington's opinion reflected the alarm of the Court at the assaults upon it. "We hold ourselves," he said, "answerable to God, our consciences and our country, to decide this question according to the dictates of our best judgment be the consequences of the decision what they may." The Court's best judgment dictated that the law was unconstitutional. When Kentucky was carved out of Virginia in 1791 to become a separate state, a compact was entered into between the two states which had a provision that all private rights and interests within the Kentucky territory should "remain valid and secure." This compact between states, said Washington, was a contract not different from one between individuals, and its obligations were equally protected by the Constitution against impairment. That neither of the two parties to the contract, Virginia and Kentucky, objected to the impairment was immaterial; the objection could be asserted by Mr. Green and all other absentee landlords.

THE DARTMOUTH COLLEGE CASE

It was not until the administration of Monroe that the United States really got around to launching the century of intensive capitalist expansion envisaged by Hamilton. Until that time the attention of the country was concentrated on securing independence and national integrity. Correspondingly, the decisions of the Supreme Court during the early period were in the main concerned with problems arising out of British and French infringements on American neutrality and out of the occupation, settling and speculation in western lands. With the defeat of Napoleon, which finally brought an end to centuries of British-French wars, and the conclusion of the War of 1812, the last armed conflict between Britain and the United States, American independence was secure. The industrial revolution, with its harnessing of steam for industrial and commercial purposes, set the stage for the meteoric development of the American capitalist system. Congress resurrected Hamilton's Report on Manufactures, passed the first American protective tariff and chartered the second Bank of the United States on the Hamilton model. Marshall's Court was prepared and willing to lend its aid in America's economic development.

Both the Marshall Court and earlier the Ellsworth Court had had opportunities to provide useful tools of constitutional law for this development and both had missed the opportunities. In *Calder* v. *Bull* the Ellsworth Court had ruled that the ban in the Constitution on *ex post facto* or retroactive laws applied only to criminal laws. Had the Court decided that it applied equally to civil laws, Marshall's Court would not have had to resort to the contract impairment clause to invalidate the laws in *Fletcher* v. *Peck* and *Green* v. *Biddle*, as well as in a number of later cases which contributed substantially to the protection of property rights and the promotion of economic expansion.

Marshall's discovery of the contract impairment clause quickly retrieved the lost opportunity of the Ellsworth Court, but it took thirty years for the Supreme Court fully to retrieve Marshall's lost opportunity. American capitalist economy rests on the corporation, a device whereby the money of many can be concentrated in the hands of a few managers for effective management and expansion. In *Strawbridge* v. *Curtiss*, in 1806, and three years later in *Bank of the United States* v. *Deveaux*, Marshall ruled that a corporation was not a "citizen" and therefore could not sue in the federal courts. Such a precedent could be disastrous to the efficacy of the federal judicial system in the protection of business interests, but it was not until 1844, after Marshall's death and under the Chief Justiceship of Roger B. Taney, that the Deveaux case was overruled and corporations were accorded the status of citizens with the right to sue in the federal courts.

In *Dartmouth College* v. *Woodward*, decided in 1819, Marshall was able to provide corporations with some of the judicial protection withheld from them by the Deveaux decision, and naturally it was the contract impairment clause that was used for this purpose. A Protestant missionary to the Indians, Eleazar Wheelock, had received from George III a royal charter to establish an educational institution, known as Dartmouth College, to educate and convert the savage Indians. The charter provided that the college should be managed in perpetuity by a board of twelve trustees who were given the authority to appoint successors to trustees who died. After Wheelock's death, his son became president, and, being a rather young man, had become infected with Republican ideas. Moreover, he lacked the necessary Congregationalist piety and favored the equality of all religions. There ensued a bitter conflict between the president and the trustees, with the result that in 1815 the trustees voted to remove the president.

The controversy now spilled over the college walls. The Republican governor of New Hampshire, William Plumer, sent a message to the legislature urging that the charter of the college be revised to introduce some measure of democratic control. Plumer sent a copy of the message to Jefferson, who replied that the idea "that institutions, established for the use of the nation cannot be touched nor modified, even to make them answer their end . . . is most absurd. . . . Yet our lawyers and priests generally inculcate this doctrine; and suppose that preceding generations . . . had a right to impose laws upon us, unalterable by ourselves; . . . in fine, that the earth belongs to the dead, and not to the living."

The Republican legislature passed a law increasing the number of trustees to twenty-one and providing for a board of overseers. The new managers promptly reinstated the ousted president and the original twelve went into court to establish their right to perpetual control. (According to one report, of doubtful authenticity, the trustees feared that they would be met with the argument that they had already forfeited their charter as there had long since ceased to be any Indians in the college. Accordingly, on the advice of their counsel, Daniel Webster, they sent across the border to Canada to import three Indians for entrance into the college. When the ordinarily brave Indians approached the town of Hanover they became panic-stricken, or perhaps decided that discretion dictated that they keep out of a Federalist-Republican war. In any event, they leaped into the water, swam ashore and disappeared into the forest—or so it is reported.)

The case reached the Supreme Court and one of the attorneys for the original trustees was Daniel Webster, then thirty-six years old and at the beginning of a phenomenally successful career at the Supreme Court bar. According to report—and here, too, there may be more apocryphy than gospel—Webster delivered an eloquent oration, generously interspersed with Latin quotations, not a word of which Marshall understood, and ended in tears with a heartrending peroration that included the famous, "It is, Sir, as I have said, a small college. And yet there are those who love it."

Marshall's opinion was a complete victory for the original board of trustees. Dartmouth College, he said, was a private corporation and the charter granted to it under the authority of George III was not a public act or law subject to subsequent modification by the legislature acting in its sovereignty as successor to the king. It was a contract between the king and the recipients of the charter, and therefore its obligations could not be impaired by a legislature subject to the Constitution of the United States. Hence, the reform law was unconstitutional and void and Eleazar Wheelock's Republican son was no longer president of Dartmouth.

The decision aroused little public attention outside of New Hampshire. On its face the case involved no more than a petty quarrel over control of a small college. But its implications were not lost upon either business interests or state officials. The states were beginning to charter industrial and commercial corporations, and the meaning of the decision was that these charters were to be thereafter forever immune to rescission or revision by the legislatures or the people. Beveridge asserts that, "It is undeniable and undenied that America could not have developed so rapidly and solidly without the power which the law as announced by Marshall gave to industrial organization." Henry Maine, English legal historian, stated that the opinion assured the security of many of the great railroad corporations and gave full play to America's economic individualism.

The direct practical consequences of the decision were soon narrowed. The state legislatures adopted laws or constitutional provisions that all corporate charters and franchises thereafter granted by the state should always be subject to legislative alteration or repeal. This provision became an implied part of every charter or franchise and therefore alteration or repeal did not impair its obligations. The principle of the decision itself was subjected to substantial modification in later Supreme Court decisions. Yet, it is undeniable that it gave great encouragement to business investments. Moreover, and perhaps more important, it provided another highly valuable tool for later Courts to use for the protection of capitalist expansion.

One of the reasons the general public gave little notice to the Dartmouth College case was that the nation's attention was riveted on two other decisions handed down during the same 1819 term of the Court, *Sturges* v. *Crowinshield* and *McCulloch* v. *Maryland*, both of which concerned the people much more closely. The former case arose out of the financial panic which covered most of the nation during that year. The Constitution grants Congress power to enact nationwide bankruptcy laws. This is a power exercised by every civilized government to relieve the hopelessly destitute of their financial burdens and afford them an opportunity to start a new life with a clean slate, upon their turning over whatever assets they have to their creditors. However, although Congress had enacted a bankruptcy law in 1800, it was repealed three years later. In the absence of a federal law, many of the states enacted insolvency laws to provide relief for their own impecunious debtors.

New York enacted such a law and its validity was challenged in a suit in the federal district court by Sturges, a Massachusetts creditor, against Crowinshield, a New York debtor. (This, too, may very well have been a feigned case.) The case reached the Supreme Court and in an opinion announced by Marshall the law was declared unconstitutional.

It should surprise no one that the provision which Marshall found violated by the New York law was the one barring impairment of the obligations of contract. He brushed aside the argument that the purpose of the provision was only to ban the issuance of cheap paper money as legal tender and that the states always had passed laws for the relief of debtors. This, he said, was not the sole purpose of the provision; its basic purpose was to secure "the inviolability of contracts." When a man borrows money he contracts to pay it back in full, and any law which says that if he cannot pay it back in full he need not do so if he turns over to his creditor whatever assets he has even if it be less than the amount of the loan impairs the obligations of that contract.

Eight years later *Sturges* v. *Crowinshield* was for all practical purposes destroyed by the Court in the case of *Ogden* v. *Saunders*. This was the first case in which Marshall suffered a defeat on a major constitutional issue, and his defeat was total. Even Bushrod Washington did not join him in his dissent. The principle of the Sturges case, the Court held, applies only in respect to insolvency laws enacted after a debt is contracted. If a loan is made at a time when there is an insolvency law on the books, then the provisions of that law are an implied term of the loan contract even if its existence is not mentioned in the contract. Hence, when the debtor takes advantage of that law there is no impairment of the obligations of the contract. Marshall's dissent was bitter. The effect of the decision, he said, was to make "prostrate . . . inanimate, inoperative and unmeaning" a vital provision of the Constitution "on which the good and the wise reposed confidently."

This was to happen in 1827 and was not anticipated in 1819. In that year all the public knew was that the Marshall Court had again elevated the rights of property over those of persons and had in the process trampled on state sovereignty. The decision of *Sturgis* v. *Crowinshield* added considerable fuel to the fire of resentment and opposition that was rising against Marshall and his Court.

The third case decided by the court in the 1819 term was *McCulloch* v. *Maryland*, the Bank of the United States case. One of the cornerstones of Hamilton's far-reaching economic program for the United States was the establishment of a national bank. In 1791 Congress enacted a law chartering the first Bank of the United States for twenty years. It was a private corporation with the government subscribing to one-fifth of its capital stock. The bank acted as the government's fiscal agent but also engaged in a widespread and quite profitable commercial banking business. On the expiration of its charter in 1811 it sought renewal, but was unsuccessful because of the opposition of the Jeffersonians. The difficulties of financing the War of 1812 induced Congress to change its mind, and in 1816 a second Bank of the United States, modeled after the first, was chartered.

The proposal for a charter had faced considerable opposition in Congress, and within two years the dire predictions of the opponents appeared to have been completely justified As a result of bad, and often dishonest, management the bank brought upon itself widespread hostility in the South and West. After first encouraging overexpansion of credit, the bank turned around and curtailed it, with the result that many state banks were ruined and thousands of small businessmen and farmers were wiped out. Because of its reckless mismanagement, wild speculation in its shares, fraudulent loans by the bank officials to themselves and defalcations by its officials, the bank itself was on the verge of insolvency in 1819. The financial panic of that year had many causes, and while the mismanagement of the bank was but one of them, in the eyes of the general public outside the Northeast, it was the sole cause.

The state legislatures took what they considered appropriate counteraction. They enacted laws imposing stringent taxes upon all banks not chartered by the particular state itself. While nominally these were revenue measures, there is little doubt that their major motivation was punitive and that they were aimed at the Bank of the United States. Such a tax law was adopted in Maryland, and upon the bank's refusal to pay, a suit for the prescribed penalty was brought by officials of Maryland against James W. McCulloch, cashier of the Baltimore branch of the bank.

The case of *McCulloch* v. *Maryland* reached the Supreme Court, and among the attorneys who argued for the bank was Webster. Two weeks after the argument, Marshall handed down his elaborate opinion upholding Webster and the bank. Constitutional lawyers and historians are generally agreed that this is his greatest opinion and, next to *Marbury* v. *Madison,* his most important. Beveridge calls some of the language of the opinion "as exalted as that of the prophets," and it has all the earmarks of careful and long preparation, considerably longer than the busy two weeks after the argument. One finds it difficult to disagree with Beveridge's suggestion that the opinion had been written before the case was even argued, and that Marshall at most made a few stylistic revisions on the basis of the argument. Webster, for his part, never had a moment's doubt as to the outcome, a certainty shared by a number of Jeffersonians in Congress who made a last ditch but vain effort to enact a law repealing the bank's charter.

The case, said Marshall, presented two principal questions: whether Congress could constitutionally charter the bank, and if so, whether the state of Maryland could constitutionally tax it. As to the first question, Marshall disposed of the contention that nowhere does the Constitution expressly authorize Congress to charter private corporations or establish a bank. The government, said Marshall, has not only express powers, but those that can reasonably be implied. The Constitution vests Congress with power "to make all laws which shall be necessary and proper" for carrying out its express powers. Even if the chartering of a bank might not strictly speaking be deemed absolutely necessary (since the government could make use of state banks, as it did in the interim between the two banks), it is nevertheless proper, that is, convenient. (This is the familiar principle of "implied powers" or "liberal construction.")

If Congress can create the Bank of the United States, may the states tax it? No, said Marshall, for if they were allowed to, they could destroy it, and the power to create the bank implies the power to preserve it and protect it from destruction. The whole question is "in truth, a question of supremacy." If the states can tax the instrumentalities of the federal government, then the declaration in the Constitution that it and the laws made under it "shall be the supreme law of the land, is empty and unmeaning declamation."

This, then, is Marshall's greatest intellectual achievement. Yet there is not an original idea in the whole long opinion. Some of what have become the most famous quotations from it were almost completely plagiarized. Said Marshall in a sentence quoted innumerable times: "Let the end be legitimate, let it be within the scope of the constitution, and all means which are appropriate, which are plainly adapted to that end, which are not prohibited, but (are) consist(ent) with the letter and spirit of the constitution, are constitutional." In 1791 Washington, before approving the act creating the first bank, requested and received from Hamilton an opinion as to its constitutionality. Said Hamilton in his opinion: "If the end be clearly comprehended within any of the specified powers, and if the measure have an obvious relation to that end, and is not forbidden by any particular provision of the Constitution, it may safely be deemed to come within the compass of the national authority." Even the most quoted (or misquoted) clause of the opinion, "the power to tax involves the power to destroy," was appropriated from Webster's argument before the Court.

Original or not, the McCulloch decision raised a storm of protest everywhere except in the commercial northeastern states. Elsewhere Marshall was attacked vigorously for not declaring the charter law unconstitutional (the attack coming from the same sources that had assailed him fifteen years earlier for asserting the right to declare an act of Congress unconstitutional). Even more vigorous was the attack based upon his again overriding states' rights in holding the Maryland taxing law to be unconstitutional. A leading Jeffersonian paper referred to the Court as "a tribunal so far removed from the people that some seem to regard it with a species of that awful reverence in which the inhabitants of Asia look up to their princes." A Mississippi newspaper editorialized that if Marshall's opinion stood, "the independence of the individual states is obliterated at one fell swoop." Spencer Roane, again writing under a pen name, hurled scorn at the five Republican appointees who joined with Marshall and Bushrod Washington. "Few men," he said, "come out of high places as pure as they went in." Virginia, he wrote ominously, "never will employ force to support her doctrines till other measures have entirely failed." (Marshall was so disturbed by Roane's attack, and particularly by the widespread charge that he controlled the Court, that he felt himself impelled to reply in the press and to seek to justify his decision, writing, of course, under an assumed name.) John Taylor of Carolina, the originator of the Kentucky Resolutions against the Sedition Law, wrote a book, *Construction Construed and Constitutions Vindicated*, in which he assailed Marshall for protecting monopolies at the expense of the rights of the people and the states. To pretend faith in Christianity and yet foster monopoly is, he said, "like placing Christ on the car of Juggernaut."

The state of Ohio did not content itself with verbal assaults. It disregarded the opinion and collected its taxes imposed against Ohio branches of the bank. Blandly ignoring an injunction issued by the federal circuit court, the state treasurer entered a branch of the bank and took away all the money he could find in the vaults, some one hundred thousand dollars. When he thereafter refused to comply with the federal court's decree to repay the money, he was held in contempt of court and thrown into prison. At the same time, the federal court officials took his keys from his pockets, entered the state treasury and removed about ninety-eight thousand dollars. The state of Ohio retaliated by enacting a statute completely outlawing the bank. The controversy lasted for about two years and finally subsided with the return of prosperity and the advent of Monroe's Era of Good Feeling.

Up to this point Marshall had succeeded in accomplishing what would seem to be an impossible task: although he had not handed down a single major popular decision but a host of highly unpopular ones, both he and his Court had come through unscathed. By the 1820's, however, it seemed that his phenomenal luck had finally run out. The decade, and particularly its first half, saw the introduction in Congress of innumerable measures designed to curb the Court and restrict its powers. The Democratic-Republican party, from Jefferson down, was convinced that something had to be done to bring the Court closer in line with the feelings of the people and the rightful claims of the states.

The Chase fiasco convinced Jefferson that there was no future in impeachment. His remedy was a constitutional amendment which would change the term of the Justices to six years, subject to reappointment by the President with the approval of both Houses. Other Democrats thought that a preferable remedy was to give the Senate the right to overrule the Court in all cases involving the constitutionality of state statutes, and in 1821 Johnson of Kentucky introduced a resolution in the Senate for such an amendment. Two years later a bill was introduced in both Houses to repeal entirely section 25 of the Judiciary Act of 1789, on which was based the Court's jurisdiction to take appeals from state court decisions. Martin Van Buren would have made the office of Supreme Court Justice elective. Less radical proposals during the same period included provisions that no state law should be declared unconstitutional except with the concurrence of all seven Justices, or five of them, or at least a majority. (*Green* v. *Biddle* was commonly believed to have been decided by three members of the Court.) Finally, there was the first proposal to pack the Court, a bill to increase the membership of the Court to ten so as to enable the President to add fresh blood to it.

None of these proposals came to aught, and one of the reasons undoubtedly was that in 1824 Marshall handed down a genuinely popular and extremely important decision in the case of *Gibbons* v. *Ogden*. Since the beginning of the century the partnership of Robert Fulton and Robert R. Livingston had enjoyed a monopoly granted by the New York legislature for the operation of steamboats on New York waters. (Livingston was of the same family as Brockholst Livingston, Jefferson's appointee to the Supreme Court. The Justice, however, died in 1823, before *Gibbons* v. *Ogden* was decided, but was succeeded by one even closer to Robert R. Livingston, Smith Thompson of New York, who was Monroe's Secretary of War and Robert R. Livingston's brother-in-law.)

Aaron Ogden had received a license from the Livingston-Fulton partnership to operate on the Hudson River. Thomas Gibbons, a partner of Ogden, broke the partnership because he refused to pay tribute to the monopoly. He obtained from the federal government an ordinary license to engage in coastwise navigation, pursuant to an act of Congress dating back to 1793. Ogden sued Gibbons for an injunction against interference with his exclusive license, and after long drawn out litigation in New York and lower federal courts, the case finally reached the Supreme Court. Gibbons' counsel included Webster, and again Webster and his client won.

The Constitution, said Marshall, grants Congress the power to regulate commerce among the several states (generally referred to as "interstate commerce"). To effect the purposes of the Constitution, this grant of power, as all other grants to Congress, must be given a broad interpretation. It is not to be limited to buying and selling; but includes transportation and navigation. The grant of power is complete and unlimited, and superior to any right in the states that might interfere with it. Since the license received by Gibbons under the Act of 1793 authorized him to navigate all coastal waters of the United States, Ogden could not exclude him from the Hudson River.

Some Jeffersonian leaders concerned with states' rights were troubled by and criticized the broad language of the opinion; or they may have felt that nothing Marshall did could be entirely right. But the American public generally was not concerned with semantics or personalities. The practical effect of the decision was to destroy a powerful and hated monopoly. The Livingston-Fulton partnership had received a similar monopoly from the state of Louisiana; and others had received monopolies in Massachusetts, New Hampshire, Vermont and Georgia. All were effectively destroyed by none other than John Marshall. Within a year after the decision the number of steamboats out of New York had increased from six to forty-three.

Gibbons v. *Ogden* was widely acclaimed. For the first time Marshall and his Court were actually popular. The popularity did not last long, but it served to brake the momentum of the campaign to curb the Court. The campaign could not thereafter gather up enough steam to get rolling again, and once more the Court had warded off disaster and was secure —until the next crisis.

THE LAST TROUBLED YEARS OF JOHN MARSHALL

Marshall's distrust of the people, intensified through the years, may have made him uncomfortable with the popularity engendered by *Gibbons* v. *Ogden*. Whatever the reason, it was not only his first but also his last popular decision. He quickly returned to form. In *Brown* v. *Maryland*, decided in 1827, he again aroused the anger of the defenders of states' rights. Maryland had passed a law imposing a license tax upon the sale by bale, package or barrel of any imported goods. Alexander Brown and his partners were indicted for having sold a package of foreign dry goods without having procured a license or paid the tax.

The statute, Marshall held, is unconstitutional. The Constitution prohibits the states from taxing imports, and so long as the goods are in their original package, they are to be deemed imports. More important, the tax is an interference with the power the Constitution grants exclusively to Congress over foreign and interstate commerce. The power of a state to tax its own citizens or their property within the state is not to be denied, but it cannot be exercised "so as to obstruct or defeat the power [of Congress] to regulate commerce."

Having restored his unpopularity in Maryland, Marshall proceeded to Missouri. In 1830 he ruled, in the case of *Craig* v. *Missouri*, that a law of that state providing for the issuance of loan certificates was unconstitutional. When Missouri became a state in 1821, the people were in a desperate financial condition. There was no money; banks had been suspended, and specie had been drained off to the eastern commercial centers. Business transactions were difficult if not impossible and taxes could not be paid. To alleviate the condition, the legislature set up loan offices where citizens could give their promissory notes and obtain loan certificates for them. The certificates could be used to pay taxes and buy salt from the state salt mines. They were made negotiable and thus served as a temporary substitute for money. No one was compelled to accept them, else they would have constituted legal tender in violation of the provision in the Constitution that no state shall make anything but gold and silver coin legal tender.

Nevertheless, Marshall held the law unconstitutional. The Constitution prohibited states from issuing bills of credit, and these so-called loan certificates were really bills of credit. The purpose of the constitutional prohibition was to prevent the states from driving out good money with bad (cheap currency) and under any other name Missouri's loan certificates were still cheap currency.

Marshall was then seventy-five years old. Bushrod Washington was gone and Andrew Jackson, who was now President, had replaced him with Henry Baldwin, a member of Congress from Pennsylvania, a man of such fiery temper and so eccentric as often to be considered insane. Todd had died in 1826, and had been replaced by federal District Judge Robert Trimble, also of Kentucky. On Trimble's death two years later, Jackson appointed John McLean of Ohio, formerly judge of that state's supreme court, and then Postmaster-General of the United States. Not a single Federalist-appointed Justice other than Marshall was on the bench. Yet Marshall was able to muster a majority in support of his decision—although it was a close majority, as Johnson, Thompson and McLean refused to go along.

Craig v. *Missouri* was an unpopular decision and revived the campaign to curb the Court. All the old resolutions were dug up and reintroduced. But it was mostly pro forma; again nothing came of any of them.

From Missouri Marshall went to Georgia and more trouble, this time on account of Indians. During Washington's administration, the government entered into a treaty with the "Cherokee Nation" of Indians in Georgia. Under the treaty the Indians owned their land and had substantial autonomy. By 1828 Georgia coveted the land, particularly as gold had been discovered on it. A statute was enacted abrogating all the Indians' laws and dividing up their lands. The Cherokees appealed to President Jackson, without avail. They then applied to the Supreme Court for an injunction to stop Georgia from enforcing its predatory statutes. While the suit was pending, a Cherokee named Corn Tassel was convicted in a state court of having murdered another Indian. Corn Tassel applied to the Supreme Court for a writ of habeas corpus on the ground that under the treaty with Washington the Cherokees were entitled to their own courts of law and could not be tried in a state court. Marshall issued the writ but the legislature of Georgia replied by adopting a resolution that "the interference by the Chief Justice of the Supreme Court of the United States in the administration of the criminal law of this state . . . is a flagrant violation of her rights." The state officials were directed not only to disregard that or any other process issuing from the Supreme Court, but to use all force necessary to resist. Five days later Corn Tassel was hanged.

The injunction suit, *Cherokee Nation* v. *Georgia*, then came to the Court for argument. The state of Georgia refused to appear and so only the Indians' counsel argued the case. In 1831 Marshall handed down the Court's decision. The Court, he said, had no jurisdiction of the case, for while the Cherokees sued as a foreign nation, they were not in fact such. It was therefore unnecessary to pass on the constitutionality of the Georgia confiscation laws.

Marshall was not yet rid of the controversy. Georgia had passed a law requiring all white persons in the Indian territory to obtain a license and take an oath of allegiance to the state. Two New England missionaries refused to obtain a license and were arrested, convicted and sentenced to four years imprisonment. They appealed to the Supreme Court and, in the case of *Worcester* v. *Georgia* (no counsel appearing for Georgia) Marshall ruled the statute unconstitutional on the ground that the jurisdiction of the federal government over the Cherokees was exclusive, and that Georgia had no power to pass laws affecting them or their territory. The conviction was therefore reversed.

Georgia again vowed defiance and resistance. Marshall is reported then to have appealed to Jackson for help, and Jackson is reported to have said: "John Marshall has made his decision; now let him enforce it." (It is unlikely that this ever happened.) The controversy was ultimately solved satisfactorily—to everybody but the Indians, that is. After a show of resistance to the Court, Georgia released the missionaries. Jackson transported the Cherokees across the Mississippi River to Indian territory. The whites kept the gold lands. And peace returned to Georgia.

This happened in 1832. Three years later peace came also to John Marshall. At the age of seventy-nine, after thirty-four years on the bench, every minute of which he was Chief Justice, John Marshall died.

THE GREATNESS OF MARSHALL

What was Marshall's true worth and what was his contribution? A British jurist, Lord Craigmyle, in a book written in 1933, said that Marshall's opinions "saved the very existence of the United States." Thirty years earlier Senator Henry Cabot Lodge called Marshall "a nation maker." On the other hand, Justice Oliver Wendell Holmes, speaking on the same John Marshall Day as Senator Lodge, said: "I should feel a . . . doubt whether, after Hamilton and the Constitution itself, Marshall's work proved more than a strong intellect, a good style, personal ascendancy in his court, courage, justice, and the convictions of his party."

If Craigmyle and Lodge are too extravagant in their evaluation, Holmes does not do Marshall full justice. If we assume that the political and economic development of the United States in the century between Marshall's death and the depression of the 1930's was good for the country and its people, then America owes Marshall a great debt of gratitude, for his achievements played a major role in that development. This does not mean that America would not have developed in the same way had Marshall never lived; but it could well have been a substantially slower development.

Marshall's contribution to America's economic expansion was twofold. His constitutional principles (inherited from Hamilton and others as they then were, and modified, qualified and even discarded as they were later to be) proved an invaluable tool for later courts to build up a wall of judicial protection around that expansion, a wall which was so sturdy that it lasted a century and was not dismantled until it was no longer needed. The Dartmouth College case made possible the corporate structure of American capitalist economy and *Fletcher* v. *Peck* its contractual base. *Gibbons* v. *Ogden* freed commerce from strangling local restraints, and *McCulloch* v. *Maryland* and *Brown* v. *Maryland* from crippling local taxation.

Secondly, and even more important, he took a Supreme Court which had been considered by the constitutional fathers as of little value and had been abandoned by Jay and Ellsworth as hopelessly impotent, and single-handedly made of it a powerful instrument for furthering, promoting and protecting economic expansion, and later, for protecting personal rights and civil liberties. It was he who brought the Court to the status that Van Buren could say of it in 1826, that there has grown up a feeling of worship and "a sentiment of idolatry for the Supreme Court which claims for its members an almost entire exemption from the fallibilities of our nature." If this sentiment enabled the Court to survive unpopular property decisions before 1937, it also enables it to survive unpopular civil liberties decisions in the 1950's and 1960's.

Marshall did not have Hamilton's great intellect and perspicacity. He certainly did not have Jefferson's genius. He had little originality and less learning. He knew little law and in a sense was not a judge at all; the far more numerous non-political decisions of the Court, the decisions on admiralty, commercial transactions, injuries, which make up the bread and butter work of any court, including the Supreme Court, were largely the work of others, principally Story. What Marshall was, was a statesman—but he was truly a great statesman.

chapter six

Taney and the Police Power

TANEY HEADS JACKSON'S COURT

Andrew Jackson placed more men on the Supreme Court than any President before him since Washington or after him until Franklin Roosevelt. Baldwin and McLean had already been serving for four years when, in 1834, Jefferson's first appointee, William Johnson, died. Johnson had been from South Carolina, and the tradition established by Washington required Jackson to appoint a southerner. He chose James M. Wayne of Georgia, a former state court judge who, at the time of his appointment, was a Democratic member of Congress. In Congress Wayne supported the Union and all measures directed against nullification. For that reason he was acceptable also to the Whigs, that somewhat strange alliance of eastern Federalists and western agrarians which, under the name of Republicans, was to dominate the American political scene from Lincoln to Hoover.

The next year, the aged, deaf and completely incompetent Duval was prevailed upon to resign—a fortunate circumstance for, although he was then eighty-three years old, he managed to live nine years longer. To succeed Duval, Jackson appointed Roger B. Taney, whom the Senate refused to confirm. Jackson then appointed Philip B. Barbour of Virginia, who had been counsel for that state in the Cohens lottery case, and had later introduced a resolution in the Senate to require concurrence of five of the seven Justices in constitutional cases.

After Taney's confirmation as Chief Justice, Jackson had five of his appointees on the seven man bench. Before he retired from the Presidency he had the opportunity to appoint two more. Perhaps taking a leaf from John Adams' Congress, Jackson's Congress enacted a law on March 3, 1837, the day before Jackson went out of office, increasing the membership of the Court to nine. Jackson immediately appointed John Catron of Tennessee and William Smith of Alabama. The former, chief judge of his state supreme court, had vigorously supported Jackson's anti-nullification policy and like Wayne was therefore acceptable to the Whigs. Smith, too, was confirmed, but he declined the appointment, and in his place, Van Buren, who was now President, appointed another resident of Alabama, John McKinley, a former United States senator. The Whigs criticized what appeared to them to be a packing of the Court with Democrats and southerners (a majority of the Court now was from below the Mason-Dixon line), but the Democrats had complete control of the Senate and McKinley was confirmed. This was the Court which Jackson chose Taney to head.

Taney was the second son of an aristocratic Maryland planter. Although primogeniture had been abolished in the South, the tradition of leaving plantations undivided to the oldest son still persisted. In England younger sons went into the army or the ministry and in America they went into law with the objective of entering politics. Like his father, Taney was a Federalist and was elected as such to the Maryland legislature. The New England Federalists' resistance to the War of 1812 and their plans to secede and conclude a separate peace with Britain alienated Taney, as it did the entire Federalist party in the South. Several years later Taney aligned himself with Jackson, who appointed him Attorney-General in 1831. In that capacity Taney proved very valuable to the President in the latter's war on the Bank of the United States. He wrote most of Jackson's message vetoing the bill to recharter the bank.

The bank's charter was due to expire in 1836, but Jackson's overwhelming triumph in winning re-election in 1832 after vetoing the recharter bill convinced him that he had a mandate from the people to bring the career of the hated bank to an immediate end. He accordingly instructed his Secretary of the Treasury, Louis McLane, to withdraw all government deposits from the bank. When McLane refused to do this Jackson kicked him upstairs to be Secretary of State and appointed William J. Duane. When Duane likewise refused, Jackson kicked him outside and appointed Taney in his place, prudently deferring the submission of the appointment to the Senate for confirmation until Taney had done what his two predecessors refused to do. The Senate retaliated by rejecting the nomination, and shortly thereafter again rejected Taney when Jackson named him to fill Duval's place on the Supreme Court. Jackson bided his time. It was clear that Marshall could not live much longer and that Jackson's Democrats would soon control the Senate. When Marshall died Jackson appointed Taney, then almost sixty years old, Chief Justice and the Senate confirmed the appointment. (Taney was a Roman Catholic, and his appointment was opposed by some Whig newspapers on that ground. However, the wave of anti-Catholic bigotry, which went under the name of Know-Nothingism, did not come until a decade later, and Taney's religion proved no serious obstacle.)

BRIDGE AND MONOPOLY

If we wish to resume the quest for symbolism on which we embarked earlier in this book, we can start out by noting as a symbol of the dawn of a new era that the first constitutional law opinion Taney wrote set forth a decision staying, if not reversing, the forward march of Marshall's broad interpretation of the Constitution. We may continue by pointing out this was accomplished by radically restricting the scope of Marshall's dearly beloved impairment-of-contract provision. We can note finally that in this case Webster's phenomenal success at the Supreme Court bar came to an end.

Charles River Bridge v. Warren River Bridge was first argued in 1831. Marshall, Story and Thompson were prepared to hold unconstitutional the Massachusetts law attacked in the case. McLean doubted that the Court had jurisdiction of the suit; Baldwin was prepared to dissent, and Johnson and Duval were absent. In earlier days these facts would not have deterred Marshall, but after the troubled 1820's he was probably sensitive to issuing decisions invalidating state laws with less than a majority of the Court concurring. Accordingly, no decision was handed down and the Court directed counsel to reargue the case. Inability to obtain a majority and changes in the Court's personnel caused further postponements so that the case was not finally decided until 1837, six years after it was first presented to the Court for decision.

In 1785 the Massachusetts legislature incorporated the Charles River Bridge Company to build a toll bridge from Charlestown to Boston and to operate it for seventy years. At the end of that time the bridge was to become the property of the state. The company was controlled initially by Federalists and later by Whigs, a party which had been formed out of a coalition of surviving Federalists and right wing Democrats. By 1828 the Jacksonian Democrats had won sufficient power in the Massachusetts legislature to incorporate the Warren River Bridge Company with authority to build a parallel bridge close by. Under its charter the Warren Bridge was to be a free bridge after six years, or as soon as the tolls collected were sufficient to cover the cost of building and operation.

The Charles River Bridge had been a highly profitable venture and the proprietors went into court to get an injunction against the impending grave threat to their monopoly. Webster argued on behalf of the Charles River Company before the Marshall Court and again before the Taney Court. The Dartmouth College decision meant that the charter granted to the Charles River Bridge Company was a contract whose obligations could not constitutionally be impaired. *Fletcher* v. *Peck* held that an implied term of all contracts is that the giver will not take back or try to take back what was given. In this case the plaintiffs had been given an opportunity to make profits by operating a bridge over the river. If the legislature could now license another company to operate a competing bridge, the plaintiffs' profits would be seriously diminished, if not completely eliminated, making worthless the contract they had received in 1785. To permit such an impairment "would destroy the security of all property and all rights derived under it." The Supreme Court must not allow this, for the prime duty of the Court was to preserve and protect private property rights.

Webster's eloquence, so effective with Marshall, fell on practically deaf ears. Less than three weeks after the reargument, Taney announced the Court's decision. (Story and Thompson dissented and McLean still felt that the Court had no jurisdiction.) The new Chief Justice's opinion breathes a fresh spirit which Marshall would have damned as the rankest radicalism. The issue, said Taney, was whether the new law impaired the obligations of the state's contract with the Charles River Company. It did so only if one read into the contract an implied undertaking that the state had granted to the company a monopoly untouchable during the life of the franchise. This Taney refused to do:

> The object and end of all government is to promote the happiness and prosperity of the community by which it is established; and it can never be assumed that the government intended to diminish its power of accomplishing the end for which it was created. And in a country like ours, free, active, enterprising, continually advancing in numbers and wealth, new channels of communication are daily found necessary, both for travel and trade, and are essential to the comfort, convenience, and prosperity of the people. A State ought never to be presumed to surrender this power because . . . the whole community have an interest in preserving it undiminished.

This is a great opinion, on a par with Marshall's greatest, although proceeding from a diametrically opposite political and economic predilection. It is not merely that Taney expressed an opposition to monopolies and refused to allow them to be created by judicial interpretation of a legislative grant not expressly doing so itself. Far more important, Taney began to spell out a concept, known as the police power, under which government could detrimentally affect private rights and interests that would otherwise normally be protected against such interference. The prime purpose of government is no longer to protect private property and promote profit-making (as it was in the philosophy of Hamilton, Marshall and practically all the fifty-five men who wrote the Constitution); it is now to promote the welfare of the community. The decision in favor of the free public bridge against the private profit-making bridge is one of the constitutional foundations of the social welfare legislation of the twentieth century.

Nor was Taney's opinion hostile to economic expansion and progress. On the contrary, he deemed his decision necessary for that purpose. If, he said, every franchise carries with it an implied grant of monopoly, the franchises granted to turnpike companies would effectively stay the development of railroad transportation. "We shall," he continued, "be thrown back to the improvements of the last century and obliged to stand still until the claims of the old turnpike corporations shall be satisfied and they shall consent to permit the States to avail themselves of the lights of modern science and to partake of these improvements which are now adding to the wealth and prosperity, and the convenience and comfort, of every other part of the civilized world."

Story's dissent predicted exactly opposite economic consequences. "I can," he said, "conceive of no surer plan to arrest all public improvements founded on private capital and enterprise, than to make the outlay of that capital uncertain and questionable, both as to security and as to productiveness." He was equally despondent about the future of the Supreme Court and of constitutional law. "There will not, I fear," he wrote to McLean, "ever in our day be any case in which a law of a State or an act of Congress will be declared unconstitutional; for the old Constitutional doctrines are fast fading away, and a change has come over the public mind from which I augur little good."

The reaction to the decision was what was to be expected. The anti-Jacksonian Whigs assailed it as vigorously as the Jeffersonians had assailed *Fletcher* v. *Peck* and *McCulloch* v. *Maryland.* As one Democratic newspaper reported, "The vested-rights class cry out bloody murder." On the other hand, to the lower economic classes, where the strength of Jackson's Democratic party lay, the decision was a glorious blow against monopoly and presaged a period of harmony between the judiciary and the other two branches of the government unknown since the days of John Adams and Oliver Ellsworth. The election of 1800 appeared to have finally caught up with the Supreme Court.

POLICE POWER AND THE COMMUNITY'S WELFARE

Another case left over from the Marshall Court was *City of New York* v. *Miln.* The rapid development of the West required considerable manpower and much of it came from the Old World. Atlantic coast ports such as New York, Boston and Philadelphia served as a gateway to the New World in the West. However, since those who came had generally expended all their money to pay for passage, substantial numbers of destitute immigrants were stranded in the eastern cities. In an effort to regulate and control what was considered an unreasonable financial burden, the state of New York passed a law requiring the master of every vessel entering the port of New York City from a port outside the state to report to the mayor the name, previous residence, age and occupation of every passenger. Miln, master of a ship, refused to comply with the statute, and the city brought a suit to recover the penalty specified in the law for noncompliance.

The case was initially argued before the Marshall Court and the Chief Justice indicated his opinion that the law was unconstitutional. It was re-argued before the Taney Court and the decision, announced by Barbour, upheld the statute, with only Story dissenting. A state, he said, has "not only the right, but the bounden duty . . . to advance the safety, happiness and prosperity of its people, and to provide for the general welfare by any and every act of legislation which it may deem to be conducive to these ends." This police power was never turned over to the federal government and therefore as to this, "the authority of a state is complete, unqualified and exclusive." In 1876, in the case of *Henderson* v. *New York*, the decision was overruled and a statute similar to the one there upheld was declared an unconstitutional infringement on Congress' power to regulate commerce. Still later Congress pre-empted the whole field of immigration, and laws and regulations such as those involved in the Miln case are now exclusively the domain of the federal government.

The permanent significance of the Miln case lies in its contribution to the development of the police power concept. The concept was not invented by Taney or his Court; it was known in Marshall's day. But then it was understood narrowly, as its name indicates, to refer to the power of the states to preserve order and safety within their borders. Under Taney the idea was broadened considerably to encompass the general well-being of the people; it became a power to provide for the welfare of the community. But not only was the scope of the concept widened; equally important, it was accorded a high constitutional status. As the opinions in the Charles River Bridge and Miln cases indicate, even if exercise of the police power transgresses on some other constitutionally protected right, such as the right to the fulfillment of the obligations of contract or to engage in interstate commerce, it is not for that reason unconstitutional. Implicit in this is the assumption that not merely are the interests of the community superior to the rights of the individual, but also that the protection of private property and the promotion of profit making are not necessarily the only or even highest and overriding ends of government—an assumption completely alien to the philosophy of Hamilton, Jay and Marshall.

Yet the introduction of the concept of the community and the obligation of the state to provide for its welfare into the decisions of the Supreme Court tempered but moderately the onward surge of expanding capitalism, a surge which was too powerful even for Taney and Jackson's other appointees to resist. Marshall had made of the Court an institution whose function it was to prevent democratic obstructions to this surge. Institutions inevitably affect and influence those who are part of it, as evidenced by the Federalist decisions of Marshall's Court during the long period when most of its members were appointees of Democratic-Republicans. If power has a tendency to corrupt, it also has a tendency to make conservative, and this is especially true of judicial power. Taney and his Jacksonian colleagues on the bench could no more resist either the surge of capitalism or their own institutionalization by the Court as fashioned by Marshall than could the latter's Jeffersonian colleagues. The Court swallows its members; it could hardly have survived otherwise.

It was not long before the Taney Court was lending its hand in aid of capitalist expansion. If in some respects it tempered that expansion, in others it greatly facilitated it and made its own contribution to America's onrushing economic development. In this development corporations were destined to play not merely a major but a critical role. Try to imagine what American economy would be if there were no General Motors, United States Steel, American Telephone and Telegraph, Standard Oil, etc.

In the case of *Louisville, Cincinnati and Charleston Railroad Co.* v. *Letson,* decided in 1844, Taney's Court overruled Marshall's decision in *Strawbridge* v. *Curtiss* and held that for the purpose of capacity to sue in a federal court a corporation is to be considered a citizen of the state that chartered it. In this case Taney's Court opened the doors of the federal courts to corporations. In *Swift* v. *Tyson* (actually decided two years earlier, in 1842), it sought to assure them of a hospitable federal law when they arrived. The Anglo-American legal system is based on the common law—that is, the decisions of judges in particular cases which are followed by later judges in similar cases and thus become the rules of law to be followed in future cases until (occasionally) overruled by a later court or (more usually) changed by a statute enacted by the legislature. Today, much—although still probably not most—of the law applied in the courts is statutory law, but for centuries statutory law was but a minute fraction of judge-made, or common law.

During the period immediately preceding the Sedition Act there was considerable discussion whether the English common law of crimes was to be applied in the federal courts. Sedition against the king was a common law crime in England and many Federalist judges contended that correspondingly sedition against John Adams or Congress was a punishable common law federal crime. Since Congress did enact a Sedition Act it was not necessary for the Supreme Court to decide the issue. In 1816 the Marshall Court finally answered the question in holding, in the case of *United States* v. *Coolidge,* that there are no common law federal crimes and punishment can be imposed by federal courts only for acts that Congress has declared to be criminal. (With few exceptions the states have adopted the same rule in respect to state crimes.)

The Coolidge case dealt only with common law crimes; in respect to non-criminal law it was generally assumed that the question had been disposed of in the Judiciary Act of 1789. Section 34 of that act provided that when a suit is brought in a federal court between citizens of different states "the laws of the several States . . . shall be regarded as rules of decision in trials at common law." This means, or was generally assumed to mean, that when a New Jersey buyer comes into New York and gives an order for goods to a New York manufacturer, if a suit on the contract is later brought in a federal court, the federal judge would decide the case in accordance with the decisions of the New York courts in similar cases.

In *Swift* v. *Tyson*, Story, announcing the Court's decision, reached a different result. The term "laws of the several States" in the Judiciary Act means only the statutes of the states (and also decisions of purely local consequences, as for example those involving real estate). In respect to business and commercial transactions, the federal court is not required to follow the state court decisions but can decide for itself what the true law is that governs the transaction.

The effect of this decision was to initiate the erection of a federal common law system, a system which lasted for a little short of a century. When a case would arise in a federal court in Ohio, the judge would not consult the Ohio state court decisions on similar cases, but would follow the decision of a Virginia or New York federal judge. Story's objective was two-fold: to assure business interests a more favorable commercial law system than might be available in the state courts, and to build up a uniform federal system of commercial law which, he hoped, the state courts would follow so that there would be certainty and uniformity throughout the land. (Actually, it did not work out that way. The state courts persisted in their misguided ways, so that in each state there were two legal systems; which was to be applied in a particular case depended on the astuteness of counsel in deciding whether to go into the state court or across the street to the federal district court, a practice which lawyers called forum shopping. Thus, instead of uniformity there came greater diversity, and instead of certainty, greater confusion.)

One further important case involving commerce should be mentioned here, although it was not decided until 1851, after there had been considerable changes in the Court's personnel. The case, *Cooley* v. *Board of Wardens*, involved the first case of featherbedding that appears to have reached the courts. When a vessel was about to enter a port, the ordinary practice was to take on a local pilot to bring the boat into the port. To save pilotage fees, however, some companies used their own pilots for this purpose. The state of Pennsylvania sought to meet this competition by enacting a law which provided that any vessel failing to take on a local pilot should pay one-half the usual pilotage fee to the Society for the Relief of Distressed and Decayed Pilots, Their Widows and Children. The law was attacked in the Supreme Court on the ground that it was an unconstitutional interference with interstate and foreign commerce. However, the Court upheld the law on the ground that no federal law had been enacted by Congress covering the point and therefore Pennsylvania was free to act to protect the needs of its pilots.

CHANGES IN COURT PERSONNEL

In the election of 1840, Van Buren was defeated by William Henry Harrison. On February 25, 1841, exactly a week before Van Buren was to go out of office, Justice Barbour died suddenly. The very next day Van Buren appointed as his successor Peter V. Daniel, federal district judge in Virginia, the post which Barbour had held before his elevation to the Supreme Court. The appointment was immediately rushed over to the Senate, still temporarily controlled by the Democrats, for confirmation. The Whigs, conveniently forgetting what had happened in the last days of John Adams, were shocked. Said one Whig paper: "The breath was hardly out of Judge Barbour's body before Van Buren hurries a successor into the Senate Chamber; and an approval of him is insisted upon, and carried at midnight by dragging Senators out of their beds. It is not an easy thing, one would think, to find a Judge fit for the Supreme Bench in 24 hours, but Mr. Van Buren found no difficulty in it. . . . Thus, in shame and dishonor, injustice and disgrace ends the career of Mr. Van Buren."

Indignantly the Whig senators walked out of the Senate chamber before the confirmation vote was taken, leaving but one of their members as an observer. The Whigs may have been the victims of their own strategy. The nomination was confirmed by a vote of 22 to 5, which was less than a majority of the whole Senate; it is possible that had they mustered their forces they might have prevented confirmation. In any event, Van Buren went out of office two days later and the Justice he appointed lived and served for nineteen years after him. During this period Daniel revealed himself to be an inveterate dissenter; even when he agreed with the decision of the majority of the Court he often found it necessary to write a separate opinion showing that while the majority had reached the right conclusion, they had done so for the wrong reasons. He also was a staunch states' righter and opposed vigorously any effort to extend the powers of Congress over internal state matters.

In December, 1843, Smith Thompson died and President Tyler was struck with a brilliant inspiration. Van Buren was then at the height of his popularity and seemed assured of the Democratic nomination for the Presidency in the election of 1844. Assuming that he himself would be the Whig choice, Tyler decided to remove this powerful rival by appointing him to the Supreme Court. In the end he was dissuaded from doing so, but as it turned out this high strategy would have been futile; the Democrats passed over Van Buren for Polk, and the Whigs chose Henry Clay over Tyler.

Tyler found it extremely difficult to fill the vacancy. He first appointed John C. Spencer, a successful New York lawyer who, however, had the misfortune of having alienated the powerful Clay faction of the Whig party. The nomination was rejected by the Senate, and Tyler then offered the position almost simultaneously though separately to two leaders of the Philadelphia bar, John Sergeant and Horace Binney. As each was approached each declined on the ground of age (both were over sixty) and each suggested that the nomination be tendered to the other. Tyler then offered the post to a Democratic member of the Senate, Silas Wright, who twice declined the offer, probably because he recognized that the Whig Senate would never confirm his appointment. Tyler next appointed Reuben H. Walworth, a New York judge of undoubted legal ability but personally unpopular, particularly to the New York Whigs. It was unlikely that the Senate would confirm his appointment, or indeed any appointment by Tyler, since the election of 1844 was approaching and the Whigs in the Senate expected Clay to be elected so that the post would go to one of their faction.

To add to Tyler's troubles, Baldwin died in April, 1844, leaving Tyler with two vacancies on the bench. Tyler never did get around to filling the second vacancy, but after the Democratic victory in the election of 1844 ruined the Whigs' plan to have Clay choose the Justices, the

Senate confirmed Tyler's appointment of Samuel Nelson, chief judge of the New York supreme court. The confirmation came in February of 1845 and Nelson took his seat in March, so that it took in all a year and a quarter to fill the vacancy left by Thompson's death.

Polk took office with one vacancy unfilled and another soon to come. Six months after Polk became President, Marshall's man Story died, his last years embittered by what he deemed the destruction of the solid doctrines of the "Old Court." Before filling the Baldwin vacancy, Polk appointed Levi Woodbury of New Hampshire to succeed Story. Woodbury had a long and distinguished career; he had been successively judge of the supreme court of his state, governor, member of the United States Senate, Secretary of the Navy under Jackson, Secretary of the Treasury under Van Buren and then again United States senator. His service on the Supreme Court was short; he died in 1851.

In filling Baldwin's place Polk had almost as much trouble as Tyler had in filling Thompson's, and for the same reasons. His first appointee, George W. Woodward, a Pennsylvania judge with ability and liberal convictions, was rejected by the Senate because he had alienated powerful elements within the Democratic party. He then offered the position to his Secretary of State, James Buchanan, who first refused it, then accepted, and then refused it again, this time for good. Finally Polk chose Robert C. Grier, a lower court Pennsylvania judge, who was to be another of the Justices to serve on the Supreme Court for some time after senility had destroyed his competence.

DORR'S REBELLION

One of the most interesting aspects of American history is the strong forward surge of political democracy coinciding with a similar surge of economic centralization and monopoly. Hamilton, Jay, Marshall and their fellow Federalists were always afflicted with a mortal fear of democracy. In all states the right to vote was limited to persons who owned substantial property, and even more stringent property qualifications were imposed upon those who sought political office. The result was that the ordinary city workers—then called mechanics—were disenfranchised. With the industrial revolution their numbers multiplied rapidly and their demands for a right to share in the selection of those who governed them became increasingly insistent. The Federalists strove valiantly to hold back the tide. Webster, addressing the Massachusetts constitutional convention of 1820, warned that all the revolutions of history which had shaken society to its foundations had been revolts against property, that equal suffrage was incompatible with inequality in property and that the grant of equal suffrage would inevitably result in assaults on wealth.

The warnings were in vain; beginning with Vermont as early as 1791, state after state began lowering and ultimately eliminating its property qualifications for suffrage. In most states the transition was relatively peaceful—more so than the later campaigns of women and Negroes for equal suffrage—with no untoward consequences beyond loud debate and hard feelings. In Rhode Island, however, the consequence was actually rebellion and violence.

The leader of the movement for universal suffrage in that state was Thomas W. Dorr. Dorr was a member of a wealthy Whig family, attended Harvard, studied law under the arch-Federalist Chancellor Kent of New York, was admitted to the bar in Providence and then, with a successful legal career before him, became afflicted with a social conscience, threw in his lot with Jackson's radical Democrats (called Loco-focoists) and soon became their leader in Rhode Island. That state still was governed under its original charter of 1663, which required ownership of land as a prerequisite of voting, thus disenfranchising practically the whole of the working class. When the ruling conservatives turned a deaf ear to the demands for electoral reform, Dorr's party called a constitutional convention, which met in 1841 and adopted a new constitution for the state. The legislature refused to recognize the legality of Dorr's convention (and there was no doubt it was illegal, as much so as the congress that adopted the Declaration of Independence or the convention that adopted the Constitution). The next year separate elections for governor were held, Samuel H. King being chosen in the legitimate election and Dorr in the Loco-focoists'.

With the sympathies of most of the nation's Democrats on his side, Dorr resorted to a show of armed force, but after an abortive assault on the Providence armory, his government collapsed and he fled the state. King declared martial law, arrested many of Dorr's followers, and had Dorr himself indicted for high treason. The conservatives, finally recognizing that they could not forever stay the tides of democracy, called a new convention and adopted a constitution which, taking effect in 1844, greatly liberalized voting requirements and enfranchised most of the townspeople and workers. Dorr thereupon returned to Rhode Island where he was immediately brought to trial, convicted and sentenced to solitary confinement at hard labor for life.

An application was then made to the Supreme Court on Dorr's behalf for a writ of habeas corpus, challenging the legality and constitutionality of his conviction, on the ground principally that under the Constitution, treason could not be committed against a state but only against the federal government. The nation, or at least the Democrats in the nation, were so shocked at the harshness of the sentence that it was freely predicted that Taney's Court would grant the writ. To the surprise of most everybody, the Court, in *Ex Parte Dorr*, unanimously held that it had no jurisdiction to issue an original writ for any prisoner held in custody under the sentence or execution of a state court.

Thus rebuffed, Dorr's followers tried again. Luther, a Loco-focoist, brought an action against one, Borden, a member of the militia, who had broken into Luther's home in order to arrest him. Borden replied in defense that he had acted pursuant to the lawful authority of Governor King and the state legislature. Luther, however, claimed that Dorr was governor and neither King nor his legislature had any legal authority. The case reached the Supreme Court in 1845, and the issue appeared to be whether the people of a state had the right to abolish an existing government against the will of the members of that government, at least where the existing charter contained no procedures for its own alteration.

It seemed, at least to the Jacksonian Democrats, that the Court could not deny Dorr's claim without repudiating the Declaration of Independence. ("We hold these truths to be self evident, that all men are created equal. . . . That whenever any form of government becomes destructive of these ends, it is the right of the people to alter or to abolish it, and to institute new government, laying its foundation on such principles and organizing its powers in such form as to them shall seem most likely to effect their safety and happiness.") Webster, in presenting the case for the King party, denied that there was such a thing as a natural right to vote or that there was within the American system of government any principle or practice of popular sovereignty.

For more than three years the Court struggled with the case of

Luther v. *Borden.* By 1849, when it finally handed down its decision, the controversy had long blown over. The Rhode Island legislature had pardoned Dorr, who, broken in health, was released from prison. Two years later, when the Democrats gained power, they enacted a law restoring his civil and political rights, and in 1854 annulled the judgment against him. When the Supreme Court announced its decision in 1849, it appeared that three of the Justices, Catron, McKinley and Daniel, (all southerners who had been appointed either by Jackson or Van Buren) did not participate in the decision, presumably because of ill health, and Woodbury (Polk's appointee) dissented.

The majority opinion was written by Taney. He stated that the questions which of two persons was properly elected governor and which of two charters is the legal constitution of a state were purely political rather than what lawyers call juridical questions. Under the Constitution the Court has no power to pass on purely political questions. Taney could not see how a court could determine the qualifications of voters, or whether those claiming the right to vote had properly participated in an election. In the states these questions were passed on by the political departments of the government, not by the courts, and this was the only sound practice. Having no jurisdiction to decide the underlying issue of Luther's suit against Borden, whether King or Dorr had legally been elected governor, the Court could not upset the state court's decision against Luther. *Luther* v. *Borden* has become a landmark case in the history of the Supreme Court, and its principle, that the Court has no power to pass upon purely political questions, though at times ignored by the Court, has been followed in innumerable cases and was not to be seriously challenged until the Reapportionment Case (*Baker* v. *Carr*) in 1962.

One aspect of the Dorr Rebellion was decided by the Court in *Luther* v. *Borden,* and that was whether the King legislature, assuming its legitimacy, could constitutionally establish martial law. If it could not, Luther was entitled to judgment irrespective of the political issues involved in the case. Where there is actual insurrection, Taney held, the legislature can constitutionally impose martial law if the civil officials are unable to preserve order.

MORE CHANGES IN COURT PERSONNEL

In 1851 Woodbury died and a Whig President, Millard Fillmore, had the opportunity to fill the vacancy. Fillmore applied to Webster for advice, delicately noting that he wanted someone who would have a "long lease," and therefore besides other qualifications, he should have "such age as gives prospect of long service." (Webster was then sixty-nine years old.) Webster suggested Rufus Choate of Boston, one of the nation's most successful attorneys. Choate turned down the offer because the work was too hard and because he could "earn in three months as much as their whole salary."

Fillmore then offered the position to and received the acceptance of Webster's second choice, Benjamin R. Curtis, also of Boston. Curtis too was a highly successful lawyer of unimpeachable Whig convictions, and the appointment was criticized in some quarters on the charge that he was merely a tool of Webster. Curtis had the proper age, forty-two, and in addition was in good health. In fact, he lived for twenty-three years after his appointment. Nevertheless, Fillmore's plan failed; after serving only six years, Curtis resigned from the bench.

In December of 1852, McKinley died, but the Democratic Senate delayed confirming Fillmore's appointee so that when Franklin Pierce took office on March 4, 1853, the vacancy was still unfilled. Pierce nominated John A. Campbell, a successful Alabama lawyer of extreme states' rights views, and the Senate confirmed him with alacrity.

This, then, was the Court which four years later was to hand down the fateful decision in *Dred Scott* v. *Sandford*. Five of the members were from the South: Taney was from Maryland, Wayne from Georgia, Catron from Tennessee, Daniel from Virginia and Campbell from Alabama. The other four were from the North: McLean came from Ohio, Nelson from New York, Grier from Pennsylvania, and Curtis from Massachusetts. And as the Court was split between North and South, so too was the nation.

chapter seven

Crisis in Court and Country

In the first years of the American republic, slavery was not a serious national problem and there was little reason to anticipate that it would ever become a nation-rending issue. There was a general agreement in the South as well as in the Middle Atlantic and New England states that slavery was an undesirable institution which should, and ultimately would, be eliminated. The Constitution protected the right to import slaves for twenty years, and it was assumed that after 1808 traffic in slaves would be outlawed. The Constitution also protected the owners of runaway slaves against emancipation in non-slave states. Nevertheless, individuals and groups, north and south, agreed that as early as possible steps should be taken to free the slaves and to prohibit the further sale and purchase of slaves.

There was an antislavery movement even in the South. Many of the southern leaders manumitted their own slaves. Taney supported state legislation protecting free Negroes from abuses, belonged to a society whose purpose it was to suppress the kidnapping and illegal imprisonment of free Negroes, and manumitted his own slaves. Between 1777 and 1804 all the states north of Maryland took action to abolish slavery within their borders, usually by gradual emancipation laws, while all the southern states abandoned the importation of slaves from abroad. By the turn of the century there was a fairly widespread belief that slavery was a dying institution.

What changed this course of events was the industrial revolution, among the consequences of which were the establishment of a host of textile mills in New England with an almost insatiable appetite for cotton, and the invention of the cotton gin, which enabled the South to satisfy that appetite. Slave labor was not feasible for the textile mills in New England cities but it was eminently practicable for the southern plantations. New England could therefore afford the luxury of morality and intensified its cries for the abolition of slavery, without abating its demands for the large amounts of raw cotton which slavery made possible.

By 1820 the lines had begun to harden perceptibly. The Missouri

Territory, having acquired sufficient population, applied for admission to the Union as a state. A statehood bill was introduced and in the House an amendment was adopted that would have forbidden the importation of slaves and ultimately have brought about the emancipation of all slaves born in Missouri. The amendment was defeated in the Senate, and the debates showed the beginnings of intense bitterness and sectional division. Fortuitously Maine applied for statehood and this made possible a compromise (usually attributed to Henry Clay) under which Maine and Missouri were both admitted, the latter with a constitution which did not prohibit slavery. The compromise law also provided that slavery would be prohibited in that part of the remainder of the Louisiana Purchase which was north of a line extending westward from the southern boundary of Missouri.

For the next half-century there was hardly a major political event in the nation that was not debated and decided against the background of slavery. In the beginning, questions of states' rights and sovereignty were viewed chiefly in terms of insolvency laws, cheap money and other measures to relieve burdened debtors from oppressive creditors or deprive honest creditors of their just claims against dishonest debtors—depending on where one's sympathies lay. Now states' rights meant the right of the South to preserve its "peculiar institution" and ultimately, if necessary, to go its own way. Originally, Congress' power to regulate interstate commerce meant only its power to promote business expansion; now it also meant its power to interfere with the transportation of slaves across state lines. Whenever a western territory sought admission as a state, the critical question was how would it affect the balance between slave and free states.

Supreme Court decisions, too, began to be examined with eyes that were rapidly becoming acutely perceptive of any slavery implications. On its surface, *McCulloch* v. *Maryland* concerned only the power of Congress to charter the Bank of the United States and of the states to tax its branches. But the decision was handed down in 1819, at the time when controversy surrounding the admission of Missouri as a free or slave state was becoming increasingly tense. In Congress the pro-slavery forces expressed concern that Marshall's broad interpretation of the powers of Congress and particularly the "necessary and proper" clause might be taken to justify interference by Congress in the field of slavery.

Later, the case of *City of New York* v. *Miln* on its face involved only the power of port cities to exclude diseased and destitute immigrants. But if the commerce clause prohibited a state from excluding immigrants it probably also prohibited the exclusion of free Negroes, and there were few things the southern states feared more than having free Negroes roaming their streets and inciting insurrection. Conversely, the same police power which New York urged entitled it to keep paupers out, was cited by the South to justify their right to exclude free Negroes. Such exclusionary laws, a southern senator argued, are a valid exercise of the states' police power and, like quarantine laws, necessary as a "protection against what is infinitely more dangerous than physical contagion—the introduction of free persons of color into a community where slavery exists, with the means of practicing upon the ignorance of these people, of deluding them into insurrection and of placing in jeopardy the lives of the people of the States."

MARSHALL'S COURT GETS INVOLVED

There is every reason to believe that, until its tragic error in 1856, the Court sought to avoid involvement in the slavery conflict. The dangers of involvement to its status and prestige were well recognized by many on and off the Court. These were pointed out vividly and with remarkable prescience by a congressman on the floor of the House in 1848. Involvement by the Court, he said, would

> hazard not its impartiality and its high moral influence only, but its constitution and even its existence. During the long period of the pendency of this question, it would be incessantly exposed to every adverse influence. Local sympathies, long cherished prejudices, and predilections of party, the known wishes of the Administration and of the National Legislature, would all conspire to bias the decision; intervening vacancies would be filled with reference to the supposed, perhaps even pledged opinion of the candidate upon this one question, and when, finally, the decision should be promulgated, the Court itself would become with the defeated party, the object of a hostility as deep-rooted, as persevering, as widely diffused and as rancorous as are at this moment the feelings and prejudices of the parties now arrayed against each other upon this great issue. Could a tribunal which relies for its support upon moral force and public opinion alone . . . enforces its decrees by no armed satellites, dispenses no patronage, and is sustained by no executive power, long withstand the malignant influence which would thus be brought to bear?

There were members of the Court who shared these fears, but any efforts on its part to avoid the maelstrom were doomed to futility. The Taney Court could no more keep itself outside the slavery conflict than the Marshall Court could avoid the conflicts around the Sedition Act and the Bank of the United States, or later Courts could stay aloof of those surrounding internal Communism or racial segregation. For better or worse, the Supreme Court is one of the nation's major political institutions and there is no way it can be insulated from the nation's major political controversies.

The Court became involved even before Taney became Chief Justice. In the case of *The Antelope*, the Court was faced as early as 1825 with the task of deciding the legality of the slave trade. An American slaver had hijacked a number of slaves from Spanish and Portuguese vessels off the coast of Africa. As the American vessel approached our shores it was intercepted by an American revenue cutter and the slaves were taken to Savannah to await determination of the complex legal questions raised by what the Spanish and Portuguese claimed had been acts of piracy.

When the case reached the Supreme Court, the United States government's attorneys argued that the Negroes should be given their freedom since they had been brought into this country in violation of the laws against the importation of slaves. The Court, in an opinion by Marshall, overruled the contention and adjudged that the slaves should be handed over to the Spaniards and Portuguese who, having first captured them in Africa, were their rightful owners. All Christian and civilized nations, said Marshall, have engaged in the slave trade; long usage and general acquiescence have sanctioned it. Whatever may be the feeling of the American public or the state of American law, neither can make illegal what is legal under international law. (*The Antelope* is interesting, too, in indicating either Marshall's influence over Story, or his skill in concealing divisions within the Court. The decision in *The Antelope* was announced by Marshall as unanimous; yet only three years earlier Story had reached a directly contrary conclusion while sitting in circuit, and had denounced the slave trade as "a breach of all moral duties, of all the maxims of justice, mercy and humanity, and of the admitted rights which Christian nations now hold sacred in their intercourse with each other.")

Four years later, the Marshall Court was called upon to decide another case involving slavery, this time the status of slaves rather than of the slave trade. The case was *Boyce* v. *Anderson*, and it grew out of a fire on a steamboat descending the Mississippi. On board were a number of slaves and they, together with all other persons on board, were able to escape to the shore. Another steamboat was coming up the river and in response to the appeals from the stranded group the captain sent a yawl to pick them up and bring them to the steamboat. The yawl upset and the slaves drowned.

Under the common law a carrier (a company operating trains, vessels, etc.) is liable for loss or damage to all merchandise carried by it, but it is not liable for loss of or injuries to passengers unless the company or its employees were guilty of negligence. In the *Boyce* case there was no proof that the crew of the yawl was careless; therefore, whether or not the owner of the slaves could recover for the drowned slaves depended on whether they were to be deemed merchandise or passengers. The owners of the slaves, Marshall ruled, could not recover for them. A slave, he said, "in the nature of things . . . resembles a passenger, and not a package of goods. It would seem reasonable, therefore, that the responsibility of the carrier should be measured by the law which is applicable to passengers, rather than that which is applicable to the carriage of common goods."

TANEY'S COURT GETS MORE INVOLVED

The first significant case decided by the Taney Court which dealt directly with the slavery issue was *Groves* v. *Slaughter*, decided in 1841. At the time the chief significance of the case appeared to be that some three million dollars turned on its outcome, and that Daniel Webster and Henry Clay were attorneys (on the same side) in the case. The Justices were divided as to the proper disposition of the case, but the division was not along sectional lines. As the division between North and South deepened, the case assumed increasing importance, and indeed had within it seeds of the Dred Scott case.

Too much of any good thing can get one into trouble, and in 1832 the state of Mississippi found itself in financial trouble by reason of the overexpansion of the slave trade and the consequent draining of fluid capital away from the state. Accordingly, a constitutional amendment was adopted prohibiting the further importation of slaves as merchandise into Mississippi. Notwithstanding this ban, slave traffic continued, largely on credit. When the notes given for the slaves became due, the buyers saw a way to escape their obligations. They insisted that since the importation of the slaves was illegal under the state constitution, the notes given for them were void and uncollectible, although they made no offer to return the slaves to the sellers—conduct that Clay in his argument before the Supreme Court called an "outrage on justice."

Webster and Clay presented two arguments in support of the creditors: first, although the Mississippi constitution said that slaves should not be imported into the state, it did not say that if they were they should not be paid for; secondly, if the constitutional provision were to be construed as to exonerate the buyer from liability for payment, it would be unconstitutional since it would be a state regulation of interstate commerce infringing upon Congress' exclusive jurisdiction. It is obvious that the second ground would bring squarely before the Court the explosive issues of the power of Congress to control or prohibit the transportation of slaves across state lines and of the power of the states to allow or to prohibit the importation of slaves into their own domains. On the other hand, if the Court decided that the Mississippi constitution required that the slaves be paid for though their importation was forbidden, there was no need to pass on these issues.

Pursuing the Court's policy of discretion, Justice Thompson (of New York) read the decision of the majority (probably written by Taney), agreeing with the first contention of Clay and Webster that the slaves had to be paid for. Then a rather strange and altogether unprecedented thing happened. To the apparent surprise of his fellow Justices, as well as every one else in the courtroom, McLean (of Ohio) took from his pocket and read a separate opinion of his own. He agreed with the conclusion of the majority of the Court in respect to the meaning of the provision in the Mississippi constitution, and agreed further that it was therefore not necessary to express an opinion in respect to the second question. But, he continued, the issue was of such public importance that he ought to state his views.

"Each State," he said, "has a right to protect itself against the avarice and intrusion of the slave dealer; to guard its citizens against the inconveniences and dangers of a slave population. The right to exercise this power by a State is higher and deeper than the Constitution. The evil involves the prosperity and may endanger the existence of a State. Its power to guard against, or to remedy the evil, rests upon the law of self-preservation; a law vital to every community, and especially to a sovereign State."

Seeing McLean throw discretion to the winds, Taney (of Maryland) felt he could not remain silent. He thereupon expressed his view that "the power over this subject is exclusively with the several States; and each of them has the right to decide for itself whether it will or will not allow persons of this description to be brought within its limits from another State, either for sale or for any other purpose; . . . and the action of the several States upon this subject cannot be controlled by Congress, either by its power to regulate commerce or by virtue of any other power conferred by the Constitution of the United States."

Baldwin (of Pennsylvania) felt he too had to state his opinion, and in doing so he expressed for the first time the suggestion that the provision in the Fifth Amendment that no person shall be deprived of property without due process of law protects property rights against confiscation or destruction by Congress. Therefore, continued Baldwin, stating a proposition that Taney made a basis of the Dred Scott decision, the only jurisdiction of Congress over slavery is to protect "the property of the citizens of the United States, which is a lawful subject of commerce among the States, from any state law which affects to prohibit its transmission for sale from one State to another."

To make the story complete, and completely confusing, McKinley (of Alabama) and Story (of Massachusetts) dissented from the conclusion of the others that the buyers of the slaves had to pay for them. They were of the view that the provision in the Mississippi constitution meant that the notes were void and uncollectible, and that this provision was not unconstitutional.

What is the explanation for McLean's strange behavior which threw the Court into such confusion and burst open the lid that had previously concealed from the people the division within the Court on the slavery issue? It should be noted that McLean and Taney were saying much the same thing—that the states may decide for themselves whether to permit or prohibit the importation of slaves; McLean simply stressed their power to prohibit, and Taney their power to permit. McLean was an ardent abolitionist, but his ardor was topped by his ambition for the Presidency. From the day he took his seat on the bench he began campaigning for the nomination, and, as a means of promoting his political ambitions, did not hesitate to write letters to the press defending or criticizing Court decisions. His opinions in the Groves case made both North and South relatively happy; the former in that it justified their efforts to prevent the spread of slavery, and the latter because it confirmed their claims of exclusive power to regulate all matters affecting slavery within their borders.

The next slavery case to be decided by the Court was *United States v. The Schooner Amistad*, also decided in 1841. *The Amistad*, a vessel engaged in the slave trade, was owned by Spanish subjects. On the high seas, the slaves mutinied, killed the captain and took charge of the vessel. They saved the lives of two of the traders on condition that the latter either take them to a free port or return them to Africa. Instead the traders steered the ship to the United States where it was seized by a naval vessel and brought into Hartford, Connecticut. The traders, acting through the Spanish embassy, demanded the return of the slaves under the provision of an existing treaty between the United States and Spain that "ships and merchandise" of any national of either country captured by pirates or robbers on the high seas and rescued by vessels of the other country would be restored to the rightful owners.

John Forsyth of Georgia, Van Buren's Secretary of State and a strong defender of slavery, made every effort to help the Spanish claimants. He instructed the federal attorney in Hartford to enter the case and press for the restoration of the slaves to the traders. The federal attorney was more than willing to cooperate. In a letter to the State Department he wrote: "I should regret extremely that the rascally blacks should fall into the hands of the abolitionists, with whom Hartford is filled." (When a copy of the letter was requested by and transmitted to a committee of the House of Representatives, this sentence was discreetly suppressed.)

The Hartford abolitionists were just as determined that the Negroes should not be returned to slavery. The abolitionists contended that whatever may have been their previous status, under Connecticut law the Negroes became free the moment they were taken off the vessel in Hartford. The abolitionists throughout the country took up the Negroes' cause because of its excellent propaganda value. The case soon became a *cause celebre*, dividing the nation across sectional lines. Each side published strong editorials in the press, and each accused the other of attempting thereby to influence the federal court's decision.

Forsyth expected a favorable decision in the district court and planned to have the Negroes shipped out of the country to Spain as soon as the decision came down and before there was any chance to appeal. Unfortunately for him, the district judge ruled that the slaves should be sent back to Africa, and the United States Attorney had to appeal. Before the case reached the Supreme Court, the abolitionists prevailed upon ex-President John Quincy Adams, then seventy-four years old and long retired from the practice of law, to act as one of the counsels for the Negroes in the Supreme Court.

Story's opinion (from which only Baldwin dissented) carefully avoided deciding the constitutionality and applicability of the Connecticut law. The treaty with Spain, he said, was not applicable since the Negroes were not pirates or robbers. Moreover, since Spain had outlawed the African slave trade, the Negroes were not merchandise and their kidnapping in Africa was therefore unlawful. Accordingly, they were entitled to their freedom and could neither be restored to the Spanish slave traders nor sent back to Africa, but could walk out into the streets of Hartford as free men.

In the following year (1842) the Court handed down its decision in *Prigg v. Pennsylvania*, a case which brought to the Court the most divisive of the issues in the slavery problem, that of fugitive slaves. The United States Constitution provides that escaping slaves shall be returned to their owners. To implement this provision, Congress in 1793 enacted a law providing for the arrest of suspected fugitive slaves. The slaves must then be brought before a judge who, upon satisfactory proof, would issue certificates for their return to their owners. Presumably also to help out, the states passed similar laws, providing that suspected fugitive slaves had to be brought before state judges who could issue the necessary certificates. To make the laws really effective, they also made it a crime to seek to remove a suspected fugitive without first obtaining such a certificate. As the laws were administered in northern states it was often found that for one reason or another the necessary certificate could not be gotten. The New York law, for example, provided for a jury trial, and New York juries apparently never were able to satisfy themselves that the Negro before them was really the slave who had allegedly escaped from the southern claimant.

Margaret Morgan, a fugitive slave from Maryland, was discovered in Pennsylvania by Edward Prigg, her master's agent. Prigg seized Margaret and the child recently born to her and brought them before a Pennsylvania magistrate to obtain the certificate required by the Pennsylvania law. The magistrate was not convinced that the person brought in by Prigg was indeed the alleged fugitive slave and refused to issue the certificate. Prigg thereupon took both the law and the slave in his own hands, and forcibly removed Margaret and her child to Maryland and back to her master's plantation. Prigg was thereupon indicted and convicted of violating the Pennsylvania law. He appealed to the United States Supreme Court on the claim that the law was unconstitutional.

All the Justices agreed that the law was unconstitutional and that the conviction must be set aside. But they apparently all found it necessary to state separately the reasoning by which they came to this conclusion. (Compare the single voice of the Marshall Court in *The Antelope*.)

The main division was between Story and Taney. The former, in the majority opinion, held that Congress had exclusive jurisdiction over the problem of runaway slaves. The states, he said, had no power to pass any laws on the subject, whether to aid or obstruct the return of fugitives. Prigg, therefore, was under no obligation to comply with the Pennsylvania law and could not be convicted for non-compliance. Taney, on the other hand, was of the view that the states could not obstruct the return of slaves, but could pass laws to assist, and in fact it was their duty to do this. He could therefore not agree with Story that all the state fugitive slave laws that had been passed were unconstitutional—only those which, like Pennsylvania's and New York's, hindered rather than facilitated the return of property to its lawful owner.

Story's opinion apparently satisfied neither the North nor the South. Antislavery leaders objected to the Court's holding that northern states could not require such safeguards as jury trials in fugitive cases. Pro-slavery advocates resented the conclusion that southern state laws for the recapture of slaves were invalid, and that northern states were under no obligation to render assistance in returning slaves.

Actually, although Prigg was released and Margaret returned to her master, the South had more to complain of than the North. Fugitive slaves generally fled north, not south. Without state assistance it was rare that they could be apprehended, and the northern states promptly made sure that, in accordance with Story's opinion, they would render no assistance. Massachusetts passed a law making it a penal offense for any state official to aid in any way the carrying out of the Fugitive Slave Act of 1793, and the act quickly became a dead letter in the North.

Five years later (1847) the troublesome problem of fugitive slaves again came to the Court in the case of *Jones* v. *Van Zandt*. Van Zandt, a former resident of Kentucky, had turned away from slavery, purchased a farm in Ohio near Cincinnati and maintained there a station of the Underground Railroad. Agents of Jones found nine of his fugitive slaves in Van Zandt's covered wagon and captured eight of them, but one escaped. The Fugitive Slave Act of 1793 imposed a penalty of five hundred dollars plus damages for harboring or concealing a runaway slave, and Jones sued Van Zandt for both the penalty and damages.

When the case reached the Supreme Court, Van Zandt was represented by two of the nation's leading abolitionist lawyers, William Seward and Salmon P. Chase, both later to be members of Lincoln's cabinet and Chase also to become Chief Justice. Their main argument was that the Fugitive Slave Act was unconstitutional. It was an obviously untenable argument, and the Court's opinion, upholding the act, made short shrift of it.

The decision brought down upon the Court the wrath of the abolitionists. Chase, having no illusions as to the legal soundness of his case, employed his argument before the Court as a propaganda medium to express a passionate protest against making free men and free states responsible for the protection of slavery, no matter what the Constitution and federal laws might say. In his argument he was indelicate enough to note that several of the Justices were themselves slaveholders and therefore were "interested parties" in the struggle over slavery.

Abolitionist editors took up the cry. At least one of them charged that "the Court was corrupt and its decisions were always in favor of slavery." The denunciations reached such a pitch that McLean, the strongest antislavery man on the bench, felt called upon to defend the Court. Writing to an abolitionist editor, he noted that the Prigg opinion had been written by Story and the Van Zandt opinion by Woodbury, both of whom were strongly antislavery. "It is," he wrote, "an easy matter to denounce the action of any Court who may differ from our own views, and thereby endeavor to lessen the public confidence in such Court. But denunciation is not argument, and however well it may be calculated to create prejudice and mislead ignorant minds and thereby promote party purposes, it is not the best mode of attaining a high and honorable object." Whatever might be their personal views on slavery, the Justices must apply the Constitution and the laws as they are written. Is it, he asked, "expected or desired that a judge shall substitute his own notions for positive law?" If this becomes so, "there will be no security for character, property or life."

McLean's attempt at defense of the Court was futile. To the abolitionists the Court was rapidly becoming the arch enemy. Attacks upon it continued without abatement. And in the meantime a storm was gathering force and would within a decade engulf the Court as it would the entire nation.

THE CLOUDS GATHER

Clay's compromise of 1820 had effected a resolution of the question of slavery in the western territories with which both North and South were able to live for thirty years. The successful prosecution of the Mexican War, however, with the consequent acquisition of tremendous additional territory raised the problem anew, and at a time when the lines had hardened immeasurably since 1820. The gauntlet was thrown down in 1846 by David Wilmot, congressman from Pennsylvania. A bill was introduced to appropriate two million dollars to enable President Polk to negotiate with Mexico for the acquisition of boundary territory. Wilmot introduced a rider or proviso that "neither slavery nor involuntary servitude shall ever exist" in the territory so acquired. The House adopted the Wilmot Proviso, which was based on the premise that Congress had the moral duty to prohibit slavery wherever its jurisdiction extended, and which was to become the battle standard of the Free Soilers and their offspring, the Republican party. In the Senate, the aged John C. Calhoun picked up the gauntlet and announced the contrary doctrine that "slavery follows the flag," that slaves were common law property of which their owners could not lawfully be deprived and that Congress therefore had no power to prohibit slavery in the territories, or anywhere else for that matter, but had a moral obligation to protect it. The Senate took no action on the Wilmot-amended bill, and the storm gathered momentum.

In 1848, in an attempt to find a way to avoid the impending clash,

John M. Clayton of Delaware introduced into the Senate a bill whose purpose it was to turn over to the Supreme Court the whole question of slavery in the territories. The bill provided specifically that in all cases involving title to slaves appeals should be allowed to the Supreme Court. Except for a few die-hards who would not risk the issue in any forum, the South soon adopted the idea and defended it with increasing enthusiasm as the only reasonable way out of the dilemma. By 1853 the Court consisted of five southerners and four northerners, and of the latter, Curtis was considered a tool of the slavery interests. "He is not," Horace Greeley's New York *Tribune* charged editorially, "a Massachusetts judge. He is a slave catching judge appointed to office as a reward for his professional support given to the Fugitive Slave bill." Hence, it appeared quite safe as well as fair to leave the issue in the laps of the judicial gods.

The northern Democrats, desperately seeking something that would stop the widening breach in their own party, also approved the idea. The Free Soilers and the abolitionists would have none of it. They had no confidence in the Court. The Justices, said Chase on the floor of the Senate, "eminent and upright as they are, are not more than other men exempt from the bias of education, sympathy and interests," and the slaveholders had taken care to see that a majority of the Court came from their class. Congress, said the future Chief Justice, echoing Jefferson and Jackson, was not bound in any way to accept the Court's interpretation of the Constitution. John Hale of New Hampshire charged that the Court's opinions were "tinted and colored by geographical position," that its decisions had tended in one direction, and that he had no doubt that it would decide in favor of slavery any case brought under Clayton's bill. While, he said, "it is considered here as a sort of patriotic effort to express great confidence in the Supreme Court, he for one had no confidence in it; its course on slavery questions had not been such "as to commend it to the friends of National Freedom." For his part the Court was "the very citadel of American slavery. . . . Upon its decisions rest the final hopes of slavery."

In 1851 the Court decided the case of *Strader* v. *Graham*, which did not add to the Abolitionists' confidence in it. The issue—the same one involved in the Dred Scott case six years later—was whether slaves whose Kentucky owner allowed them to go into Ohio to work thereby acquired their freedom in accordance with Ohio laws. The Court held that their status depended on the laws of the state from which they came (Kentucky) and not of Ohio, and since it was unlikely that slave states would enact laws emancipating slaves simply because they were taken outside the state, the decision was a complete victory for slavery. The abolitionists attacked it and the Court vigorously. "The history of the particular case," said the New York *Evening Post*, "illustrates the stupidity and danger of leaving to this tribunal the arbitration of issues that belong to the legislature or to the forum of popular discussion. . . . The Court needs reorganizing; instead of four members allotted to the free States they should have six." The anti-slavery forces in Congress retaliated against the Court by voting down a measure to increase the salaries of the Justices, even though Curtis complained that "their salaries are so poor that not one judge on the bench can live upon what the Government pays him."

In 1820 Clay had worked out a compromise that lasted for thirty years; in 1850 he tried again. With the aid of Webster, and over the opposition of Chase and Seward in the North and Calhoun in the South, he prevailed upon Congress to accept another compromise. California would be admitted to the Union as a free state; the territories of New Mexico and Utah would be organized without mentioning slavery, and in return the South would get a new and stringent fugitive slave law to replace the now completely ineffectual 1793 statute. (It was this last provision that enraged the Free Soilers and abolitionists.)

The Missouri Compromise had lasted some thirty years, but its days were numbered. The South was committed to Calhoun's principle that slavery follows the flag and would not allow the organization of any new free territory. Accordingly they defeated every bill to organize the Nebraska territory, which was north of the dividing line fixed in the Missouri Compromise. Stephen Douglas finally proposed his principle of "popular" or "squatter sovereignty," which would allow the settlers to decide for themselves whether to be free or slave. He also agreed to divide the territory into Kansas and Nebraska, with the former presumably becoming a slave state and the latter, free. This implicitly nullified the Missouri Compromise, but that did not satisfy the South, and they demanded an express repeal of the 1820 act as part of the bargain. Douglas felt he had no alternative but to yield; his bill was accordingly amended and after considerable struggle pushed through to passage. The Kansas-Nebraska Act infuriated the North as probably no other measure ever did, for it was the first time the clock was turned back; American territory formerly closed to slavery was now opened to it.

THE COURT IS ENGULFED

This, then, was the situation when the Dred Scott storm broke on the nation. The case had been in the courts on and off for eleven years, at first obscurely and inconspicuously, but with each succeeding year gathering public attention until, by the time it was decided, it had become almost the major political issue in the nation.

Dred Scott, a slave, had been purchased by Dr. John Emerson, a physician attached to the United States Army in Missouri, a slave state. In 1834 Emerson was transferred first to the free state of Illinois and then to the Wisconsin Territory, where slavery was forbidden by the Missouri Compromise of 1820, and in each case took Scott along with him. In 1838 Emerson returned to Missouri with Scott, who by this time was married and had two children. Emerson thereafter died, and in 1846 Scott sued Emerson's widow in the Missouri courts on the ground that his residence in a free state and a free territory had emancipated him. The Missouri supreme court ruled that his return to Missouri reestablished his slave status, even if it had been suspended during his absence.

At this time Mrs. Emerson married Dr. C. C. Chaffee, an abolitionist representative from Massachusetts. As an abolitionist member of Congress, Chaffee could obviously not own a slave, but instead of emancipating Scott directly, he conceived of the idea of using Scott to obtain a determination by the Supreme Court of the constitutionality and effect of the Missouri Compromise. (Ironically, after the decision was announced the abolitionists charged that it was a feigned case cooked up by slavery interests.) Since it would be unseemly for an abolitionist congressman to be sued, Scott was nominally sold to Mrs. Emerson's brother, J. F. A. Sandford of New York. (Three months after the final decision came down, Scott was manumitted.)

The only way to get the case into the federal courts was on the basis of diversity of citizenship. Accordingly, Scott brought suit in the federal circuit court, in Missouri, alleging that Sandford was a citizen of New York, and he, Scott, was a citizen of Missouri. Sandford defended the suit, and the court held that Scott indeed was a citizen of Missouri and therefore could sue in the federal courts. It also held, however, that under Missouri law Scott was still a slave. Scott thereupon appealed to the Supreme Court.

For a number of reasons argument of the case was delayed until February, 1856. It was taken up in conference by the Justices in May. A majority of the Court quickly agreed that neither the question of Scott's citizenship nor of the constitutionality of the Missouri Compromise would be passed on, but that the decision of the circuit court would be affirmed on the basis of *Strader* v. *Graham*, which had clearly held that when a slave is brought back from a free state where he was taken by his master to the slave state from which he came, his slave status re-attaches. It appears, however, that McLean had written a vigorous dissenting opinion in which he upheld the power of Congress to exclude slavery from the territories. Moreover, he was going to use this dissenting opinion as a political manifesto in an effort to obtain the Republican nomination for the Presidency. Upon learning McLean's intentions, his associates on the bench hastily decided that they needed more time for consideration, and directed that the case should be re-argued in December, well after the 1856 Presidential elections.

In the meantime public tension around the case developed at an alarming rate. The pro-slavery interests exerted all kinds of pressure on the Court. At dinners, receptions and social functions, the Justices were individually taken aside, flattered and importuned to settle the issue once and for all by a full decision that Congress could not exclude slavery from the territories. Alexander H. Stephens, congressman from Georgia and later Vice-President of the Confederacy, was extremely persistent, particularly with Wayne, also from Georgia, with whom he was on closest terms of friendship. The political excitement was intense and some of the Justices were advanced in age—Taney was eighty, Wayne, sixty-seven, McLean, seventy-two, Catron, seventy-one, Daniel, seventy-three—and not quite vigorous enough to resist the pressures.

In December, 1856, the case was re-argued. Again a delay, this time of two months, elapsed before the matter was taken up in conference by the Justices. Shortly before the day set for the conference, President-elect Buchanan wrote to his good friend Catron, asking whether a decision could be expected before March 4, the inaugural date. Catron wrote back that the case would be decided at a conference on February

10, that the decision would be announced late in February, but that it "would not help" with the inaugural, "since the question of the power of Congress over slavery in the territories would not be determined." In the meantime, however, Wayne became convinced that the expected dissenting opinions of McLean and Curtis (what a surprise to the abolitionists who had called him a tool of the slavery interests!) would assert the power of Congress to exclude slavery from the territories. Nelson had been instructed by Taney to prepare an opinion based on *Strader* v. *Graham*, and had done so; but Wayne convinced Taney and the other southern Justices that this should be scrapped, and instead Taney should write the Court's opinion deciding with a finality he was sure the nation would accept that Congress had no power to bar slavery anywhere.

Grier was reluctant and urged further delay. Catron thereupon wrote to Buchanan suggesting that he exert some influence with Grier. The President-elect accepted the suggestion and wrote to Grier—exactly what is not known since the letter has not been located. Whatever it was, it proved effective. Partly because of Buchanan's letter and partly because he did not want the nation to see the Court divided purely on sectional lines, Grier (of Pennsylvania) decided to cast his lot with the Taney-Wayne wing of the Court. He replied to the President that the decision would not be handed down until March 6, two days after the inauguration, but that there will be "six, if not seven (perhaps Nelson will remain neutral) who will decide the Compromise law of 1820 to be of non-effect." With this letter in his pocket, Buchanan piously stated in his inaugural address that the question of slavery in the territories "is a judicial question which legitimately belongs to the Supreme Court of the United States before whom it is now pending. . . . To their decision, in common with all good citizens, I shall cheerfully submit, whatever this may be."

Two days later the decision was announced. Grier had been right in his prediction; Nelson remained neutral and read the opinion which he had expected would be the majority opinion, affirming the circuit court decision on the basis of *Strader* v. *Graham*, and refusing to decide whether Dred Scott was a citizen or the 1820 act was unconstitutional. Nelson remained isolated; all the other eight Justices were decidedly unneutral. The majority decision was written and read by the Chief Justice; the other four southern Justices and Grier concurred in it; McLean and Curtis dissented.

The first question, said Taney, was whether the circuit court had jurisdiction of Scott's suit. This depends on whether Scott is a citizen of Missouri, there being no doubt that Sandford was a citizen of New York. Scott, Taney held, was not a citizen of Missouri or of any other state; as an African Negro he could not be a citizen of any state, regardless of whether he was slave or free.

African Negroes, he said,

> are not and were not intended to be included under the word "citizens" in the Constitution, and can therefore claim none of the rights and privileges which that instrument provides for and secures to citizens of the United States. On the contrary, they were at that time considered as a subordinate and inferior class of beings, who had been subjugated by the dominant race, and whether emancipated or not, yet remained subject to their authority, and had no rights or privileges but such as those who held the power and the government might choose to grant them. . . . They had for more than a century before been regarded as of an inferior order, and altogether unfit to associate with the white race either in social or political relations; and so far inferior that they had no rights which the white man was bound to respect. . . .

Since, therefore, Scott was not a citizen, the circuit court had no jurisdiction and his case must be dismissed. At this point, Taney, according to the usual principles of judicial procedure, should have ended his opinion. But as Marshall in *Marbury* v. *Madison* had delivered a political manifesto after deciding that the Court had no jurisdiction over the suit, so too did Taney. Even if, he said, Scott could sue, he would lose his case because his sojourn in the Wisconsin Territory did not make him free. This was because the provision in the Missouri Compromise making the northern part of the territory free was unconstitutional; Congress could not exclude slavery from any territory. The Fifth Amendment provides that no person may be deprived of his property without due process of law, and slaves are property. Congress could no more provide that a man shall lose his slaves by taking them to the territories than lose his horses by taking them there. (It should be noted that not only was it unnecessary for Taney to pass on the constitutionality of the Missouri Compromise in view of his holding that the Court had no jurisdiction of the suit, but in addition the whole law had been repealed three years earlier in the Kansas-Nebraska Act—a rather unique situation for a court to declare a law unconstitutional after it had been repealed.)

McLean and Curtis dissented in separate opinions holding that Scott was a citizen, the Missouri Compromise was constitutional, and that Congress could exclude slavery from the territories. Even before the case reached the Supreme Court, McLean had written to a friendly newspaper telling the editor what position he would take. His dissent was published in the press the day after the decision was handed down and received national publicity before the text of the Chief Justice's majority opinion was received by the press.

Curtis, for his part, after reading his dissent from the bench, gave the original to the Court clerk and the only copy to a newspaper reporter, and then, as it was the last day of the term, left for home. On his way home, Curtis picked up information leading him to believe that Taney had delayed filing his opinion with the clerk of the Court to enable him to revise and change his opinion to reply to the Curtis dissent—and this was not according to the rules of the game. Curtis, thereupon, wrote to the clerk of the Court asking for a copy of the Court's majority opinion. The clerk presented the letter to Taney who forbade him to send Curtis a copy. When the clerk so wrote Curtis, the latter wrote to Taney asking for an explanation and renewing his demand. Taney replied that Curtis had no business to give his dissenting opinion to the press. Moreover, Curtis could scarcely require a copy for official use since "you announced from the bench that you regarded the opinion as extra-judicial, and not binding upon you or anyone else." Curtis wrote back that as a member of the Court he had a right to examine any opinion handed down by it, and besides he had been advised that the opinion had been "revised and materially altered."

Taney waited a month before replying, during which time all the opinions were officially published. Then he wrote to Curtis vehemently denying that he had changed one historical fact or one principle of constitutional law in the opinion after he had read it from the bench. When Curtis finally got hold of Taney's published opinion he marked out the alterations and changes he said had been made after Taney had read the opinion from the bench, and these amounted to eighteen pages.

Feeling that his dignity had been irreparably compromised, Curtis sent his resignation to the Attorney-General. The latter drafted for Buchanan a laudatory letter of acceptance praising Curtis' work on the bench, the usual protocol required of Presidential letters accepting resignations. (Curtis, too, had followed protocol by stating that his reason for resigning was inadequate compensation rather than hurt feelings.) When Buchanan got the draft, he struck out all the laudatory remarks, leaving it a curt acceptance of Curtis' resignation.

AFTERMATH OF DRED SCOTT

Buchanan had expressed the hope that the nation would accept the decision whatever it might be; Taney had believed that the question of slavery in the territories would be settled for all time. Their miscalculations have seldom been equaled in American history. Even before the decision was announced, but after Buchanan's inaugural address, Greeley's *Tribune* editorialized: "You may 'cheerfully submit,' of course you will, to whatever the five slaveholders and two or three doughfaces on the bench of the Supreme Court may be ready to utter on this subject. But not one man who really desires the triumph of freedom over slavery in the territories will do so."

When the decision was announced the wrath of the northern press appeared boundless. The fires, moreover, were spread by the fact that the northern papers had the full text of the dissenting opinions, but for two weeks thereafter had only newspaper reporters' accounts based on memory as to what Taney had said for the majority. It was widely reported that Taney had said that the Negroes "had no rights which the white man was bound to respect." What was not reported was that Taney stated this not as his own opinion but as the views of the constitutional fathers when they used the word "citizen" in the Constitution seventy years earlier.

The Republican and abolitionist press had a field day. "The Court has rushed into politics," wrote the *Tribune*, "voluntarily and without other purpose than to preserve the cause of slavery. . . . Their cunning chief led the van, and plank by plank laid down a platform of historical falsehood and gross assumption, and thereon they all stood exultingly thinking or feigning to think that their work would stand during the remainder of their lives at least." The decision, it reported, "has been heard and commented upon with mingled derision and contempt. If epithets and denunciation could sink a judicial body, the Supreme Court of the United States would never be heard of again."

The New York *Independent* picked up the cry of defiance. "The decision of the Supreme Court is the Moral Assassination of a Race and Cannot be Obeyed," read the head of an editorial which said that "If the people obey this decision, they disobey God." The New York *Evening Post* said that a "majority of its members have consented to become parties to a combination with their administration to transfer the political control of the government to the hands of the slave oligarchy." Even the conservative New York *Times* noted that while all looked with respect and some degree of reverence on the Court, "the circumstances attending the present decision have done much to divest it of moral authority and to impair the confidence of the country."

This is a fair sampling of the reaction of the New York press, which in turn fairly reflects the reaction of the northern press generally. The southern press naturally exulted and the loyal administration papers elsewhere defended the decision against the "sedition, treason and insurrection" contained in the opposing editorials.

The northern clergy reacted in the same way as the northern press. The dissenting opinions were everywhere read from church pulpits. A St. Louis paper reported that the decision "has roused the lately torpid Northern pulpit into a factitious frenzy on the stale Negro question and incited the preachers to a fresh crusade against the judges." (One preacher, however, accused those who attacked the decision of hypocrisy in view of the discrimination practiced against free Negroes in the northern states.)

The decision and the Court were assailed with corresponding vehemence in the halls of Congress. On the floor of the Senate Seward ridiculed as sheer mockery Buchanan's promise to accept the decision. Either on the basis of inside information or a shrewd guess, he charged that the President "approached or was approached by the Supreme Court," arranged with it "to hang the millstone of slavery on the neck of the people of Kansas, and knew very well when he blandly promised to abide by the will of the Court just what its decision would be."

Lincoln expressed a somewhat more conservative view. Before the case reached the Supreme Court he had taken the position in political speeches that the issue of slavery in the territories was one for the Supreme Court to decide. After the decision was announced he criticized it as erroneous. Obedience and respect, he said, were due to the decisions of the Court on constitutional questions, but only when the issues involved were fully settled, and he did not consider them fully settled by the Dred Scott decision. Since the Court had often overruled its own decisions, he pledged himself to do all he could to make the Court overrule itself in this case. What he clearly had in mind was the reorganization of the Court—later to be called packing—so that an antislavery majority would control. In some of the later debates with Douglas, he took an even stronger stand and adopted Jefferson's position that the President and Congress had equal power with the Court to decide constitutional issues for themselves. He read from Jefferson's letters denouncing the idea that judges were the final arbiters on all constitutional questions and were to be held in higher esteem than other men. The Constitution, he said, "has erected no such single tribunal, knowing that to whatever hand confided, with the corruptions of time and party, the members would become despots." Our judges "are as honest as other men and not more so. They have, with others, the same passions for party, for power and the privilege of their corps. . . . Their power is the more dangerous as they are in office for life, and not responsible, as the other functionaries are, to the elective control."

Whether the Civil War could have been averted had there been no Dred Scott decision is a matter that can only be left to the speculation of historians. If war was not inevitable, the decision made it so. It also elected Lincoln to the Presidency. The northern Democrats could not accept the full sweep of the decision that slavery followed the flag and based their platform on the "squatter sovereignty" idea of their candidate, Stephen A. Douglas. The southern Democrats wanted no retreat and insisted that the party platform embody the exact language of the decision. When this was refused they broke off and nominated John C. Breckenridge. The split in the Democratic party elected Lincoln, who had considerably less than a majority of the popular vote.

The Dred Scott decision did not destroy the Court. Had it come a half-century earlier, under otherwise the same circumstances, it most probably would have. But Marshall had done his work well. He had established for the Court such a position in the American scheme of things that even so egregious a blunder as the Dred Scott decision could only shake and weaken it, but not topple it. It took more than a decade for the Court to recover, and during that period it played a decidedly subdued role in influencing American history.

THE LAST DAYS OF TANEY

Taney hung on to life and to the Chief Justiceship for seven years after *Dred Scott* v. *Sandford*. His health was feeble and he could participate only occasionally in the activities of the Court. However, neither his mental vigor nor his determination failed, and to the very end he staunchly defended the position he had taken.

After war broke out, Taney came into a direct clash with Lincoln. Maryland did not secede from the Union, but in a border state Confederate sentiment was strong and much aid and comfort was given to the southern cause. Lincoln found it necessary to issue orders subjecting to military arrest and court martial persons engaged in disloyal activities, and as to them he suspended the privilege of habeas corpus. John Merryman, an ardent secessionist, was arrested by the military authorities and brought to Fort McHenry in Baltimore. A writ of habeas corpus was obtained from Taney directing General Cadwalader, commander of the fort, to produce Merryman in the Baltimore federal court. Cadwalader refused to comply on the ground that Lincoln had suspended the right to habeas corpus. With a sublime but quite unrealistic trust, Taney sent a court marshal to arrest the general for contempt of court. The brave marshal appeared at the entrance of the fort and informed the sentry that he had a warrant for the arrest of the commanding general. What the sentry's reply was has unfortunately not been recorded, but the upshot was that the marshal returned to Taney with the warrant but without the general. Taney mercifully relieved the marshal of further obligation for the general's arrest, but wrote a paper, which became known as the opinion in the case of *Ex parte Merryman*, in which he held that under the Constitution, Congress alone, and not the President, had the power to suspend the right to habeas corpus. Taney sent a copy of the opinion to Lincoln who submitted it to his Attorney-General. The latter gave Lincoln an advisory opinion to the effect that Taney was wrong and that the President had the power to suspend the writ. Lincoln, accordingly, disregarded Taney's opinion and allowed the military action against Merryman to proceed. (Merryman was later released, but only because it was thought no longer necessary to keep him in prison.)

The issue in the Merryman case was to come up again in *Ex parte*

Milligan, and was hotly debated as a conflict between a rule of law and military necessity. (The same issue was to arise ninety years later when Truman seized the steel mills.) The evidence is clear that Taney's opinion was, at least in part, motivated by a lack of sympathy for the war. Indeed, during the remaining three years of his life he waged his own private war against the Union. He dissented from the decision in the Prize Cases that held (by a five to four vote) that Lincoln had the constitutional power to impose a blockade on the South. He wrote a number of other opinions in cases not before the Court, simply to have them ready for use should the occasion arise. One declared the conscription act unconstitutional. Another dealt similarly with the Emancipation Proclamation. A third found the Legal Tender Acts to be unconstitutional. He never had the opportunity to use any of them, although ironically the issue of the Legal Tender Acts did come to the Court in the 1863 term, in the case of *Roosevelt* v. *Meyer*. Unfortunately, Taney was ill and did not come to Court at any time during the whole term. The other Justices decided that the Court had no jurisdiction of the case, and so Taney could not use his already prepared opinion. The next year, the frustrated and embittered Taney died at the age of eighty-eight.

TANEY AND MARSHALL

A century and three-quarters have elapsed since the Supreme Court was established by the Judiciary Act of 1789. During that period, although the Court has had fourteen Chief Justices, the administrations of two of them, Marshall and Taney, covered a period of sixty-three years, or more than a third of the total number of years served by all fourteen. History has been generous to Marshall; it has been unkind to Taney. Towards the end of Marshall's career, even a political enemy, Martin Van Buren, called him "in all human probability, the ablest judge now sitting upon any judicial bench in the world." The sentiment, or others equally laudatory, has been echoed innumerable times since then. In contrast, on Taney's death, Charles Sumner predicted on the floor of the Senate that his name would be "hooted down in the pages of history." Sumner's prophecy, until recently at least, has proved only moderately exaggerated.

Why has Marshall been the beneficiary of indiscriminate adulation and Taney the victim of indiscriminate disparagement? Both served long terms as Chief Justice, Marshall thirty-four years and Taney twenty-eight, and thus had the opportunity to influence greatly the history of the Supreme Court and the course of constitutional law. While Marshall far more than any other man fashioned the Court after his own desires and made of it a major political instrument, Taney, whose origin was as aristocratic as Marshall's was humble, achieved for the Court (until the catastrophe of 1857) a position of confidence and respect on the part of the common people by bringing into it some part of the spirit of Jacksonian democracy. In addition, he was a much abler judge than Marshall, and constitutional law owes more to his keenly analytical decisions than to Marshall's majestic generalities, which in any event were rarely original and have long since lost all but minimal practical significance.

In recent years the scales have shifted somewhat. Marshall's achievements have begun to be subjected to a more searching and less adulatory scrutiny and the result has been some depreciation of his stature. This process is likely to continue, although not to such a degree as to threaten seriously his position in history. A corresponding closer examination of Taney's contributions has resulted in a more generous appraisal of them with a consequent enhancement of his stature and the elevation of his status.

There are several reasons for both the long-time disparity in the treatment of the two men and the recent partial rectification. In the first place, until fairly recently (Charles Beard may be said to mark the turning point) American history has been written from a strongly Federalist-conservative bias; compare, for example, the treatment accorded in school history books to Washington and Lincoln on the one hand and Jefferson and Jackson on the other. In the second place, during the same period nationalism had been the highest good in the American hierarchy of values, and Marshall was a nationalist par excellence, while in Taney regionalism was equally important. Marshall, unlike many of his co-Federalists in New England, was willing to endure Jeffersonianism rather than see a dissolution of the Union; Taney was committed to the belief that the southern states had the moral and legal right to go their own way in peace. As Edward Corwin acutely noted, Marshall considered the Supreme Court to be an organ of the national government for the vigorous assertion of its powers; Taney considered it an impartial umpire between equal sovereignties, the national government and the states.

The best of all possible worlds would come about, in Marshall philosophy, by rapid and boundless economic expansion. The surest way to achieve this is by allowing individual initiative free rein, and this can be done only by protecting property and property rights through forcefully restraining the predatory envy of the lower classes. To secure these ends governments are instituted among men deriving their just powers from the good, the wise and the rich. Taney, though also committed to the judicial protection of property rights, believed that "the object and end of all government is to promote the happiness and prosperity of the community." His ideas of the community and the obligations that government owes to it were completely beyond Marshall's realm of contemplation. Taney made of the concept of police power, barely known and severely limited by Marshall, an invaluable instrument for the effectuation of government's obligations to the community and a vehicle for social welfare legislation. To Marshall the Constitution, and particularly the commerce and impairment of contracts provisions, sanctified and immortalized Adam Smith's *Wealth of Nations;* Taney's development of the police power, a term not even found in the Constitution, provided the principal constitutional basis for America's present modified welfare state.

In short, Marshall was in complete harmony with the temper of the century of American history from the time of his death in 1835 until the coming of Roosevelt's New Deal, Taney with that of the twentieth century from the time of the coming of Franklin Roosevelt. This explains at least in part why Marshall has been universally uncritically idolized until recently and why Taney is beginning to come into his own.

Fate has decreed, however, that Taney can never achieve full redemption. He is forever damned by his commitment to slavery and the innate inferiority of the Negro race. The community whose welfare the state was obliged to promote was limited to persons with white skins. Marshall is remembered by *Marbury* v. *Madison*, the Dartmouth College case and *McCulloch* v. *Maryland;* Taney will always be remembered by *Dred Scott* v. *Sandford*. As the Court historian, Hampton Carson, noted, that "damned spot" will not "out" (although in 1937 Felix Frankfurter expressed the hope that eventually it will be "intellectually disreputable to see him predominantly as the judicial defender of slavery"). Marshall, too, was a southerner and his views on slavery and the Negro race were not substantially different from those of Taney; he favored the return to Africa of all Negroes, free as well as slave. But Taney was Chief Justice at a time when slavery had become not only the chief but almost the only national issue. Perhaps Marshall would have somehow been able to avoid involving the Supreme Court in the titanic struggle. Taney willingly brought it into the fray. It was not merely his misfortune to have chosen the losing side; that, in time, his reputation could have lived down, as, for example, in the case of Robert E. Lee. His tragedy was that he did not recognize the evil and inevitable doom of the division of the human race into superior and inferior beings, into owners and owned, and that he staked the existence of the nation and the Court on that division. Rightly or wrongly, the evil that Taney did in the Dred Scott case will continue to live long after him.

chapter eight

Reconstruction and Reaction

LINCOLN AND HIS JUDGES

When Curtis left the Court, Buchanan was called upon to select a successor. Since Curtis had been from Massachusetts, tradition demanded that his replacement come from New England. For a brief moment Buchanan toyed with the idea of breaking with tradition and appointing a southerner, William L. Yancey of Alabama. This would have converted a Court in which a majority was from the South into one in which two-thirds were and would have replaced with a slavery man one of the two lone dissenters in the Dred Scott case. It requires no exceptional power of imagination to picture the frenzy that would have gripped the North had this happened. Fortunately, Buchanan's discretion subdued his valor, and he settled on a considerably less provocative choice, Nathan Clifford of Maine. Clifford had been speaker of the Maine house of representatives, state attorney-general, member of Congress and Attorney-General in Polk's cabinet. His chief qualification for the post was that he was a loyal, hard-working Democrat who came from New England. The New York *Tribune* commented that "the process of deterioration goes on, and the Supreme Court is gradually becoming a mere party machine, to do the bidding of the dominant faction and to supply places to reward party hacks." Greeley was hardly an unbiased observer, but there was considerable opposition to the appointment even among the members of the New England bar. However, party discipline prevailed, and Clifford was confirmed by the close vote of 26 to 23.

Before he left the White House, Buchanan had another opportunity to fill a vacancy on the bench, this one caused by the death of Daniel in May, 1860. After considerable deliberation Buchanan chose his own Secretary of State, Jeremiah S. Black, who had formerly been his Attorney-General and before that chief judge of the Pennsylvania supreme court. Daniel had been from Virginia and this was a break with tradition, but a necessary one. The southern states had already begun seceding, and qualified persons from the South were not available. Black's outstanding legal ability and judicial experience made him as fit for the post as Clifford was not; but by this time Lincoln had been elected to the Presidency and the Republicans were not going to allow Buchanan, who had but one month longer in office, to appoint a midnight judge. By a vote even closer than the one which resulted in Clifford's confirmation, Black was rejected, and the vacancy remained for Lincoln to fill.

When Lincoln took over the White House he was faced with matters of more immediate urgency than filling the vacancy on the bench. By the time he got around to it, almost a year later, there were two more vacancies to take care of; McLean had died and Campbell felt impelled to resign and follow his state, Alabama, out of the Union. (Wayne of Georgia felt no such compunction, and stayed on until his death in 1867.) Lincoln was reluctant to fill all the vacancies, since he hoped that peace would return soon and with it the errant southern states, and he wanted to keep places on the bench open for them. However, of the six Justices still in office, only two were less than seventy years old, and two, Taney and Catron, were so enfeebled that they could devote little energy to the performance of their duties. Lincoln could postpone no longer, and in 1862 made three appointments to the bench.

Two years later, when Lincoln was faced with the need to appoint a successor to Taney, he explained in a letter to a friend the factors considered by him in making his selection. When important administration action (in this case emancipation and legal tender) is to be passed upon by the Court, the appointee should be one who will vote to sustain the action. "We cannot," wrote Lincoln, "ask a man what he will do, and if we should, and he should answer us, we should despise him for it. Therefore, we must take a man whose opinions are known."

At first blush this frank expression of court packing would seem to be shocking. If Marshall and Taney were right in their protestations that they simply applied the Constitution as it was written and the law as it had been decided, the sole criterion for a Supreme Court Justice would be his legal competence. Actually, what Lincoln did was simply to recognize the reality that when the Supreme Court acts on political issues it is a political institution, a fact which no observer uninfluenced by the bias of the legal craft or the apologetics of Federalist-tinted history can readily deny. This does not mean that no factor other than political orientation is considered by a President making an appointment; nor that no President has ever appointed a person affiliated with a political party other than his own. (Party affiliations are only rough approximations of political belief.) It also does not mean that the traditions of the institution and the personalities of some of its dominating leaders may not influence a person after he joins the Court, with the result that his actions on it may disappoint the President who appointed him (as Lincoln himself would have been had he lived). It does mean that rarely has a President willingly (occasionally an appointment is forced upon a President) appointed a person whose views on important political issues sharply opposed his own, no matter how high his excellence as a judge; nor are many Presidents likely to do so. Presidents have become more sophisticated than the simple backwoods lawyer from Illinois and do not say openly what Lincoln said, but there is little reason to doubt that their motivations are similar.

Lincoln, in any event, appointed no one to the Court whose known positions on the major political issues of the day were not in substantial harmony with his own. To fill the vacancy left over by Buchanan, he selected Noah H. Swayne of Ohio. Swayne had no previous judicial experience and little else that would seem to qualify him for appointment to the nation's highest tribunal. He was a successful lawyer who had earlier served in the state legislature and had been federal district attorney at Columbus. He was, however, one of the original members of the Republican party, had been active as counsel in fugitive slave cases, and, above all, had the strong backing of the two powerful senators from Ohio.

To fill the other two vacancies, Lincoln selected Samuel F. Miller of Iowa and David Davis of Illinois, two of the most interesting appointments ever made to the Court. (Lincoln was to make a third the following year.) Miller was little known outside the Midwest, but his reputation there was so high that although he had no previous judicial office, or for that matter public office of any kind, his appointment was urged by the lawyers of Iowa, Minnesota, Kansas, and Wisconsin, by the governor, the senators and representatives from Iowa, and by a petition signed by 129 out of 140 congressmen and 28 out of 32 senators. Only a remarkable person could have achieved such endorsement, and Miller was one.

He started his professional career not as a lawyer, but as a duly matriculated and licensed physician. After ten years of successful medical practice he decided to study law and was admitted to the bar at the age of thirty-one. He became leader of the Republican party and, turning down numerous public offices, devoted his non-professional energies to fighting for abolition.

He was forty-six years old when appointed to the Court and he remained on the bench until his death twenty-eight years later. In some ways he might be described as the poor man's John Marshall. Marshall had little legal education and what Miller had came late, with the result that neither was much of a legal scholar. Both were able to compensate with their commitment, their skill at argument and logic, their prodigious work habits and their personalities. (Chief Justice Chase was to call Miller "beyond question the dominant personality" on the bench.) Miller wrote over seven hundred opinions during his twenty-eight years on the bench, more than any other Justice before or after him. The concern of both Marshall and Miller was chiefly with constitutional law questions and neither could abstain from writing an opinion whenever such a case arose. The principal difference between them was that Miller was more concerned with the welfare of society as a whole than with the protection of vested property interests. (He was, however, no more liberal than his colleagues in cases involving Negroes' rights.)

Miller was unable to shape the decisions of the Court in accordance with his own philosophy for several reasons. First, unlike Marshall, he was not Chief Justice. Second, the day that one person could consistently dominate the other Justices so that they or a majority of them would do his will ended with Marshall's death; thereafter, the members of the Court were individuals with independent, strong wills. Finally, and perhaps most important, during Miller's stay on the bench, expanding capitalism dominated America as during no other period in its history; even Marshall, had he been so inclined, could not have stayed that surge. The result was that Miller became a perpetual dissenter, second, after William Johnson, in a line that was to include the first Harlan, Holmes, Brandeis, Stone, Black and Douglas. It was Miller who was to complain after a conference of the Justices in which his liberalism again found itself in a minority, that "It is vain to contend with judges who have been, at the bar, the advocates of railroad companies, and all the forms of associated capital, when they are called upon to decide cases where such interests are in contest. All their training, all their feelings are from the start in favor of those who need no such influence."

The principal qualification of the second of Lincoln's interesting appointments was that he was a close friend of the President. When Lincoln was elected President, Davis accompanied him on his journey to Washington, and after the President's death, Davis became administrator of his estate. At the time of his appointment to the Supreme Court Davis was a minor state court judge in Illinois.

Politically, Davis was even left of Miller. In 1872 he was nominated for the Presidency by the national convention of the Labor Reform Party on a platform that called for a national currency "based on the faith and resources of the nation and interchangeable with 3.6 percent bonds of the Government," an eight-hour day law, and the payment of the national debt "without mortgaging the property of the people to enrich capitalists." Davis accepted the nomination and was also candidate for nomination at the Liberal Republican convention, where he received ninety-two and a half votes on the first ballot. At that point, however, he decided to withdraw from the contest and so informed both parties. While on the Court he had no hesitation in expressing himself on political issues, and was undoubtedly uncomfortable in the conservatism of the bench. After fifteen years of service he resigned to enter the Senate, to which he had been elected by a coalition of Democrats and Independents.

In 1863 Congress enacted a law increasing the membership of the Court to ten in order to provide a seat for the Far West. For this post Lincoln selected Stephen J. Field, one of the ablest, most conservative and certainly most colorful persons who ever sat on the Supreme Court. Field was a member of a remarkable family. His father, an obscure Congregationalist minister in a small Massachusetts town, had nine children. One became a Justice of the Supreme Court. Another, Cyrus W., conceived of and promoted the laying of the first transatlantic cable. A third, David Dudley, became one of the nation's most successful lawyers. Jay Gould, James Fiske and Boss Tweed were among his clients, yet he devoted his energy, imagination and learning to completely revise and modernize both civil and criminal procedure in New York, and make of them models followed not only in numerous states but in Britain as well. A fourth son, Henry Martin, become a prominent clergyman and hero of the novel *All This and Heaven, Too*. A daughter became the mother of David J. Brewer, himself to become a Justice of the Supreme Court and sit with his uncle.

At the age of thirteen, Stephen Field accompanied his sister, the wife of a missionary, to Turkey to learn Oriental languages and ultimately qualify for a professorship at American University. He remained in the Near East and acquired a command of the Greek, Turkish, French and Italian languages. He returned to America, entered Williams College, graduated at the top of his class, and studied law in his brother's office. On admission to the bar he entered into partnership with his brother, but after a while he tired of it, traveled in Europe, and finally decided to settle in California. He arrived in San Francisco in 1849 with ten dollars in his pocket. The next year he was already a member of the state legislature. Within one short term he secured the enactment of a law reorganizing the state judiciary, drafted codes of civil and criminal procedure which, though based on his brother's work, were adapted to conform to Spanish customs and miners' practice, drafted and secured the enactment of a comprehensive and liberal exemption law for debtors, and codified the current mining practices into a statute which became the basis of mining law in California and other western states, and later was adopted by Congress for all territories. After this short stint in the legislature, he returned to private practice and quickly became one of the most successful members of the California bar. In 1857 he was elected to the state supreme court, and two years later he became its chief judge. Four years later, on the unanimous recommendation of all the senators and congressmen of the Pacific coast states as well as the governor of California, Lincoln appointed him to the Supreme Court.

But there was more to his career than this. Shortly after he had set himself up in a small mining town, he was elected mayor and went around carrying a six-shooter both to enforce his authority and protect himself (a practice that he continued long after he joined the Supreme Court of the United States). For he also speculated in land and put up zinc houses which he rented at what his tenants considered exorbitant rentals. He got into a dispute with a state court judge who disbarred him and committed him to jail for contempt of court, but the California supreme court reversed the conviction and reinstated Field.

After Field came to Washington at least one, and possibly two, attempts were made on his life. In 1865 he received in the mail a package which turned out to contain an infernal machine and a copy of a decision he had handed down dispossessing a large number of squatters on what were formerly Mexican lands and whose titles were clouded by allegations of fraud and forgery. More serious in its outcome was his feud with David S. Terry, his associate on the California supreme court and predecessor as its chief judge. In 1859, United States Senator David C. Broderick wrote a letter stating that Terry was the only honest man on the California supreme court bench, but when he later retracted the statement insofar as it excepted Terry, the latter challenged him to a duel and killed him.

About thirty years later, Terry was counsel for one Sarah Hill who claimed to have been the secret wife of a deceased millionaire mine owner, who had also been United States senator. The California court upheld the claim and in the meantime Terry had married his client. Justice Field, sitting as federal circuit court judge, ordered the cancellation of the alleged secret marriage contract on the ground of forgery. In rage, Mrs. Terry in open court asked Field how much he had been paid for his decision, and Field held her in contempt of court. When Terry reportedly drew a bowie knife at Field, the latter ordered him arrested and committed to jail for six months. (Field's action was upheld by the Supreme Court in the case of *Ex parte Terry*.) A deputy United States marshal, named Neagle, was thereupon assigned to protect Field, although the gun-toting Justice protested that he needed no bodyguard. One day the following year, 1889, Field stopped at a railroad station for breakfast and came upon Judge and Mrs. Terry. Terry came up to the luncheon stool on which Field was sitting and slapped his face with the back of his hand. Neagle thereupon shot Terry dead. Although Terry was unarmed, his wife reportedly had a bowie knife and revolver in her purse. Opinion was divided on whether the killing was justified. There was sworn testimony that Terry had vowed that he would kill Field, and while some felt that the killing of Terry was unmitigated murder, Field, though arrested, was released. Neagle, too, was arrested by state police, but the federal circuit court ordered him released without trial, and, in the case of *Ex parte Neagle*, the Supreme Court, with two Justices dissenting, affirmed the habeas corpus order and Neagle, too, was exonerated.

One further incident in the long life of Stephen Field should be told. It occurred in 1897, after he had been on the bench for thirty-four years. In 1870, during the course of the Legal Tender cases it became obvious that Grier had become senile. The rest of the story should be told in the words of Charles Evans Hughes, who reported it in his book *The Supreme Court of the United States*.

A committee of the Court waited upon Justice Grier to advise him of the desirability of his retirement and the unfortunate consequences of his being in a position to cast a deciding vote in an important case when he was not able properly to address himself to it. Justice Field [too] tarried too long on the bench. It is extraordinary how reluctant aged judges are to retire and to give up their accustomed work. They seem to be tenacious of the appearance of adequacy. I heard Justice Harlan tell of the anxiety which the Court had felt because of the condition of Justice Field. It occurred to the other members of the Court that Justice Field had served on a committee which waited upon Justice Grier to suggest his retirement, and it was thought that recalling this to his memory might aid him to decide to retire. Justice Harlan was deputed to make the suggestion. He went over to Justice Field, who was sitting alone on a settee in the robing room apparently oblivious of his surroundings, and after arousing him gradually approached the question, asking if he did not recall how anxious the Court had been with respect to Justice Grier's condition and the feeling of the other Justices that in his own interest and in that of the Court he should give up his work. Justice Harlan asked if Justice Field did not remember what had been said to Justice Grier on that occasion. The old man listened, gradually became alert and finally, with his eyes blazing with the old fire of youth, he burst out:

"Yes! And a dirtier day's work I never did in my life!"

That was the end of that effort of the brethren of the Court to induce Justice Field's retirement; he did resign not long after.

(But not without some difficulty. His brother, the clergyman, called to Washington for the purpose, prevailed upon him to write a letter of resignation. However, no sooner had the brother left Washington than Field tried to withdraw the letter, but the President, on the advice of Field's associates, promptly sent Field a letter of regretful but firm acceptance of the resignation.)

This was Justice Stephen J. Field. All in all, quite a remarkable man.

Lincoln had now appointed four Justices to the bench. The death of Taney in 1864 enabled him to add a Chief Justice. To this post he appointed Salmon P. Chase, who not only had no previous judicial experience, but had not practiced law for fifteen years. Lincoln chose Chase for several reasons. He wanted to make sure that the emancipation and legal tender measures would be upheld when they reached the Court. He sought to put an end to Chase's increasing efforts to become President (although Lincoln was realistically not too sanguine that the appointment would achieve this). Finally, Chase was still a powerful leader of the radical wing of the Republican party and Lincoln's acceptance of his resignation as Secretary of the Treasury six months earlier (accepted, to Chase's chagrin and astonishment, after four previous offers to resign had been declined) threatened to alienate that wing of the party.

As a lawyer, Chase had defended runaway slaves so often that he became known as the "attorney general for fugitive slaves." He became United States senator from Ohio, and in that capacity opposed both the Compromise of 1850 and the Kansas-Nebraska Bill of 1854. Thereafter, he was elected governor of the state, and upon the formation of the Republican party became one of its leaders. He sought the Republican party Presidential nomination in 1860, but his views were deemed too abolitionist, and the convention settled upon the more moderate Lincoln. The latter made him his Secretary of the Treasury, and while Chase accepted the position, he resented the President's preference of Seward for the top post in the cabinet. His relations with Lincoln were always strained, and while in the cabinet he and Secretary of War Edwin M. Stanton maintained close relations with the anti-Lincoln radical Republicans in Congress. Nevertheless, he was a person of outstanding ability and was invaluable to the President in the financing of the war. His elevation to the Chief Justiceship did not end his ambition for the Presidency, but his moderate conduct in presiding over the impeachment of Andrew Johnson infuriated his former radical associates and left him without any political support in his last effort to achieve the nomination in 1872. He died the following year, Chief Justice of the United States, but still only a would-be President.

Lincoln had now appointed five of the ten members of the Court. Six months after the appointment of Chase, Catron died, and since Congress would not allow Johnson to make any appointments to the Court, Lincoln's appointees constituted a majority of the Court. Lincoln, of course, did not live to see his Court in operation.

WAR AND PEACE

Ex parte Milligan, one of the most important decisions in American constitutional law and the history of civil liberties, was a war case decided after peace had come. During the war Lincoln had authorized the creation of military commissions to try persons accused of aiding the enemy, violating the rules of war or engaging in other disloyal activities. In 1864 Lambdin P. Milligan, a civilian resident of Indiana, was arrested by the military police after making a public address which allegedly incited to insurrection. Indiana was not one of the states that had seceded, and although southern parts of the state had earlier in the war been invaded by Confederate forces, by 1864 it was far out of the actual war zone. Milligan was charged with inciting to insurrection and conspiring to free prisoners of war confined in a nearby fort. He was tried and found guilty by a military court and was sentenced to be hanged. Avoiding the error made by Marbury, Milligan's lawyers applied for habeas corpus not to the Supreme Court but to the federal circuit court in Indiana, and from that court the case went up to the Supreme Court.

By this time the war was over and Justice Davis was frank enough to admit in his opinion that during the war "the temper of the times did not allow that calmness in deliberation and discussion so necessary to a correct conclusion of a purely judicial question." All the Justices agreed that the trial and conviction were illegal since the President had no constitutional power to substitute a military for a civil trial, with its right to a jury, in an area which was not in rebellion and against a person who was not in the military forces. Had Davis' opinion stopped there, it would have aroused little controversy for it would have had little practical significance, since it is highly unlikely that in wartime the Congress would refuse to enact a law conferring jurisdiction on military tribunals if the President, in his capacity of commander in chief of the armed forces, informed Congress that such a measure was necessary.

But Davis went further than was required by the case before the Court, and as so frequently happens (e.g., *Marbury* v. *Madison, Dred Scott* v. *Sandford*), it was that unnecessary excursion which made trouble for the Court. Lincoln had acted although Congress had not passed any law suspending civil trials in Indiana; nevertheless, Davis held that under the Constitution Congress would have no more power to do so than the President. "The Constitution of the United States," said Davis, "is a law for rulers and people, equally in war and in peace, and covers with the shield of its protection all classes of men, at all times, and under all circumstances. . . . Martial law can never exist where the courts are open, and in the proper and unobstructed exercise of their jurisdiction." Chase, with the agreement of Wayne, Swayne and Miller, dissented in respect to the second point and expressed the opinion that Congress did have the power to suspend civil trials in "time of public danger." (It is interesting to note that all five of Lincoln's appointees agreed that his conduct in authorizing the suspension of trials had been unconstitutional.)

Even before the Milligan case was argued President Johnson had commuted the defendant's sentence to life imprisonment, and after the Court's decision Milligan was released from prison. The importance of the case at the time it was argued is indicated by the fact that Milligan's counsel before the Court included David Dudley Field, the Justice's brother, James A. Garfield, later to be President of the United States, and Jeremiah S. Black who had almost become a Supreme Court Justice himself. Its significance in the development of American liberties has been universally recognized by constitutional authorities, some of whom, however, do not agree with its conclusions. It breathes the spirit of the American commitment to the subordination of the military to the civil government. (One of the grievances against George III, which the Declaration of Independence cites as cause for the separation from Britain, was that "He has affected to render the military independent and superior to the civil power.")

Yet when the Milligan decision became public it was denounced with unrestrained vehemence by those who asserted and fought for the civil rights of Negroes. Horace Greeley's New York *Herald* compared the decision with the Dred Scott case, a motif that was echoed in many Republican papers, as in the one which said: "Like the Dred Scott decision, it is not a judicial opinion; it is a political act." Another Republican party organ predicted that "the hearts of traitors will be gladdened by the announcement that treason vanquished on the battlefield and hunted from every other retreat, has at last found a secure shelter in the bosom of the Supreme Court."

There were, of course, the usual accompanying demands for appropriate action. There were proposals to abolish the Court, reform it, pack it, require unanimity in constitutional cases, etc. There were even demands to impeach the Court, but Thaddeus Stevens, the leader of the radicals, decided instead to impeach the President, "from whom," he said, "all evils flow."

Shortly after the Milligan case was decided the Court handed down two other decisions that infuriated the radical Republicans and pleased the Democrats. In *Cummings* v. *Missouri* it invalidated a state statute that barred from the right to vote, hold office, teach, preach or practice law any person who did not first take an oath that he had not supported or favored the Confederacy. In *Ex parte Garland* it invalidated a federal statute requiring a similar oath of any attorney seeking to practice in the federal courts. In both cases the ground for invalidation was that the statutes were *ex post facto*, that is, they retroactively imposed punishment for conduct which was not punishable when committed. A second ground was that they were bills of attainder, i.e., legislative determinations of guilt on the part of a person or class of persons without a judicial trial. Both decisions were by five to four votes; all the pre-Lincoln appointees voted to invalidate the statutes, all the Lincoln appointees except Field voted to uphold them. As usual, these unpopular decisions evoked strident attacks upon the Court and demands for its reform.

REVENGE OR REDRESS?

The Milligan, Cummings and Garland decisions, all significant milestones in the development of American liberties, tend to corroborate the almost universally held view that the Reconstruction Congress and its chief architects, Thaddeus Stevens and Charles Sumner, were evil people motivated solely by hatred for the South and a consuming passion for vengeance, tempered only by a venal desire to milk the South financially by burdening it with an army of political parasites consisting of deserving Republican politicians from the North. Stevens has been the subject of more denunciation in American history books than perhaps any other American since Benedict Arnold.

History has been generous to Lincoln; it has been less than just to Stevens. It must always be kept in mind that to Lincoln the purpose of the Civil War was to preserve the Union. After his election a delegation of southern leaders met with him to seek to evolve a compromise on the slavery issue. Lincoln refused to open the territories to slavery—having just been elected by Free Soilers and abolitionists he could hardly do less. But he did offer to make slavery secure in the states that had it and to institute vigorous enforcement of the Fugitive Slave Law. His letter to Greeley stating that if he "could save the Union without freeing any slave" he "would do it," just as he would free all the slaves if that would save it, has been extolled in conventional history as a great expression of statesmanship. It is at least equally reasonable to condemn it as an amoral perversion of means and ends, which makes of a particular form of political association an idol for whose preservation millions of human beings would be willingly sacrificed. If the sole purpose of the Civil War was to preserve the Union, then in addition to the millions of black slaves whose liberties Lincoln was willing to barter, the lives of hundreds of thousands of white soldiers, north and south, who died in it were also sacrificed to the idol of nationalism. (There is, of course, no question that Lincoln was personally opposed to slavery and condemned it as morally evil.)

Stevens was consumed with a passion, not for nationalism or vengeance, but for equality. The same idea or ideal of equality—that every human being is and should be in the eyes of God and the law the equal of every other human being—motivated his struggle in 1835 for a free common school system in which the child of the poor could receive a basic education along with the child of the wealthy. It also motivated his struggle thirty years later to achieve full equality to the freed Negro slaves. To emancipate them from physical slavery without assuring them equality was to him but part of the mission which alone could justify the blood spilled at Gettysburg and Antietam. To Lincoln, on the other hand, once the preservation of the Union had been secured at Appomattox, what remained to be done was to "bind up the nation's wounds."

History has also been less than just to the Reconstruction Congress which Stevens dominated as completely as Marshall had dominated his Court. It has been the victim of what W. E. Du Bois, in his book *Black Reconstruction in America,* called "the propaganda of history." One need only glance through the history text books that were until comparatively recently universally used and even today are in widespread use in the elementary and secondary schools to note the villification of the Reconstruction Congress, "radical" Republicans, and "carpetbaggers," and the romanticization of the vanquished southern leaders, the Ku Klux Klan and the moderate, forgiving Republicans. There were certainly vengeful and venal persons in the Reconstruction Congress as in every Congress; but its pervading spirit was neither vengeance nor venality; it was to insure by law and military force the complete equality of the newly freed Negro.

The Civil War was barely over when every one of the southern states began to enact a wide array of "black codes," all with the common objective of keeping the Negro as close to his ante-bellum status as possible. Even return to de facto slavery was sought. Every means was used to have Negroes convicted of some crime and then, when they were unable to pay their fines, to have them farmed out to whites to work off the fines. As one reputable historian put it, "Almost every act, word or gesture of the Negro, not consonant with good taste and good manners as well as good morals, was made a crime or misdemeanor, for which he could first be fined by the magistrates and then consigned to a condition of almost slavery for an indefinite term, if he could not pay the bill."

The South, defeated though it was in the war, was now even less willing to give the Negro equality, and least of all the right of suffrage. Everywhere he was disenfranchised, or, more accurately, nowhere was he enfranchised. In 1864 Lincoln wrote cautiously to the newly elected governor of Louisiana that "now you are about to have a convention, which, among other things, will probably define the elective franchise, I barely suggest, for your private consideration, whether some of the colored people may not be let in, as for instances, the very intelligent, and especially those who have fought gallantly in our ranks. . . . But this is only suggestion, not to the public, but to you alone."

In the same year Charles Sumner boldly demanded the ballot for all Negroes as full equals with whites. "The ballot," he said,

> is a schoolmaster. Reading and writing are of inestimable value, but the ballot teaches what these cannot teach. It teaches manhood. Especially is it important to a race whose manhood has been denied. The work of redemption cannot be complete if the ballot is left in doubt. . . . Give the freedman the ballot and he will be educated into the principles of the government. Deny him the ballot and he will continue an alien in knowledge as in rights. . . . For generations you have shut him out from all education, making it a crime to teach him to read for himself the book of life. Let not the tyranny of the past be an apology for any further exclusion.

There were many who, like Lincoln, honestly believed that the newly freed slaves were not yet ready for the ballot, and that education must precede the franchise. However, aside from the fact that there were many thousands of poor whites enjoying the ballot who were as uneducated as the Negroes, was the more important fact that if the South had its way the Negro would never acquire the education which would qualify him for the ballot.

The Reconstruction Congress sent northern "carpetbaggers" to the South not to milk it nor as a means for political patronage (although, of course, patronage was inevitably involved in the selection of personnel, as it often is in the selection of personnel even for the Supreme Court), but simply because no southern legislature or officials would make secure the Negro's newly won freedom or help him achieve equality or civil rights. The oaths invalidated in the Cummings and Garland cases were imposed not out of vindictiveness but in an effort to exclude from positions of influence those most likely to use that influence to bring back the ante-bellum status of the Negro. The military tribunals condemned in the Milligan case were set up because in the southern civil courts it was impossible for a Negro to get justice (a decision in favor of a Negro against a white was a rarity), or for a white man who violated the rights of a Negro to be punished. Whether these measures would have been effective had the Supreme Court allowed them to stand, and if so whether they would in any event have been justifiable, are entirely different questions. The point sought to be made here is only that there is a side to the history of the Reconstruction Congress other than the conventional one, and that there is a defensible explanation of the dissent of such a libertarian as Davis in the Garland and Cummings cases and for the bitter opposition to those decisions and the Milligan decision on the part of Stevens, Sumner and their colleagues in Congress.

THE CONSTRUCTIVE ACCOMPLISHMENTS OF THE RECONSTRUCTION CONGRESS

The Reconstruction Congress is remembered chiefly for its errors and misdeeds, but its constructive achievements were truly remarkable. It was responsible for the adoption of the Thirteenth Amendment, which finally and universally abolished slavery. Shortly after the ratification of the amendment, it enacted a civil rights law. The law provided that all persons born in the United States are citizens, and, without regard to race, color or previous condition of servitude, shall have equal rights to enter into contracts, sue and be sued, give evidence in court, buy and sell property, and in general have equal rights under law.

Johnson vetoed the bill because he feared that under its terms Chinese, Indians and gypsies, as well as Negroes, might be made citizens. In addition, he questioned the wisdom of making former slaves citizens. "Four million of them," he said, "have just emerged from slavery into freedom. Can it be reasonably supposed that they possess the requisite qualifications to entitle them to all the privileges and equalities of citizens of the United States?" The bill, he said, was an interference with states' rights, and was likely to serve as an undesirable precedent, for if Congress may guarantee equal rights to Negroes, may it not grant them the right to vote, hold office and marry white persons? Congress, however, passed the bill over his veto.

Because the constitutionality of the law was questioned, the Reconstruction Congress decided to make assurance doubly sure and in 1868 obtained the adoption of the Fourteenth Amendment. This Amendment consists of five sections, only the first and last of which are of permanent importance. The first section provides that: "All persons born or naturalized in the United States and subject to the jurisdiction thereof, are citizens of the United States and of the State wherein they reside. No State shall make or enforce any law which shall abridge the privileges or immunities of citizens of the United States; nor shall any State deprive any person of life, liberty or property without due process of law; nor deny to any person within its jurisdiction the equal protection of the laws." (For shorthand, the three operative provisions are generally referred to as "privileges or immunities," "due process," and "equal protection.") The fifth section authorized Congress to enforce the amendment by appropriate legislation.

In 1869 Congress passed the Fifteenth Amendment and in 1870 the requisite number of states ratified it. The amendment provides that "The right of citizens to vote shall not be denied or abridged by the United States or by any State on account of race, color or previous condition of servitude." Congress is empowered to enact appropriate enforcing legislation.

Also in 1870 and 1871 Congress passed two more laws, the second civil rights or Enforcement Act, and the Ku Klux Klan or Anti-Lynching Act. Their general purpose was to make effective the Fourteenth and Fifteenth Amendments and remove all doubt as to the constitutionality of the 1866 law. In substance they re-enacted that law, and penalized action under color of law and conspiracies by two or more persons to interfere with the free exercise of rights under the federal Constitution or laws.

Finally, in 1875 Congress passed the last civil rights law it was to enact for more than eighty years. This law provided that all persons within the United States shall have equal access to and use of inns, public conveyances on land or water, theaters and other places of public amusement, without discrimination on account of race or color. Violation of the law by any person was made a misdemeanor, and in addition the person discriminated against could sue for damages.

The fate of these measures was not to be decided by the Supreme Court for more than a decade, and in the meantime events were to occur that would greatly influence that determination.

RECONSTRUCTION AND THE COURT

To the radical Republicans the efficacy of Reconstruction depended upon the establishment of military governments in the South. Simultaneously with the enactment of the various civil rights laws, Congress proceeded to adopt a series of statutes (all over President Johnson's veto) providing for military governments in the southern states. The opponents of these laws immediately sought to get a judicial determination that they were invalid. In 1867 the state of Mississippi sought to sue Johnson in the Supreme Court for an injunction to prevent his enforcement of these laws by means of setting up a military government in that state. The Court, however, in the case of *Mississippi* v. *Johnson,* decided that it had no jurisdiction to issue an injunction against the President in the performance of his official duties.

Undaunted, the South tried again. This time the state of Georgia sued Secretary of War Stanton to enjoin him from establishing a military government in Georgia. Again, this was of no avail. The Court, in *Georgia* v. *Stanton,* ruled that it would not decide whether the law establishing military governments in peacetime was constitutional. It held that the controversy was purely political (as the one arising out of the Dorr Rebellion) and therefore not subject to determination in the federal courts, which can pass on only the rights of persons or property.

It seemed, however, that the Court would not be able to escape passing judgment on the military establishment laws. In 1867 Congress passed a law providing that appeals could be taken to the Supreme Court from the circuit courts in all cases where a person claimed that he was being deprived of his liberty in violation of the United States Constitution or laws. The purpose of this statute was to provide additional protection to Negroes in the South. Ironically, it now became a means whereby the Court might destroy one of the foundations of Reconstruction; for under this statute an appeal was taken to the Supreme Court not by a Negro, but by a white named McCardle who had been arrested and held for trial by a military commission in Mississippi. McCardle applied for a writ of habeas corpus from the federal circuit court on the ground that the act establishing the military commission was unconstitutional. When the circuit court denied his application, he appealed to the Supreme Court in accordance with the terms of the newly enacted statute.

When the case first came to the Supreme Court, Johnson's Attorney-General Henry Stanbury (whose earlier nomination to fill the vacancy caused by Catron's death had been rejected by the Senate) appeared before the Court and stated that he agreed with McCardle that the laws were unconstitutional, that he therefore could not in good conscience defend the appeal and that Congress should get its own lawyer to argue the case.

Congress did so, but it also decided to take more vigorous and effective action. Rumors were afloat that the Court would hold the Reconstruction Laws invalid by a vote of five to three. (Wayne had died the previous year.) Accordingly, the House Judiciary Committee reported out and the House passed a bill requiring a two-thirds vote of the Court to invalidate any federal law. The measure was defended editorially by the Indianapolis *Journal*, which commented: "The Reconstruction Acts are full of the rights and liberties of millions of men; and to have these stricken down by the decision of some old fossil on the Supreme Court whose political opinions belong to a past era, would be an outrage on humanity."

After some consideration the Senate decided not to enact the bill, nor another one, sponsored in the House by Stevens and in the Senate by Lyman Trumbull, which would have deprived the Supreme Court of jurisdiction in any suit arising out of the Reconstruction Acts. One of the reasons that no action was taken was that in the meantime the decision in *Georgia* v. *Stanton* was made public and it was generally assumed that in the McCardle case also the Court would hold that the controversy was political and therefore outside its jurisdiction. To the surprise and consternation of Congress, the very next week the Court came out with its first decision in *Ex parte McCardle* holding that it did have jurisdiction and would consider and decide the case.

Congress reacted quickly, but except for the Court's cooperation the reaction would not have been quick enough. A bill was speedily introduced which repealed the 1867 statute providing for appeals to the Supreme Court in habeas corpus suits and forbade the Court to exercise jurisdiction even in appeals which had already been filed. There was plenty of time for the Court to hand down a decision in the McCardle case while the measure was being debated in Congress. But by that time the impeachment of Johnson was well under way (Chase was absent from the Court because of his need to preside over the trial in the Senate), and the Court, as so often in the past, may have again decided to substitute discretion for valor. For whatever reason, although all the questions in the case had been fully argued by the attorneys, the Court helpfully withheld its decision while the bill was debated, passed, vetoed by Johnson and passed again over his veto. Then, in the second *Ex parte McCardle* case in 1869, it ruled that in view of the new law it had no jurisdiction and accordingly dismissed the appeal. Thus once more the Court was able to avoid passing on the constitutionality of the Reconstruction Acts.

ABOUT FACE ON LEGAL TENDER

Lincoln had appointed Chase Chief Justice in order to make as sure as possible that the two major war measures, the emancipation and the Legal Tender Act, would be upheld by the Supreme Court. Lincoln could safely assume—or believed he could—that a long-time abolitionist as Chase was would not upset the emancipation. And since Chase himself, as Secretary of the Treasury, had been the chief architect of the Legal Tender Act, that too was secure. The adoption of the Thirteenth Amendment removed the emancipation from danger, but the Legal Tender Act faced a more uncertain future and almost met its death at the hands of none other than Chase himself.

Chase's chief responsibility as head of the Treasury was to finance the war. To help accomplish this Congress in 1862 enacted a law authorizing the issuance of paper money ("greenbacks") which were declared to be legal tender with which people could pay their debts and which creditors would be compelled to accept. As these greenbacks continued to be issued (almost a half billion dollars were issued during the war) their value in terms of gold exchange continued to depreciate. The banks and business interests, and others in the creditor classes, naturally opposed being compelled to accept payment either of principal or interest in depreciated currency. Conversely, the debtor classes, and these included not only the farmers but also the railroads which had floated bonds in large amounts to finance their rapid expansion, supported the law. The constitutionality of the law was generally assumed; practically every state court that had considered the question upheld it. Hence, when a suit testing its constitutionality came before the Supreme Court in the case of *Hepburn* v. *Griswold* in 1867, there was little doubt about the outcome, and a speedy decision upholding its constitutionality was universally expected.

When after two years passed and no decision had yet been handed down, the administration of Grant, who was then President, began feeling uneasy. Uneasiness was followed by concern and then by consternation, for rumors were widespread that the Court would invalidate the law. The delay, it later transpired, resulted from the inner tensions of the Court and particularly the difficulties it was having with Grier. Of the eight members of the Court, four—Chase, Nelson, Clifford and Field—voted to declare the law unconstitutional. Miller, Swayne and Davis voted to uphold it. Exactly where Grier stood was not clear. At first he agreed with the latter three and had he so voted, this would have resulted in a tie vote, thus affirming the lower court which had upheld the law. Then he apparently changed his mind and appeared to side with Chase. It was clear to all the Justices that Grier had now become so senile that he had no idea what the whole question was about. They accordingly prevailed upon him to retire from the Court, leaving seven Justices split four to three against the law.

In 1870 the decision in *Hepburn* v. *Griswold* finally was announced. The majority opinion was written by Chase. He recognized the incongruity of his voting against a law for which he was chiefly responsible, but he apologetically explained that in the excitement and exigencies of war clear and careful deliberation was not always possible. He held that Congress had no power to issue paper money, even to finance a war. He accepted Marshall's principle of implied powers, that Congress may enact all appropriate means to carry out express powers. But he held that the ultimate decision as to what are appropriate means to carry out the express powers is the responsibility of the Supreme Court, rather than Congress, and that the issuance of paper money was not within that category even to finance a war.

The effect of this decision, if it were allowed to stand, would have been that not only the Civil War Legal Tender Act but all similar future acts as well were unconstitutional. This would have wrought havoc with America's financial system and its capitalist expansion. It would have brought hopeless bankruptcy, not only to millions of small farmers and merchants, but to every railroad in the country as well. There is hardly any doubt that Congress would not have allowed the decision to stand and some effective measures would have been taken to nullify it. Action by Congress, however, became unnecessary by reason of a fortuitous circumstance.

After Catron died in 1865, Congress enacted a law reducing the size of the Court to seven (effective on the death of two more Justices) to make sure that Johnson would have no opportunity to name anybody to the Court. With Grier's resignation, the Court was now down to seven; but in April, 1869, after Grant had become President and while the Court was engaged in the long drawn out internal conflict over *Hepburn* v. *Griswold*, Congress passed a law increasing the membership of the Court to nine, the number at which it has since remained. On the day the decision was announced, Grant nominated to the Court William Strong of Pennsylvania and Joseph P. Bradley of New Jersey. As soon as both were confirmed and took their seats, the Attorney-General of the United States made a motion that the question decided in *Hepburn* v. *Griswold* be reconsidered by the Court. The three dissenters and the two new Justices voted in favor of reconsideration; Chase, Nelson, Clifford and Field, now a minority, voted against reconsideration. In the new case, *Knox* v. *Lee*, the same five to four vote overruled the Hepburn decision and upheld the Legal Tender Act as a proper exercise of the war power. (Thirteen years later, in *Julliard* v. *Greenman*, the Court was to uphold even peacetime legal tender laws—a decision indispensable to the economic expansion of the nation.)

The charge has been made, and vigorously denied, that Grant packed the Court to obtain a reconsideration and reversal of the Hepburn decision. Those who deny it assert that the matter was one purely of coincidence. In any event, the two persons nominated by Grant were not selected by chance. Both were railroad lawyers, Strong's principal client being the Philadelphia and Reading Railroad, and Bradley's, the Camden and Amboy Railroad of New Jersey. Strong had earlier been a Democratic member of Congress and Bradley was not only lawyer for the Camden and Amboy but actively involved in its management as secretary of its board and member of its executive committee. Both Justices reportedly divested themselves of their railroad stock on ascension to the Court, but, as Miller later noted, it is not quite so easy to divest oneself of long-standing loyalties. (Bradley was later to prove one of the strongest members of the bench, on a par with Miller and Field.)

Had Lincoln been alive in 1870 he might well have felt that Chase had betrayed the trust placed in him. Grant had no reason to be disappointed in his choices. Strong and Bradley fought valiantly and effectively. One month after their confirmation, Miller wrote to a friend:

> We had a desperate struggle in the secret conference of the court for three weeks involving the legal tender question. The Chief Justice has resorted to all the stratagems of the lowest political trickery to prevent their being heard, and the fight has been bitter in the conference room. . . . The excitement has nearly used me up. It has been fearful; and my own position as leader in marshalling my forces, and keeping up their courage against a domineering Chief, and a party in court [Field?] who has been accustomed to carrying everything their own way, has been such a strain on my brain and nervous system as I never wish to encounter again.

Supreme Court Justices are human.

HAYES-TILDEN AND RECONSTRUCTION'S END

But a few years after the Reconstruction Court reversed itself and upheld the Legal Tender Act, the Court was again in trouble. The disputed Hayes-Tilden election of 1876 catapulted the Court, or five members thereof, into partisan politics and simultaneously doomed the Negroes' struggle for equality for many decades. When the first reports of the election came in it appeared that the Democratic candidate, Samuel J. Tilden of New York, had won a sweeping victory over Rutherford B. Hayes. But the votes of four states, South Carolina, Florida, Louisiana and Oregon, seemed to be in sufficient doubt for the Republicans to challenge the Democratic claim to have carried them. If all four states were swung to Hayes, he would be elected by an Electoral College majority of one vote, 185 to 184. With both parties claiming the four states, Congress finally created an electoral commission of fifteen to decide the contest. The commission was to consist of five senators, five representatives and five members of the Supreme Court. The original intent was to have seven of the members of the commission from each party, and the fifteenth to be Justice Davis, generally considered nonpartisan. At the last moment, however, the Illinois legislature elected Davis to the Senate and he resigned from the Court. To replace him on the commission, Bradley, whose pre-Court politics had been Republican, was chosen.

It is quite likely that it would have been preferable if the disputed election had been submitted to the Court as a whole for determination, following the practices in the states and in many foreign nations. But the principle announced in the Dorr Rebellion case (*Luther* v. *Borden*) that the Court would not pass on purely political questions, particularly those involving contested claims to elected office, was too firmly established to allow this. Instead, following the precedent established by Washington in the cases of the invalid pensioners' claims, the five Justices were selected to serve as commissioners in their individual capacities.

It might also have been better if the Justices had followed the precedent of Washington's appointees and had declined to serve (although the critical nature of the situation may have well made this impossible). For just as the ten senators and representatives split strictly along party lines on every disputed question that came up during the hearings, so too did the five Justices, the Democratic Clifford and Strong voting with the Democrats, and the Republican Field, Miller and Bradley voting with the Republicans.

Yet, it seemed that literally at the eleventh hour Bradley was prepared to act as it was expected that Davis would act—in a purely nonpartisan manner. The day before the decision on the Florida contest was to be announced, Bradley had prepared an opinion in favor of the Democratic electors. This would have resulted in an eight to seven vote in favor of Tilden in that state, and any one of the four contested states would have been enough to elect him. However, when Bradley read his opinion the next day, the second half of it had been changed and it now ended with a decision for the Republican electors.

What was the explanation for the midnight switch? Bradley later said simply that further reflection had caused him to change his views. Perhaps so, but it is also likely that he was aided in making the change.

At midnight or later, Bradley was visited by two top Republican party leaders, Senator Frederick Frelinghuysen and Secretary of the Navy George M. Robeson, both from his native state of New Jersey.

What Frelinghuysen and Robeson told Bradley that helped him change his mind is of course not known. Yet it may well have been news that a settlement had been worked out between the Republican leaders and the Democratic leaders in the South under which the South would accept the election of Hayes in return for the withdrawal of all remaining federal troops from the South and the end of Reconstruction. That such an arrangement was made is hardly open to serious question; it was evidenced in part by a written agreement, and one of its signers on behalf of the Republicans was Stanley Matthews of Ohio, who five years later was himself to be a member of the Supreme Court.

The bargain was made and kept by both sides. The electoral commission by a vote of eight to seven awarded all four states to Hayes. A brief effort at revolt by some northern Democrats, who talked of a filibuster in the House to prevent or delay the declaration of the election of Hayes, was quickly squelched by the southern Democrats. For his part, Hayes promptly withdrew the remaining federal troops from the South, and adopted a policy of reconciliation (although he would not go so far as to approve a bill passed by the Democratic Congress in 1877 to repeal the Civil Rights Enforcement Act). The Republicans in Congress too remained faithful to the bargain. No further civil rights laws were passed; the South was left to the (white) southerners and the turbulent decade of Reconstruction came to an end.

If the President and the leadership of both political parties were now willing to leave the destiny of the southern Negro in the hands of the southern white-controlled state governments, it would have been unrealistic to expect the Supreme Court successfully to challenge that decision. That not only Bradley but at least the other four Justices who served on the electoral commission became aware of the settlement and its terms is more than merely probable. And if they knew, it is almost equally certain that the other Justices knew too. In any event, the settlement of the Hayes-Tilden dispute marked the beginning of the decline and fall of civil rights, and the Supreme Court played a significant role in that process. But before this is recounted, some important changes in its personnel must be related.

FOURTH CHOICE FOR CHIEF JUSTICE

On the death of Chase in 1873, Grant was called upon to select a new Chief Justice. In line with his custom of appointing close friends and political cronies to high positions, he offered the post to Senator Roscoe Conkling of New York. Conkling's only objective qualifications for the post (aside from the fact that he was a lawyer) were his undisputed leadership of the Republican party in New York and his complete control of an effective state political machine which he built up almost entirely on federal patronage. He was, however, wise enough to recognize his own limitations and declined the honor. Grant's next selection was even worse. He nominated for the office of Chief Justice his Attorney-General, George H. Williams of Oregon. Williams not only had no affirmative qualifications for the post, but in addition was corrupt and was later compelled to resign from the cabinet. Even at the time of his nomination, his career was associated with scandal. Williams did not have the good sense of Conkling to decline, and when the selection became public the nation was shocked. "The nomination surprised and disgusted every lawyer in the United States who has the honor of his profession at heart" was the typical comment of one newspaper. Conkling tried to get Grant and Williams off the hook by proposing a bill to abolish the post of Chief Justice—one senator remarked dryly that this was no longer necessary since the nomination of Williams had already achieved that. Finally, Grant and Williams saw the light, and at the latter's request Grant withdrew the nomination.

Grant's next choice, though no more successful, was only slightly less objectionable. Caleb Cushing, then seventy-four years old, was undoubtedly a person of high legal ability as well as long judicial experience, having been a member of the Massachusetts supreme judicial court and before that Attorney-General of the United States. But he had many disqualifications as well. First was his advanced age. In addition, he was a man of exceedingly unstable character as well as an opportunist in politics. The editorial comment of the Springfield *Republican* was typical. "His reputation," it said, "is that of a man who has never allowed principle or conscience to stand in the way of gain." Again Grant found it necessary to withdraw the nomination.

Finally the President selected a person whom the Senate was willing to confirm and the nation to accept. The appointee was Morrison R. Waite, and the reason he was acceptable was thus stated by the New York *Tribune*: "After the previous shocks, the people are prepared to accept, with something like equanimity, any appointment which should not be scandalous." Waite's appointment was not scandalous; little else could be said for it. "An honest man and a fair lawyer," as one newspaper summarized it, "and that is as much as we can reasonably expect from the President." The Senate agreed, and Waite was confirmed by a vote of 63 to 6.

Waite was virtually unknown outside his own state of Ohio and was little known there. He had no previous judicial service, and only a little public experience of any kind. He had served a single term in the state legislature, had been chairman of the state constitutional convention and a member of a three-man delegation appointed by Grant to represent the United States at Geneva in connection with the arbitration of certain claims arising out of the Civil War. He was a successful lawyer, numbering among his clients important banks and insurance companies, but had never argued a case before the Court he was appointed to head. Principally, like Bradley and Strong, his clients were railroads, and he participated in their management and control as director and officer, as well as representing them in law suits. However, on the Supreme Court Waite turned out to be not only highly competent, but surprisingly liberal in economic (though not racial) cases, including those involving railroads.

HARLAN: GREATNESS BY ACCIDENT

To make this chronicle of the Supreme Court and its members complete, reference must be made to Ward Hunt, appointed by Grant in 1872 to fill the vacancy caused by the retirement of Nelson. Hunt had been a highly respected and able member of the New York court of appeals but played no role on the Supreme Court. In Warren's three volume history of the Supreme Court not more than half of a sentence is devoted to his appointment (and that, in a footnote), and another half to his resignation fully nine years later. The explanation lies in the fact that for the last five of these nine years Hunt was completely incompetent mentally, and in order to get him off the bench Congress had to pass a special law allowing him to retire on full salary.

Davis' resignation to enter the Senate enabled Hayes to make an appointment to the Court almost as soon as he was inaugurated, and he nominated to the position John Marshall Harlan of Kentucky. The nomination was purely a political one but it brought to the bench, almost by accident, one of the giants in the history of the Court. Harlan, a southerner, former slave owner, opponent of the Emancipation Proclamation, bitter foe of the Civil War amendments (Thirteenth, Fourteenth and Fifteenth) and a critic of the Civil Rights Laws, became a great liberal and by far the most uncompromising and vigorous champion of the rights of the Negroes to equality during the entire thirty-four years he was on the bench.

Harlan had entered politics in Kentucky immediately upon his admission to the bar in 1853. Although first a Whig, he soon joined the anti-Catholic, anti-foreigners Know-Nothing party and took an oath to vote only for native Protestants. Hugo Black in the 1920's joined the Ku Klux Klan, the twentieth century descendant of the Know-Nothing movement, but Black was only a nominal member, while Harlan became an active and ardent champion. He proved to be an eloquent orator and stumped the state on behalf of Know-Nothing (officially "American Party") candidates. His speeches were described as "orthodox . . . Know-Nothing scripture"—anti-foreign, pro-slavery and anti-Catholic in just the right proportions. But the Know-Nothing party quickly faded from the political scene, and Harlan moved over to the Unionist party. He favored slavery, supported the Dred Scott decision and vigorous enforcement of the Fugitive Slave Law, but like his father, he was unreservedly nationalist—his father had christened him John Marshall. Hence, when the war broke out, he volunteered for service with the Union forces.

On his father's death in 1863 he retired from the army with the rank of colonel, and returned to the practice of law and politics. He accepted the nomination for state attorney-general on the Union ticket and won. The fact that Kentucky, a loyal state, was nevertheless subjected by Lincoln to military rule caused the downfall of the Unionist party. In 1864 Harlan supported the candidacy of General George McClellan and campaigned against Lincoln. At the end of the war he became one of the leaders of an experimental new party, the Conservative Union party, which tried to steer a middle course between the pro-Confederate Democrats and the radical Republicans. When that party met disaster at the polls, Harlan drifted into the Republican party, almost by chance: his legal associates were mainly Republicans and his law partner, Benjamin Bristow, was to become Grant's Secretary of the Treasury.

This accidental drifting into the Republican party was to shape Harlan's future life both politically and intellectually, the former because it ultimately enabled him to become a member of the Supreme Court, the latter because it changed his entire thinking in respect to Negroes and Negro rights. The only chance that the Republicans in Kentucky had to break the domination of the Democratic party was to enlist the support of the newly franchised Negro voters. For three years, from 1868 to 1871, Harlan found himself campaigning for Negro votes and found himself defending the very civil rights measures and Constitutional amendments he had formerly condemned. By the end of this period he had become completely committed not only politically but intellectually to the pro-civil rights position. It is also true, however, that his education was helped along by the widespread lynchings, floggings, robberies and terrorizing of Negroes which the Democratic state administration was either unwilling or unable to halt.

Harlan quickly became the leader of the Kentucky Republican party. In the Presidential nominating convention of 1876 he led his state delegation into the Hayes camp, thus making possible his nomination. Upon Hayes's election, Harlan was offered his reward in the form of an appointment as ambassador to Great Britain, "the very best mission" in Hayes's words. Harlan, however, could not financially afford to accept the post, and declined. Hayes then offered to pay his political debt to Harlan by appointing him to the vacancy on the Court caused by Davis' resignation. This time Harlan accepted and, although his nomination was questioned by some Republicans in view of his pro-slavery past, the Senate confirmed the appointment. (Harlan was a deeply religious Justice. According to a colleague on the bench he went to bed every night with a Bible clutched in one hand and a copy of the Constitution in the other.)

Harlan was appointed in 1877. Three years later, on the retirement of Strong after ten years on the bench, Hayes appointed William B. Woods, who, born in Kentucky, had settled in Alabama after the war and had been appointed a federal circuit judge by Grant. In the same year Swayne resigned because of disability, and Hayes nominated Stanley Matthews as his successor. As chief negotiator for the Republicans,

Matthews had been responsible for the successful outcome of the contested Hayes election and the appointment may have been the reward for his efforts. Matthews had been counsel for Jay Gould and even while in the Senate he acted as lawyer for large railroads and vigorously supported and promoted legislation favoring the railroad interests. These facts led to widespread public opposition to the appointment and the Senate refused to confirm it. After Garfield succeeded Hayes he renewed the nomination, and although the Senate judiciary committee disapproved it, the Senate after bitter debate voted confirmation by the margin of one vote.

Earlier in the same year, 1881, Clifford resigned. He had been senile and incompetent for a number of years but, true to his party to the last, he refused to resign in the hope that a Democratic President would be elected so that his successor would also be a Democrat. When Garfield defeated Hancock in 1880, Clifford gave up and resigned. To succeed Clifford, President Arthur appointed Horace Gray of Massachusetts, a member of a wealthy and aristocratic Boston family, a legal scholar and the chief justice of the state's supreme court.

In 1882 Hunt was retired from the bench, and Arthur, to the surprise of most lawyers, appointed Conkling. A storm of protest was raised, but the Senate confirmed the appointment. Again, however, Conkling declined, and Arthur selected Samuel Blatchford, also of New York, who had been federal district and circuit court judge for fifteen years.

These were the Justices who presided over the interment of the Negro's struggle for equality.

JUDICIAL REPEAL OF RECONSTRUCTION

The judicial process of nibbling away at civil rights protection for Negroes had begun even before the end of Reconstruction effected by the settlement of the Hayes-Tilden dispute. In 1875 in the case of *United States* v. *Cruikshank*, the Court reversed convictions, under the Anti-Ku Klux Klan or Civil Rights Enforcement Act of 1870, of a mob of Ku Kluxers who tried to break up a Negro meeting by force. The federal government, Chief Justice Waite said for the Court, has no power to punish violence against Negroes by private persons. The Fourteenth

Amendment prohibits only the *states* from depriving persons of life, liberty or property without due process of laws, not private individuals. The responsibility to punish such crimes rests exclusively with the states themselves.

In *United States* v. *Reese,* the Court in the same year declared unconstitutional another section of the 1870 act. Two Kentucky election inspectors were indicted under the law for refusing to count votes cast by Negroes in a municipal election. The Court held the statute unconstitutional because it did not specifically say that its provisions were limited to denials to vote on account of race, color or previous condition of servitude, and that was the only type of denial that the Fifteenth Amendment prohibited.

After 1877, what was previously nibbling away at the objectives of the Reconstruction Congress became in effect judicial nullification. In *Hall* v. *DeCuir,* decided in 1878, the Court held unconstitutional an act passed by the Reconstruction legislature of Louisiana *forbidding* railroads to discriminate against passengers because of race or color. This, said the Court, interferes with interstate commerce.

In 1883 the Court, in the case of *United States* v. *Harris,* held unconstitutional the key provision in the Anti-Klan Act. Twenty members of a Tennessee lynch mob seized four Negro prisoners held by a state deputy sheriff and beat them severely, killing one. They were indicted under a provision of the act prohibiting a conspiracy by two or more persons to deprive others of their civil rights. This, the Court said, was unconstitutional. The Fourteenth Amendment applies only to deprivations by the states, and does not authorize Congress to enact any law making it a federal crime for private persons to lynch Negroes or otherwise deprive them of their civil rights.

The *coup de grâce* came later in the same year in the Civil Rights cases. A number of individuals were indicted under the Civil Rights Law of 1875 for denying hotel and theater accommodations to Negroes because of their race, and a railroad was indicted for refusing to allow a Negro woman to ride in a railroad car. (The hotel and theater were in San Francisco and New York; only the railroad was in a southern state, Tennessee.) The Supreme Court threw out the indictments and declared the 1875 act unconstitutional.

This act, as the other civil rights laws, the Court said, was adopted under the section of the Fourteenth Amendment empowering Congress to enact appropriate legislation to enforce the amendment. But the enforcement clause can be no broader than the amendment itself, for a river can rise no higher than its source. The first section of the amendment declares that no *state* shall deny to any person the equal protection of the laws. The amendment invalidates state laws and state acts that deny the equal protection of the laws and authorizes Congress to enact legislation to implement that invalidation. It does not, however, permit Congress to penalize infringement of civil rights committed by individuals.

There was also an attempt to justify the act under the Thirteenth Amendment which prohibits slavery even by private individuals. The argument was that racial discrimination is a "badge" of slavery. The Court, however, rejected the argument.

Harlan delivered a powerful dissent. He pointed out that both the Fugitive Slave Law of 1793 and that of 1850 imposed penalties against private persons. Both laws had been upheld as constitutional in *Prigg* v. *Pennsylvania* and *Abelman* v. *Booth*. If laws of Congress enacted to enforce the Constitutional provision protecting slavery against infringement by private persons are valid, why are similar laws to enforce the Constitutional provision securing equality for the Negro not equally valid? Moreover, the Thirteenth Amendment not only prohibited slavery but empowered Congress to enact laws forbidding the incidents of slavery, in the tradition of the Black Codes, and racial discrimination in public accommodations is such an incident of slavery.

In these cases the Court nullified the efforts of Thaddeus Stevens and his associates in the Reconstruction Congress to confer by law upon the Negro not merely freedom but equality as well. In 1896, in *Plessy* v. *Ferguson*, the Court went further and protected the rights of the southern states to take positive steps to prevent by law the grant of equal treatment to Negroes even by whites who might voluntarily wish to accord them such treatment.

Post-Reconstruction Louisiana enacted a law requiring all railroads to have separate coaches for whites and colored passengers and making it a criminal offense for a person of one race to sit in a coach reserved for members of the other race. A man named Plessy, who was one-eighth Negro, one of his eight great-grandparents having been of African descent, entered a coach reserved for whites; the conductor ordered him to sit in the coach for colored passengers. When Plessy refused, he was arrested for violation of the law. With only Harlan dissenting, the Supreme Court upheld the validity of the law.

Plessy argued first that enforced racial segregation was a badge of slavery and thus prohibited by the Thirteenth Amendment. This argument was futile for the Court had already interpreted the amendment to bar no more than involuntary servitude. His second and principal argument was that legally enforced separation of Negroes from whites necessarily implied inferiority of Negroes to whites and thus denied to Negroes the equal protection of the laws secured by the Fourteenth Amendment.

The Court held that laws separating Negroes and whites do not imply the inferiority either of Negroes or of whites. If enforced separation stamps the colored race with a badge of inferiority, it is not because of anything in the law but because the colored race chooses to put that construction on it. Legislation is powerless to overcome social prejudices or to eradicate racial instincts. If one race is inferior to the other socially the Constitution of the United States cannot put them on the same plane. So long as the Louisiana statute did not require the railroad to put Plessy in a coach whose accommodations were physically inferior to those of coaches reserved for white passengers, Plessy was not discriminated against or denied the equal protection of the laws; and therefore he had no cause to complain to the Supreme Court.

Harlan's dissent was even more powerful than the one in the Civil Rights cases:

> The white race deems itself to be the dominant race in this country. And so it is, in prestige, in achievements, in education, in wealth and in power. So, I doubt not, it will continue to be for all time, if it remains true to its great heritage and holds fast to the principles of constitutional liberty. But in view of the Constitution, in the eye of the law, there is in this country no superior, dominant, ruling class of citizens. There is no caste here. Our Constitution is color-blind, and neither knows nor tolerates classes among citizens. In respect to civil rights, all citizens are equal before the law. . . . The law regards man as man, and takes no account of his surroundings or of his color when his civil rights as guaranteed by the supreme law of the land are involved.

He concluded,

> The destinies of the two races in this country are indissolubly linked together, and the interests of both require that the common government of all shall not permit the seeds of race hate to be planted under the sanction of law. What can

more certainly arouse race hatred, what more certainly create and perpetuate a feeling of distrust between these races, than state enactments, which, in fact, proceed on the ground that colored citizens are so inferior and degraded that they cannot be allowed to sit in public coaches occupied by white citizens? That, as all will admit, is the real meaning of such legislation as was enacted in Louisiana.

It would be incorrect to assume that during this period the Court handed down no decisions in support of civil rights. In *Strauder* v. *West Virginia* and *Ex parte Virginia* it upheld the right of Negroes to serve on juries, at least in cases in which a Negro was tried for a crime. In *Ex parte Yarborough* it upheld the power of Congress to protect the rights of Negroes to vote in federal (as distinguished from state) elections. But these were minor in their immediate practical consequences and constituted almost negligible aid to the Negro in his slow and tortuous march towards equality. After 1877 Congress decided to leave in the hands of the states the responsibility for securing the rights of Negroes and on the Supreme Court only Harlan fought, steadfastly but vainly, against the Court's endorsement of that decision, although it meant the frustration of the clear objectives of the Thirteenth, Fourteenth and Fifteenth Amendments.

The truth of the matter is that in the second half of the nineteenth century the nation was not prepared to accord equality to the Negro, or at least to make a determined effort to do so. Its conscience was appeased by its having granted him freedom. After the first flush of the war had passed, the attention of the people was concentrated on getting rich and doing so quickly. Capitalist expansion was the motif of America in the next three score years. Negro rights would have to wait until a third great war had come and gone.

During this period the Supreme Court faithfully reflected the spirit of the nation. Its task was the protection of capitalist expansion; all else was secondary. However, ironically, even to this the Negro made his contribution—unconsciously, unintentionally, yet effectively. For (along with Marshall's broad concept of interstate commerce) the chief weapon used by the Supreme Court in protecting capitalist expansion was the very one that had proved so ineffective in achieving its intended purpose of securing equality for the Negro—the Fourteenth Amendment.

chapter nine

The Flowering of Court-Protected Capitalism

With the Civil War over and the troublesome problem of slavery presumably satisfactorily solved, the nation settled down to the business of getting rich quick. In the period between the crisis of Fort Sumter and that of October, 1929, the United States engaged in an almost frenzied rush to exploit its physical and human resources in the interest of acquiring wealth. Even the First World War did not seriously interrupt the mad pace. The period was to see the elevation of the acquisition of wealth to the highest level in the hierarchy of American values, and to accord to millionaires the prestige and reverence which in the old world was reserved to royalty and the church. Jefferson's agrarianism was interred at Appomattox along with the system of slave labor, practicable in an agrarian economy but economically wasteful and inefficient in an industrial and commercial capitalist society. Hamilton was about to come into his own.

In the development the Supreme Court played its part; but perhaps because by its nature it is often tardy in reflecting the temper of the times, its earliest post-war opinions appeared to be more concerned with states' rights than with economic expansion. It would not be long before it would recognize the validity and effectuate the philosophy of Hamilton and Marshall that such expansion required the promotive aid of the national legislature and the protective aid of the national judiciary. But its earliest decisions after the war indicated mostly a reaction from the nationalism which had just triumphed on the battlefields.

This reaction explains in substantial part the various restrictive civil rights decisions that were handed down even before the Hayes-Tilden settlement, as well as the 1871 decision in *Collector* v. *Day*, in which the Court held that the salaries of state judges or other state officials could not be subjected to federal income tax laws. In *McCulloch* v. *Maryland*, Marshall had held that instrumentalities of the federal government could not be taxed by the states, and in *Collector* v. *Day*, the Court applied the converse. In the former case it was the patent purpose of the tax to destroy the Bank of the United States. In the latter, while the purpose of the tax was obviously not to destroy, the Court apparently held a genuine apprehension that if an immediate halt were not put to the federal government's assertion of power to tax state instrumentalities and officials, that power might be used, in conjunction with the powers conferred by the Civil War amendments, as an attack on the existence of the states themselves.

It was probably the same reaction against nationalism and the desire to protect the states in the internal control of their affairs that explains more than anything else the decision handed down in 1873 in the Slaughterhouse Case. In 1869 the Louisiana legislature enacted a law granting to a single corporation a twenty-five-year monopoly in all commercial slaughtering in the city of New Orleans. How much the legislature's motivation was venal and how much it was a real concern with a serious health condition growing out of the multitude of individual butchers who did their own slaughtering is a matter on which there is considerable difference of opinion. The company that received the monopoly was subject to detailed regulation by the state authorities; it was required to serve all without discrimination and the rates it could charge were fixed by state authorities. Nevertheless, it enjoyed a monopoly, and influential leaders of the carpetbag legislature that granted the monopoly quite likely received some material as well as spiritual reward for protecting the health of the residents of New Orleans.

The displaced butchers of New Orleans brought suit to invalidate the monopoly. Their attorney before the Supreme Court was John A. Campbell of Alabama who twelve years earlier had resigned from the Court to join his state in its withdrawal from the Union. The monopoly, he contended, imposed "involuntary servitude" upon the ousted butchers in violation of the Thirteenth Amendment, and it abridged their privileges and immunities, deprived them of their liberty and property without duc process of law and denied them the equal protection of the laws, all in violation of the Fourteenth Amendment. In a five to four decision the Court overruled all the claims and upheld the law. The majority opinion was written by Miller, with the concurrence of Clifford, Davis, Strong and Hunt. The dissenters were Chase, Field, Swayne and Bradley.

The purpose of the Thirteenth Amendment, said Miller, was to achieve freedom for the Negro, and of the Fourteenth to insure him citizenship and accord him equality. While neither are strictly limited to Negroes and undoubtedly forbid as well Mexican peonage or the Chinese coolie trade, their purpose certainly was not to restrict the states in their police power to enact regulations necessary for the protection of the health and comfort of the people. The law did not consign the independent butchers to a condition of involuntary servitude nor did it deprive them of the privileges and immunities secured by the Fourteenth Amendment.

The only privileges and immunities contemplated by the amendment, said Miller, were rights or privileges that owe their existence to the federal government. Examples of these are the right to vote in federal elections, the right to petition the federal government, the right of access to federal buildings, offices, and courts of justice, etc. The right to engage in the slaughterhouse business or in any other lawful occupation (not connected with the federal government) was a natural right, not created by the federal government and one which would exist even if there were no federal government, and therefore was not protected by the "privileges or immunities" clause.

What this interpretation of the "privileges or immunities" clause does, if looked at realistically, is simply to read it out of the Constitution. For, so interpreted, there is no need for it at all. Federally created rights are protected against state infringement by virtue of the clause in the Constitution making the Constitution and federal statutes the supreme law of the land. It was by virtue of that provision that the state of Maryland could not injure or tax the federally created Bank of the United States. Similarly, the supremacy clause prohibits the state from passing laws interfering with federal elections, the right to petition the federal government or access to federal courts of justice. Because this decision limits the privileges or immunities clause to federally created rights where it is not needed, the clause has become practically a dead letter in American constitutional law.

The Slaughterhouse opinion has been almost universally acclaimed as a great liberal opinion, and the acclaim has come no less from constitutional lawyers and scholars with a strong liberal bias. If so many wise and good people say so, then it must be so. The fact that it was written by one of the two most liberal men on the Court and concurred in by the other (Davis) lends much weight to this evaluation, although it must be noted that the decision upheld a state-created monopoly, and the only popular decision that Marshall ever wrote struck down such a monopoly. It is quite possible that with remarkable foresight, Miller sought to insure that the Fourteenth Amendment would always be kept as an effective means to secure equality for the Negro and not be diverted to promote business interests or protect them against necessary state regulation. This supposition would seem to be corroborated by Conkling's criticism of the decision on the floor of the Senate on the ground that the committee which drafted the Fourteenth Amendment had intended to include not only the Negro struggling upward from bondage, but also corporations and business interests striving for emancipation from state legislative interference.

If this was Miller's purpose he failed woefully on both counts. His judicial repeal of the privileges or immunities clause withheld from the Court a means which it could have used to protect the rights of Negroes. For example, in the Cruikshank case but two years later, the Court (without dissent by Miller or Davis) held that the right of Negroes to assemble peaceably was a natural right not created by the federal government and therefore the action of the Ku Klux Klan in violently preventing them from exercising that right was not within the scope of the privileges or immunities clause. Conversely, the constitutional immunity to legislative regulation that Miller sought to keep from business and industry they quickly acquired through the employment of the due process clause. In his opinion Miller brushed aside with a few words the argument based on the due process clause, thus leaving it practically intact for future use. In truth it may be said that the only thing slaughtered in the Slaughterhouse cases was the right of the Negro to equality.

In fairness to Miller it should be noted that whatever he said or held in the Slaughterhouse decision would have made no difference in the course of events. Had the Supreme Court been willing to accord equality to the Negro it could have done so by using the equal protection clause, as it was to do seventy-five years later when it was willing. On the other hand, had Miller destroyed the due process clause as completely as he did the privileges or immunities clause, the Court would have found other equally effective means to protect expanding capitalism; Marshall did quite well with the impairment of obligations and interstate commerce clauses. When the New Deal Court was ready to call a halt to judicially protected laissez faire it was able to do so notwithstanding the large body of constitutional law that had grown up around the due process clause. Realistically, the Slaughterhouse decision was neither a great decision nor an evil one. It was a futile decision, as was the Dred Scott decision before it and the Schechter Poultry Corporation decision after it, and as are all other decisions that attempt single-handedly to reverse the course of America's economic, social and political evolution.

THE INFANCY OF DUE PROCESS

The due process clause ("nor shall any State deprive any person of life, liberty or property without due process of law") ultimately evolved as probably the most effective means employed by the Court to restrain state interference with capitalist expansion. (The interstate commerce clause was the only close rival.) The Court, however, was slow in discovering its great potentialities, and this is understandable. Before the adoption of the Fourteenth Amendment this provision was already to be found in the Constitution, specifically in the Fifth Amendment. That amendment provides that persons tried for serious crimes must first be indicted, that they shall not be tried more than once for the same crime, nor compelled to testify against themselves in criminal cases "nor be deprived of life, liberty or property without due process of law." It had long been assumed by lawyers generally that just as the guarantees in the Fifth Amendment preceding the due process clause referred only to criminal cases, so too did that clause, and that it meant only that no person should be punished except in accordance with law and after a fair trial. However, in the Dred Scott case Taney applied the provision to a law enacted by Congress, the Compromise of 1820, holding that by prohibiting slavery in the territories Congress unconstitutionally deprived the slave owners of their property without due process of law.

In the Slaughterhouse case the counsel for the displaced butchers vainly tried to use the same argument. He asserted that being denied the right to engage in the cattle slaughtering business deprived the butchers of their property without due process of law. The next forward step came in 1877, in *Munn* v. *Illinois*, and *Chicago, Burlington and Quincy Railroad Company* v. *Iowa*, also known as the Granger cases, which paradoxically also represented the last futile effort to stay the rising tide of American capitalist economy.

RATE REGULATION AND PUBLIC PURPOSE

The railroads were in the lead in the rush to get rich after the war, and the methods they used for this purpose could not even charitably be said to have been characterized by high ethical scruples. In the agricultural West, particularly, grievances against the railroads were loud and bitter. The freight rates charged by the roads were considered by the farmers to be so extortionate that at times they burned their corn for fuel rather than ship it. Other abuses complained of included discrimination in rates and service, granting of rebates to powerful shippers and free passes to state legislators and other influential political figures, slashing freight rates at competitive points and making up the loss at non-competitive points, railroad control of grain elevators and warehouse facilities, retention of railroad land for speculative purposes, and corrupt activities in politics. Before the age of motor transportation the railroads possessed a complete monopoly on inland transportation and intended to enjoy all its fruits.

In 1867 Oliver H. Kelley, an official of the Department of Agriculture, organized the National Grange of the Patrons of Husbandry for social and educational purposes. With the panic of 1873 its interests quickly changed. Its local units, or granges, became forums for farmer protests against manufacturers of farm machinery, grain warehousemen and railroads. Within a few years state granges were able to capture several legislatures in the Middle West and secured the passage of what became known as Granger laws, setting maximum rates for railroads, grain warehouses and elevators. The constitutionality of these laws was challenged in a number of cases which collectively became known as the Granger cases, the most important of which was *Munn* v. *Illinois*. The decision was announced in 1876 by Chief Justice Waite, with a dissenting opinion by Field.

The challenge was based squarely on the due process clause of the Fourteenth Amendment. The refusal of the legislatures to allow the railroads and grain elevator owners to charge as much as the traffic would bear was claimed to have the effect of depriving them of their liberty and property without due process of law. The railroads and some of the elevator owners were corporations but the Court simply disregarded that aspect of the case and proceeded on the implicit assumption that a corporation is a "person" whose liberty and property were protected by the due process clause. Nevertheless, the Court held the laws to be constitutional. If property is devoted to a public use then it is subject to public regulation. Railroads and other carriers of goods or persons have long been deemed to be what are today called public service corporations, that is they serve the whole of the public and generally enjoy a monopoly for that reason. Grain elevators and warehouses, the Court held, are in the same category. Moreover, said Waite, it is for the legislatures, not the courts to decide what rates should be charged. "For protection against abuses by legislatures [in fixing rates], the people must resort to the polls, not to the courts."

Field, in his dissent, deplored the majority's decision. "If this be sound law," he said, "if there be no protection, either in the principles upon which our republican government is founded, or in the prohibitions of the Constitution against such invasion of private rights, all property and all business in the state are held at the mercy of a majority of the legislature."

Constitutional lawyers with a liberal bias have universally acclaimed *Munn* v. *Illinois* as great or almost as great as the Slaughterhouse decision. It is true that the Court upheld the power of legislatures to control monopolistic enterprises by regulating their rates, and in addition disavowed any judicial veto over the rates so regulated. Yet, examined more closely and more realistically, *Munn* v. *Illinois*, too, is not all on the side of the angels. Here but four short years after Miller had so thoroughly established that the sole purpose of the Fourteenth Amendment was to protect the newly freed slave, the lowly Mexican peon and the Chinese coolie, the Court, including Miller, accepted without debate a case involving neither slave, peon nor coolie. It took it for granted that the Chicago, Burlington and Quincy Railroad, as well as any other corporation, was a "person," an assumption the average, intelligent man on the street, unsophisticated in law, would find ludicrous. Lincoln is reputed to have asked a friend how many legs a dog would have if you called his tail a leg. When the friend replied, five, Lincoln said, no; calling a tail a leg does not make it a leg. The Supreme Court of the United States is more potent; if it calls the Chicago, Burlington and Quincy a person, it is a person. The only justification for the holding is that the term "person" was used in the Fourteenth Amendment in a legal sense, and lawyers understood it to include corporations. Historically, this is far from certain. But even if it were so, acceptance of the premise that the English-speaking people of the United States are subject to the esoteric meanings attributed by lawyers to words used in a Constitution adopted by all the people would mean that ours is a government not of men, nor of laws, but of lawyers.

Moreover, to paraphrase Tennyson, though much was given, much abided. The legislatures were authorized to regulate businesses affected with a public interest; but impliedly they might not regulate other businesses. They could not, for example, regulate the price of gasoline, ice or theater tickets—as the Court was later to hold. It was not until the great depression of the 1930's that the Court was to liberate itself from the shackles of this distinction and hold that in the interests of the general community the legislature could regulate the price of milk, even though milk dealers do not run railroads.

What was said of the Slaughterhouse decision is equally true here. *Munn* v. *Illinois* was neither a great decision, nor an evil one; it was largely a futile decision. That which was useful in promoting the Adams Smith-Herbert Spencer philosophy of economics enshrined by post-Civil War America was retained; the rest, in the main conveniently forgotten. Corporations remained persons after *Munn* v. *Illinois;* the due process clause continued to be available for the protection of business interests, and the prices charged by non-public businesses could not be controlled by legislatures. On the other hand, barely a decade passed before the Court was to hold that, notwithstanding Waite's brave words, it was for the Court and not for the legislatures to decide whether rates fixed by them were adequate to assure capital reasonable profit on its investments. This came about, however, after there were important changes in the personnel of the Court.

FULLER: THE MAN NOBODY KNEW

Chief Justice Waite died in March, 1888, towards the end of Grover Cleveland's first administration. (His estate was so small that a fund had to be raised to provide for his widow.) If at the time, Felix Frankfurter wrote a few years ago, "a poll had been taken among lawyers to determine the choice of a successor, I do not suppose a single vote would have been cast for Melville W. Fuller." Fuller's biographer, Willard L. King, was even more vivid in his description of the reaction to Fuller's appointment. "Many Easterners," he wrote, "persisted in regarding Fuller's appointment to this high office as somewhat comparable to the selection of a Dalai Lama, the great religious ruler in Tibet. When the Great Lama dies, the Buddhist authorities select his successor from the children in the country born at the time of his death, into one of whom his spirit has supposedly entered. A child of an obscure family from a remote part of Tibet is thus likely to be elevated to the most exalted office in the country."

The actual explanation for Fuller's appointment is much simpler, although in some respects hardly less bizarre. Fuller was not Cleveland's first choice; nor, for that matter, his second, third, or fourth, and perhaps not even his fifth, sixth or seventh. His first choice appears to have been Edward J. Phelps, then ambassador to Great Britain. But Phelps had done his job as ambassador to the British too well. He made speeches lauding them highly. While this is common and indeed expected of ambassadors, it infuriated the Irish vote in America. Patrick Collins, a Democratic leader in the House and later mayor of Boston, advised Cleveland that the nomination would not sit well with the Irish Americans; and since the election of 1888 was approaching, and the Irish generally voted the Democratic ticket, Cleveland discreetly decided against sending the nomination to the Senate.

Senator Joseph C. Blackburn suggested the name of John G. Carlisle, then Speaker of the House of Representatives and a powerful orator. At the time, however, Cleveland had doubts concerning Carlisle's integrity. "I won't," he said, "appoint a man to be Chief Justice of the United States who might be picked up in the street some morning." (Cleveland must have later changed his estimation; during his second term, he made Carlisle his Secretary of the Treasury.)

The President's next choice appeared to be Senator George Gray of Delaware. Twenty-seven of Gray's fellow Democrats in the Senate petitioned for his appointment, but the Democratic majority in the Senate was extremely narrow, and Cleveland felt he could not afford to lose as strong a man as Gray in the Senate.

While all this deliberation was going on, the election of 1888 was drawing closer. It promised to be a very close race and if, as it actually turned out, Cleveland were not re-elected, it was quite probable that the Republicans in the Senate would delay the confirmation of any of his nominees until the new President took over and could appoint a deserving Republican to this high post. The tightness of the election also convinced Cleveland that he should appoint someone from Illinois; when Davis of that state had resigned to enter the Senate, he was replaced by Harlan of Kentucky, and this affronted the Illinois political leaders who were thus left without a representative on the bench.

The leading lawyer in Chicago was W. C. Goudy. Goudy was also Democratic boss of the city, and Melville Fuller was one of his protégés. Goudy wanted the appointment, but he had two strikes against him, which in those days were apparently enough. In the first place he was a railroad lawyer, and Cleveland felt that the Court already had its full quota of these. In the second place, Goudy was sixty-four years old.

Woods had died in 1887 and to replace him Cleveland had nominated a former professor of mathematics and of metaphysics, Confederate Army colonel, senator from Mississippi and Secretary of the Interior, whose classically oriented parents had named him Lucius Quintus Cincinnatus Lamar. Lamar was then sixty-two years old, and there was a law on the books allowing a Justice who served for ten years on the bench to retire at full pay at the age of seventy. The Senate took the position that no man who passed his sixtieth birthday should be appointed to the Court, since, as had happened, senility might set in by the time he was seventy and inability to obtain a pension would deter retirement. (The incident of Hunt, for whom a special law had to be enacted, was fresh in the minds of the Senate.) Perhaps because of courtesy to a former colleague and the fact that Lamar was only two years past sixty, his confirmation was voted. But Goudy had not been a member of the Senate and was four years past sixty, and these facts convinced Cleveland that Goudy would not be confirmed.

The logical choice from Illinois was John Schofield, formerly member of the supreme court of that state and at the time a judge of the federal district court. He was of the right age and had all the necessary qualifications. Accordingly, Cleveland sent an emissary to Schofield to sound him out for the position. Tearfully, Schofield replied that he would give his right arm to be Chief Justice, but unfortunately he would have to decline. It seems that his wife, a woman of sterling character, was a child of the frontier and had never mastered the really unnecessary and decadent custom of wearing shoes. The emissary sympathized deeply with Schofield, but also agreed with him that it would just not be right for the wife of the Chief Justice of the United States to walk around the streets of Washington and attend Presidential receptions in her bare feet.

By this time it was already May; the election was drawing ever closer and Congress would soon adjourn. Cleveland was becoming desperate. Some years earlier he had made the acquaintance of Fuller and a modest, though far from close friendship developed. Fuller was used primarily as the go-between through whom Goudy transmitted to the President his recommendations on patronage, and through whom the President cleared with Goudy proposed appointments. Cleveland had also used Fuller to get reports on proposed appointments, and he had been consulted on and had warmly approved the selection of Schofield. Fuller was himself a lawyer, and while not on the very top rung of the ladder of success even in Chicago—the national newspapers had nothing in their "morgues" on him, and he was not listed in any national "who's who"—still he was fairly successful, was of the right age (he was fifty-five) and apparently had nothing against him. There was no time for further delay, so, first getting the embittered Goudy's reluctant endorsement, Cleveland offered the post to Fuller, and the latter accepted. And that is how Melville Weston Fuller, the man nobody knew, became Chief Justice of the United States.

Fuller's story is that of a young man who achieved success through hard work, perseverance, ability and marriage to the daughter of a bank president. Born in Maine, he attended Bowdoin College and Harvard Law School, and then, to forget a thwarted love affair, migrated to Chicago where he set up his law office. He entered politics, joined the Democratic party and served a short term in the state legislature. His law practice was insufficient to support himself, his wife and his two children, and even supplemented by the rents on his wife's real estate, he could barely make ends meet. Within a year after his second child was born, his wife died of tuberculosis. Mortgaging the real estate inherited from her, he was able to pay off his debts and construct a small building where he set up his office. His practice picked up slowly, but the real change occurred when he moved his residence opposite the home of the president of Chicago's largest bank. This proximity enabled him to meet, fall in love with and marry the latter's daughter. He soon became attorney for his father-in-law's bank, and from that point on his success was assured. His father-in-law, too, was active in Democratic politics, and

Fuller, under the mentorship of both his father-in-law and Goudy, rose to a position of leadership within the party and in the Chicago bar. Other than his stint in the state legislature and his election as a delegate to the Democratic national convention, he held no political office, executive, legislative or judicial, before he became Chief Justice of the United States.

FULLER'S FELLOWS

Fuller was confirmed before the 1888 election, but Cleveland's Republican successor, Benjamin Harrison, was able to make four appointments to the Court during his single term in the White House. Within three weeks after Harrison's inauguration, Stanley Matthews died and Harrison named David J. Brewer of Kansas to succeed him. Brewer was the son of Justice Field's sister, and had studied law in the office of David Dudley Field. He settled in Leavenworth, Kansas, and almost immediately became a judge in the state court. He was promoted to the supreme court of the state, then to the federal circuit court, from which, after five years of service, he was named to the Supreme Court. Brewer adopted the political, economic and judicial philosophy of Justice Field, and matched him in his ultra-conservatism. Early in his career on the bench he stated his philosophy succinctly. Dissenting with his uncle in *Budd* v. *New York,* he said: "The paternal theory of government is to me odious. The utmost possible liberty to the individual, and the fullest possible protection to him and his property, are both the limitation and duty of government."

After Miller's death in 1890 Harrison appointed Henry Billings Brown of Michigan to the Court. Brown's selection was urged upon the President by Howell E. Jackson, who had been Harrison's colleague in the Senate, and thereafter served with Brown in the federal circuit court. Before that Brown had been a successful lawyer in Detroit. Charles A. Kent, Brown's good friend and biographer, stated that Brown's life showed how a man "without perhaps extraordinary abilities," might attain "the highest judicial position by industry, by good character, pleasant manners and some aid from fortune."

Bradley died in 1892 and Harrison appointed as his successor George Shiras, Jr., of Pittsburgh. Shiras was a successful lawyer, numbering among his clients such important corporations as the Baltimore and Ohio Railroad. Shiras had no previous judicial experience and his appointment was strenuously opposed in the Senate, but in the end it was confirmed.

In the election of 1892 Cleveland made a successful comeback and defeated Harrison for the Presidency. Between the election and Cleveland's inauguration (then March 4) Lamar died after but five years on the bench. Harrison thus had the opportunity of making his fourth appointment to the Court in as many years. (F. D. Roosevelt was to go through his entire first term without making a single appointment.) Howell E. Jackson had been responsible for Brown's appointment to the bench, and Brown now reciprocated the kindness by prevailing upon Harrison to appoint Jackson to the vacancy. Although his native state of Tennessee remained loyal, Jackson himself held office under the Confederacy. In 1880 he ran as a Democrat for a seat on the state legislature and won by a narrow margin. Within a few days after taking office he found himself elected to the United States Senate (at that time senators were elected by the state legislatures). A deadlock had occurred and to the surprise of everyone a Republican legislator nominated Jackson, and to his own surprise as well he was elected. Thirteen years later he was again surprised to find himself elevated to the nation's highest tribunal, again by a Republican, the first Republican to name a Democrat to the Supreme Court since Lincoln appointed Field. Jackson was to live only two years after his elevation, but his last days were dramatic as well as tragic, as will be related later in this chapter.

In the summer of 1893 Blatchford died and Cleveland appointed Edward Douglass White of Louisiana. Of Irish descent, White had been educated in Jesuit schools and was a devout Roman Catholic. His father, a rich sugar planter, had been governor of Louisiana, and White inherited both his father's plantation and his avocation for politics. He served in the Confederate army, became a state senator, then a judge of the state supreme court and then a member of the United States Senate. Although he was named to the Supreme Court by Cleveland on February 19, 1894 and the Senate confirmed him the very same day, he did not resign from the Senate until March 8th, more than two weeks later. The reason for the delay was that the Senate was in the midst of a bitter debate on the continuation of the sugar bounty in which, as a sugar plantation owner, White was directly interested. (Actually, the bounty was discontinued, but as compensation the tariff on raw sugar was restored.) Even the Democratic New York *World* was shocked and called White's conduct "a disgraceful spectacle" rendering him unfit to be a Justice of the Supreme Court of the United States. White, however, calmly took his seat on the bench.

DUE PROCESS TRIUMPHANT

With the ascent of Fuller to the Chief Justiceship due process was ready to come into its own. In *Chicago, Milwaukee and St. Paul Railroad* v. *Minnesota*, Fuller's Court in 1890 struck a mortal blow at the brave words of *Munn* v. *Illinois* that "For protection against abuses by legislatures, the people must resort to the polls, not to the courts." When a public service commission fixes rates for a railroad, the Court held, it must not deprive it of its property without due process of law, and if it fixes rates that are not reasonable in that they will not enable the company to earn a reasonable profit, it is violating the due process clause of the Fourteenth Amendment. And, said the Court, it is for the courts (and, thus ultimately for the Supreme Court) to decide finally which rates are reasonable and which are not.

Two years later, in *Budd* v. *New York*, an attempt was made to maintain some life in *Munn* v. *Illinois*. A majority of the Court held that if the rates are fixed by the legislature itself, they would not be reviewed by the courts; but if they are fixed by public service commissions, they would be reviewed and set aside if found to be unreasonable. The effort was futile; the mortal blow had already been struck and all that remained was to bury the corpse. Brewer wanted to do it then and there. In his dissent, in which he expressed the economic philosophy in which paternalism in government was odious, he urged that *Munn* v. *Illinois* should be completely abandoned and railroads be given a free hand in fixing their rates.

The Court was not then willing to go that far; nor did it ever abandon the principle of *Munn* v. *Illinois* that rates fixed by railroads and other public service corporations were subject to governmental regulation. What it did do in 1894, in the case of *Reagan* v. *Farmers' Loan and Trust Company*, was to hold that whether rates are fixed by a commission or by a legislature, the Court will decide for itself whether or not they are unreasonable. And in 1898 in *Smythe* v. *Ames*, the Court not only reiterated the principle that all rates that are not reasonable are confiscatory in violation of the due process clause, but held also that in order for a rate to be reasonable it must assure the railroad or utility a fair return on a fair valuation of its investment.

These decisions enthroned the due process clause as a means whereby the Court asserted for itself the power, unknown in any other nation in the world, to pass judgment on economic measures adopted by the legislative branches of the government. Illustrations of how this censorial power has been exercised will appear in the next two chapters. But it must not be inferred that in all cases, or perhaps even the majority, the corporation or other business interest asserting that it has been deprived of its property without due process of law has prevailed in the Supreme Court; nor that the Court has ever accepted the complete laissez-faire philosophy urged by Brewer. Had it done so, it could not have survived. Indeed, its next great crisis occurred because it seemed to have lost all or most of its self-restraint in the exercise of this censorial power. In periods of prosperity, when the urge to make money fast is universal, the public has been quite tolerant in allowing the Court to use its power to prevent what it deems undue interference with the profit-making efforts of business. But even then, there are outer limits beyond which the Court may not transgress, as the Income Tax case, shortly to be recounted, illustrates.

A reasonable argument can be made that there should be an independent branch of government having the power and responsibility to step in when other branches of the government seek to confiscate the property of its citizens. What the Fuller Court did, however, was to go much further than merely claim the power to forbid confiscation. It held that even if the legislature does not confiscate a corporation's property, no matter how liberal a meaning is given to the word confiscation, but simply does not allow it to make as much profit in its business as the corporation would like to make, the Court has the right to step in and pass judgment. If the Court, made up overwhelmingly of persons who have spent their pre-judicial lives in defending corporations engaged in the pursuit of profits, feels that the legislature's action does not permit the corporation to make what the Court deems to be a fair profit, then the due process clause authorizes it to set aside the legislature's action. This was the contribution of the Fuller Court. It was Marshall's success in building up the Supreme Court to a high status of public esteem and acceptance that enabled the Fuller Court and its successors to exercise this economic censorial power without a major public protest until the great depression of the 1930's.

DUE PROCESS AND LABOR UNIONS

As the Court was expanding the due process clause as a judicial instrument for the protection of industry and commerce, it was severely limiting the potential use of due process as an instrument for the protection of persons charged with crime. Despite all learned efforts to prove the contrary, it is not likely that there was any substantial understanding, either in 1791, when the due process clause was written into the Fifth Amendment as a restriction on the federal government, or in 1868, when it was placed in the Fourteenth as a restriction on the states, that it would authorize the Court to invalidate laws regulating business. It was understood only to assure persons charged with crime that they would receive a fair trial in accordance with the law of the land. But it was to be a half-century after *Munn* v. *Illinois*—just about the time the due process clause was to lose its effectiveness as a protector of business interests—that it was to begin to acquire effectiveness as a protector of persons accused of crimes.

Waite was still Chief Justice when the Court stopped in its tracks any effort to make of the Court a censor of state criminal trials through the use of the due process clause. The case was *Hurtardo* v. *California*, decided in 1884. The Fifth Amendment provides that all serious crimes shall be prosecuted only after a grand jury has handed down an indictment. In 1879 California adopted a new constitution for the purpose of modernizing its government. One of the changes was to allow a trial of a felony charge simply after an examination and commitment by a magistrate. After a man named Hurtardo had been tried, convicted and sentenced for murder, his lawyer appealed to the Supreme Court on the claim that the right to grand jury consideration of an accusation was an aspect of due process of law within the scope of the Fourteenth Amendment.

The Court rejected the appeal. The Fifth Amendment specifically provides for indictment by grand jury (in federal court cases) as well as for trials in accordance with due process of law. If due process means that there must be a grand jury indictment in all cases there was no reason to spell it out specifically; the only logical conclusion was that due process was not intended to encompass indictment by grand jury. And if that is so, the use of the same term in the Fourteenth Amendment must be presumed to have been with the intent that it should have the same limited meaning. Since the Fourteenth Amendment does not specifically provide that a state must proceed by grand jury indictment, but only by due process, Hurtardo was not deprived of any constitutional right and must hang.

The logic seems irrefutable. The only trouble with it is that the same logic applied equally to judicial censorship of the regulation of business. In *Chicago, Milwaukee and St. Paul Railroad* v. *Minnesota*, the state of Minnesota claimed that it had the right, under its police power, to regulate railroad rates in the interest of the public. But, said the Supreme Court, rates cannot be fixed so low that the railroad will not make a reasonable profit, for the due process clause of the Fourteenth Amendment prohibits the taking of private property for public use without just compensation. But the same Fifth Amendment which specifically requires grand jury indictment as well as due process of law also expressly states that private property shall not be taken for public use without just compensation. If indictment is not encompassed in due process, logic requires a similar conclusion in respect to taking of private property for public use, which is also specifically provided in the Fifth, but not the Fourteenth Amendment.

The answer lies in history. As Justice Holmes said in what has now become a triusm, "a page of history is worth a volume of logic." In the history of the United States the major concern of the Supreme Court until the last quarter-century has been the protection of property rights. This is what Hamilton and his colleagues at the Philadelphia Convention of 1787 conceived to be the primary function of government. Hamilton's disciple, John Marshall, so shaped the Supreme Court that the judicial branch of the government could effectively carry out that function. Fuller's Court, as White's, Taft's and Hughes's after him, acted faithfully in accordance with that concept.

Another case decided by the Fuller Court illustrates the same conclusion. In the Chicago, Milwaukee and St. Paul Railroad case, and in *Smyth* v. *Ames*, the Court undertook to supervise closely the actions of state legislatures and public service commissions to make sure that regulated railroads and utilities were getting a fair deal, going so far as to involve itself in complicated financing and accounting problems, a function at which judges, no matter how learned, are not specially competent. But it is the business of high court judges to supervise criminal proceedings and to make sure that the accused gets a fair trial. Yet, in *Spies* v. *Illinois*, arising out of the Haymarket riot in Chicago, the Fuller Court decided that the due process clause did not empower it to impose the same censorial supervision over the criminal trial of labor agitators and anarchists as over rate regulation by state legislatures and public service commissions. (In the Sacco and Vanzetti case the Taft Court was to refuse to intervene on exactly the same grounds.)

A long, drawn-out strike in the McCormick Harvester Company culminated on May 3, 1886 in a riot in which the police killed or wounded a half-dozen labor demonstrators. On the following day, when the police broke up a mass meeting held in Haymarket Square to protest against this massacre, someone threw a bomb into their midst; seven persons were killed and over sixty injured. The actual perpetrators of the crime were never apprehended, but a criminal judge in Chicago held that anarchists who incited violence were equally guilty with those who threw the bomb, and accordingly eight known anarchists were arrested, tried and convicted of murder. One was sentenced to imprisonment and the other seven to death.

The convicted anarchists appealed to the United States Supreme Court. According to Governor John P. Altgeld, who examined the record of the trial very carefully, "the judge conducted the trial with malicious ferocity." There is no doubt that the judge allowed nothing to stand in the way of conviction. The record showed that he permitted some men to serve on the jury even though they candidly admitted that they had made up their minds before hearing a word of testimony that the defendants were guilty. One of the arguments presented by the anarchists' lawyers to the Supreme Court was that trial by an impartial judge and jury was one of the privileges and immunities which the Fourteenth Amendment protected against state infringement, but the Slaughterhouse decision had adequately taken care of that claim. As for due process of law, the Supreme Court simply could not supervise the details of criminal trials in state courts, and if the Illinois supreme court found that the anarchists had been fairly tried and justly convicted, that was good enough for Fuller's Court. (In 1894, Governor Altgeld, convinced that there had been a miscarriage of justice, pardoned the three defendants who were still alive, and thereby committed political suicide.)

In 1895, in the case of *In re Debs,* the Fuller Court was again to show that neither logic nor consistency with previous decisions seriously interfered with judicial protection of property interests. The case grew out of the bitter Pullman Car strike which originated with Pullman's refusal to discuss grievances with representatives of his employees living in the paternalistic model town of Pullman, Illinois. Under the leadership of Eugene V. Debs, the American Railway Union voted a boycott against all Pullman cars. The newly organized General Managers' Association of Railroads promptly championed Pullman's cause and transportation was paralyzed throughout the north. Richard Olney, United States Attorney-General, a former railroad lawyer whose loyalties to his erstwhile clients had not abated, prevailed upon President Cleveland to take action. The President sent a regiment of soldiers into Chicago, although Governor Altgeld protested that the state militia was adequate to preserve order and protect property. At the same time, Olney appointed a prominent railway attorney as special counsel for the federal government to go into the federal courts and obtain an injunction against the strikers' interference with the delivery of mails or obstruction of interstate commerce. The federal district judge in Chicago issued a blanket injunction which not only forbade interfering with the mails and obstructing the railroads, but also the urging of any worker to strike or stay away from his job. There is hardly the slightest doubt that the purpose for which the injunction was obtained was to break the strike, and it proved quite effective.

Debs deliberately defied the injunction. He was prosecuted for conspiracy, but the prosecution failed. Then he was held in contempt of court and was sentenced to six months imprisonment. He appealed to the Supreme Court, but the conviction was affirmed in a decision written by Brewer. Today the Taft-Hartley Law authorizes the federal government to go into court to get an injunction against strikes that "imperil the national health or safety." But in those days there was no law that permitted the government to intervene by injunction in a purely private labor dispute which involved the government no more than it involved any other shipper who used the railroads for transportation. This, however, did not deter Brewer or his associates.

Even if there is no law on the books specifically empowering it to do so, Brewer said, the government may sue to prevent an injury to the general welfare resulting from a strike's disruption of interstate commerce. But in a previous case involving the Credit Mobilier scandal the Court had emphatically rejected this same proposition. There, indeed, the federal government was directly involved for it had in substantial part financed the operations of the Credit Mobilier. Moreover, there Congress had adopted a resolution expressly directing the Attorney-General to sue both for the government and on behalf of the general public. Yet there the Court held the government could not sue, and here it reached a directly contrary conclusion.

The point of the matter is that while there are many factors which often restrict the power of the Supreme Court to decide a specific case before it the way its members would like to decide it, low upon the list are the prior decisions of the Court itself. No court in the United States is less hampered by the need to follow precedent than the Supreme Court. Actually, it is not too much to say that the Court has rarely decided an important constitutional law case in a particular way for no other reason than that it had been decided in that way in previous cases. There is, perhaps no better illustration of this than the Income Tax cases.

THE INCOME TAX CASES

During Cleveland's administration a bill was passed imposing a tax of 2 per cent on incomes above four thousand dollars a year. An income tax had been enacted during the Civil War and there was no question as to its general constitutionality. In *Collector* v. *Day* it had been held by the Supreme Court that the salaries of state officials could not be subjected to the tax, but as to others, there was no serious question that the law was valid, and taxes under it were paid, without challenge, until the law expired. However, a quarter of a century had passed since that decision, and financial interests felt that the Fuller Court might be more sympathetic to their grievance.

The strategy of attacking the law was devised by William D. Guthrie, a young New York attorney who was later to become one of the nation's leading corporation lawyers. The usual way of testing the validity of a tax is to pay the tax under protest and then sue the government to get the payment back. In this way the suit is between the taxpayer and the government. But Guthrie thought of a better way. The Farmers' Loan and Trust Company prepared to pay the tax on its income in accordance with the law, when Pollock, one of its stockholders, demanded that it not do so because the law was unconstitutional. Oh, no, said the bank, the tax is perfectly constitutional and like all good, law-abiding citizens we are going to pay it. Pollock then engaged an array of the highest paid counsel in the country to bring suit against the bank for an injunction to prevent it from paying this unconstitutional tax. (The value of Pollock's stock in the bank is not known; but it is far from improbable that the fees paid to his attorneys for bringing the suit exceeded it by many times.) The bank thereupon instructed its attorney to fight Pollock's unpatriotic suit, up to the Supreme Court if necessary.

The case reached the Supreme Court with almost phenomenal speed. Did the Court throw the suit out on the ground that it was a feigned case? It did not. It proceeded to hear the appeal and decide it with an alacrity rather unusual in cases involving constitutional issues of such transcendent importance. (In fairness, it should be noted that by invitation of the Court the Attorney-General had the opportunity to and did argue in defense of the law.) In April, 1895, within a month after the argument, the decision was handed down in the first *Pollock* v. *Farmers' Loan and Trust Company* case. Jackson was seriously ill with tuberculosis at the time and did not participate in the case so that only eight Justices passed on it.

All eight Justices agreed that insofar as the tax included income received from state or municipal bonds it was unconstitutional. This was but an extension of the ruling in *Collector* v. *Day*, which in turn had been an extension, or the converse of Marshall's ruling in *McCulloch* v. *Maryland*. To the extent that the tax included income on real estate, the Justices were divided six to two. Ever since *Hylton* v. *United States*, in which a century earlier the Court upheld a federal tax on carriages, it was universally assumed that a tax on persons or on *land* was a direct tax which, under the Constitution, had to be distributed among the states according to population (and not according to wealth). White and Harlan were of the opinion that a tax on the *income of land* was not the same as a tax on the land itself; that only the latter was a direct tax, and the former an indirect one which did not have to be apportioned according to population. The other six Justices disagreed, and the law was held unconstitutional in respect to land income.

The most important part of the tax, however, was the tax on general income. Stock in corporations is not real property, but, like a carriage, personal property; and if the Carriage Tax decision was to be followed, the tax on corporate income was constitutional. On this point, the Justices divided four and four. The procedure in the Supreme Court is that when the Justices are evenly divided, no opinions are written, no votes are recorded, but the decision of the lower court is deemed affirmed. Hence, it cannot be said with certainty which four Justices voted to uphold and which to invalidate the tax. Since White and Harlan had held that even a tax on real estate income is constitutional, obviously they were two of the four who voted to uphold the tax on personal property income. However, two days before the decision was announced, the Chicago *Tribune* printed a seven column story detailing what, it said, had happened in the Justices' conference room while they were considering the case, and predicted exactly what the outcome would be. Its report proved so accurate that there is little doubt that one of the Justices must have leaked the story. (This was not the last time that Justices would leak to the press accounts of what transpired in the priestly secrecy of their conference room.) In fact, when the decision was finally announced, some Washington correspondents, instead of sending a complete account to their newspapers, simply wired, "Chicago *Tribune* story all straight." The *Tribune* reported that besides Harlan and White, the two Justices who voted to uphold the law insofar as it affected personal property were Brown and Shiras. The *Tribune* was so accurate in all other aspects of its account, that it is safe to assume that it was accurate in respect to this one too.

The outcome of the first Pollock suit was unsatisfactory all around; it left the constitutionality of the main part of the law completely up in the air. Pollock accordingly made a motion, which the Court granted, that the case should be reargued and again considered by the Court. In the meantime efforts were made to get the incapacitated Jackson to resign so that a physically fit appointee could take his place and break the deadlock. The difficulty with this was that Jackson had been on the bench only two years and therefore was not eligible for a pension. Jackson's brother wrote to Fuller that a bill should be passed for his benefit as had been done for Hunt. Although such a bill was introduced, Fuller did not press for its enactment as he was informed that Jackson's end was very near.

But Jackson was not quite ready to die. Three weeks later he wrote to Fuller that his physicians were more optimistic about his chances of recovery and that no action should be taken on the retirement bill. After the first decision was announced, Jackson wrote Fuller that he felt sufficiently strong to come to Washington to hear the reargument and participate in the decision, and that his physicians had agreed that he could do so.

The case was reargued in May of 1895 and Jackson, who actually was dying at the time, sat through the argument. The decision in the second *Pollock* v. *Farmers' Loan and Trust Company* was handed down ten days later. In the short interval, however, it almost seemed that even if Jackson survived long enough to participate in the decision, there might again be an eight-man Court. During the night a week after the conclusion of the reargument, Field, then eighty years old, suddenly experienced such severe internal pains that he felt that his end had come. Writing to Fuller the next morning when he felt considerably better, the true conservative-to-the-end said: "What gave me additional pains was the thought that if I did not survive, our action in reference to the Income Tax case would be entirely defeated." Presumably a Federalist Providence had spared him, but there was no point taking unnecessary risks. Referring to his experience, he wrote, "I mention it to you simply to make a suggestion that it might be well, considering my condition, that the decision of the Income Tax case be announced as soon as practicable." Fuller accepted the suggestion and the decision was issued three days later. (Jackson died two and a half months later, but Field held on for four more years.)

When the decision was announced, it became known that Jackson was among those who believed the tax on personal income to be constitutional. With him, besides Harlan and White, was Brown. But that was only four. At the end of the first argument four of the Justices had held the personal income tax to be constitutional and with Jackson added this would have made a majority. Someone had changed his mind in the interim, and ever since historians have speculated who this was. If the Chicago *Tribune* account was correct, it was Shiras, and no evidence has ever been presented which effectively disproves the account.

The majority opinion was written by the Chief Justice, as is usually the practice in major constitutional cases, particularly when an important federal law is declared unconstitutional. The statement in *Hylton* v. *United States* and the widespread if not universal view of judges and legal scholars since then that the only direct taxes are capitation taxes (on each person) and land taxes Fuller held to be incorrect. (As a writer was later to say, the nation had unknowingly been going through "a century of error.") The fact that these judges and scholars included such renowned and conservative persons as Story and Chancellor Kent proved only that even the wisest and best of us can make mistakes. Under the Constitution, said Fuller, taxes must be uniform; and that means that as far as the federal government is concerned everybody must pay the same tax, not the rich pay more and the poor none at all.

Field wrote a concurring opinion (for convenience the two Pollock cases are considered as one) with the eloquence and fervor of one to whom protection of property and wealth was not merely the principal purpose of government but of life itself. "The present assault on capital," he said, "is but the beginning. It will be but the stepping-stone to others, larger and more sweeping, till our political contests will become a war of the poor against the rich; a war constantly growing in intensity and bitterness. If the Court sanctions the power of discriminating taxation, and nullifies the uniformity mandate of the Constitution, it will mark the hour when the sure decadence of our government will commence."

The dissenters, each of whom wrote a separate opinion, were no less fervent. Harlan's dissent was particularly emphatic. The result, he said, "is one to be deeply deplored. It cannot be regarded otherwise than as a disaster to the country." White, too, warned of the disastrous consequences of the decision.

The dying Jackson added his voice of disagreement. "The practical operation of the decision is not only to disregard the great principles of equality in taxation, but the further principle that in the imposition of taxes for the benefit of the government, the burden thereof should be imposed upon those having most ability to bear them. This decision in effect works out a directly opposite result. . . . It is in my judgment, the most disastrous blow ever struck at the constitutional power of Congress."

Finally, Brown:

The decision involves nothing less than a surrender of the taxing power to the moneyed class. . . . Even the spectre of socialism is conjured up to frighten Congress from laying taxes upon the people in proportion to their ability to pay them. [Joseph H. Choate, in arguing the case before the Court, warned that if it approved this law along with "its iniquitous exemption of four thousand dollars," then the "communistic march goes on."] While I have no doubt that Congress will find some means of surmounting the present crisis, my fear is that in some moment of national peril this decision will rise up to frustrate its will and paralyze its arm. I hope it may not prove the first step towards the submergence of the liberties of the people in a sordid despotism of wealth. As I cannot escape the conviction that the decision of the Court in this great case is fraught with immeasurable danger to the future of the country, and that it approaches the proportion of a national calamity, I feel it my duty to enter my protest against it.

King, Fuller's biographer, has set forth an interesting table relating the Justices' votes to the economic status of the states from which they came. When the income tax bill was in Congress all the wealthy commercial and industrial states voted against it, while the poor southern and mid-western agricultural states voted for it. Exactly the same thing happened in the Supreme Court, as can be seen from the following table.

Justice	*State*	*Wealth per Capita by 1890 Census*
AGAINST CONSTITUTIONALITY OF THE TAX		
Fuller	Illinois	$1,324
Field	California	2,097
Gray	Massachusetts	1,252
Brewer	Kansas	1,261
Shiras	Pennsylvania	1,177
FOR CONSTITUTIONALITY OF THE TAX		
Harlan	Kentucky	$ 631
Brown	Michigan	1,001
Jackson	Tennessee	502
White	Louisiana	443

In view of the exemption of four thousand dollars it is clear, said King, that no substantial part of the tax would have been collected in the home state of any of the dissenting Justices. This table may help explain Shiras' vacillation, for the per capita wealth in his state was higher than that of any of those represented by the Justices who voted for the tax, but lower than those represented by the Justices who voted against it.

Brown was, of course, right in predicting that Congress would find some way to nullify the decision (it did it through the adoption of the Sixteenth Amendment), as it always has when a decision of the Court shocks the conscience of the nation. The Dred Scott decision was in that category. So too were to be the decisions that sought to frustrate Roosevelt's efforts to cope with the depression. The Income Tax decision falls in the same class. Few decisions of the Court received such widespread and almost spontaneous condemnation from all but the organs of the top economic class. There was the usual talk of impeachment, of reconstituting the Court, of withdrawing its power to declare acts of Congress unconstitutional, etc. Coupled with the rate regulation and the Debs decisions it convinced the farmers and the workingmen generally that in Field's war of the poor against the rich the Court was on the side of the rich.

Even the legal profession, the most conservative of all professions, was amazed at the decision. The editor of the staid *American Law Review* asserted that "it appears, at least from one of the opinions which was rendered, that the Justice who rendered it [Field] proceeded with an imagination inflamed by the socialistic tendencies of the law, as involving an attack upon private property; a consideration which lay totally outside the scope of his office as a judge interpreting the Constitution. It is speaking truthfully, and therefore not disrespectfully, to say that some of the judges of the Court seem to have no adequate idea of the dividing line between judicial and legislative power, and seem to be incapable of restraining themselves to the mere office of judge."

In 1909, during the administration of William Howard Taft, Congress was debating a tariff bill, and one of the senators proposed to add to it exactly the same income tax bill that had been invalidated in the Pollock case. In support of the proposal, another senator said, "I am not one of those who regard the judgment of the Supreme Court as an African regards his particular deity."

The proposal was defended on the ground that the Court's decision was obviously incorrect and unacceptable to the people of America, that if the issue were again to come before the Court it would surely overrule its previous decision, and the way to bring it to the Court was to reenact the law. President Taft agreed that the Court's decision was wrong, but objected to the procedure of reenactment. "For the Congress to assume," he said, "that the Court will reverse itself, and to enact legislation on such an assumption, will not strengthen popular confidence in the stability of judicial construction of the Constitution. It is much wiser policy to accept the decision and remedy the defect by amendment in due and regular course."

Congress accepted Taft's urgings and went through the slow process of amending the Constitution, even though the cost to the nation by reason of the delay amounted to hundreds of millions of dollars. Such expensive deference to the prestige of the Court on the part of Congress and the people would have been inconceivable a century earlier. John Marshall had done his work well.

A postscript needs to be added here. When Jackson was away from the Court during his last illness, but before his return to vote in the Pollock case, he wrote to Fuller telling him that he had received from the Internal Revenue department a circular calling for a report of income in accordance with the recently enacted law. "Does that Act," he asked, "include our salary as members of the Supreme Court? Under the Constitutional provision that the salary [of federal judges] should not be reduced during the term of office can the salary or any portion thereof be taxed? It seems to me that it cannot. That Congress cannot do indirectly what it is prohibited from doing directly. What is your view and that of the members of the Court on this subject."

The Pollock decision made it unnecessary for Fuller to reply to the question. A later Court, however, could not avoid it. The Sixteenth Amendment nullified the Pollock decision and authorized Congress to levy taxes on income "from whatever source derived." If language can be made unambiguous and unqualified, this would seem to be it. But not to the Supreme Court. In 1920, in the case of *Evans* v. *Gore*, the Court answered the question put by Jackson to Fuller, and in a way which would have gratified Jackson had he been alive, for it adopted his reasoning. "From whatever source derived," the Court, in effect, said, means from whatever source derived except judges' salaries. (Other exceptions were also discovered. In the same year, the Court held in *Eisner* v. *Macomber*, that when a corporation distributes its profits in the form of stock rather than cash dividends, that does not constitute income within the taxing authority granted by the Amendment.) The reason this is so, said the Court, is that the Amendment was intended only to remove the requirement of apportionment, not to make taxable what previously was constitutionally untaxable. If you tax a judge's salary, you are reducing it in violation of the Constitution.

Holmes and Brandeis dissented on the ground that "the exemption of salaries from diminution is intended to secure the independence of judges on the ground, as it was put by Hamilton in the *Federalist*, that 'a power over a man's subsistence amounts to a power over his will. . . .' But this is no reason for exonerating a judge from the ordinary duties of a citizen, which he shares with all others."

The decision was subject to considerable criticism. Van Devanter, who wrote the opinion, said that the constitutional limitation was not for private benefit but "in the public interest." Henry W. Edgerton, then a professor of law but who later became one of the most liberal of all judges ever to serve on a federal court, commented drily that "the only interests which the decision served were those of the judges of the United States courts, including the Supreme Court, in escaping taxation."

Five years later, in 1925, the Court, in *Miles* v. *Graham*, extended the rule of *Evans* v. *Gore* and held that the salaries of federal judges could not be taxed even if they were appointed after the tax law had been adopted. Since, the Court held, the salaries of federal judges are tax exempt under the Evans decision, the salary to which the judge was appointed was the salary stated by Congress, undiminished by taxes. This extension caused Congress expressly to provide that the salaries for all judges thereafter to be appointed should be subject to income taxes. The efficacy of this statute came to the Court for determination after the Rooseveltian-induced Revolution of 1937, and in the 1938 case of *O'Malley* v. *Woodrough*, the Court, in an opinion by Frankfurter, not only upheld the provision but for good measure overruled *Evans* v. *Gore* and *Miles* v. *Graham*, so that today federal judges, no matter when appointed, pay income taxes just like everybody else. (Pierce Butler dissented sadly: "Another landmark has been removed.")

chapter ten

Harlan, Holmes and Hughes

Death came to Jackson shortly after the Pollock decision, though income taxes were not to come to the United States for almost twenty years longer. To succeed him, Cleveland appointed Rufus W. Peckham, a successful New York lawyer, who had become a member of the state's highest court. Peckham was a trustee of the Mutual Life Insurance Company and retained his post for ten years after becoming a Justice of the Supreme Court. He finally resigned from the company in 1905, but only because of public criticism resulting from a state legislative committee's investigation, conducted by Charles Evans Hughes, which revealed monopolistic and unethical, if not corrupt, practices on the part of the company.

Peckham's economic and political philosophy is indicated by his opinion in *Budd* v. *New York*, when that case was decided by the New York court of appeals. His forty-page opinion was written with scarcely controlled emotion. He attacked the statute setting rates for grain elevators as "vicious in its nature, communistic in its tendency." Speaking of the opinion in *Munn* v. *Illinois*, in which the Court noted that in England Lord Hale had long ago upheld the regulation of rates of callings affected with a public interest, Peckham, as Max Lerner points out, implied rather broadly that Hale's "paternalism" in economics was of a piece with his belief in witchcraft. (Brandeis later commented that Peckham's "major premise was God damn it," meaning thereby that emotional predilections somewhat governed him on many issues.)

Field was finally prevailed upon to resign from the Court in 1897, having achieved his ambition of serving longer than any Justice before him, including John Marshall. In his letter of resignation Field pointed out not only this fact but also that in his early years he had sat on the bench with Justice Wayne, who in turn had been on the bench with Marshall "thus binding into unity nearly an entire century of the life of this Court." After his letter was sent, it became known that President McKinley planned to appoint as his successor Joseph McKenna of California. McKenna, who was McKinley's Attorney-General, had been born in Philadelphia of Irish parents who migrated to California when he was eleven years old. He was educated in Catholic schools and entered politics as soon as he was admitted to the bar. He served as county attorney and state legislator, and was elected to Congress after having twice been defeated, reportedly because of his religion. In the House he became a member of the Ways and Means Committee and formed a fast friendship with its chairman, William McKinley. His political conservatism is indicated by the fact that he was one of the forty-one representatives who voted against the Interstate Commerce Act. Harrison appointed McKenna to the federal circuit court in California, and after five years service he resigned to join McKinley's cabinet as Attorney-General. His appointment to the cabinet, according to rumor, was motivated by McKinley's desire to rebut the reports that he was friendly to the anti-Catholic American Protective Association. McKenna had been reluctant to give up his life position on the federal bench for a cabinet post because of his lack of financial means to maintain his family in Washington, but was prevailed upon to accept when McKinley promised to appoint him to the first vacancy that occurred on the Supreme Court.

Before Field's resignation became effective, Chief Justice Fuller received a letter from a federal district judge in California protesting against the proposed appointment of McKenna:

> I know the estimate in which the Attorney General is held by the judges who were associated with him in the Circuit Court of Appeals in this circuit and what is said of his qualifications among lawyers who practiced before him. He had no standing at the Bar at the time he was appointed circuit judge. He had never been connected with an important case nor appeared in any Federal court, nor, as I am informed, in the Supreme Court of the state. He was without legal training, or knowledge or acquaintance with the literature of the law. Nor did he develop any of the qualities required by the office of judge during the time he held it. His associates in the Circuit Court of Appeals were under the necessity of revising his opinions and correcting his syntax and mistakes of grammar. I believe that such portions of his opinions as did not require correction will be found to have been taken mainly from the briefs of counsel. His capacity for work is shown by his record as judge. When he retired from the bench he left more than thirty cases undecided that had been taken under advisement by him, and these reached back over a period of some two and a half years.

A letter such as this has the tenor of having been written by one nursing a personal grudge against McKenna, a supposition which is not rebutted but perhaps even fortified by the writer's statement that his relationship with McKenna had always been friendly. In any event,

Fuller decided to check on the report and wrote to another federal judge (a Republican) on the west coast in whom he had confidence. The report he got back verified in all details the first letter. "My relations with Judge McKenna," the second judge wrote, "have always been pleasant and I bear no animosity toward him, but his unfitness for a judicial office is glaring and well known to the judges and lawyers of the circuit."

Fuller had no choice but to turn over these letters to McKinley. The President wrote back asking Fuller to see him. What happened at their meeting is not known, but it is probable that he told Fuller that he had promised the post to McKenna and could not go back on his word. In any case, the President sent the nomination to the Senate, where it evoked violent opposition. The press, too, was hostile. Said the New York *World*: "The man's unfitness by reason of a lack of learning, a lack of capacity, a lack of fruitful experience and a lamentable lack of that high integrity which is the most essential qualification of a Supreme Court Justice, is attested by the indignant protest of the judges and lawyers in his own part of the country." A petition was sent by a number of leading San Francisco lawyers in which McKenna was accused of being "slow and incompetent . . . a man of confused ideas" whose "record on the bench is disgraceful." Nevertheless, the Senate confirmed the nomination, perhaps because his deficiencies were somewhat mitigated when compared to those of some of the respected Justices then in the Court. Field was senile; Gray, suffering from kidney trouble, frequently fell asleep during argument of cases; and so too did Shiras who was himself entering dotage. McKenna had the advantage of comparative youth; he was only fifty-five.

One thing should be said for McKenna: he appeared to be fully aware of his own limitations. In his first years, he attached himself to his coreligionist White, a highly competent jurist, and generally voted with him when the Court divided. His associates were aware of his inadequacies, and in the beginning Fuller took care to assign to him the simpler cases to write opinions. Later, however, he showed considerable independence and a progressivism which would have shocked McKinley as Peckham's conservatism would have pleased him.

McKenna remained on the Supreme Court twenty-seven long years. His personal honesty was never questioned, and while it cannot be said that he ever became a great Justice, his career on the bench certainly belied the dire predictions made on his nomination. A real liberalism and integrity is to be found in many of his decisions and opinions. The career of McKenna, as that of Waite before him, seems to indicate that there is something in the Supreme Court and its traditions that brings out whatever latent capabilities its members possess.

TRUSTBUSTING AND THE COURT

The rapid pace of capitalist expansion during the last third of the nineteenth century began to provoke popular alarm. As Harlan said in a later decision, "there was everywhere among the people generally a deep feeling of unrest. The nation had been rid of human slavery . . . but the conviction was universal that the country was in real danger from another kind of slavery, namely the slavery that would result from the aggregation of capital in the hands of a few—controlling, for their own advantage exclusively, the entire business of the country."

Opposition to trusts and monopolies was not aroused so much by the aggressive and even corrupt practices which so often accompanied them—these were looked on with a tolerance characteristic of the frontier spirit of the American people—as by the fear that the natural resources of the country were being ruthlessly exploited and exhausted by a group of men who used them for the aggrandizement of their own fortunes. Effective, too, was the hostility of the rapidly growing labor unions to powerful corporations and the opposition of small farmers and of small businessmen, the latter often faced with a choice of surrender or ruin.

Beginning with the Populists, the cry that trusts must be regulated spread quickly among the western states, and state laws with that objective began to be passed. The demand then spread to the Democratic party generally and thence to the Republican party. By 1888 both major parties found it politic to include anti-trust planks in their national platforms. The result was that in 1890 Congress almost unanimously enacted the Sherman Anti-Trust Law. This declared illegal and made a misdemeanor "every contract, combination in the form of trust or otherwise, or conspiracy in restraint of trade or commerce among the several states or with foreign nations."

The Congress and the people had, however, not taken the federal courts into account. An attempt was made to dissolve the powerful sugar trust, which controlled 98 per cent of the sugar refining in the country. In *United States* v. *E. C. Knight Company*, decided in 1895, the Court threw out the government's suit.

The opinion was written by Fuller. The act, he said, can be constitutionally enforced only in respect to interstate commerce. Commerce is primarily transportation. Goods do not become part of interstate commerce until they start their movement from one state to another. "Contracts, combinations, or conspiracies to control enterprise in manufacture, agriculture, mining, production in all its forms, or to raise or lower prices or wages, might unquestionably tend to restrain external (i.e., interstate and foreign) as well as domestic trade, but the restraint would be an indirect result, however inevitable and whatever its extent." Since refining of sugar, like all manufacturing processes, is purely local, it is not part of interstate commerce and therefore the Sherman Act cannot apply to it.

Harlan dissented vigorously—but alone. He suggested that American capitalism had expanded far too greatly to be effectively controlled by state legislatures whose powers were severely limited geographically. It is quite clear that the Knight decision practically nullified the intention of the American people to control the trusts and monopolies.

In fairness to the Fuller Court it must be stated that its lack of enthusiasm for the Sherman Anti-Trust Act was shared by the first three administrations committed to its enforcement. Richard Olney, Cleveland's Attorney-General, believed the law to be "no good," and although the government's brief in the Knight case was signed by him, he was far from unhappy at the outcome of the case. It seems that there was, if not sabotage, then certainly no fervor in enforcing the act by the Department of Justice during the decade it was on the books before Theodore Roosevelt became President. The Department took the position that the act was aimed only at "unreasonable" restraints of trade and only against monopolies which were against the public interest. It is not surprising therefore that during Harrison's administration only four civil suits and three criminal prosecutions were brought under the act. In Cleveland's second administration there were six civil and two criminal cases; in McKinley's, three civil suits and no criminal prosecutions. By contrast, Theodore Roosevelt's administration saw nineteen civil and twenty-five criminal prosecutions; and Taft's, in a single term, thirty-five civil and forty-five criminal cases.

The Knight decision evoked anger among the people generally, but with the tolerance or apathy of the administration, the captains of industry went about their work of concentrating more and more economic power in fewer and fewer hands. In 1899 the Standard Oil Company was formed. At about the same time the Copper Trust and the Smelters' Trust were organized. The next year the National Sugar Refining Company came into existence with a capital greater than the total national debt in Washington's day; and at the opening of the new century J. P. Morgan completed the building of the United States Steel Corporation with a capital of more than a billion dollars.

Roosevelt was as earnest in his efforts to control the trusts as his immediate predecessors were not. Although he had little faith in the efficacy of the Sherman Act—it was, he once said, about as effective as a papal bull against a comet—he was infuriated at the federal courts for their hamstringing whatever enforcement the government attorneys sought to effect. The courts, he later said, "had for a quarter of a century been . . . the agents of reaction and by conflicting decisions which, however, in their sum total were hostile to the interests of the people, had left both the Nation and the States well-nigh impotent to deal with the great business combinations."

When, therefore, on the death of Gray in 1902, Roosevelt was called upon to appoint a Justice of the Supreme Court, he was as determined that the appointee should be sympathetic to trust busting as Lincoln had been that his appointee should be sympathetic to emancipation and legal tender. ("I may not know much about law," Roosevelt later said, "but I do know that one can put the fear of God into judges.") Roosevelt was attracted to Oliver Wendell Holmes, Jr., then chief justice of the Massachusetts supreme judicial court. Holmes was a scholar, and it was the destiny of Massachusetts to provide the Court with scholars: Story, Gray, Holmes and Frankfurter—the Court's four outstanding legal scholars (only Cardozo was on a par with them) all came from Massachusetts. But Roosevelt wanted above all to make sure of Holmes's views on anti-trust legislation. Fuller, White, Peckham and Brewer, Roosevelt considered hopeless, Harlan had dissented in the Knight case and could therefore be relied upon. There was hope for McKenna, Brown and even Shiras. The new appointee, therefore, might hold the balance of power. Lincoln had compunctions about asking a prospective Justice how he stood on a particular issue, but Roosevelt apparently felt less restraint. He wrote to his friend, Henry Cabot Lodge, to inquire whether Holmes could be trusted, and authorized him to show the letter to Holmes. Whether he did so is not known, but what Lodge replied to Roosevelt apparently assured him, for he did nominate Holmes. What kind of man Holmes was and what happened to Roosevelt's expectation must be deferred until we recount the Supreme Court's involvement in America's brief excursion into imperialism.

DOES THE CONSTITUTION FOLLOW THE FLAG?

William Randolph Hearst's declaration of war on Spain brought in its wake a number of consequences, not all of which were or could have been anticipated. One of them was the acquisition of the Presidency by Theodore Roosevelt. Another was the acquisition of colonies by the United States. America had no experience on either score and both proved to be rather trying, to America generally and to the Supreme Court particularly. Our concern for the moment is with colonialism in the country and the Court.

We had vowed before we fired the first shot that we wanted no conquests and no colonies; that our war was solely to liberate the oppressed Cubans, Puerto Ricans and (later) Filipinos from their Spanish tyrants. "Forcible annexation," said McKinley, "cannot be thought of. That, by our code of morality, would be criminal aggression." But that was before Roosevelt and his horseless Rough Riders marched up San Juan Hill, Gridley fired when ready and Lieutenant Rowan carried the message to Garcia. It is always easier to disown wealth before one has it. The American people engaged in a struggle with their conscience as brief as the one with Spain and the outcome was just as successful. "Manifest Destiny" and "Don't haul down the flag," were the battle cries of the Republicans in the election campaign of 1900, and to make the point even clearer the hero of San Juan Hill was chosen to run with McKinley. McKinley and Roosevelt scored a smashing victory over William Jennings Bryan and his anti-imperialism platform.

America was quite happy with its new possessions; but there were complications. Neither the Declaration of Independence with its sentimental romanticism about how governments derive their just powers from the consent of the governed, nor the Constitution with its provisions for citizenship and franchise, contained any guides for a colonial power. It was all fine for Cuba, Puerto Rico and the Philippines to become part of the United States, but they produced great quantities of sugar, and since the Constitution forbids any tariff on goods shipped from one part of the United States to another, this would mean that Cuban and Puerto Rican sugar must be admitted duty free—an outcome devoutly not desired by the newly established and judicially sanctified sugar trust. Moreover, the Constitution guarantees freedom of speech and trial by jury, and forbids cruel and unusual punishment. Did this mean that the bandit Aguinaldo could preach his insurrectionary doctrines to the Filipinos, or that Filipino criminals had to be tried by a jury (imagine a Filipino jury convicting a Filipino!) or that American soldiers could no longer use the "water cure" in pacifying captured Filipinos? In other words, does the Constitution follow the flag?

Naturally, under the American system, the answer to these questions had to come from the Supreme Court. In a series of cases known as the Insular cases the Court did supply the answer. At first it was a rather confusing and unclear answer, but in the end it turned out to be quite satisfactory to everybody (except, of course, the Filipinos and the Puerto Ricans). As Mr. Dooley pointed out at the time, the Supreme Court followed the election returns, and the returns in November of 1900 were quite clear and convincing.

The first of the Insular cases was *Downes* v. *Bidwell*, and the question before the Court was whether a Congressionally imposed tariff on imports from Puerto Rico to continental United States was constitutional. The Court was faced with the difficulty of overcoming a dictum by John Marshall that "The District of Columbia or the territory west of the Missouri are not less within the United States than Maryland or Pennsylvania." However, even Marshall could not stand in the way either of "Manifest Destiny" or of adequate protection for America's sugar growers. By a vote of five to four the Court upheld the tariff, although the five Justices could not agree on which theory gave the tariff law its validity.

A number of other cases followed, and ultimately a theory first presented by White was adopted in *De Lima* v. *Bidwell* and became the judicial premise of American colonialism. According to this theory, insular possessions are of two categories: incorporated and unincorporated; and what constitutes incorporation is to be determined by the

Court. Incorporated territories, such as Alaska before its statehood, are deemed part of the United States for almost all purposes except representation in Congress and participation in Presidential elections. Unincorporated territories, such as Puerto Rico, had less rights. Still they are not foreign countries, and therefore tariff laws do not automatically apply to their exports to the United States. But they are not part of the United States either, and therefore Congress may, if it wishes, enact laws imposing tariffs on their exports to the United States.

This may appear confusing, and it is. As Fuller noted, "If an organized and settled province of another sovereignty is acquired by the United States, Congress has the power to keep it like a disembodied shade, in an intermediate state of ambiguous existence for an indefinite period; and more than that, after it has been called from that limbo, commerce with it is absolutely subject to the will of Congress, irrespective of constitutional provisions."

Harlan, who dissented along with Fuller, Brewer and Peckham, expressed his concern in a letter to the Chief Justice. "The more I think of these questions," he wrote, "the more alarmed I am at the effect upon our institutions of the doctrine that this country may acquire territory inhabited by human beings anywhere upon the earth and govern it at the will of Congress and without regard to the restraints imposed by the Constitution upon governmental authority. There is a danger that commercialism will sweep away the safeguards of real freedom."

De Lima v. *Bidwell* was decided in 1901. The effect of the decision and others that followed and further developed the incorporation theory was that the tariff followed the flag to the extent that a lobby in Washington was strong enough to prevail upon Congress to enact a special tariff law for a particular commodity. Three years later, in *Dorr* v. *United States*, the Court was called upon to decide whether the Constitution followed the flag. The Fifth Amendment guarantees criminal prosecution of felonies by a grand jury indictment, and the Sixth assures a jury trial of the charge. Was a Filipino charged with a felony entitled to be tried by a jury? No, said the Court with only the redoubtable Harlan dissenting. Organic acts of Congress are the constitutions of the insular possessions, but Congress in passing them and the Court in interpreting them are completely bound by the Bill of Rights only if the particular territory is incorporated into the United States. If it is not, then the natives are entitled only to "fundamental" rights guaranteed by the Constitution; not to "procedural" rights. Trial by jury is in the latter category, and therefore, Sixth Amendment or no, residents of the Philippines could not claim trial by jury unless Congress enacted a special law extending that right to them.

The upshot of these cases is that America, during its relatively brief flirtation with imperialism, was able to have its pie and enjoy the taste too. It could pride itself on at last becoming a world power, along with Britain, France and the others. At the same time it was not unduly encumbered by such embarrassments as free trade and civil and political rights for people who not only did not possess the wisdom and civilization of citizens of Boston or Topeka, but did not even speak the American language. The Supreme Court helpfully provided America with a legal justification for this highly satisfactory solution of a difficult problem. The Court's decisions were subjected to criticism in the Democratic and anti-imperialist press, but there can be little doubt that they reflected the overwhelming sentiment of the American people in the two decades before the First World War.

THE APPOINTMENT OF HOLMES

If Oliver Wendell Holmes, Jr., had lived for no longer than what, at the time of his birth was the normal life expectancy, it is probable that few except a small group of legal scholars would have ever heard of him. Holmes was a state court judge before Roosevelt brought him to Washington, and his twenty-year career on the state bench was a successful one. A number of the opinions he wrote became important precedents in law, and his lectures on *The Common Law,* published in book form, became a recognized classic within the legal profession. But even there, his stature as an architect of civil law did not approach that of Cardozo, who left the New York state court for the Supreme Court at about the same age and after having served about the same length of time as Holmes. Cardozo's reputation rests primarily on his accomplishments as a state court judge; Holmes's as a Supreme Court Justice. To the average literate American in 1902 the name Oliver Wendell Holmes would certainly have meant the poet, not the judge. (Indeed, this was probably true even until his death in 1935; Holmes's fame really came after he died, as a by-product of the Court Revolution of 1937.)

A President can acquire greatness in a short time; Lincoln did it in four years (although he received substantial assistance from John Wilkes Booth) and Kennedy may have done it in less (with the same kind of assistance). A Supreme Court Justice needs many years to achieve fame even within the legal profession. Every one of the giants in the history of the Court—Marshall, Story, Taney, Miller, Harlan, Holmes, Brandeis and Black—served more than twenty years on the bench. A long life is an indispensable requisite for judicial fame, and Holmes was well blessed in that respect. He was sixty-one years old when the Senate confirmed his nomination and he was ninety-one when he retired. His place in American history is based on those thirty years.

Holmes's father was not only a poet and wit, but a physician and medical researcher with notable achievement to his credit. Holmes was brought up as an intellectual aristocrat in the highly cultured Boston circle that included Ralph Waldo Emerson ("Uncle Waldo"), Theodore Parker and Wendell Phillips. He attended Latin school and Harvard, graduating just as the Civil War broke out. He quickly enlisted and shortly thereafter received a wound in the region of the breast from a bullet which narrowly missed both the heart and lung. Returning to the battlefront after recuperation to take part in the battle of Antietam, he was again wounded, this time through the neck. After another leave from the war to be healed, he returned, only to be wounded again by a piece of shrapnel which splintered the bone, tore the ligaments of his heel and for a while threatened the loss of a leg. On the not unreasonable premise that three serious wounds were enough, he was mustered out of the army in 1864 with the well-earned rank of lieutenant-colonel.

After leaving the army, Holmes returned to Harvard to study law. He was admitted to the bar in 1867 and rapidly became prominent in his profession. Before he was thirty he became a lecturer in constitutional law at Harvard and assumed the editorship of the *American Law Journal.* Later he edited Kent's *Commentaries on American Law* and delivered a series of lectures which were published under the title *The Common Law.* The publication of the book led to a professorship at Harvard, but after one term he resigned to accept appointment to the Massachusetts supreme judicial court. He remained on the bench for twenty years, during the last three of which he was chief justice.

An assassin's bullet was responsible for Holmes's great career on the United States Supreme Court. As Gray's life was drawing to a close,

McKinley decided to appoint as his successor Alfred Hemenway, a leading Boston lawyer and law partner of McKinley's Secretary of the Navy. McKinley inquired of Hemenway whether he would accept, and upon receiving an affirmative reply, promised him the post. But McKinley was assassinated and Roosevelt did not feel himself obligated to fulfill the promise.

At the last moment Holmes almost lost the appointment for himself. On the centenary of Marshall's ascension to the Chief Justiceship, innumerable laudatory speeches were made, and Holmes, as chief judge of Massachusetts, was called upon to make one too. In this speech—a quotation from it appears toward the end of our chapter "The Reign of John Marshall"—Holmes seemed to belittle Marshall's reputed greatness, suggesting that it lay not so much in his own qualities as in his good fortune in being Chief Justice at an opportune period in American political history. This was almost sacrilege, and the super-nationalist President began to get second thoughts on the contemplated appointment. It was only on being reassured by Lodge of Holmes's soundness that Roosevelt decided to go ahead and send the nomination to the Senate, where confirmation came quickly and without difficulty.

Holmes's advanced age during most of his long service on the bench occasionally caused embarrassing situations. Like so many other Justices in their late sixties and seventies, he often dozed off during the lawyers' presentation of their cases. (In fairness it should be noted that many of the presentations of cases in the Supreme Court were so boring as to have a potently soporific effect even on younger Justices.) He developed a skill of knitting his brow as if in rapt attention to counsel's argument and closing his eyes better to concentrate, and under this mask of deep concentration, peacefully dozing off. On one occasion, a particularly long-winded attorney was presenting a tedious argument, and Holmes escaped into sleep. Some indefinite time later he opened his eyes. Astonished that the lawyer was still droning on, Holmes blurted out in a whisper loud enough for everyone in the courtroom to hear, "Jesus Christ!" replaced his mask of concentration and went back to sleep.

Roosevelt was able to make two more appointments to the Court. In 1903 the feeble Shiras resigned (but lived for more than twenty years longer). Before McKinley's death, when Roosevelt did not regard himself as a likely candidate for the Presidency in 1904, he had declared himself "in honor bound" to make William Howard Taft either President or Chief Justice. (All his life Taft said he would rather be Chief Justice than President.) After Roosevelt became President, and thus a candidate for re-election in 1904, there was an additional reason to put Taft on the Supreme Court: Roosevelt's political enemies within the Republican party were beginning to mention Taft as a possible candidate.

Accordingly, when Shiras informed Roosevelt that he planned to retire, the President immediately cabled to Taft, then governor of the Philippines, offering him the post. The latter immediately cabled back declining the offer, stating that he felt that he had to finish his task in the Philippines. Roosevelt wrote back insisting that he accept, but Taft was able to call upon the other commissioners and leading Filipinos to protest and Roosevelt had to yield temporarily. However, he did not give up. Of a sudden, Fuller discovered that he was about to retire. He woke one morning to read in the press a story from an unidentified source "close to the White House" that Taft had refused the appointment to Shiras' post because he wanted to complete his mission in the Philippines but that "Chief Justice Fuller may soon wish to retire and Governor Taft would be a suitable man for the vacancy." In all innocence, Roosevelt sent an emissary to Fuller to inquire whether there was any basis for the story that appeared in the press. Fuller, who suspected Taft of being responsible for it, refused to take the hint and replied that there was none.

Upon Taft's refusal to accept the Shiras vacancy, William R. Day of Ohio was named to the post. Day came from a long line of judges. His father had been chief judge of the Ohio supreme court, his grandfather a member of that court, and his great-grandfather chief judge of Connecticut. On his admission to the bar in Canton, Ohio, Day became a close friend of William McKinley, another young Canton lawyer. When McKinley was President, he made Day Assistant Secretary of State and then Secretary. In 1899, in accordance with his family traditions, he resigned to become a judge of the federal circuit court of appeals, where he served for three years until his elevation to the Supreme Court.

The second appointment was made in 1906 upon the resignation of Brown. Again Roosevelt offered the position to Taft, but this time he did not insist upon acceptance, as he had decided to make Taft his successor in 1908. Taft might have compromised on an Associate Justiceship, but his wife would not. Her heart was set on the Presidency for her husband, and while she might have been prevailed upon to allow him to take the post of Chief Justice, for which he yearned, she was not prepared to settle for less. Taft, to whom the prospect of the Presidency had become a nightmare, developed an acute and almost morbid interest in Fuller's health. He wrote to his wife wistfully: "If the Chief Justice would retire, how simple everything would be." But the Chief Justice would not retire, notwithstanding another storm of published rumors. Elihu Root remarked drily to the President that Fuller would "stay indefinitely" and that "they will have to shoot him on the day of judgment."

Unable to get Taft, Roosevelt appointed William H. Moody of Massachusetts. Moody had gained national fame as prosecutor in the case of Lizzie Borden, the Fall River spinster who took an axe and gave her mother forty whacks. He served several years in Congress, and was appointed by Roosevelt first to be Secretary of the Navy, then Attorney-General, and finally Supreme Court Justice. In the latter post Moody was able to serve only for three years, being compelled to retire because of physical incapacity. (As in the case of Hunt, Congress had to enact a special law allowing him to retire on full pay though he served less than ten years.)

RETURN TO TRUSTBUSTING

When Holmes arrived in Washington, he and Roosevelt quickly developed a warm friendship which, however, came to an abrupt end within two years. The cause of the split was the case of *Northern Securities Company* v. *United States*. J. P. Morgan and James J. Hill formed the Northern Securities Company as a holding company to merge control of the Northern Pacific and Great Northern Railroads. On direction of the President, the Department of Justice brought suit to dissolve the merger on the ground that it was a combination in restraint of trade in violation of the Sherman Act. An injunction was issued by the federal circuit court in Minnesota and the company appealed to the Supreme Court.

The injunction was sustained, but by the closest vote. As Roosevelt predicted, Harlan, Brown and McKenna, the liberal wing of the Court, upheld the government's suit. So, too, did Day, Roosevelt's then latest appointment. Fuller, White and Peckham, also as Roosevelt predicted, voted against the government. To the President's surprise, however, the swing vote was not that of Holmes but of Brewer. He voted to sustain the injunction, although he disassociated himself from Harlan's liberal opinion. He stressed that the scope of the law was limited to "unreasonable restraints of trade," but he agreed that the Northern Securities combination represented an unreasonable restraint.

Roosevelt was shocked to find Holmes among the conservatives. To add insult to perfidy, Holmes did not content himself with voting with them and joining in White's dissenting opinion, but insisted on writing a separate dissenting opinion which sounded almost as a declaration of war against Roosevelt's trustbusting efforts. The act, he said, was not violated merely because the owners of large blocks of stock in two railroads decide to form a partnership, any more than it would be violated if two small grocers decided to become partners. So long as they do not use illegal means to wipe out competitors, the fact that the indirect effect of their merger is to create a practical monopoly does not make the merger illegal. The last paragraph of his opinion could have been written by Peckham, and would have delighted Field. Harlan's opinion, he said, would "disintegrate society into individual atoms." If that were the intent of Congress in enacting the Sherman Act, "I should regard calling such a law a regulation of commerce as a mere pretense. It would be an attempt to reconstruct society. I am not concerned with the wisdom of such an attempt but I believe that Congress was not entrusted by the Constitution with the power to make it." (Naturally, Fuller, White and Peckham concurred in Holmes's dissent.)

Death spared Lincoln the witnessing of Chase's betrayal in the Legal Tender cases, but Roosevelt was very much alive when the Northern Securities case was decided. He was infuriated with Holmes. "I could carve out of a banana," he is reported to have cried, "a Justice with more backbone than that." Roosevelt was not a man to conceal his feelings. The honeymoon with Holmes was over, and Holmes was to know it. The incident, as Holmes wrote later, "broke up our incipient friendship, as he looked upon my dissent in the Northern Securities case as a political departure (or, as I suspect, more truly, couldn't forgive anyone who stood in his way). We talked freely later but it was never the same after that, and if he had not been restrained by friends, I am told he would have made a fool of himself and would have excluded me from the White House."

In the end it was Brewer who was triumphant in trust busting cases. In 1910 the government moved against the Standard Oil Company and the American Tobacco Company. Both were ordered dissolved, but in the Standard Oil case the Court finally and formally adopted Brewer's theory that while the Sherman Act went beyond transportation, nevertheless it outlawed only those combinations or agreements that "unreasonably" restricted commerce. Harlan, whose liberalism age did not wither, alone disagreed and issued his last dissent, which, as Charles Evans Hughes said, "was not a swan song but the roar of an angry lion." Harlan denounced the "rule of reason" as a piece of "judicial legislation" and "a perversion of the plain words of the Act in order to defeat the will of Congress." The Act, he said, unequivocally and unqualifiedly declared illegal "*every* contract, combination or conspiracy in restraint of trade, not every *unreasonable* contract, combination or conspiracy." But Harlan's protest was in vain. The "rule of reason" became the rule of decision in later cases, as well as the guiding principle for the Department of Justice in instituting legal proceedings.

POLICE POWER, DUE PROCESS AND LIBERTY OF CONTRACT

Perhaps the most notable constructive achievement of the Taney Court had been the extension of the concept of the states' police power as a means of justifying a judicial hands-off policy in respect to efforts to promote social welfare through legislation. The Fuller Court sharply restricted the scope of the police power, and for this purpose expanded the principle of due process by incorporating into it a new concept, called liberty of contract. Marshall had exploited the ban on laws impairing the obligations of contract for all it was worth, but the decision in *Ogden* v. *Saunders*—over his vigorous dissent—that a state insolvency law is valid in respect to debts contracted after its enactment, showed the limitations of that provision. The decision held that a contract cannot be deemed impaired before it is made, and therefore a law which restricts contracts to be made after its enactment is not unconstitutional under the impairment of contracts clause.

What was needed was some theory which would give effect to Marshall's dissent in the Ogden case, that is, would extend the impairment prohibition to future as well as existing contracts. The Fuller Court supplied the theory in 1905 in the case of *Lochner* v. *New York*, using the due process clause to police the states' exercise of their police power.

The progressive movement which flourished during Roosevelt's administration saw the enactment of laws in many states seeking to ease the burdens of the working classes. As part of its labor laws, the state of New York enacted a statute limiting the working hours of bakers to sixty hours weekly and ten daily, and declared it a misdemeanor for any employer to permit a baker in his employ to work more than those hours. Lochner was prosecuted under the act, fined fifty dollars and appealed all the way up to the Supreme Court of the United States.

In a five to four decision, the Court threw out the conviction. Peckham, writing for the majority, held that the law interfered with the right of the employer and the employee to contract with each other as they wished. The right to make a contract, even one to work for twelve or fourteen hours daily, is a part of the liberty which neither bakers nor anybody else can be deprived of without due process of law. Peckham rejected the argument that the statute was authorized by the police power of the state to legislate for the health and welfare of its citizens. The police power, he ruled, must be exercised within the limits of the due process provision, which means that the law must be reasonably related to health and safety, and it is for the Court to decide in each case whether a particular law is so related. Peckham and his four associates could not be convinced that a healthy baker would suffer unduly if he worked for more than ten hours a day or sixty hours a week.

Harlan wrote a dissenting opinion in which White and Day joined. Employer and employees, said Harlan, are not on equal footing and it is therefore unrealistic to say that the employees voluntarily contract to work for what the legislature found to be hours that endanger their health. It is for the legislature to decide whether ten hours a day and sixty hours a week is the safe limit, and unless the legislature's determination is clearly beyond reason the Court may not interfere. Harlan cited medical authorities, the New York Labor Statistics Reports and average hours of workers in foreign countries as well as other states all showing that work days for bakers in excess of ten hours were considered injurious to health. Hence, he said, the statute could not be said to lack a reasonable basis, and its constitutionality under the police power should be upheld.

Holmes, disappointing Fuller as a year earlier he had disappointed

Roosevelt, wrote a separate dissenting opinion which showed that he was a master stylist with an outstanding talent for penning aphorisms, and could write as imperiously for states' rights and liberalism as Marshall could for nationalism and conservatism.

> This case is decided upon an economic theory which a large part of the country does not entertain. If it were a question whether I agreed with the theory, I should desire to study it further and long before making up my mind. But I do not conceive that to be my duty, because I strongly believe that my agreement or disagreement has nothing to do with the right of a majority to embody their opinions in law. . . . The Fourteenth Amendment does not enact Mr. Herbert Spencer's *Social Statics*. . . . A Constitution is not intended to embody a particular economic theory whether of paternalism . . . or of laissez faire. . . . I think that the word liberty in the Fourteenth Amendment is perverted when it is held to prevent the natural outcome of a dominant opinion, unless it can be said that a rational and fair man necessarily would admit that the statute proposed would infringe fundamental principles as they have been understood by the traditions of our people and our law.

Then comes the magisterial dismissal not only of Peckham's majority opinion, but even more, perhaps, of Harlan's authority-laden dissenting opinion: "It does not need research," he said in a tone that would have done credit to Marshall, "to show that no such sweeping condemnation can be passed upon the statute before us."

Measured by the standards of constitutional law prevailing in 1905, there can be little doubt that Harlan's opinion is superior to Holmes's in everything but style and quotability. The underlying principle of both was identical: the Court should not invalidate a law enacted by a state under its police power unless it patently bears no reasonable relation to health or safety. Implicit in Holmes's opinion but almost explicit in Harlan's is the assumption that except in rare and extreme cases, the fact that a democratically elected state legislature has enacted a law in an area which has some relevance to health and safety is almost a guarantee that it is not patently unreasonable. Holmes rested on this implicit assumption; Harlan did not content himself with this, but in addition presented medical and statistical evidence to show that in fact the particular law in issue was reasonable.

Holmes's was the voice of the distant future, Harlan's of the more immediate future. After 1937 the Supreme Court would no longer delve into the factual basis of laws limiting hours of labor or otherwise regulating working conditions. If the statute is not irrational on its face—and no legislature in the past quarter-century has enacted so irrational a statute regulating working hours or conditions—the Court will usually not even consider the case but will dismiss an appeal without bothering to hear argument from the lawyers. Lawyers today rarely advise their clients to undergo the expense of an appeal doomed to failure. The Court today treats such appeals even more summarily than Holmes would have treated Lochner's appeal.

But the very fact that Holmes's was a dissenting opinion is conclusive proof that in 1905 the Court was not ready to accord such carte blanche to state legislatures. The era of judicial laissez faire had not yet arrived. For another thirty-five years the Court would still insist on being shown. States seeking to induce the Court to uphold their laws enacted under the police power would have to present factual evidence that the laws were reasonable. This was shown clearly three years later in the case of *Muller* v. *Oregon.*

The case involved the constitutionality of an Oregon law limiting the hours of women workers in factories and laundries to ten hours daily. To sustain the law in the Supreme Court the state of Oregon engaged as co-counsel, a highly successful Jewish lawyer from Boston, Louis Dembitz Brandeis. (Brandeis was engaged at the initiative of the National Consumers' League after Joseph H. Choate, certainly one of the nation's half-dozen leading corporation lawyers, declined the retainer. He did so because he could see no reason why "a big husky Irishwoman should not work more than ten hours a day in a laundry if she and her employer so desired.")

Brandeis presented a brief to the Supreme Court so different from any other previously presented to the Court that the type became known in legal circles as a "Brandeis brief." It contained but two pages of legal argument; over a hundred pages were devoted to an economic and sociological presentation of the case. Taking his cue from Harlan's dissenting opinion in the Lochner case, Brandeis presented to the rather surprised Court a vast array of evidence drawn from hundreds of reports, domestic and foreign, of legislative committees, statistical bureaus, commissioners of hygiene and factory inspectors, all showing that as a matter of fact long hours are dangerous to women's health, safety and morals, and that short hours result in social and economic benefits. (It should be pointed out, however, that to be on the safe side Brandeis' co-counsel submitted a conventional, legal brief.)

In the light of such an array of proof, even the Fuller Court could not hold that there was no rationality to the action of the Oregon legislature. In a unanimous decision the Court upheld the law. The opinion, written by Brewer, made special reference to Brandeis' brief, and incorporated a summary of its findings.

Brewer stated specifically that the Court was not overruling the Lochner case, but was deciding differently only because that case involved men while the Muller case concerned the weaker sex. But once the door was opened, it was not easily closed. In 1917, in the case of *Bunting* v. *Oregon*, the Court, in a five to three decision, overruled the Lochner case and upheld another Oregon law which imposed a maximum ten-hour work day for all mill and factory workers, men as well as women. As Brandeis, in presenting the Muller case, wisely decided not to rely on Holmes' magisterial "it does not need research to show," so too the attorney for Oregon in the Bunting case (Felix Frankfurter, another Boston Jew) played it cautiously and presented a "Brandeis brief" to show that long hours of work were injurious also to men.

THE COURT AND LABOR UNIONS

It is not easy to explain Harlan's opinion in *Adair* v. *United States*, a scant three years after *Lochner* v. *New York*. The Adair case involved the constitutionality of a provision in the Erdman Act, adopted in 1898 in an effort to prevent a repetition of the Pullman strike and to bring some order in the jungle of labor relations in railroads. A forerunner of the later Railway Labor Act, it sought to set up an arbitration procedure for the settlement of controversies concerning wages, hours of work, and conditions of employment on railroads traveling between states. One of its provisions outlawed the "yellow dog" contract (an agreement by a worker not to join a labor union) imposed as a condition for getting a job. Another provision made it a misdemeanor for a railroad or any of its agents to fire a worker solely because he joined a labor union. It was under this provision that Adair, a railway agent, was tried and convicted.

In a six to two decision (Moody being ill), the Court held the provision unconstitutional on the ground that it interfered with the liberty of both the railroad and the worker to contract that non-joining of a union shall be a condition of employment. The majority opinion was written by the same Harlan who wrote so cogent a dissenting opinion in the Lochner case. The difference between the two cases, said Harlan, was that in the Lochner case there was a direct and substantial relation between hours of labor and the state's police power to protect the health and safety of bakery workers, whereas in the Adair case there was no such relation between Congress' power to regulate interstate commerce and the joining or non-joining of unions by railroad workers.

McKenna and Holmes disagreed, writing separate dissenting opinions. Holmes's opinion is shorter, much better written and far more readable. McKenna's is superior as a legal opinion. (Holmes does not cite a single decision in his opinion.) Both are based on the same premise: that unsettled labor conditions can lead to strikes which in turn interfere with interstate commerce, and therefore Congress has the power to impose such regulations of employer-employee relations as will minimize the occasions for strikes. Holmes expressed his skepticism as to the real advantage of labor unions to workers, but, he said, that was a decision to be made by Congress, not by the Court.

In the same year (1908) organized labor suffered another serious setback at the hands of the Supreme Court, and this time without even the consolation of a dissenting opinion. In *Loewe* v. *Lawlor*, more popularly known as the Danbury Hatters case, the Fuller Court held that a union which organized a boycott against a company in an effort to compel it to unionize could be sued by the company for triple damages under the Sherman Anti-Trust Law as a combination in restraint of trade; accordingly, it upheld a judgment for a quarter of a million dollars obtained by Loewe and Company against the United Hatters Union.

When the Sherman Act was being considered in Congress, Samuel Gompers, president of the American Federation of Labor, was assured by the sponsors of the bill that it was not intended to and did not encompass activities by labor unions. Indeed, an amendment expressly so stating was prepared and had general approval, but was not pushed, primarily because it was felt unnecessary as the only purpose of the bill was to prevent industrial monopolization and price-fixing. Organized labor was therefore astounded and furious when the Danbury Hatters decision was announced.

Undoubtedly, by law and logic the decision of the Court was correct. No matter what may have been said by influential senators and representatives to Gompers, it is the duty of the Court to enforce a law as it is written, unless its meaning as written is unclear or ambiguous. The language of the Sherman Act was quite clear and unqualified; it said "Every combination in restraint of trade" is illegal, and it can hardly be doubted that a boycott of a manufacturer is a combination in restraint of trade. The union's grievance could only be that the Court was more scrupulous in adhering strictly to the words of the law when the defendants were labor unions than industrial or financial trusts. Fuller, for example, found the law much less clear and unqualified in the sugar trust case than in the Danbury Hatters case, and Holmes's dissent in the Northern Securities case is quite difficult to reconcile with his concurrence in the Danbury case. An industrial combination violated the act only if it "unreasonably" restrained trade—though the act does not use the word "reasonable" or "unreasonable"; but the test of reasonableness had no relevance where the combination was by unions seeking to establish a closed shop.

In the case of such comparatively respectable unions as the Railway Workers and the United Hatters the Court was content to authorize respectable countermeasures, such as firings or suits for damages. But the graver the evil, the more drastic the countermeasures required to meet it. With so militant a union as the Western Federation of Miners, mainstay of the Industrial Workers of the World (IWW), more drastic measures were called for, and in *Pettibone* v. *Nichols* and *Moyer* v. *Peabody*, the Court sanctioned them too.

In December, 1905, former Governor Frank Steunenberg of Idaho was assassinated by a bomb placed at the gate in front of his house. The Western Federation of Miners had been engaged in a campaign to unionize the miners in Idaho and Colorado, and Steunenberg had aroused their enmity by what they considered his oppressive hostility to them. Accordingly, it was immediately assumed that they were responsible for his death. George Pettibone and Charles Moyer, officers of the Federation, were seized in Colorado by state officials acting under orders of the governor, held incommunicado for several weeks without any charges and then shipped over the border to Idaho in a sealed and heavily guarded train where, along with IWW leader William (Big Bill) Haywood, they were indicted for the murder of Steunenberg.

While Pettibone and Moyer were in custody, they applied to the federal circuit court for a writ of habeas corpus on the ground that they had been illegally kidnapped. When the case came to the Supreme

Court, it was held (in an opinion by Harlan) that they were not entitled to habeas corpus since they were now being legally held for trial on a charge of murder, and it was immaterial that they had previously been kidnapped and held incommunicado by collusion between the governors of Idaho and Colorado. Only McKenna dissented. To his untutored mind kidnapping was kidnapping, whether committed by a common criminal or the governor of a state. To the argument of the majority that the kidnapping was past history and that habeas corpus could not be granted now since an indictment had been handed down and the defendants were now being held in lawful custody, McKenna asked how they could have applied for it earlier when they were being held under close guard and not permitted to communicate with anybody.

Ultimately, Moyer, Pettibone and Haywood were brought to trial and acquitted. Moyer then sued the governor of Colorado and the head of the state militia for false imprisonment. This time, when the case of *Moyer* v. *Peabody* reached the Supreme Court, even McKenna did not dissent. In an opinion by Holmes the Court held that in time of public danger the governor of a state has the right to act without resorting to ordinary judicial procedures; that he can declare a state of insurrection, call out the militia and, if necessary, order them to shoot to kill; and therefore he can take the less drastic measure of subjecting persons he believes dangerous to preventative arrest. So long as the governor acted in good faith, he cannot be held liable even if actually there was no real danger of insurrection (as there was not in Colorado at the time) and even if the person arrested had committed no crime and was in fact not a dangerous person at all.

Laws seeking to outlaw "yellow dog" contracts again came to the Court for adjudication in 1915 in the case of *Coppage* v. *Kansas.* This time a state law rather than federal law, was involved, and the law made it a criminal offense for an employer to require an applicant for employment to sign an agreement that he would not join a union. In a six to three decision, with Holmes, Hughes and Day dissenting, the Court followed the Adair case and held the law unconstitutional. The state of Kansas sought to justify the law as an exercise of its police power for the promotion of the general welfare, but Pitney, for the majority, held that its real purpose was that of "levelling the inequalities of fortune," and this, he said, the due process clause of the Fourteenth Amendment does not permit.

ALMOST CHIEF JUSTICE

The Supreme Court in the first year of Taft's Presidency was in a sorry plight. Four of its members, including the Chief Justice, were over seventy years of age. In addition, Moody was too ill to attend Court at any time during the October, 1909 term. The Court calendar was overloaded with cases which had grown "stale" as a result of the Court's slowness in handling its business. Taft was furious over the unwillingness of "those old fools" to retire. But ultimately even Supreme Court Justices die, and some retire. Peckham died in 1909; Fuller and Brewer in 1910; and Harlan in 1911. In addition, Moody's ill health compelled him to retire in 1910. The result was that in his single four-year term, Taft was able to appoint a Chief Justice and five Associate Justices to the Court. In a way, too, Taft was responsible for three Chief Justices. By his own being he was responsible for one, since he later became Chief Justice. He promoted White to the Chief Justiceship, and appointed Hughes to the Court, an appointment which must have in part at least contributed to Hughes's later appointment as Chief Justice.

Taft's first selection was Horace H. Lurton, a Cleveland-appointed judge of the federal circuit court of appeals, who earlier had been a judge of the Tennessee supreme court. Lurton died in 1914 and thus served only for four years. Taft's second appointment was a far more significant one.

Charles Evans Hughes already had had a brilliant career as teacher, lawyer and public servant when Brewer died. He had graduated from college and law school with highest honors. He interrupted a rapidly rising legal practice to accept a professorship in law at Cornell University. After two years he returned to legal practice, although he continued as lecturer in law at Cornell and later at New York Law School. In 1905 he was selected by the New York legislature to investigate the cost of gas. Shortly thereafter the legislature engaged him to conduct an investigation of life insurance companies, an investigation which resulted in a thorough reform of state insurance legislation and which earned him a national reputation. In 1906 he was retained by the federal government to investigate Sherman Anti-Trust Law violations by railroads engaged in transporting coal. In the same year he was nominated by the Republican party to run for governor of New York against William Randolph

Hearst. Although every other Republican on the state ticket was defeated, Hughes won and was re-elected in 1908. His administration as governor was distinguished by the initiation of far-reaching reforms, both legal and administrative, including the establishment of a public service commission, the enactment of laws protecting women and children in factories and the adoption of stricter election laws.

While Hughes was governor, Taft visited him at Albany, and two days later confided to a friend, "I don't know the man I admire more than Hughes. If I ever have the chance, I shall offer him the Chief Justiceship." It was quite probable that Taft would soon have the chance, for Fuller by this time was quite ill and not likely to live long. Unfortunately for Hughes, as it had been for Taft, Fuller delayed in dying. Brewer died before the Chief Justice, and there was therefore another vacancy to be filled first. Taft offered the position to Hughes, and, recognizing that Hughes was being widely talked about as a possible Presidential candidate, indicated in his letter that he intended to appoint Hughes Chief Justice on Fuller's death. Then, almost as an afterthought, he added that this should not be taken as a commitment. Hughes wrote back accepting the appointment and acknowledging his understanding that there was no commitment as to the Chief Justiceship.

When Fuller died a few months later Taft intended to give the Chief Justiceship to Hughes, going so far, it is reported, as placing the nomination in the hands of the Vice-President to be presented to the Senate when Taft would give the word. On Saturday, December 10, 1910, Taft called the White House reporters into his office to tell them that he had made a decision regarding the Chief Justiceship and that the nomination would go to the Senate on Monday. Toward the evening of the next day, a telephone call came to Hughes asking him to come to the White House. Then suddenly, something happened. Less than a half-hour later, even before Hughes had finished dressing, another telephone call came from the White House cancelling the request. The next morning, Taft again called in the reporters and told them that he was sending to the Senate the nomination of Edward D. White to be Chief Justice.

There never has been a satisfactory explanation for Taft's change of mind. What is most probable is that the switch came about as result of a visit to the President by six members of the Senate Judiciary Committee. Hughes, they said, had never argued a case before the Supreme

Court, and had sat on its bench only two months. The older and more experienced Justices, they said, would resent being presided over by a junior member who had just been admitted to the club. (It would have been different, if Hughes had not been a member of the Court at all; it was the usual procedure to name outsiders to head the Court.) That, combined possibly with a report by White's backers that the selection of Hughes would arouse the ire of Roosevelt, seems to have been responsible for what might be called the midnight non-appointment.

To fill the post left vacant by White's promotion, Taft appointed Joseph R. Lamar of Georgia, a former railroad attorney, who served on the supreme court of his state. On Moody's retirement, Taft appointed Willis Van Devanter of Wyoming, railroad lawyer, assistant Attorney-General and federal circuit judge, in that order. Van Devanter was later to become one of the four ultra-conservatives on the bench during Hughes's Chief Justiceship. At the time, however, he was moderately liberal and, despite his career as a railroad attorney, wrote an opinion in the Second Employers' Liability cases in 1911 upholding the right of Congress to regulate virtually every phase of the relationship between railroads and their employees. His chief difficulty was what his equally conservative and friendly colleague, George Sutherland, was later to call "pen paralysis" and what less friendly commentators were to call sheer laziness. During his long tenure on the bench, he wrote extremely few opinions.

On Harlan's death in 1911, Taft appointed Mahlon Pitney, a former congressman and a member of the supreme court of New Jersey. With Pitney's appointment, Taft's nominees constituted a majority of the Court. Two years later Lurton died, and Wilson, who was then President, appointed to the post his Attorney-General, James C. McReynolds of Tennessee. McReynolds at the time was considered a liberal, even a radical. But like Van Devanter, he was shortly to become quite conservative, and became the second of what irreverant reporters were to call "the Four Horsemen" of the 1930's.

LIBERAL INTERLUDE

With the confirmation of Hughes, the Court acquired a bloc of four Justices generally liberal in political and economic issues, Harlan,

Holmes, McKenna and Hughes. Harlan's death the year after Hughes's appointment quickly reduced the quartet to a trio. However, the three were sometimes able to enlist two or more of their associates to accompany them in a leftward decision, so that the half dozen years during which Hughes was an Associate Justice can be considered a moderately liberal period in the history of the Court.

The first major opinion Hughes wrote indicated in which section of the Court's political spectrum he would most often be found. The case, decided in 1911, was *Bailey* v. *Alabama* and involved one of the many peonage laws enacted in the south to subvert the Thirteenth Amendment's ban on slavery. Lenze Bailey, an Alabama Negro, had contracted to work on a farm for a year at twelve dollars a month. After about thirty days he quit and failed to return the fifteen dollars that had been advanced to him. Under Alabama law this was a crime if done with intent to defraud, and failure to complete the contract or refund the advance was considered prima facie evidence that when he received the advance the worker fradulently intended not to carry out the contract. Moreover, to make sure that some honest-looking Negro might not deceive an innocent jury, Alabama law provided that on trial the defendant could not rebut the inference by testifying under oath that he had really intended to go through with the contract when he made it. Bailey, under the circumstances, was naturally found guilty and sentenced to 136 days at hard labor for failure to return fifteen dollars.

Hughes's opinion for the majority of the Court struck down the law as violative of the Thirteenth Amendment. Charitably, he refused to impute any motive on the part of the legislature to evade the amendment's ban or to oppress. But, he said, these were the natural effects of the statute; it was "an instrument of compulsion peculiarly effective as against the poor and the ignorant, its most likely victims."

What is astounding about this case is not that a half-century after the Civil War two of the nine Justices would dissent and vote to uphold the law, but that one of these two (the other was Lurton) should be Holmes, who twice almost lost his life in that war. Not content with noting his disagreement, he insisted on writing a dissenting opinion that smacked of the kind of unrealistic legalism which might have been appropriate if Lenze Bailey had had a corps of Wall Street lawyers examine his contract to work for twelve dollars a month before he signed it.

In 1915, Holmes and Hughes joined in a dissent in the case of *Frank*

v. *Mangum,* in which the court held that it was unable to do anything about what was clearly a judicial lynching of a New York Jew in a Georgia mill town that reeked with anti-Semitism and hatred for "foreigners" from New York. Leo Frank had been convicted of murdering a girl who had worked in a pencil factory that he managed. The trial was held in such an atmosphere that it was apparent that the jury stood in danger of themselves being lynched by the mob should they have shown any inclination to acquit Frank. What was said in respect to the Haymarket riot case is equally applicable here: the untrusting scrutiny which the Supreme Court visited upon rate regulating commissions to make certain that railroads and utilities were being allowed a fair profit contrasts sharply with the trusting acceptance it gave to state courts' assurances that a lone, hated defendant had really received a fair trial. (Eight years later, in *Moore* v. *Dempsey,* Holmes was to have the satisfaction of writing an opinion for the majority of the Court which, for all practical purposes, overruled *Frank* v. *Mangum.* McReynolds, along with Sutherland, dissented and stated that *Frank* v. *Mangum* should be followed. "The fact," he said, consciously or unconsciously hurling back at Holmes his dissent in *Bailey* v. *Alabama,* "that petitioners are poor and ignorant and black naturally arouses sympathy; but that does not release us from enforcing principles.")

In 1915 too Hughes wrote an opinion in *Truax* v. *Reich* for the whole Court except McReynolds, declaring unconstitutional an Arizona law requiring employers to hire not less than 80 per cent of their workers from among American citizens. The equal protection clause of the Fourteenth Amendment, which applies to all persons and not merely to citizens, does not permit a state to deny to lawful inhabitants the right to earn a livelihood merely because they are not citizens.

During the same year, in the case of *Guinn* v. *United States,* the Court declared unconstitutional as an obvious subterfuge to evade the Fourteenth and Fifteenth Amendments, the so-called "grandfather clauses"—provisions in southern election laws exempting from the states' literacy requirements for voters persons who either themselves had been eligible to vote on January 1, 1866 or were direct lineal descendants of such persons. (Negroes were not eligible to vote in the south on January 1, 1866.)

Merlo J. Pusey, Hughes's biographer, summed up with fairness the Justice's achievements during the six years he was on the bench. "In protecting civil liberties," says Pusey, "Hughes had been more alert to realities than Holmes. By broadly interpreting the states' police powers, he had sought to make the law the servant and not the master of the people's will. Without jeopardizing federalism, he had taken the lead in forging the commerce clause into a potent tool for congressional control over the national aspects of our economy. One observer concluded that Hughes' opinions ranked 'among the most important and able pronouncements upon the principles of constitutional law that have come from the Supreme Court during its entire history.' "

Pusey is right too in suggesting that when, in 1916, Hughes resigned from the Court to run for the Presidency (a step he always regretted), "he was well launched upon what promised to be one of the great judicial careers in America." Hughes returned to the bench as Chief Justice in 1930 and retired in 1941. Had he served continuously from the time of his original appointment in 1910 until 1941, he might well have achieved the status, in the eyes of the legal profession generally, of the greatest of all Justices, not excluding Marshall. He had all the qualities of greatness, except long years of continuous service.

chapter eleven

Holmes and Brandeis Dissenting

BRANDEIS AND THE BRAHMINS

On January 28, 1916, Woodrow Wilson dropped a bombshell into the relatively quiet world of Capitol politics. Without taking a single senator into his confidence, he announced the nomination of Louis D. Brandeis to succeed the deceased Lamar. Perhaps most typical of the comments of the conservative press was the statement of the New York *Tribune* that it must be "a ghastly joke." But it was no joke; Wilson was serious and determined and throughout the period of more than four months during which the nomination was hotly discussed in the press and debated and redebated in Senate subcommittee, committee and finally on the floor, Wilson never wavered.

Brandeis was born in Louisville, Kentucky, in 1856. His parents were part of a small band of Jews from Bohemia who fled to America after the collapse of the Revolution of 1848. His parents became attached to Lincoln's cause and his maternal uncle, Louis Dembitz, whose name he received, was an ardent abolitionist. Although his father had established himself and become a successful merchant, he was wiped out in the panic of 1873, and Brandeis was compelled to work his way through Harvard Law School by tutoring youngsters. After graduation he practiced briefly in St. Louis but then returned to Boston where, within a period of ten years, he gathered a large and wealthy clientele and won a high position in the community.

Possessed of a brilliant mind, he was well traveled and had absorbed European culture. (Before his father lost his money, the family spent three winters in Europe, where Brandeis attended school.) Interested in the arts and music, acquainted with the Old Masters, he was taken into high Boston society as one of their own. He became a player-member of the Dedham Polo club, and when he married at the age of thirty-four, the first person to call upon his wife was the acknowledged leader of Boston society. There was no doubt about it. Louis Brandeis had arrived; he was one of the Boston Brahmins.

Then something startling happened. Brandeis suddenly became

plagued with a social conscience. This was not as surprising as it would at first seem; his family had always participated in progressive and reformist campaigns, but the incident that brought Brandeis back to reform appeared to be the bitter and bloody Homestead strike of 1892. He told his new bride, Alice Goldmark, that henceforth they were to live a frugal life so that he could devote himself in large measure to public service, and his wife, herself a reformer, readily agreed.

As early as 1890, he showed his legal brilliance in a path-breaking article, "The Right of Privacy," written with his law partner Samuel Warren. Later, drawn into a labor dispute as attorney for an employer, he became convinced of the justice of the workers' grievances and prevailed upon his client to effect a satisfactory settlement. From that time on he acted as "the people's attorney" in every controversy affecting the public into which he was drawn or entered. Out of his experience as arbitrator in the New York garment workers' strike, he drew up a protocol for continuous collaboration between the industry and the workers. His experience as counsel to the Massachusetts State Board of Trade enabled him to devise an arrangement for gas utility rates under which the stockholders were to receive increased returns on their investment as the rates charged to consumers were lowered. He initiated and launched a plan for savings bank life insurance, widely used today not only in Massachusetts but in other states as well, whereby insurance became available to the lower classes at a substantial saving in premium.

At the opening of the twentieth century he entered into the struggle over the regulation of railroad rates, and to prepare himself adequately he became a master of the subject of railroad management. When the New York, New Haven and Hartford Railroad directors, controlled by Morgan and Mellon, opened up a spectacular career of buying and consolidating, Brandeis, speaking as "the people's attorney" for the Public Franchise League, began a searching inquiry into their operations and disclosed the inefficiency of their monopolistic control of New England transportation.

He served first as counsel for shippers, then as counsel for the government in contests before the Interstate Commerce Commission over advances in freight rates. He wrote a series of articles for *Harper's Weekly*, later reprinted as a book, and *Other People's Money*, which exposed the monopolistic practices of bankers in business, and the inefficiency of their management, making recommendations later put into effect by the Clayton Anti-Trust law and the Federal Trade Commission Act. He became counsel for Gifford Pinchot and Norman Hapgood, then of *Harper's Weekly*, in their charges of waste and fraud in the disposition of public lands in the West and Alaska under the administration of Secretary of the Interior Richard A. Ballinger.

He presented innumerable arguments on behalf of public interests before law courts, Congressional and state legislative committees, and public service commissions. His argument of the Oregon hours law case was typical of many; in each case he prepared himself thoroughly and became a master of the subject before he argued his case. Somehow or other he also found time to become active in a leadership role in the Zionist movement and later, along with his close friend, Rabbi Stephen S. Wise, became one of the founders of the American Jewish Congress.

Had Brandeis devoted his tremendous talents and energies exclusively to the profitable practice of law, there can hardly be any doubt that he would have become one of the most financially successful lawyers in the history of the legal profession. (His earnings from his law practice before he ascended the bench averaged seventy-three thousand dollars annually.) Moreover, he would have retained the admiration and esteem of the Boston Brahmins who so graciously accepted him into their small circle. Instead Brandeis took a road which may have endeared him to the common people but certainly alienated the upper classes, who not unnaturally looked at him as something of an ungrateful renegade. When Wilson, on that calm Friday in January, announced that Brandeis had been selected for the Supreme Court, the fury of the wealthy and the conservatives broke out.

The New York *Sun* called the appointee "utterly and even ridiculously unfit." The New York *Press* called the appointment "an insult to members of the Supreme Court." In a more restrained tone, the New York *Times* complained that Brandeis was "essentially a contender, a striver after changes and reforms. The Supreme Court by its very nature is the conservator of our institutions." The Boston *Morning Globe*, summing up the case against Brandeis, listed four principal objections: He was "a radical, a theorist, impractical with strong socialistic tendencies." He was "given to extravagance in utterance, inspired by prejudice and intolerance." He was a " 'self-advertiser,' reckless in his method of seeking personal exploitation." And he did "not possess the 'judicial temperament' that would fit him for the duties of the Supreme Court judge." (The charge that Brandeis did not possess a "judicial temperament" was probably the single one most frequently urged against the appointment.)

Former President Taft, to whom the Supreme Court was a sacred shrine, declared that the appointment was "a fearful shock. . . . It is one of the deepest wounds that I have had as an American. . . . He is a muckracker, an emotionalist for his own purpose, a socialist." Taft joined a group consisting of the president and former presidents of the American Bar Association (which included, besides Taft, such prominent figures as Elihu Root and Joseph H. Choate) in presenting a petition to the Senate stating that they felt "under the painful duty to say that in their opinion, taking into view the reputation, character, and professional career of Mr. Louis D. Brandeis, he is not a fit person to be a member of the Supreme Court of the United States."

Not to be outdone, the Boston Brahmins presented their petition. Fifty-five of the top crust of Boston society, headed by A. Lawrence Lowell, president of Harvard University, sent a petition to the Senate stating that they did "not believe that Mr. Brandeis has the judicial temperament and capacity which should be required in a judge of the Supreme Court."

Walter Lippmann, writing in the *New Republic*, explained the opposition by the fifty-five Bostonians on the ground that Brandeis was "a rebellious and troublesome member of the most homogeneous, self-centered and self-complacent community in the United States." A Boston lawyer, Arthur D. Hill, who did not agree with A. Lawrence Lowell and his fifty-four cosigners, said that most of the feeling against Brandeis could be explained by the fact that he was "an outsider, successful, and a Jew." (Brandeis was not the first Jew to be proposed for service on the Supreme Court; Fillmore had offered a place on the bench to Judah P. Benjamin.)

There were, of course, counter-voices. The Democratic and liberal press warmly defended the nomination. A number of prominent lawyers—none quite as prominent as the presidents of the Bar Association—sent to the Senate a letter endorsing the appointment. At Harvard Law School, nine of the eleven members of the faculty disagreed with the president of the University and endorsed the appointment, and other endorsements came from a variety of sources. However, measured by prestige on the American scene, the opponents far outweighed the proponents.

The hearing dragged on for more than four months. But all the shouting and the tumult apparently signified nothing. In the vote in subcommittee, and again in committee and finally on the floor of the Senate, the division was strictly according to party lines—all Democrats (except one in the Senate) voted to confirm; all Republicans (other than the three Progressives) voted against confirmation. Since there were many more Democrats than Republicans in the Senate in 1916, when the final vote was taken, Brandeis was confirmed with ease, 47 to 22. On June 5, 1916, he took his oath of office and joined the Supreme Court of the United States.

Shortly thereafter, Hughes resigned from the bench in order to run for President, and Wilson appointed as his successor John H. Clarke of Cincinnati. Clarke had been a railroad lawyer and then a federal judge who was known for his liberal views. Whether or not Brandeis himself suggested Clarke to Wilson, he warmly applauded the appointment, and on the bench Clarke proved to be a foremost liberal.

THE RETURN TO DUE PROCESS

With the resignation of Hughes, the White Court in large measure returned to the spirit of the Fuller Court with its great concern for the protection of business and property interests and its use of the due process clause as a restraint on the reformist inclinations of state legislatures. Almost invariably, Brandeis found himself dissenting; usually he was joined by Holmes and, during the five years that Clarke was on the bench, also by him. Brandeis' dissents, like Harlan's before him, were radically different from Holmes's. They were far less readable, stylistically inferior, and almost completely lacking in the brilliant aphorisms on which the fame of Holmes rests. On the other hand, they were not written in the magisterial tone which characterized the opinions of both Marshall and Holmes. Where Holmes simply dismissed the economic conclusions of the majority opinions as irrelevant, Brandeis carefully mustered facts and statistics to establish their unsoundness.

He utilized his dissenting opinions as educational instruments in the field of social and economic realities.

The case of *Adams* v. *Tanner*, decided in 1917, is illustrative. The state of Washington, on the basis of a popular referendum, enacted a law prohibiting employment agencies from charging fees to workers, although permitting them to charge fees to employers with whom the workers were placed. Adams, operator of a private employment agency, sued in the federal court for an injunction to prevent enforcement of the law. The attorney-general of the state of Washington submitted a Brandeis-type brief and asserted that the business of employment agencies that impose their fees on the workers is "non-useful, if not vicious, because it compels the needy and unfortunate to pay for that which they are entitled to without fee or price, that is, the right to work." (Chief Justice White was not impressed by the weighty brief. "Why," he said, "I could compile a brief twice as thick to prove that the legal profession ought to be abolished.")

In a five to four decision, the Court held the statute to be unconstitutional. McReynolds, writing for the majority of the Court, asserted that while the abuses of which employment agencies were found by the legislature to be guilty might justify regulation of the business, they did not justify destruction, and forbidding it to charge fees to the workers in effect destroyed it. The right to engage in the business of employment agent is protected by the due process clause of the Fourteenth Amendment and the statute was therefore unconstitutional.

McKenna wrote a one-sentence dissenting opinion in which he stated that he deemed the law to be within the state's police power. Brandeis wrote a long dissenting opinion, concurred in by Holmes and Clarke, in which he paid little attention to judicial precedents (the only basis for the majority opinion) but stressed the economic and sociological facts that gave rise to the statute. Supporting each statement with text and footnote citations to reports and writings, he showed the widespread practices of charging extortionate fees, discrimination, misrepresentation of conditions of employment, fee splitting with foremen and many other abuses and oppressions. He showed that no less than half of the states had attempted to control the evils by one way or another. All in all, his opinion revealed the painstaking research into the factors underlying the controversy which had caused Dean Roscoe Pound of

Harvard Law School to remind the Senate Judiciary Committee that besides being a reformer, social scientist and economist, Brandeis was also "a very great lawyer."

Towards the end of the same year (1917) Brandeis again found himself speaking for the liberal trio of himself, Holmes and Clarke, in a case involving the rights of workers. In *Adair* v. *United States* and *Coppage* v. *Kansas* the Court had earlier held that neither Congress nor a state legislature could outlaw yellow dog contracts. In *Hitchman Coal and Coke Company* v. *Mitchell,* the Court went further. In a six to three decision, it held that an employer whose workers had signed a yellow dog contract could get an injunction against a union (the United Mine Workers) to compel it to stop soliciting the workers to join the union. The union could not do this, said Pitney, even if no violence or threat of violence is employed, because the agreement between the company and the workers was a legal contract, and by seeking to enroll the workers, the union was inducing them to breach their contract, and this the law would not allow it to do.

Brandeis' dissent challenged the correctness of Pitney's legal principles. But it did not stop there. It considered the vital need of strengthening the bargaining power of workers in bituminous mines and labor's need for security and economic independence. To the argument that by threatening to call a strike if the company did not agree to a closed shop, the union was guilty of coercion, Brandeis replied that "If it is coercion to threaten to strike unless plaintiff consents to a closed union shop, it is coercion also to threaten not to give one employment unless the applicant will consent to a closed non-union shop." In each case economic necessity is used as a lever to achieve economic advantages, and fairness would require that if its use by the employer is legal, so too should be its use by the union.

In 1921 Brandeis again had occasion to speak for the dissenting trio in a case restricting the right of workers to use the economic weapons of strike and boycott to improve the conditions of labor. The Fuller Court had held in the Danbury Hatters case that the Sherman Anti-Trust Law was applicable to union boycotts in support of organizational activities. To overcome this, Wilson's first term liberal Congress provided in the Clayton Anti-Trust Act that labor unions were to be deemed exempted from the act and that injunctions were not to be used in labor disputes except where necessary to prevent irreparable injury.

Samuel Gompers, president of the American Federation of Labor, called the measure "labor's charter of freedom," but he did not reckon with the White Court.

The plant of the Duplex Printing Press Company in Michigan had been struck by the International Association of Machinists in an effort to gain a closed shop, an eight-hour day and a higher scale of wages. The union announced a boycott of the company's presses and threatened strikes against those who purchased or handled the blacklisted presses. In *Duplex Printing Press Company* v. *Deering*, the Court held by the now usual six to three vote that notwithstanding the provisions of the Clayton Act, the company could get an injunction against the union forbidding it from boycotting its presses. In an opinion by Pitney the Court held that the act applied only to action by the workers employed by the company, and not to action by the sixty thousand members of the International who had no personal controversy with the company. Such action was an illegal combination or conspiracy in restraint of trade made unlawful by the Sherman Act, and not legalized by the Clayton Act. Brandeis wrote a dissenting opinion for himself, Holmes and Clarke in which he argued that the very purpose of the provision in the Clayton Act was to make legal union activity that the Supreme Court had declared to be illegal under the Sherman Act.

In *Hammer* v. *Dagenhart* the dissenting trio of Holmes, Brandeis and Clarke were able to convince McKenna to go along with them, but still lacked one vote to make them a majority. This was the first Child Labor Law case and involved the constitutionality of a law enacted by the Wilson Congress in 1916 to prohibit the interstate transportation of goods produced in factories in which children under fourteen worked or in which children between fourteen and sixteen worked more than eight hours a day. Many states had passed such laws, but many others had not, with the result that companies in the latter states enjoyed a competitive advantage. To equalize the situation, Congress enacted a law barring the products of child labor from transportation across state lines.

Mr. Dagenhart, the father of two children, one under fourteen and the other under sixteen, decided that the law deprived him and his children of constitutionally guaranteed rights and brought suit to enjoin the government from enforcing the act. The earning capacity of his two children must have been fabulous, for he apparently was able to engage a corps of the highest priced attorneys in the country to bring his case to the Supreme Court. With such legal talent, it is not surprising that he won his case, and his children were free to return to the factory and work ten and twelve hours daily.

Manufacturing, said Day for the majority of the Court, is not commerce, and therefore Congress has no power to regulate it. (So, it will be remembered, it was held in the sugar trust case.) True, here Congress was not directly prohibiting factory employment of children, but it was indirectly doing it by forbidding transportation of their product across state lines, thus making it economically impracticable to employ children. In three previous cases the Court had upheld acts of Congress which respectively forbade interstate transportation of lottery tickets, intoxicating liquors and women for immoral purposes (the Mann Act). These decisions did not faze Day and his colleagues. In those cases, he said, the evil remained to be effectuated when the interstate transportation took place: the lottery tickets were still to be used, the whiskey drunk and the women debauched. Here, however, whatever evil there was—assuming that permitting children to engage in lawful employment is an evil—has already been done. The coal mined or the clothes made by the children were not different from any other coal or clothes and were completely pure and innocent.

This time it was Holmes who spoke for the minority. Had Brandeis written the dissenting opinion, there would undoubtedly have been a mass of evidence to show that the evil of child labor did not end when the product—or what Holmes called "the product of ruined lives"—was finished, but that it continued and multiplied in the product's transportation to other states where it competitively compelled somewhat more humanitarian employers likewise to hire child workers. But Day's opinion was so obviously faulty (it is one of the most severely criticized opinions in the history of the Court) that Brandeis' acute economic and sociological analysis was unnecessary. More valuable was Holmes's eloquent and moving pen. After reciting the numerous precedents in which the Court had held that the power of Congress to regulate transportation was not limited by the fact that it indirectly affected local conditions, and that the wisdom and morality of legislation was for Congress and not the Court to determine, he said that "if there is any matter upon which civilized countries have agreed . . . it is the evil of premature and excessive child labor. I should have thought that if we were to introduce our own moral conceptions where in my opinion they do not belong, this was preeminently a case for upholding the exercise of all its powers by the United States, rather than defeating such exercise."

Hammer v. *Dagenhart* represents the nadir of the White Court. It must not, however, be assumed that during the generally conservative period between Hughes's retirement in 1916 and White's death in 1921 there were no liberal decisions. It was during this period that *Bunting* v. *Oregon,* which in effect overruled the Lochner case, was decided. In this period, too, the quartet of Holmes, Brandeis, Clarke and McKenna was joined by White in the case of *Wilson* v. *New* to uphold the Adamson Law, which established an eight-hour day for workers on interstate railroads. During the same five years, the Court in *Buchanan* v. *Warley* unanimously invalidated a municipal ordinance that forbade Negroes to occupy houses in blocks the majority of whose residents were white. It should, however, be pointed out in respect to the last case that the basis for the Court's decision was not the discrimination against Negroes but the principle that the right of a white owner to sell his property to whomever he wanted was a liberty of which he could not be deprived without due process of law. In other words, it was not the personal liberty of Negroes that the Court was protecting, but the property rights of whites.

These decisions were the exception rather than the rule. Between the time Hughes left the bench and Taft came to it, even a score card would not enable one to tell the difference between the White Court and the Fuller Court. (The Taft Court would be even more conservative.) During this period too the Supreme Court was for the first time faced with large numbers of cases involving the constitutional guarantee of freedom of speech and press, and in these political cases it proved to be as illiberal as in the economic cases.

CLEAR AND PRESENT DANGER

The First World War and the Russian Revolution brought in their wake an intense, though brief period of fear bordering on panic in the United States, similar, both in intensity and brevity, to the extreme fear accompanying the war between Revolutionary France and England in

Adams' administration and the Korean War in Truman's administration.

The intensity of the hysteria that pervaded the country during the First World War is indicated by some of the rumors that floated around and were taken seriously. A phantom ship sailed into our harbors with gold from Bolshevik Russia with which to corrupt the country; submarine captains landed on our coasts, went to the theaters and spread influenza germs. A German spy was landed by U-boat with large funds to engage in sabotage and assassination. (He turned out to be a law-abiding plumber from Baltimore carrying a bag of innocent plumbing tools.) Another spy was caught in a house on the beach one night signaling to German submarines. (He had to be released when it turned out that he was simply changing a light bulb in his room.) The Attorney-General told of hundreds of reports of fires started by enemy agents, infecting of foods with poison and ground glass, sabotage of Red Cross supplies, and similar activities. There was hardly a fair sized community in the country which did not report at least one German spy.

Throughout the country organizations and societies, with memberships running into the hundred thousands, were formed to suppress sedition and treason. One of them carried a full-page advertisement in leading newspapers from coast to coast offering to make every man a spy chaser on the payment of a dollar membership fee. None of these organizations uncovered a single spy, but they did cause considerable injury to innocent men.

The inevitable consequences of panic and hysteria are oppression and repression. So it was in 1798-1800 and was to be in 1949-1954. So too it was in 1918-1921. The only difference was that the second oppression and repression were more severe than the first and the third more severe than the second. In each case, the Supreme Court or its Justices became directly involved.

The first case to involve sedition in connection with the First World War arrived at the Supreme Court in 1919 after the war was over. This was *Schenck* v. *United States* in which Holmes, speaking for a unanimous Court, first expressed the famous "clear and present danger" test. A number of Socialists were indicted for having printed and circulated among men who had already been drafted and were awaiting induction into the armed forces a leaflet which argued that the draft was unconstitutional and that the government had no power to send American citizens to kill the people of other lands. It contained a good deal of similar language regarding the cold-blooded ruthlessness of mercenary capitalist Wall Street and urged the recipients to "assert your rights" and not to allow themselves to be intimidated. There was nothing in the leaflet urging the recipients to resist conscription, nor was any evidence presented to show that anyone who had received the leaflet had actually refused to report for induction.

Nevertheless, the Socialists' claim that the conviction violated their constitutional right of free speech was rejected and the conviction upheld. The most stringent protection of free speech, said Holmes, would not protect a man from the penal consequences of falsely shouting "Fire!" in a theater and thus causing a panic. The question in every case is whether the words used are used in such circumstances and are of such a nature as to create a clear and present danger that they will bring about evils that Congress has a right to prevent. It is a question of proximity and degree. Here there was a clear and present danger that some of the recipients of the leaflet would in fact be induced by it to resist induction into the armed forces, and therefore penalizing the language does not violate the First Amendment.

The clear and present danger test has been widely hailed as a great, libertarian contribution to constitutional rights. Yet it should be noted that actually it represented a retreat. Jefferson, in his Virginia Statute for Religious Liberty, had stated that "it is time enough for the rightful purposes of civil government for its officers to interfere when principles break out into overt acts against peace and good order." According to the Holmes formula, civil government could rightfully interfere when there was a clear and present danger that overt acts would break out, even though they have not yet done so. The ban of the First Amendment on laws abridging freedom of speech is absolute; it makes no exception for speech that presents a clear and present danger. At best the clear and present danger test is a compromise, intended to afford some constitutional check on the power of government to punish speech it deems evil.

Realistically, it can hardly be expected that any formula of words can protect the liberties of a detested and feared minority in a period of panic. The Court after the First World War quickly forgot about the test almost as soon as it was formulated and uniformly affirmed all convictions of Socialists, Communists, pacifists and assorted radicals.

(Thirty years later, lip service was paid to the test, but the practical results were the same.) It was enough for the Court that the defendants had an evil intent and that their words had a tendency, no matter how remote, to cause evil deeds.

In one case, Eugene V. Debs, oft-time Socialist candidate for the Presidency, was convicted of attempting to cause insubordination in the armed forces and to obstruct recruiting. The conviction was based on a speech Debs had made at a Socialist convention in which he denounced capitalism and pointed to the war as one of its evils. During the course of the speech he praised a number of individuals who had been convicted of resisting the draft. Perhaps his most extreme statement was: "You need to know that you are fit for something better than slavery and cannon fodder." The Supreme Court, in *Debs* v. *United States*, affirmed the conviction. The unanimous opinion was written by none other than Holmes himself, and in it he made no mention, other than a simple citation of the Schenck case, of the very clear and present test that he had announced but a week earlier, relying instead on evil tendency and evil intent. Debs began his ten-year sentence when he was sixty-three years old, and the following year polled almost a million votes for the Presidency. His sentence was commuted in 1921 by President Harding.

In *Schaefer* v. *United States*, the editors of a German-language newspaper were convicted of making false statements with the intent to interfere with the government's military operations and to promote the success of its enemies. Their offense consisted in the publication of an editorial entitled "Yankee Bluff" which derided American war efforts. The Supreme Court affirmed the conviction, finding that the derision of American efforts could have had evil influence in that it might have chilled the ardor of patriotism of some readers and caused them to relax their war efforts. That, said the Court, must have been the evil intent of the defendants, and although it could not be shown that the article actually had that effect, it was enough to show that such might be its tendency. Brandeis, Holmes and Clarke dissented.

In *Pierce* v. *United States*, the Court upheld the conviction of three Socialists who had distributed a pacifist pamphlet written by a prominent Episcopal clergyman. The defendants were charged with making false statements, in violation of the Espionage Act, in that the pamphlet asserted: "Our entry into it [the war] was determined by the certainty that if the allies did not win, J. P. Morgan's loans to the allies would be repudiated, and those American investors who bet on his promises would be hooked." The Court held that the government did not have to prove the untruth of this statement, since its untruth was known to the jury as to all loyal Americans. Moreover, the statement was so obviously false that it could not be doubted that the defendants knew it was false and therefore acted with an evil mind in circulating it. As for the evil effect of the publication, the Court held that the jury's finding that it would have a natural tendency to cause insubordination, disloyalty, and refusal to enlist was conclusive, and it was not necessary to prove that any particular person was in fact influenced by the pamphlets to act disloyally or resist the draft. Brandeis and Holmes dissented.

In *Abrams* v. *United States*, the defendants, five young men and a young woman, were indicted on the basis of two sets of poorly printed leaflets, one in English and the other in Yiddish, which they threw out of the window of a loft building on Houston Street in lower New York City. The leaflets, denouncing President Wilson for sending American troops into Russia, stated: "Workers in the ammunition factories, you are producing bullets, bayonets, cannon, to murder not only the Germans, but also your dearest, best, who are in Russia and are fighting for freedom." One of the pamphlets, signed "Revolutionists," ended with the call: "Awake! Awake! You Workers of the World!" It added: "P.S. It is absurd to call us pro-German. We hate and despise German militarism more than do your hypocritical tyrants. We have more reason for denouncing German militarism than has the coward in the White House."

The Supreme Court affirmed the conviction on the ground that the plain purpose of the leaflets was to incite dissatisfaction, sedition, riots, and revolution for the purpose of obstructing the government's military efforts in Europe. Of course, if that was their purpose it was evil enough; and it mattered little that there was nary a chance that their purpose would be achieved by the quixotic act of throwing a fistful of hand-printed leaflets into the air. Recognizing that under the Court's decisions the test of guilt was evil intent, counsel for the misguided young would-be revolutionaries contended that it was not their purpose to hinder the war against Germany. They were, he claimed, as opposed to the German government as was the federal court (which was to convict them) and the Supreme Court (which was to affirm the conviction). Their sole purpose was to create disaffection from the government's policy of sending the armed forces to suppress the revolution in Russia, a country with which we were not at war and presumably on friendly terms.

Of this argument the Court made short shrift. A worker in a munitions factory, it said, could not possibly know whether the particular shell he was making would go to Germany or to Russia, and if he refused to make it because he believed it would go to Russia, he was obstructing the war effort if the shell was actually intended for Germany. The defendants must have known this, and therefore they had an evil purpose and an evil mind and were rightfully convicted.

Holmes wrote what undoubtedly was his most eloquent and most famous dissent. If Holmes's reputation as a great liberal rests upon any one opinion it is upon his dissent in the Abrams case:

> In this case sentences of 20 years imprisonment have been imposed for the publishing of two leaflets that I believe the defendants had as much right to publish as the Government had to publish the Constitution of the United States now vainly invoked by them. . . . When men have realized that time has upset many fighting faiths, they may come to believe even more than they believe the very foundations of their own conduct that the ultimate good desired is better reached by free trade in ideas—that the best test of truth is the power of the thought to get itself accepted in the competition of the market.

Brandeis concurred in the dissent.

It could not be expected that, during the period of intense fear and patriotism coming with the declaration of war, juries would often acquit defendants charged with obstructing the war effort or committing sedition against the United States. Acquittals by juries, if there were any at all, were as rare as under the Sedition Act of 1798. But a more dispassionate and courageous reaction might have been expected from the Supreme Court, particularly as all the cases reached it after fighting had ended and the United States had emerged victorious. How the Court actually reacted is best summarized in the following sentence from Clarke's dissent in the Schaefer case, a sentence no less applicable to all the Court's decisions in the First World War's sedition cases: "To me it seems simply a case of flagrant mistrial, likely to result in disgrace and great injustice, probably in life imprisonment for two old men, because this Court hesitates to exercise the power, which it undoubtedly possesses, to correct, in this calmer time, errors of law which would not have been committed but for the stress and strain of feeling prevailing in the early months of the late deplorable war."

In short, if the Supreme Court was the guardian of individual liberties, it failed miserably in the fulfillment of its function during the period immediately following the First World War. Apparently the only case in which the Court reversed a conviction was one in which the Attorney-General himself asked it to because he became convinced that the defendants (some twenty-seven South Dakota farmers who had petitioned government officials that the draft quota for their county was too high) should never have been indicted in the first place, much less convicted. But the truth of the matter is that the Court was not then the guardian of personal liberties; it would be almost another score of years before the Court would fully assume that office. In 1920 the Supreme Court was still what Marshall had conceived it to be—the protector and gaurdian of property. And that was to be its role during the decade in which William Howard Taft was Chief Justice.

TAFT BECOMES CHIEF JUSTICE

Taft once said that his idea of heaven was a great court inhabited exclusively by angelic judges. Taft was thus the only mortal known to history who attained not only heaven but the heaven of heavens—for he presided over this angelic court—ten years before his death. Yet, it must be admitted that if anyone merited achieving heaven on earth, Taft did. No man desired the position of Chief Justice more than Taft, none was more qualified or worked harder and more patiently to attain it.

Almost from the time he graduated from Yale, Taft set his heart on becoming a member of the Supreme Court. His almost worshipful attitude toward judges is well reflected in his comment that it was well that the judge should be clothed in a robe not only to indicate to the general public that his function is "different from and higher than that which man discharges as a citizen in the ordinary walks of life; but also in order to impress the judge himself with the constant consciousness that he is a high-priest in the temple of justice and is surrounded with obligations of a sacred character."

Taft was graduated from Cincinnati Law School in 1880 at the age of twenty-three and immediately entered politics. Within a year he became assistant county prosecutor, and then in quick succession assistant county solicitor and superior court judge. The Republican Benjamin Harrison succeeded the Democratic Grover Cleveland in 1889 and immediately Taft, then only thirty-two years old and but nine years out of law school, began pulling strings for an appointment to the Supreme Court. Although he had the ardent backing of the governor of Ohio, Taft had to settle for becoming United States Solicitor-General. While this post is below that of Attorney-General and does not entail a place in the cabinet, it affords much better opportunity to prepare for service on the Court, since it is the Solicitor-General who usually is responsible for the presentation of cases to the Court on behalf of the government.

After three years as Solicitor-General, Taft was appointed by Harrison to a federal circuit judgeship, a position he held until 1900, when he resigned to become the first civil governor of the Philippines. Part of this time, from 1898 to 1900, he was also dean of Cincinnati Law School. In 1904 Roosevelt brought him home to become Secretary of War and then his heir to the Presidency. As President, Taft at first continued Roosevelt's progressive policies, but soon reverted to his natural conservatism. The result was a bitter split between Taft and Roosevelt which led to the election of Woodrow Wilson in 1912. Taft then became a member of the Yale law faculty. During the First World War he returned partly to public life as co-chairman of the War Labor Conference Board. In 1921 White died and the moment of Taft's attainment of his life's ambition appeared at hand.

Even before White's death Taft had approached Harding, informing the newly elected President that "many times in the past the Chief Justice [White] had said he was holding the office for me and that he would give it back to a Republican administration." There were, however, two serious obstacles in the way of Taft's appointment. One was Charles Evans Hughes and the other, George Sutherland. Hughes, now Harding's Secretary of State, had an even higher claim to the office than Taft, but fortunately he immediately made it clear that he would not accept the post if it were offered him, and to show that he was in earnest he even threatened to resign as Secretary of State if the post of Chief Justice were to be offered him. Sutherland proved a more formidable obstacle. He had been Harding's right hand man throughout the campaign and Harding had in fact promised him the Chief Justiceship.

For a while Harding tried to stall, suggesting that the post remain unfilled until another vacancy occurred so that the two names could be sent to the Senate simultaneously. But Taft was impatient; he was almost sixty-four and time refused to stand still. He enlisted the aid of Attorney-General Harry M. Daugherty and other party leaders who lobbied persistently until Harding finally yielded, and about a month and a half after White's death, sent Taft's name to the Senate for confirmation.

During the 1920 campaign Taft wrote an article for the *Yale Review* which gives a good indication of his view of the role of the Supreme Court. He wrote,

> Mr. Wilson is in favor of a latitudinarian construction of the Constitution of the United States to weaken the protection it should afford against socialistic raids upon property rights. . . . He has made three appointments to the Supreme Court. He is understood to be greatly disappointed in the attitude of the first of these [McReynolds] upon such questions. The other two [Brandeis and Clarke] represent a new school of constitutional construction, which if allowed to prevail, will greatly impair our fundamental law. Four of the incumbent Justices are beyond the retiring age of seventy, and the next President will probably be called upon to appoint their successors. There is no greater domestic issue in this election than the maintenance of the Supreme Court as a bulwark to enforce the guaranty that no man shall be deprived of his property without due process of law.

Wilson was able to appoint only three Justices during the eight years of his two terms. Harding, in his two years as President, was able to appoint a Chief Justice and three Associate Justices, an annual rate unequaled by any President before or since. This came about through the successive resignations in 1922 of Clarke, Day and Pitney. Clarke's resignation enabled Harding quickly to repay his debt to Sutherland. The latter had been leader of the Utah Republican party and had served in the Senate from 1905 to 1917, where he consistently opposed the progressive policies of Roosevelt and Wilson. During the campaign of 1920 he became attached to Harding's personal headquarters and after the election continued as his one-man brain trust.

Harding's second appointee was Pierce Butler of Minnesota, Roman Catholic, highly successful railroad attorney, and regent of the University of Minnesota. In the latter capacity, he had been responsible for the discharge of three members of the faculty with whose economic views he disagreed. His confirmation was strenuously opposed by Senators George W. Norris of Nebraska and Henrik Shipstead of Minnesota. "The appointment of Judge Cary of the United States Steel Corporation," said Norris, "would not in our opinion be more unfitting or improper than the appointment of Mr. Butler." The debates lasted two months, but in the end the Senate confirmed the nomination by the overwhelming vote of 61 to 8.

Harding's last appointee was Edward T. Sanford of Tennessee. Sanford had not been connected prominently either with politics or with corporate interests. He had been Assistant Attorney-General and then for fifteen years a federal district court judge. He died in 1930, after serving on the bench for seven years.

About half-way through Taft's term as Chief Justice, the aged McKenna retired and Coolidge appointed Harlan F. Stone to succeed him. Stone had been a highly successul corporation lawyer; his income from his law practice exceeded one hundred thousand dollars a year. However, most of his adult years before entering government service were spent first as professor and then as dean of Columbia Law School, where he was in frequent disagreement with the politically ambitious Nicholas Murray Butler, president of the university. His only government service before Coolidge appointed him Attorney-General in 1924 was as a member of a three-man special board of inquiry to pass on claims of conscientious objectors during the First World War.

The factors motivating Coolidge's appointment of Stone to be Attorney-General were probably similar to those that motivated the appointment of Judge Kenesaw Mountain Landis to be commissioner of baseball after the "Black Sox" scandal. To overcome the disastrous public relations effects of the scandal, baseball needed a man whose reputation was unsullied. Similarly, to meet the public displeasure with the scandal-ridden administration of Attorney-General Daugherty, Coolidge needed someone highly respectable, and who could be more respectable than the dean of a leading law school?

How it came about that Stone should be appointed to the Supreme Court after less than a year of service as Attorney-General is a matter of speculation. (During this short period he reorganized the Federal Bureau of Investigation and placed at its head J. Edgar Hoover, then a young lawyer.) It has been asserted that when Coolidge appointed Stone Attorney-General he intended to elevate him to the Court at the first opportunity. On the other hand, Stone's biographer, Alpheus Thomas Mason, indicates that there may well have been some basis for the widespread newspaper reports that Stone was "kicked upstairs," partly for his cleaning up of the Justice Department, but even more for his vigorous enforcement of the Anti-Trust Law, particularly against the Aluminum Trust—a vigor which much displeased Secretary of the Treasury Andrew W. Mellon. Whatever the cause, Stone was nominated and was confirmed in February of 1925.

DUE PROCESS AND PROPERTY RIGHTS

Taft became Chief Justice in 1921 and his Court took up where the White Court left off. Taft himself quickly showed that not only had he learned well from his predecessor but that he would better the instruction. He had been barely confirmed when he wrote the opinion of a bare majority of the Court in the case of *Truax* v. *Corrigan.*

During the turbulent period in labor relations before the First World War there was a growing feeling that court injunctions in labor disputes were being used to break strikes. It was this feeling that resulted in the provision in the Clayton Anti-Trust Law exempting labor unions and labor disputes from the ban on combinations in restraint of trade and prohibiting court injunctions against peaceful picketing. In the Duplex Printing Press case, decided shortly before Taft ascended the bench, the Court practically repealed this provision of the act. In *Truax* v. *Corrigan* Taft's Court did the same to similar provisions in state laws.

An Arizona law provided that no injunctions should issue against peaceful picketing. A strike took place in a restaurant in Bisbee, Arizona, and Truax, the owner, went to the state court for an injunction, claiming that the picketing by the strikers had drastically diminished his business and adversely affected his property. The Arizona supreme court refused to issue the injunction, holding the anti-injunction law to be constitutional. In a five to four decision, the Supreme Court overruled the state court and held the law unconstitutional. Taft's opinion stated that even peaceful picketing might be unlawful and could therefore be enjoined; that permitting an injunction in non-labor cases and not permitting it in labor cases would be discriminatory, and that the statute denied to Mr. Truax the equal protection of the laws and deprived him of his property without due process of law.

Pitney, who himself had written the majority opinion in the Duplex Printing Press case, could not accept its extension to nullify state laws, and wrote a dissenting opinion in which Clarke joined. "I cannot believe," he said, "that the use of the injunction in such cases is so essential to the right of acquiring, possessing and enjoying property that its restriction or elimination amounts to a deprivation of liberty or property without due process of law." Brandeis and Holmes wrote separate dissenting opinions, each typical of its author. Brandeis' was a massive survey of the history of judicial treatment of labor disputes in England, Australia and the United States, coming to the conclusion that the labor injunction had generally been used not to protect property but to make it "dominant over men," that through it the government had thrown its power on the side of the employer, and that the denial of the injunction simply helped equalize the struggle. Holmes's opinion was concise and aphoristic. It is not, he said, the purpose of the Fourteenth Amendment "to prevent the making of social experiments that an important part of the community desires, in the insulated chambers afforded by the several states, even though the experiments may seem futile or even noxious."

Felix Frankfurter, then professor of law at Harvard, commented editorially in the *New Republic* on Taft's opinion. "This decision of the Supreme Court," he said, "is fraught with more evil than any which it has rendered in a generation. . . . For all the regard that the Chief Justice of the United States pays to the facts of industrial life, he might as well have written this opinion as Chief Justice of the Fiji Islands." Frankfurter pointed out that the history of the labor injunction was only a little more than thirty years old, yet to Taft "the world never was without it, and therefore the foundations of the world are involved in its withdrawal."

Taft's attitude towards organized labor and labor's attitude towards Taft is indicated in a letter he wrote to his brother the year after the Truax case. "The only class," he wrote, "which is distinctly arrayed against the Court is a class that does not like the courts at any rate, and that is organized labor. That faction we have to hit every little while, because they are continually violating the law and depending on threats and violence to accomplish their purpose."

The year after the Truax case, Taft made it quite clear that his Court had no intention of retreating from *Hammer* v. *Dagenhart* or of permitting Congress in any way to interfere with the natural and God-given right of children to labor in mines and mills. After the Hammer case was decided, Congress enacted as part of its revenue laws a statute imposing an additional tax of 10 per cent of the profits of any mine in which children under the age of sixteen and any factory in which children under fourteen were employed. No one could deny the power of Congress to impose excise taxes on mines and factories. While it could not regulate mining and manufacturing, since these were purely local activities (as was held in the sugar trust case and in the Hammer case), the power of Congress to levy excise is not limited to taxes on goods in interstate commerce.

In *Bailey* v. *Drexel Furniture Company*, Taft, speaking for all the Justices except Clarke, held the tax unconstitutional as a patent attempt to evade the Hammer decision. "A court must be blind," said Taft, "not to see that the so-called tax is imposed to stop the employment of children." The Court had said that Congress could not directly prohibit child labor, and the Court would not allow it to do so indirectly through use of the taxing power.

These two child labor cases illustrate excellently how small an obstacle prior precedents of the Court are to Supreme Court Justices when they really want to reach a particular result. Before *Hammer* v. *Dagenhart* was decided the Court had held that Congress could bar interstate transportation of lottery tickets, women and liquor; but in the Hammer case it held that Congress could not bar interstate transportation of child-made products. Before the Bailey case the Court had held that Congress could tax white oleomargarine at one-quarter of a cent a pound, and yellow oleomargarine at ten cents a pound, although the Court had to be blind not to see that the purpose of the difference was to discourage the sale of oleomargarine as a competitive substitute for butter. In that case (*McCray* v. *United States*) the Court held that it could not enter into the motives of Congress in enacting a law which Congress had constitutional authority to enact. But in *Bailey* v. *Drexel Furniture Company* Taft had no difficulty in holding that the motive of Congress could very well invalidate an otherwise valid statute. A disinterested observer can hardly help concluding that the attitude of the Justices towards lottery tickets, immoral women, liquor, yellow-colored oleomargarine and child labor has some relationship to their ability to recognize or overlook prior precedents.

(Why neither Holmes nor Brandeis dissented in *Bailey* v. *Drexel Furniture Company* is puzzling. One suggested explanation was that, recognizing they were in the minority, they decided to yield to Taft's importunings not to register their dissent lest the prestige of the Court be injured. Taft, like Marshall before him and Hughes after him, was obsessed with the notion that the prestige and influence of the Court would be seriously lessened if the public were to become aware of the sharp differences among the Justices on important constitutional issues. He considered it his special duty as Chief Justice to "mass" the Court, i.e., achieve unanimity, and he exerted all his personal charm and good humor in this direction, often with notable success. Even if this explanation, offered in a biography of Brandeis by Alpheus Mason, were valid, it would not explain the persistence of Holmes and Brandeis in not dissenting after Clarke's refusal to go along showed that unanimity was in any event unattainable.)

Even Taft could not accept the Court's next major disregard of precedent. In *Adkins* v. *Children's Hospital* he found himself in the rare role of a dissenter. Congress, whose relationship to the District of Columbia is similar to that of state legislatures to the states, enacted a law setting up a board to determine minimum wages for women employed in the District. The law was enacted under the police power and made express reference to the relationship between wages and the health and morals of women. Similar laws had been passed in many states (a number of them filed briefs in the Adkins case) and of the twenty-nine state court judges that had passed on such laws, only two had been of the opinion that they were unconstitutional.

Children's Hospital in Washington brought suit to prevent enforcement of the law which required it to pay some scrubwomen the minimum wage fixed by the Washington board. The suit was joined by a Miss Lyons, an elevator operator employed in a hotel at thirty-five dollars a month who alleged she was discharged because the hotel could not pay the higher minimum fixed by the board.

Frankfurter argued the case for the District of Columbia, as he had argued the Oregon hours law case (*Bunting* v. *Oregon*); but this time he was not successful. The Supreme Court, by a vote of five to three (Brandeis disqualifying himself, as he had in the Bunting case) held the law unconstitutional. The opinion by Sutherland relied on *Lochner* v. *New York* for the holding that a state could not under the police power deprive Miss Lyons and other women of the freedom to contract to work for thirty-five dollars a month if they so wished. Miss Lyons, Sutherland pointed out, was "of full age and under no legal disability," and therefore could not be deprived of her liberty to contract for any wage she saw fit to accept. "In principle," he said, "there can be no difference between the case of selling labor and the case of selling goods." In each case, the Constitution protects the rights of the parties to get the best price their individual bargaining abilities can achieve. Moreover, under the statute the board was required, in fixing minimum wages, to consider the amounts necessary to maintain women in good health, provide them with a minimum standard of living and protect their morals; but it was not required to take in account the needs of the employer, the amount he could afford to pay, or whether the women's services were worth the amounts fixed by the board. This deprived the employers of their property without due process of law, since it might compel them to pay for the services more than they were worth.

Taft dissented in an opinion, in which Sanford joined, based upon the assertion that the Lochner decision had been in effect overruled by the Muller and Bunting cases, and that it was these cases rather than the Lochner case that should be followed. He could not accept the view of Sutherland that there is a constitutional difference between a law fixing maximum hours and one fixing minimum wages.

Holmes dissented in a separate opinion in which he noted that liberty of contract, which had started as an "innocuous generality," had now become a "dogma." To Sutherland's claim that the act was discriminatory since it provided minimum wages only for women, Holmes remarked caustically: "It will need more than the Nineteenth Amendment to convince me that there is no difference between women and men." Frankfurter had submitted A "Brandeis brief" showing the large number of states and foreign countries that had enacted minimum wage laws for women. Sutherland dismissed it as "proper enough for the consideration of lawmaking bodies," but the judicial question "cannot be aided by adding heads." Holmes, however, held that the evidence was not only relevant but cogent in establishing that the act of Congress was reasonable and therefore not unconstitutional.

In *Burns Baking Company* v. *Bryan* Taft was again with his usual colleagues in the majority, and Holmes and Brandeis were again lone dissenters, Clarke having left the Court and Stone having not yet arrived. A Nebraska law attempted to prevent short-weighting and deception in the sale of bread by requiring that every loaf baked or sold in the state be of standard weight—half-pound, pound, pound-and-a-half or an exact multiple of a pound. (Most hurried marketing housewives could not tell the difference between a thirteen-ounce and a pound loaf.) A baking company brought suit to prevent enforcement of the act.

Again precedent proved a poor prop for reliance. In 1913, during the Hughes liberal interlude, the Court (in *Schmidinger* v. *Chicago*) had held that the making and selling of bread was a permissible subject for regulation by the state, that the state could fix standard sizes and weights of loaves, and that it could compel bakers to state the weight of each loaf. But that was in 1913. In 1924, Butler, speaking for all the Justices except Holmes and Brandeis, held that, notwithstanding the contrary views of the Nebraska legislature, the setting of maximum weights for loaves was not really necessary to protect consumers against fraud and deception, and therefore the law was unconstitutional. Brandeis replied to this sharply in the last sentence of his dissent. Butler's decision, he said, "is an exercise of the powers of a super-legislature—not the performance of the constitutional function of judicial review."

The question of what is an industry "clothed with a public interest" again came to the Court in 1927 in the case of *Tyson Brothers* v. *Benton*. To prevent "scalping" in the resale of theater tickets, New York passed a law requiring the licensing of ticket brokers and prohibiting the resale of any theater ticket at higher than a fifty cent mark-up. In a five to four decision, Sutherland held the law unconstitutional on the ground that the selling of theater tickets is not affected with a public interest and is therefore not subject to state regulation. The law violated the liberty of the broker and the theater goer to contract for the purchase of the ticket at any price they saw fit.

Holmes, Brandeis, Stone and Sanford dissented. The concept of business affected with a public interest had been brought into constitutional law in *Munn* v. *Illinois*, the grain elevator rate case. Holmes and Brandeis (though not Stone or Sanford) were ready to discard it. "The notion," said Holmes, "that a business is clothed with a public interest and has been devoted to the public use is a little more than a fiction intended to beautify what is disagreeable to the sufferers. The truth seems to me to be that, subject to compensation when compensation is due, the legislature may forbid or restrict any business when it has sufficient force of public opinion behind it."

The Taft Court could also use precedent when precedent was useful. A union seeking to organize producers of Indiana limestone placed in its constitution a provision that no union workers should work on any limestone cut by non-union workers. When members of the union refused to handle stone cut by the unorganized Bedford Cut Stone Company, that firm went to court for an injunction. In *Bedford Cut Stone Company* v. *Journeymen Stone Cutters' Association*, the Supreme Court, in a decision written by Sutherland, held that it was entitled to the injunction. The case of *Duplex Company* v. *Deering* had decided that the Clayton Anti-Trust Act did not exempt union activities and it was the duty of the Court to follow that precedent.

Brandeis dissented in an opinion with which Holmes concurred. "The Sherman Law," he said, "was held in *United States* v. *United States Steel Corporation* to permit capitalists to combine in a single corporation fifty percent of the steel industry of the United States dominating the trade through its vast resources. The Sherman Law was held in *United States* v. *United States Shoe Machinery Company* to permit capitalists to combine in another corporation practically the whole shoe machinery industry of the country, necessarily giving it a position of dominance over shoe manufacturing in America. It would, indeed, be strange if Congress had by the same Act willed to deny to members of a small craft of workingmen the right to cooperate in simply refraining from work, when that course was the only means of self-protection against a combination of militant and powerful employers. I cannot believe that Congress did so." (Taft called Brandeis' dissent "one of his meanest opinions.")

THE TAFT COURT AND PROPERTY RIGHTS

Taft retired from the Court in 1930 and died shortly thereafter. On his retirement, Frankfurter, in an article in *Current History*, reviewed the achievements of his Court.

"Since 1920 the Court has invalidated more legislation than in fifty years preceding. Views that were antiquated twenty-five years ago have been resurrected in decisions nullifying minimum wage laws for women in industry, a standard-weight bread law to protect buyers from short weights and honest bakers from unfair competition, a law fixing the resale price of theatre tickets by ticket scalpers in New York, laws controlling exploitation of the unemployed by employment agencies and many tax laws. . . . Merely as a matter of arithmetic this is an impressive mortality rate. But a numerical tally of the cases does not tell the tale. In the first place, all laws are not of the same importance. Secondly, a single decision may decide the fate of a great body of legislation. . . . Moreover, the discouragement of legislative efforts through a particular adverse decision and the general weakening of the sense of legislative responsibility are destructive influences not measurable by statistics."

Measured by his own standards, Taft did his work well. Yet towards the end of his life he became obsessed with the fear that his accomplishments would not last. Radicalism was on the march and it threatened to engulf his beloved Court. Even the election of Herbert Hoover to the Presidency did not reassure him. "The truth," he said, "is that Hoover is a Progressive, just as Stone is, and just as Brandeis is and just as Holmes is."

Taft's greatest fortune was that he died in 1930. It is almost frightening to imagine the agonies he would have suffered if he had lived during the second term of Franklin Roosevelt, particularly if he were then still Chief Justice. In two respects he was like Louis XV: the deluge came after him, and he was largely responsible for it. Had he cast his considerable influence with Holmes, Brandeis, Clarke and Stone, rather than with McReynolds, Van Devanter, Sutherland and Butler, the future of the Court might have been radically different.

Under Taft Marshall's property-protecting Court sowed the seeds of its own destruction. The last act was to be delayed some seven or eight years and even at that required an unprecedented national catastrophe to bring it about so soon. But its end was inevitable. The type of Court that Marshall had conceived and Taft perfected simply could not survive in a twentieth-century America. Taft's due process, liberty of contract and interstate commerce decisions were the seeds that blossomed into the suicidal decisions of the Hughes Court majority in the 1930's. The Court that Taft worshiped ceased to exist after 1937.

This is fairly well recognized, but what is even more remarkable and not at all generally recognized is that under Taft the Court also sowed the seeds of its own rebirth. If Taft and his colleagues were responsible for the destruction of the pre-1937 Court they were also responsible for the creation of the post-1937 Court. As the mission of the former was the protection of property rights, so that of the latter has been the protection of individual liberties; and it was the activities of the Taft Court that made possible the carrying out of this mission. Frankfurter was correct when he stated that under Taft the Court invalidated more social welfare legislation than in the preceding fifty years. But that is only half the story. He did not state what was no less true, that under Taft the Court protected individual liberties to an extent far greater than had been done in the entire preceding history of the Court since its establishment in 1789. And in doing so, it showed itself to be not merely resourceful but truly creative. It effectively opened the door of the Supreme Court to protect individual liberties against impairment by the states, and did so after that door had apparently been sealed for all time by none other than the great liberal Miller, in his Slaughterhouse decision.

THE TAFT COURT AND PERSONAL LIBERTIES

In 1915, during the liberal first half of the White Court, a majority of the Justices could find no way to interfere with the judicial lynching of Leo Frank. In 1923 the Taft Court found that after all the Constitution did enable it to outlaw judicial lynchings. The case was *Moore* v. *Dempsey*, in which the following facts appeared. A group of Negro sharecroppers met in a church in Phillips County in eastern Arkansas, near the Mississippi border, to discuss the employment of counsel to protect their rights against their white landlords. The white citizens of the community got word of the meeting and descended upon the church. Gunfire broke out, and a white man was killed. A posse of white men was formed to hunt down the Negroes and avenge the white man's death. Many Negroes were caught, tortured, and slain. Finally, saner heads prevailed; when five captured Negroes were about to be lynched, a "Committee of Seven," representing the more responsible white citizenry, prevailed upon the mob to disperse by solemnly promising them that the Negroes would be hanged after trial. To make sure that this "solemn promise" would be carried out, the committee called Negro witnesses and had them whipped and tortured until they promised to testify as the committee wanted them to. The courtroom was filled with angry white citizens; outside hundreds more milled about, shouting threats at anyone who interfered with the desired result. The trial of all five Negroes before an all-white jury took about forty-five minutes. Five minutes later the jury returned a verdict of guilty of murder in the first degree against all the defendants.

In the Supreme Court, Holmes, who had dissented in the Frank case, was now able to speak for a majority of the Court, with only McReynolds and Sutherland dissenting. He declared the conviction unconstitutional as a denial of life and liberty without due process of law. A mob dominated trial is not a fair trial, and the Fourteenth Amendment guarantees a fair trial to all.

In the same year (1923) Holmes and McReynolds found themselves in reversed positions, the former seeking to uphold a state infringement upon personal liberties and the latter deciding against it. Only Sutherland was consistent, joining Holmes in dissent in the second case as he had joined McReynolds in dissent in the first.

Meyer v. *Nebraska* arose out of the excessive nationalism and xenophobia that characterized the period immediately following the First World War. This was a time when many Americans believed that the welfare of our country demanded the elimination of cultural differences. Then the preservation of the "American type" was deemed of paramount importance. Homogeneity was the goal sought and its attainment was pursued through a variety of ways. One was the establishment of a restrictive immigration system based upon national quotas. Another, with which we are here concerned, was the enactment of a number of state laws controlling private education. The validity of these laws came to the Supreme Court for determination in a number of cases. The first of these, *Meyer* v. *Nebraska,* proceeded from a prosecution under a state statute—one of several enacted in a number of mid-western states—that prohibited the teaching of foreign languages in elementary private or parochial schools.

In reversing the conviction of the defendant, a teacher of German in a Lutheran parochial school, McReynold's decision for the majority of the Supreme Court recognized as valid the desire of the legislature to foster a homogeneous people with American ideals, prepared readily to understand current discussion of civil matters. Nevertheless, the

Court held, this objective could not constitutionally be achieved by penalizing the learning of a foreign language.

Two years later the Court decided the famous Oregon parochial school case, *Pierce* v. *Society of Sisters*. In 1922, largely under the influence of Ku Klux Klan elements, the people of Oregon enacted a law aimed at eliminating parochial and private schools. While it did not expressly outlaw these schools, it sought effectively to achieve the same end by requiring all children, with limited exceptions, to attend only public schools.

The attorney-general of Oregon urged in support of the law that the notorious and alarming increase in juvenile crime could be attributed to the lack of public school education by many children; that religious prejudices might result from religious segregation; that subversive economic doctrines might be taught in non-public schools; and that a system of compulsory public education was necessary to encourage the patriotism and insure the loyalty of future citizens.

This time the Supreme Court was unanimous. Relying on *Meyer* v. *Nebraska*, the Court, in an opinion again written by McReynolds, held the Oregon statute unconstitutional on the ground that it unreasonably interfered with the liberty of private and parochial schools to do business, and of parents to direct the religious upbringing of their children.

It is interesting to note that technically the liberty protected in the Meyer decision was the property right of German language teachers to engage in that lawful occupation, and in the Pierce decision, the property right of proprietors of private schools to engage in the profit-making business of teaching children. The Court used for the protection of personal rights the forms of due process adjudications perfected by the Fuller Court for the protection of property rights. But whatever the form, the substance was clear; the Supreme Court for the first time in its history asserted its power to employ the due process clause to protect individual freedoms, such as freedom of religion and freedom of teaching.

During the same year, the Court extended the principle of due process to encompass protection of freedom of speech from unconstitutional infringement by the states. The case of *Gitlow* v. *New York* arose under a New York statute punishing the advocacy of criminal anarchy. Gitlow was one of the leaders of the left wing which in 1919 broke away from the Socialist Party to become the Communist Party. Like the revolutionaries of 1776, Gitlow and his associates felt it necessary to declare the causes that impelled them to the separation. There, however, the similarity ended; their declaration of independence, the *Left Wing Manifesto*, consisted of thirty-four closely printed pages the effect of which was far more likely to induce sleep than revolutionary activity. There were the usual calls to "mass strikes," "expropriation of the bourgeoisie" and establishment of a "dictatorship of the proletariat." In a seven to two decision (Holmes and Brandeis dissenting) the Supreme Court affirmed Gitlow's conviction of advocating revolution on the ground that the legislature of New York was not forbidden by the Constitution to make it a crime to utter words it deemed dangerous, whether or not there was any real likelihood that in a particular case the utterance would in fact provoke revolution, anarchy, or other unlawful acts.

Gitlow v. *New York* is one of the landmark cases in the history of constitutional law; it is one of the half-dozen or so most important cases decided by the Supreme Court. Its importance has been obscured by the fact that the actual holding was to affirm the conviction of a radical who had exercised freedom of speech; but this was merely incidental. (By the time the case reached the Supreme Court Gitlow had already been pardoned by Governor Alfred E. Smith.) The importance of the case lies in the fact that for the first time the Court proceeded on the assumption that the liberty in the due process clause included liberty of expression. In the Meyer and Pierce cases the Court employed the fiction that it was really protecting property rights, even though it seemed rather incongruous to suggest that an order of Roman Catholic nuns were motivated by a desire to gain financial profit in operating a parochial school. In the Gitlow case, there was no way to bring in the profit motive. The Court took the bold step of holding that personal freedoms, no less than property rights, were entitled to constitutional protection against state infringement. The First Amendment forbids Congress to abridge freedom of religion, speech, press and assembly. What the Taft Court did in the Gitlow case was to impose the same prohibition on the states and to assert its own right and duty to protect Americans against violation of the prohibition.

In *Fiske* v. *Kansas*, decided in 1927, the Court showed the practical consequence of its holding in the Gitlow case. An IWW organizer was indicted under a criminal syndicalism statute similar to the New York law under which Gitlow was convicted. The pamphlets he distributed urged abolition of the wage system, but there was no evidence that he advocated violent means for this end. The Supreme Court unanimously reversed the conviction, holding that his constitutionally protected freedom of speech, press and assembly had been violated.

In the Slaughterhouse decision Miller had held that the sole purpose of the Fourteenth Amendment was to protect the newly freed slaves. The Waite Court fairly well nullified the usefulness of the amendment for that purpose. The Fuller Court created out of the due process clause an effective instrument for the protection of property rights. It was the Taft Court that created out of the same clause an effective instrument for the protection from infringement by the states of the First Amendment rights of freedom of religion, speech, press and assembly.

History has not been fair to Taney. Neither has it—at least as written by persons with a liberal bias—been entirely fair to Taft. If he is to be held responsible for the Court's laissez faire decisions in the field of business regulation, social welfare and labor unionization, he is entitled equally to the credit for the pioneering decisions in the field of fundamental liberties of expression. In the former case the Taft Court was simply following the path made by the Fuller Court; in the latter it was opening new frontiers. In the long run of history its decisions in the Meyer, Pierce, Gitlow and Fiske cases are likely to overshadow those in the Truax, Bailey, Adkins and Wolf Packing Company cases. The evil the latter cases did was to be buried in the Revolution of 1937. The good done by the former cases was to be preserved and extended after 1937.

chapter twelve

Bloodless Revolution

HUGHES RETURNS AS CHIEF JUSTICE

After Charles Evans Hughes slighted Hiram Johnson and lost California and the Presidency by four thousand votes, he resumed his long-interrupted practice of law. The election of Harding in 1920 brought him back to public service as Secretary of State, first for Harding and then Coolidge. He resigned in 1925 and again took up his law practice, soon becoming perhaps the highest paid attorney in the nation, with fees amounting one year to no less than four hundred thousand dollars. These fees, moreover, were earned while he devoted less than his full working time to legal practice. On resigning from the State Department he became a member of the Permanent Court of Arbitration at the Hague, and also, two years later, a member of the Permanent Court of International Justice. During this period also he wrote a book, *The Supreme Court*, which quickly became something of a classic.

With Taft's retirement from the bench in 1930, Hoover's appointment of Hughes was not only natural but inevitable. Despite his obvious qualifications for the post of Chief Justice (only Taft equaled him in that respect), his liberal record during his earlier service on the bench, and the fact that in 1920 he had led the (unsuccessful) fight against the expulsion of five duly elected Socialists from the New York State Assembly, the nomination was bitterly opposed by liberals and progressives throughout the nation. One of the reasons was that Hoover's secretary had tipped off the press that the President had decided to elevate Stone, a report which gladdened the hearts of liberals, and conversely bitterly disappointed them when it failed to eventuate. A second reason was that Hughes had sat silently by during the period of the scandalous actions of some other members of Harding's cabinet, particularly Albert B. Fall, Edwin Denby and Harry M. Daugherty. Many persons found it difficult to believe that the cabinet offices were so insulated from each other that the top cabinet member should be completely unaware of what was going on in the other offices. But by far the most serious objection to Hughes was that he was an extremely successful Wall Street lawyer. After the administration of Taft, the idea of a Wall Street lawyer occupying the highest judicial office in the United States was anathema to the liberals and progressives.

In the Senate the lead against confirmation was taken by George W. Norris of Nebraska. The proponents of the nomination asserted that only Hughes's (undeniable) legal qualifications were relevant since Justices applied the Constitution as it was written and not in accordance with their own economic predilections or political biases. The opponents dismissed this argument with scorn. "We have," said Norris,

> "a legislative body, called the House of Representatives, of over 400 men. We have another legislative body, called the Senate, of less than a hundred men. We have, in reality, another legislative body, called the Supreme Court, of nine men; and they are more powerful than all the others put together. . . . There has not been a criticism of the Supreme Court anywhere, even on the floor of the Senate, for several years because we have set it up on a pedestal beyond human criticism. . . . We have made idols of them . . . they have black gowns over their persons. Then they become something more than human beings. . . . We have tried to make plain that the power of the Supreme Court has been steadily growing; that, like human beings, they have been reaching out for more and more power until it has become common knowledge that they legislate and fix policies."

Senator Tom Connally of Texas took up the attack. "The great questions that now confront us," he said, "are economic questions, questions as to whether the powers of the Federal Government and of the State governments are adequate to control and regulate the great aggregated masses of wealth which are rapidly seizing upon and controlling many of the necessities of life of the people of the Nation." That would be the contest facing the Court in the immediate future, and there was grave danger in having during that period a Court presided over by a Wall Street lawyer who had previously appeared before the Court almost invariably on behalf of wealthy corporations. Connally agreed with Norris' statement that Hughes "looks through glasses contaminated by the influence of monopoly, as it seeks to get favors by means which are denied to the common, ordinary citizen."

William E. Borah, Burton K. Wheeler, Carter Glass and other senators joined in the attack. The Supreme Court, Borah charged, had become an "economic dictator" and the Senate should not permit the President to add to the Court a man holding extreme views "which exalt property rights over all other rights."

The debate, though bitter, was short. Three days after the Judiciary Committee reported the nomination favorably, the Senate confirmed it by a vote of 52 to 26. Hughes's biographer, Merlo Pusey, is probably right in his explanation of the bitter opposition to a person whose record on the whole was overwhelmingly liberal and progressive. "America was in the first throes of the great depression of the thirties. The Insurgents were striking more at the Taft Court and the Hoover Administration than at Hughes as an individual. For the moment Hughes was made an unwitting symbol of the philosophy which they believed to be responsible for the country's economic convulsions. The strange thing is that the men who claimed to be 'liberals' chose as their target one of the greatest champions of human rights in the current century."

ROBERTS AND CARDOZO

That Pusey's explanation has validity is indicated by the events following Hughes's confirmation. The very next day, the Senate insurgents launched an attack on "judge made law," "government by injunction," and "Federal judicial interference in the internal concerns of the states." Constitutional amendments aimed at stripping the Court of its power to declare acts of Congress unconstitutional were proposed, as were suggestions that federal judges, including those of the Supreme Court, be elected by popular vote.

The crusade against the Court was resumed a few weeks later when, to fill the vacancy caused by the death of Sanford, Hoover nominated John J. Parker of North Carolina. Parker, a Republican, was federal circuit court judge, and in that capacity had brought upon himself the bitter opposition of organized labor by upholding yellow-dog contracts and injunctions against strikers, although in both cases he was merely following precedents established by the Supreme Court.

The opposition to Parker exceeded in bitterness even that to Hughes, and in the end the Senate refused confirmation by a narrow margin. Hoover's second choice was Owen J. Roberts of Philadelphia. He had been a member of the law faculty at the University of Pennsylvania and assistant city district attorney. During the First World War he had been appointed by the United States Attorney-General to prosecute espionage cases. He gained national fame in 1924 as the prosecuting attorney in the Teapot Dome scandal, and this fact, together with the natural reactions following the rejection of Hoover's first choice, resulted in his speedy confirmation by the Senate.

Two years later, Holmes retired from the bench, and Hoover had the opportunity of making another appointment. This is an accurate statement as far as it goes; it would not have been accurate had it said that Hoover had the opportunity of making another selection. For if any President had a Supreme Court Justice thrust upon him Hoover did. He certainly did not want to appoint Benjamin Nathan Cardozo but his refusal to do so would have outraged the nation—and not merely the liberals and progressives. Cardozo was the one man in the country who could fittingly succeed Oliver Wendell Holmes.

Unlike Holmes, Cardozo achieved his greatness before he went to Washington. He was sixty-two years old when he became a member of the Supreme Court, just about a year older than Holmes had been upon his ascension. But whereas Holmes served on the Supreme Court for thirty years, Cardozo could serve only six. Had Cardozo enjoyed Holmes' good fortune, it is a reasonable supposition that he would have outshone the latter in greatness and in fame.

Cardozo was the son of Albert Cardozo, a Sephardic Jew whose ancestors had come to this country before the Revolution. The older Cardozo was one of the New York judges appointed by William M. Tweed, the corrupt boss of Tammany Hall, and resigned under a cloud when Tweed was deposed. The present writer recollects that when he was in law school a legend floated around that because of the scandal surrounding his father's name, Benjamin Cardozo vowed that he would never marry (he died a bachelor) but would devote his life to redeeming the name. This was legendary, but it was a fact that so great was the esteem he achieved in New York that when he ran for high judicial office and again when he was nominated for the Supreme Court, by tacit agreement not a single newspaper mentioned the incident concerning his father.

Cardozo had been tutored in his youth by Horatio Alger, graduated from Columbia College and entered Columbia Law School. He did not stay to complete the course; because he had two sisters to support, he sought and obtained admission to the bar as soon as he completed a year of law studies. For twenty-two years he practiced law as a lawyers' lawyer, an unusual professional activity even in New York. The result was that although unknown to the general public he became well known and tremendously respected by bench and bar. Much of his legal practice consisted of arguing cases before the New York court of appeals, the state's highest court. Most New York lawyers must wait many years before they receive their first opportunity to argue a case before the court of appeals; when Cardozo had been a lawyer for but twelve years, he had accumulated enough experience to publish a book on the practice of that court. In 1913 he was elected as an anti-Tammany candidate to a lower court justiceship, but after he served only six weeks a vacancy occurred on the court of appeals, and the judges of that court all joined in a request to the governor to designate Cardozo to fill the vacancy. After serving in a temporary capacity, he was elected permanently to the post and in 1927 was elected, without opposition, to become its chief judge.

While on the New York bench he wrote *The Nature of the Judicial Process*, a little book that took its place as a classic of the law along with Holmes's *The Common Law*, and also *The Growth of the Law*, the *Paradoxes of Legal Science* and *Law and Literature*. More important even than these were the many opinions, all written in a high and perhaps somewhat over-elegant literary style that lawyers and judges by the thousands have since sought to emulate, which adapted the ancient feudal common law to the needs of a twentieth-century industrial society.

On Holmes's retirement there arose a truly spontaneous demand by bench and bar that Cardozo be named to succeed him. On the Court, Stone waged a one-man campaign, motivated equally by his great admiration for Cardozo and his fear that Hoover would further injure the Court's prestige by appointing a conservative. Hoover was more than reluctant. There were already four easterners on the bench; of these two were from New York, and Hoover thought the geographical imbalance should be corrected by appointing a westerner or mid-westerner. Hoover expressed the same objection when Senator Borah of Idaho pressed for Cardozo's nomination. Stone responded to the objection by offering to resign—an offer, which when it became public, served to increase the demand for Cardozo's appointment. Borah responded by telling Hoover that Cardozo belonged as much to Idaho as to New York. To both, as undoubtedly to others, Hoover pointed out that an objection had been made in an influential quarter that Cardozo was not "socially acceptable" and that he was a Jew and the Court already had one Jew. (It was widely reported that McReynolds had urged Hoover not to "plague the Court with another Jew.") Stone replied that the truly highest circles would accept Cardozo but would not accept the objector. Borah replied that "The way to deal with anti-Semitism is not to yield to it," adding: "Just as John Adams is best remembered for his appointment of John Marshall to the Supreme Court, so you, Mr. President, have the opportunity of being best remembered for putting Cardozo there."

But still Hoover resisted. Stone became discouraged. "Just why," he commented, "the opportunity to do an outstanding and fitting thing should seem so unattractive, I do not understand." In the end, however, the unanimity of the pressure was too great even for Hoover to resist, and ultimately he yielded. Cardozo was nominated and speedily confirmed.

HOPE

Hughes's first entry to the Supreme Court in 1910 inaugurated a period of comparative liberalism, and his re-entry in 1930 appeared to be the harbinger of another revival of liberalism. On the right, the Praetorian Guard of laissez faire capitalism—McReynolds, Van Devanter, Sutherland and Butler—were as stalwart and as uncompromising as ever. On the left, so too were the *avante garde* of Brandeis, Stone and Holmes-Cardozo. In the center were Roberts and Hughes, the former perhaps slightly more conservative than Sanford, but the latter far more liberal than Taft. There appeared to be good reason for liberals and progressives to be moderately optimistic as to the future course of the Court.

The early decisions of the Hughes Court lent substance to these modest expectations. In 1931 it handed down two decisions evidencing a determination to carry on the function of the Taft Court in protecting personal freedom from state infringement and guaranteeing to Americans that the liberties of expression secured by the First Amendment against impairment by Congress would be equally secured against impairment by the states. In *Stromberg* v. *California* it upset a conviction of the operator of a children's camp who every day raised a camp-made reproduction of the red flag of Soviet Russia, which was also the flag of the Communist Party of the United States. The defendant had been indicted under a state statute making it a felony to display a red flag "as a sign, symbol or emblem of opposition to organized government." The Court held that exhibition of a flag is a part of political discussion within the guarantee of freedom of speech. The display of a symbol may communicate ideas no less than the articulation of words. The majority opinion was written by Hughes; only McReynolds and Butler dissented.

In *Near* v. *Minnesota,* Hughes again spoke for the majority of the Court in a decision upholding freedom of expression, although this time Van Devanter and Sutherland joined McReynolds and Butler in dissent. In that case the Court passed on the constitutionality of what the press called the Newspaper Gag Law. This was a statute authorizing the suppression by court injunction of obscene, scandalous, and defamatory newspapers and periodicals. The *Saturday Press,* published in Minneapolis, printed a series of articles charging that a Jewish gangster controlled all gambling, bootlegging and racketeering in the county and that the chief public officials, the chief of police and the prosecuting attorney, were either corrupt or grossly neglectful in the performance of their duties. The prosecuting attorney replied by suing under the "gag law" to suppress the newspaper, and he succeeded in obtaining a court order directing destruction of all printed issues for the past two months and forbidding any further publication of the newspaper.

The Supreme Court set aside the injunction and declared the statute unconstitutional. Except in rare cases, as when the government during wartime seeks to prevent the publication of the sailing dates of transports or the location of troops, the First Amendment guarantee of the freedom of the press bars previous restraints upon publication. The states may constitutionally enact criminal libel laws providing for the punishment *after* publication of egregiously defamatory matter; but they may not by suppression, through injunction or otherwise, interfere in advance with publication. Whatever else freedom of the press may mean, its history shows conclusively that at the very least it bars previous restraints upon publication.

In economic affairs the early decisions of the Hughes Court lent additional and more important weight to the promise of progressivism. True enough, the case of *New State Ice Company* v. *Liebman* appeared to be a setback. The state of Oklahoma, reflecting local emergency conditions, enacted a law requiring a certificate of public convenience and necessity of any new company desiring to enter the ice business. The New State Ice Company procured such a certificate and invested a half million dollars in the erection of a plant. Liebman, a free lance dealer, set up a competing plant without procuring a certificate.

By a vote of six to three (Brandeis, Stone and Cardozo dissenting) the Court, speaking through Sutherland, held the law unconstitutional. Under the Fourteenth Amendment the states can regulate only those businesses affected with a public interest, and that term must be construed strictly in the light of its traditional meaning. Only transportation and public utilities were businesses affected with a public interest; and this category did not include the ice business.

New State Ice Company v. *Liebman* was a setback; yet it really did no more than reaffirm the holding in the Burns Baking Company case that the business of selling food, or ice to preserve food, was not one affected with a public interest and therefore not subject to state regulation. But whatever was lost in the New State Ice case, and far more, was won back two years later in *Nebbia* v. *New York*. In the former case all that the proponents of the Oklahoma law hoped for was that the category of businesses affected with a public interest would be broadened at least in the presence of an economic emergency. In the Nebbia case the Court (with the Praetorian Guard, of course, dissenting) threw the entire concept out of the window.

The majority upheld a New York law regulating the price of milk. No industry, whether within or without the traditional category of businesses affected with a public interest, is immune from control for the public good. The state's police power, the Court held, reviving Taney's long dormant concept of community welfare, authorized New York to take such steps as it deems appropriate to correct existing maladjustments in the price structure. "The Constitution," the majority opinion stated, "does not secure to any one liberty to conduct his business in such a fashion as to inflict injury upon the public at large or upon any substantial group of people." (McReynolds was so furious in his dissent that he rashly disclaimed the incantation so frequently intoned by the priests of the judicial temple—and recited in the majority opinion—that the Court is not concerned with the wisdom of a law but only with its constitutionality. "But plainly," McReynolds declared, "I think this court must have regard to the wisdom of the enactment.")

The same year (1934) saw another five to four decision whose implications appeared no less radical. The depression had hit the farm areas particularly hard. In so formerly prosperous a state as Minnesota, the annual cash income of farmers fell in 1932 to an average of $141. During the same year more than half of the farms in the state were either mortgaged or foreclosed. On occasions mobs of farmers took the law into their own hands and forcibly prevented foreclosure sales from taking place. The situation seemed rapidly to be degenerating into anarchy, and the governor warned that unless the legislature granted some relief he would be compelled to declare martial law. He issued an order directing all sheriffs to refrain from foreclosure proceedings until the legislature had an opportunity to act. The legislature, in turn, quickly and without a dissenting vote enacted a law giving courts the power to postpone mortgage foreclosures. Creditors prompty attacked the moratorium in the courts as an impairment of the obligations of contract.

In *Home Building and Loan Association* v. *Blaisdell*, the majority of the Supreme Court upheld the law. The opinion seemed to rely on a legalism: the statute, it said, did not impair the *obligation* of Minnesota mortgages, that is, the duty to pay them, but only the *remedy* of foreclosure. That had been given by the legislature, and what the legislature gave it could take back. Emergency does not create power; nor does it increase granted power. But it may furnish the occasion for the exercise of power, and the Minnesota emergency furnished the occasion for the legislature temporarily to withhold from creditors the remedy of mortgage foreclosure. Although no special concurring opinions were written, Stone and Cardozo were unhappy with Hughes's emphasis on emergency and the temporary nature of the moratorium.

Sutherland, for the minority, conceded that war might be an emergency justifying legislative action otherwise subject to objection, but not depressions. "The present exigency," he said, "is nothing new. From the beginning of our existence as a nation, periods of depression, of industrial failure, of financial distress, of unpaid and unpayable indebtedness, have alternated with years of plenty." The Constitutional remedy was laissez faire; "self-denial and painful effort" had always worked before, and would work now again if only allowed to. If not, the Constitution was in grave danger. "If the provisions of the Constitution be not upheld when they pinch as well as when they comfort, they may as well be abandoned." Historically, it should be noted, Sutherland was undoubtedly right. It certainly was one of the major purposes of the Constitutional Fathers to prevent just this type of legislative interference with the rights of creditors, and it was one of the principal functions of the Court fashioned by Marshall to effectuate that purpose.

ANXIETY

Franklin D. Roosevelt took office at the depth of the depression. To meet the emergency he immediately called a special session of Congress. "One Hundred Days" (technically, 104) later the Congress adjourned, having enacted more important pieces of legislation and instituted more new policies than any previous legislature in American history. Emergency situations call for emergency measures. The country cried for leadership; Roosevelt showed that he was prepared to supply it, and Congress was quite content not to stand in the way. Most of the bill drafting was done, not, as usually, by Congressional committees, but by a "brain trust" under the professorial leadership of Felix Frankfurter, who in turn often sought and received guidance from Brandeis. Indeed, although he disagreed with some parts of the New Deal, to a substantial extent Brandeis may be said to have been its intellectual godfather, and Roosevelt, communicating with him through Frankfurter, placed great reliance upon his advice and encouragement.

During the Hundred Days Congress enacted the Emergency Banking Law, almost unanimously in both Houses, in a single day. It confirmed the President's action in closing all the banks in the country—which had effected a Presidential moratorium on debts—and gave him further emergency powers to control foreign exchange, gold currency movements and banking in general. Another act authorized the creation of a Civilian Conservation Corps; another, the Federal Emergency Relief Administration. The National Industrial Recovery Act (NIRA) was adopted and the establishment of a Public Works Administration (PWA) authorized. The Emergency Farm Mortgage Act and the law establishing the Home Owners Loan Corporation (HOLC) were enacted to give relief to the hard pressed farm and home owners. The Agricultural Administration Act sought to raise the income of farmers. The Tennessee Valley Authority (TVA) was created to expand both our natural resources and employment opportunities for the jobless; and the President was empowered to devalue the dollar by reducing its gold content in an effort to halt the steady deflationary process that had started in Wall Street on that Black Thursday when the bottom fell out of the stock market.

The Nebbia and Blaisdell cases engendered great hopes in the framers and champions of the New Deal. While these did not involve the acts of Congress passed during the Hundred Days, but only state laws adopted to meet the same depression, nevertheless, the statutes embodied two of the major means employed by the New Deal, regulation of competition to stabilize the disintegrating price structure, and a moratorium on the enforcement of financial obligations, particularly through mortgage foreclosure.

Particularly encouraging about the two decisions was the identities of the authors of the majority opinions in both cases. The Nebbia opinion was written by Roberts; the Blaisdell, by Hughes. Brandeis, Stone and Cardozo could, of course, be relied upon, and McReynolds, Van Devanter, Sutherland and Butler were hopeless. But Nebbia and Blaisdell gave promise that Hughes and Roberts would be found on the side of the angels, and in constitutional law as in baseball there is no practical difference between a score of five to four and one of nine to nothing.

The Nebbia and Blaisdell decisions were handed down in the early part of 1934, just about a year after the Hundred Days. A year later, specifically on January 7, 1935, the New Deal experienced its first setback at the hands of the Court, serious in itself but far more serious in what it portended. The case was *Panama Refining Company* v. *Ryan*, quickly dubbed by the press, the "Hot Oil" case.

The oil industry had long been suffering from overproduction and wasteful competition. Excessive exploitation of the oil fields created fears that this important natural resource might be quickly depleted. Several states attempted to regulate drilling for oil; in some the militia was called out to enforce shutdowns in the fields. But there was no uniform policy among the states, and a shutdown in one state only served to encourage greater production in others. In desperation some of the state governors called upon the federal government for help. Congress and the President responded in two ways. The NIRA authorized codes of fair competition, and one was adopted for the oil industry which fixed production quotas for the various states, but left it to each state to allocate its quota among its own producers. Another section of the act dealt specifically with oil production and authorized the President to prohibit under penalty of law the movement in interstate commerce of any oil produced in excess of the quotas fixed by the state legislature.

With only Cardozo dissenting, the Court held the latter provision unconstitutional. The opinion was written by Hughes and its basis was that Congress could not delegate to the President the undefined and unlimited power to create a crime by Presidential proclamation that in his uncontrolled discretion "hot oil" should not be transported across state lines. Such a provision conferred legislative powers on the Executive, in violation of the constitutional separation of powers. This was the first federal statute ever set aside on that ground. The legal proposition was so unanticipated that the government's brief of 227 pages and 200 more of appendix devoted only 13 pages to the subject.

Hughes's opinion caused considerable consternation and apprehension. In a twentieth-century economy it is simply impossible for Congress to spell out in detail the guideposts to be used by the multitude of administrative bodies in the regulation of industry. If the decision stood, no New Deal measure was safe.

Cause for anxiety came again the next month in the case of *Norman* v. *Baltimore & Ohio Railroad*. This involved a resolution adopted by Congress in June of 1933 declaring unenforceable and against public policy contract provisions requiring repayment of loans in gold. The resolution made such contracts dischargeable dollar for dollar in any legal tender currency, which of course meant the devalued dollar. A holder of a railroad bond bearing an interest coupon payable in gold of face value of $22.50 demanded repayment in the sum of $38.10 which was the current value in legal tender of $22.50 in gold coin. In a companion case, the holder of a similar bond that had been issued by the United States Treasury for $10,000 demanded payment of the government in the sum of some $17,000 in devalued currency.

The cases were argued early in January, 1935. The legislation had become effective a year and a half earlier. The government's entire monetary policy depended upon the outcome of the case. But the Court delayed announcing a decision. So intense was the excitement caused by the delay that on successive weekends the Court ordered the clerk to announce that no decision in the case would be forthcoming on the following Monday. (Stone commented drily that he did not like this "communique" procedure.) The Friday before Monday, February 18, no such announcement was made and the world of finance waited anxiously until the following Monday when the decision was announced.

Over the bitter dissent of the Praetorian Guard, Hughes, who wrote the opinion, and four of his colleagues agreed that the gold clause resolution was constitutional insofar as it applied to private contracts, so Mr. Norman was not entitled to any more than his $22.50 in legal tender. However, Hughes said for the majority, in respect to government bonds, Congress could not modify its own obligations, and that section of the resolution was unconstitutional. Apparently recognizing (although not saying so) that to compel the government to pay $17 for every $10 it owed would result in financial catastrophe, Hughes found a technical way out. Although the government had breached its contract, the bondholders were not damaged and suffered no loss. While the dollar was devalued, prices of commodities had plummeted even further, so that even a devalued dollar could buy more goods than a gold dollar could when the plaintiffs bought their Liberty Bonds.

The workings of the American judicial system are puzzling to foreigners. Robert Jackson, later himself to be a member of the Court, reported that shortly after the decision was announced he was in Sweden and was faced with the following questions by Swedish lawyers and bankers:

"How could you Americans let your national monetary and economic policy be dependent on the outcome of a lawsuit between private parties over a difference of $15.60?"

"How could American business intelligently function over a year and a half while such basic questions were pending in the Court? Why could you not learn the answer earlier?"

"Why should within one of a majority of your Court hold that a private contract between two citizens should deprive the nation of power to change its monetary policy?"

"And why, anyway, should lawyer-judges be supreme over the national parliament, the President, the Treasury, and the whole government in a matter so vital to economic life?"

In its practical effect the decision was a victory for the government, and the four dissenters so regarded it. Besides reading his written dissent which spoke of the "spoilation of citizens" and the "impending legal and moral chaos," McReynolds, according to a report in the New York *Times*, delivered a twenty minute extemporaneous denunciation. "The Constitution," he said dramatically, "is gone. . . . In one breath it is said Congress has no power to repudiate a government obligation. In the next breath, it is said, it is true you have but sixty cents and you were promised a dollar, but . . . there is no damage. . . . Here we have a monetary system the extent—I almost said wickedness—of which is almost beyond comprehension."

But though a victory in its practical consequences, the decision caused considerable consternation within the New Deal. Ordinarily, if the Court found that the plaintiffs could not recover because they suffered no damage, it would not go into the constitutional question. It is one of the oft-recited (and, since *Marbury* v. *Madison*, oft-violated) rules of the Court not to declare a law unconstitutional except where necessary for the disposition of the case. Stone refused to go along with Hughes's opinion and wrote a special concurring opinion in which he asserted this rule. Consternation was caused by the fact that Hughes and Roberts went out of their way (it was assumed that concurrence by Brandeis and Cardozo was the price that had to be paid for the practical victory) to declare unconstitutional one of the major pillars of the entire New Deal structure. The future appeared ominous. High hopes had given way to anxiety, and anxiety was quickly to give way to despair.

DESPAIR

The feared first blow was not long in coming. But the person who struck it was not Hughes, who had written the grudging opinion in the Blaisdell case and the ominous opinion in the Gold Clause cases. It was rather Roberts, who had written in the Nebbia case an opinion so broad in its scope and language as to justify the entire rationale of the New Deal program. On May 6, 1935 the Court handed down its decision in *Railroad Retirement Board* v. *Alton Railroad*, and it was discovered that not only had Roberts joined the ultra-conservatives on the Court, but had become their spokesman.

In 1934 Congress had adopted the Railroad Retirement Act. Its purpose was to provide for the retirement of superannuated railroad employees with a pension. This was done by a form of compulsory insurance whereby contributions of the railroads and their employees were pooled to provide an annuity to all employees, varying according to the length of service.

Roberts' opinion for the five to four majority threw out the entire act. It was, he held, beyond the power of Congress to set up a compulsory pensions system for railroads. This did not constitute the regulation of commerce. Congress could, of course, take appropriate measure to insure the safety of railroad transportation, and this might well include compulsory retirement of over-age workers, but it could not provide them with pensions at the railroads' expense. The act, said Roberts somewhat contemptuously, is based on "the contentment and satisfaction" theory of social progress. Disguised as a measure to regulate railroad transportation, its provisions "are really and essentially related solely to the social welfare of the worker." The five members of the majority were not fooled. Social welfare is not for Congress. The provisions of the law were "remote from any regulation of commerce as such," and the entire law must be thrown out as constitutionally impure.

Hughes wrote a stiff opinion for himself and the other three dissenters. The Court, he said, had long upheld federal laws imposing liability on railroads for injuries suffered by their workers in the course of employment. The Retirement Act was no different. "The fundamental consideration which supports this type of legislation is that industry should take care of its human wastage, whether that is due to accident or age."

The Railroad Retirement case was decided on May 6, 1935. Three weeks later the Court closed its current term on a day which liberals dubbed "Black Monday." On that day the Court handed down three decisions striking hard blows at Roosevelt's New Deal, and the worst of it was that in all three cases the Court was unanimous. There was not a single dissent; in fact, one of the three opinions was written by the chief champion himself, Louis Brandeis.

This was the case of *Louisville Joint Stock Company* v. *Redford*, holding unconstitutional the Frazier–Lemke Act. In June, 1934 Congress had adopted the Farm Mortgage Foreclosure Act to enable farmers to borrow money from the government to forestall loss of their farms in foreclosure proceedings. At the same time it adopted the Frazier–Lemke Bankruptcy Act. This provided that a bankrupt farmer might demand a reappraisal of his property under foreclosure and be allowed to buy it back at the new, greatly devalued figure, paying for it over a six-year period with interest at only 1 per cent. If the holder of the mortgage objected, the law provided that the farmer had the right to halt the foreclosure proceedings and keep the farm for five years on payment of a reasonable rental.

Speaking for a unanimous Court, Brandeis declared the law unconstitutional for violating the ban in the Fifth Amendment on any federal statute depriving a person of property without due process of law. The objection to the statute, Brandeis held, was that it was a clear case of class legislation, transferring the property of the creditor class to the debtor class without any compensation for the former. "The Fifth Amendment," he said, "commands that, however great the nation's need, private property shall not be thus taken even for a wholly public use without just compensation. If the public interest requires, and permits, the taking of property of individual mortgagees in order to relieve the necessities of individual mortgagors, resort must be had to proceedings by eminent domain; so that through taxation, the burden of relief afforded in the public interest may be borne by the public."

The second case was *Humphrey's Executor* v. *United States.* One of the difficulties in which Roosevelt found himself on taking over was that the various governmental commissions and departments were staffed by men, appointed by Harding, Coolidge and Hoover, who were completely unsympathetic to the aims and purposes of the New Deal, and some of them did not hesitate to wage internal war against it. The laws setting up these agencies provided for fixed terms for their holders, and the impatient President could not wait until the terms expired. If any of the holdovers could be shown to have committed some clearly wrongful act, they could be removed for cause, but—as had been established in the unsuccessful impeachments of Justice Chase and President Johnson —disagreement with the policies of the dominant political faction does not legally constitute a wrongful act or course of conduct.

One of these office holders was William E. Humphrey, a member of the Federal Trade Commission appointed by Hoover. Roosevelt issued an order declaring him removed from office on the ground of disagreement between Humphrey's policies and those of the administration in the carrying out of the purposes of the Federal Trade Commission Act. (Only nine years earlier, in the case of *Myers* v. *United States,* Taft, speaking for the majority of the Court, had held that the power to appoint implies the power to remove, and that a postmaster appointed by the President could be removed by him.)

Humphrey sued to regain his post. Before the case reached the

Supreme Court, he died. The action was continued by his widow as a suit for salary and the Court not only ordered that she be paid his salary but forbade future dismissals of duly appointed and confirmed members of commissions such as the FTC. The Myers decision did not embarrass the Court or its spokesman, Justice Sutherland, the ablest of the ultra-conservative members. The Myers case involved a postmaster, who was purely an executive official; Humphrey was a member of a regulatory commission exercising a quasi-judicial function. Nor was Sutherland fazed by the fact that Taft's opinion in the Myers case made no distinction between executive and quasi-judicial officials, but on the contrary expressly stated that the same Presidential right, and in fact duty, of removal existed in all cases.

The concurrence in this decision by the liberal members is understandable. Removed from the context of the particular situation which gave rise to it, the decision was one which liberals would ordinarily applaud. Brandeis (along with Holmes and McReynolds, but not Stone) had dissented in the Myers case and was naturally gratified when the substance of his dissent was adopted by the Court in the Humphrey case. "If men on the Federal Trade Commission," and similar government agencies, he said in a confidential interview, "are not allowed to exercise their independent judgment we should have in effect a dictatorship or a totalitarian state. What would happen to us if Huey Long were President and such a doctrine prevailed?"

Of the three decisions handed down on Black Monday the Humphrey opinion appears to have infuriated Roosevelt the most. He took it almost as a personal affront. It seemed to him that the Court went out of its way to rebuke him for doing what Taft had said it was the right and duty of Presidents to do. Instead of saying frankly that the Court had changed its mind, it implied that Roosevelt had flouted the Constitution. Beyond that, it appeared to be a judicial attempt to hamstring the President in carrying out the mandate he had so overwhelmingly received from the people. His reaction to the Humphrey decision was very similar to Jefferson's reaction to *Marbury* v. *Madison*, and for the same reason: to both it seemed that a Court representing a discredited administration was seeking to encroach upon the Presidential prerogative and frustrate the will of the people by foisting upon the new administration the discarded remnants of the old. Rexford G. Tugwell, one of Roosevelt's chief brain trusters, suggests that it was the Humphrey decision that may have motivated Roosevelt's choice of a particularly humiliating means for curbing the Court.

The third decision handed down on May 27, 1935 was by far the most dramatic and newsworthy. It was the *Schechter Poultry Corporation* v. *United States*, the case that killed the NRA.

The National Industrial Recovery Act had been passed by Congress some two months after Roosevelt's inauguration. At the time it was the keystone of his recovery program. Whatever its failings and deficiencies, it can hardly be doubted that more than anything else it had burst forth as a beacon of hope and courage in a sea of despond and demoralization. Its purpose, in the words of Roosevelt's message to Congress, was to set up "the machinery for a great co-operative movement throughout all industry in order to obtain wide re-employment, to shorten the working week, to pay a decent wage for the shorter week, and to prevent unfair competition and disastrous overproduction." It sought to accomplish this through self-government in industry.

The act provided that the President should have authority to approve codes of fair competition in each trade or industry if they were proposed by a truly representative section of the trade or industry and were not designed to promote monopolies or oppress small enterprises. When so approved by the President, all engaged in the trade or industry were required to comply under penalty of the law. One section of the act required that every code should insure the free right of collective bargaining, bar yellow-dog contracts, and impose upon employers the obligation of complying with maximum hours and minimum wages for the trade or industry as fixed by the President.

The act was adopted in the dark days of 1933 when even to the Republicans Roosevelt appeared as a savior. By 1935 disillusionment had set in. The press had become overwhelmingly hostile to the whole New Deal experiment, and the NRA became the chief whipping boy. So many trades and industries had brought themselves under the act that effective administration and supervision was impossible. The inherent weaknesses and deficiencies became apparent in the course of administration. The act had a two year expiration date, and was scheduled to terminate on June 15, 1935. Had the Court not intervened, the act would have undoubtedly been either completely dropped or, more likely, radically revised. But this was not allowed to happen.

The Department of Justice had recognized early that ultimately the constitutionality of the act would have to be decided by the Supreme Court and it kept hunting around for a good test case to bring up. Unfortunately for it, it tarried too long, and the case which did reach the Court, very much against the Department's wish, was a very poor one.

The test case involved the Live Poultry Code. The Schechter brothers of Brooklyn, operators of a small poultry market, were indicted and convicted for violation of both the labor and trade practice provisions of the code, the labor provisions by paying substandard wages and imposing excessive hours, and the trade practice provisions by selling sick chickens. The federal circuit court of appeals held the wage and hour provisions of the code unconstitutional, but it upheld the trade practices provisions. Had it invalidated these as well, the government would probably not have appealed to the Supreme Court and would have continued to shop around for a better case—one involving a major industry whose unfair trade and labor practices would be shown seriously to affect the national economy. Unfortunately for the Government it had won part of its case, and the Schechter brothers exercised their option of appealing, particularly as they suddenly found themselves graced with the voluntary legal services of one of the top Wall Street law firms.

The Supreme Court held the entire NRA unconstitutional. The opinion was written by Chief Justice Hughes, and two grounds were stated for it. In the first place, he said, the act involved a delegation of power to the President in violation of the principles set forth in the "Hot Oil" case. In the second place it went beyond the powers of Congress for it sought to regulate as interstate commerce what were purely local activities subject only to state regulation. Fuller's sugar trust decision had held that manufacturing was not interstate commerce, and therefore, said Hughes, the fixing of wages and hours in manufacturing (or retail selling) cannot be justified under the provision in the Constitution empowering Congress to regulate interstate commerce. Congress, he held, can regulate local activities when they *directly* affect interstate commerce, but not when they do so only indirectly.

Roosevelt called a press conference. It lasted almost an hour and a half, and most of it was devoted to the Schechter decision. Its effect, he said, was to take the United States back to the "horse and buggy" days. This phrase was picked up by the press and hurled back at the President with scorn and derision. Nevertheless, it did symbolize the realistic implications of the decision. The question the nation had to decide, Roosevelt said, was "whether in some way we are going to restore to the Federal Government the powers which exist in the national governments of every other nation in the world to enact and administer laws that have a bearing on and general control over national economic problems and national social problems."

Reality was undoubtedly on Roosevelt's side. Reliance on separate legislation in forty-eight separate contiguous states was impossible in the mid-twentieth century. The alternative faced by the country was not national regulation or state regulation; it was national regulation or no regulation at all. If (as Cardozo said in his concurring opinion) the NRA was "delegation run riot"; Hughes's opinion in the Schechter case was laissez faire run riot. That may have been the way to run a country in 1789; it decidedly was not the way to do so in 1935.

DISASTER

The next term of the Supreme Court convened in the fall of 1935 and it soon took up where the previous term had left off. During the summer, however, Brandeis, Stone and Cardozo must have done some hard thinking and apparently came up with second thoughts. Whatever the cause, thereafter they were to be found in their more natural habitat on the left. Hughes, for his part, wavered as if he were in the middle of a tug of war between the two factions of the Court. Roberts, on the other hand, had found himself a home with the ultra-conservatives, and these, of course, remained as steadfast as Gibraltar.

The first major bastion of the New Deal to fall in the new term was the Agricultural Administration Act. This had been enacted during the Hundred Days for the purpose of raising depressed farmers' income by according parity to agricultural products, that is, giving them a purchasing power with respect to the manufactured goods that farmers bought equivalent to that which they had in the period of 1900-1914, which was taken as the normal period. Since the cause of depressed prices for farm products was considered to be overproduction, the Secretary of Agriculture was authorized to make agreements with individual farmers under which they would receive benefit payments for reducing the acreage of their crops or their production of livestock. The revenue for these payments was to be raised through a "processing tax" paid by the first processor of the basic commodities for the domestic market.

Whatever may have been the economic validity of the AAA, it gave all appearances of working. During the two and a half years of its existence basic farm prices increased by about 100 per cent. Whether this was a case of cause or of coincidence may be a matter of dispute; but it is indisputable that the farmers felt it was the former, for every referendum revealed that they overwhelmingly favored continuation of the program. At least some financial interests, too, were of the opinion that the program had salutary effects on the entire economy. "It is hardly deniable," said a report issued by the National City Bank of New York in October, 1935, "that the impetus to the general business improvement originated on the farms, in the improved relationship between farm and industrial prices, which gave farm products a greater value in exchange for the products of industry."

In the case of *United States* v. *Butler*, the constitutionality of the law was attacked. The argument against it by George Wharton Pepper, former Republican Senator from Pennsylvania, was reminiscent of Joseph H. Choate's appeal to the Court to invalidate the income tax in order to stop the march of communism. "I am standing here today," Pepper told the Court, "to plead the cause of the America I have loved; and I pray Almighty God that not in my time may 'the land of the regimented' be accepted as a worthy substitute for 'the land of the free.' "

On January 6, 1936 the Court announced its decision and Pepper found that his prayers had reached the ears of a receptive deity. "Judges," Governor John Winthrop of Massachusetts Bay Colony had said in 1644, "are Gods upon earth." The gods on the Supreme Court bench, or two-thirds of them anyway, answered Pepper's prayer and held the AAA unconstitutional.

Undoubtedly, said Roberts for the majority, Congress has the power to levy excise taxes on the processing of agricultural products. Likewise, it has the power to subsidize agriculture, as it has to subsidize manufacturing and commerce; this was the underlying thesis of Hamilton's famous Report on Manufactures. But, said Roberts, it cannot do both, for then it reveals that the processing tax is not really a tax at all but a devious means of regulating agricultural production, just as the tax in the case of *Bailey* v. *Drexel Furniture Company* was a subterfuge employed to regulate child labor. Agriculture is not commerce; it is not subject to regulation by Congress. The AAA must fall because

> it is a scheme for purchasing with Federal funds submission to Federal regulation of a subject reserved to the states. . . . Congress cannot invade state jurisdiction to compel individual action; no more can it purchase such action. . . . It must follow that it may not indirectly accomplish those ends by taxing and spending to purchase compliance. . . . It does not help to declare that local conditions throughout the nation have created a situation of national concern; for this is but to say that whenever there is a widespread similarity of local conditions, Congress may ignore constitutional limitations upon its own powers and usurp those reserved to the states.

Stone's dissenting opinion, in which Brandeis and Cardozo joined, is almost universally deemed by constitutional lawyers to be devastating. According to Roberts, said Stone, the government could subsidize the farmers but could not condition the subsidy on acreage reduction. The logic of this was that the

> Government may give seeds to farmers, but may not condition the gift upon their being planted in places where most needed or even planted at all. The Government may give money to the unemployed, but may not ask that those who get it shall give labor in return, or even use it to support their families. It may give money to sufferers from earthquake, fire, tornado, pestilence or flood, but may not impose conditions—health precautions designed to prevent spread of disease. . . . All that, because it is purchased regulation infringing state powers, must be left for the states, who are unable or unwilling to supply necessary relief.

Roberts' opinion, continued Stone, represents a "tortured construction of the Constitution. . . . While unconstitutional exercise of power by the executive and legislative branches of the government is subject to judicial restraint, the only check upon our own exercise of power is our own sense of self-restraint. . . . For the removal of unwise laws from the statute books appeal lies not to the courts but to the ballot and to the processes of democratic government. . . . Courts are not the only agency of government that must be assumed to have capacity to govern."

Roberts strongly resented the tone of Stone's dissent and even went so far as to complain to the Chief Justice that this was not the way to treat a Court colleague. Hughes refused to intervene, but suggested that Roberts approach Brandeis. Roberts may have done so, and it is possible that on Brandeis' urging, Stone softened the tone of the original draft of his opinion. If so, one can judge from the final version the intensity of feeling in the original.

The next blow struck at the New Deal came in May, and this time the sacrificial victim was the Bituminous Coal Conservation Act of 1935. The purpose of the law was to bring some order and stabilization in the chaotic coal mining industry. If any industry was national in its consequences, the coal industry was, and the soft coal industry was one of the first to bring itself under the NRA. After that act was declared unconstitutional in the Schechter case, Congress passed the Guffey Act to save whatever could be saved, for there was substantial unanimity of opinion that wherever else NRA may have failed, it had effected substantial improvements in the coal industry.

The new law declared that the production and distribution of soft coal directly affected interstate commerce and that regulation of production and prices was unnecessary to promote such commerce. A commission was set up, and codes to regulate prices and trade practices were authorized. A separate part of the act dealt with labor relations and sought to assure free collective bargaining. Provision was also made in respect to maximum hours and minimum wages. Finally, with the Supreme Court ever in its consciousness, Congress provided that if any provision of the act should be declared unconstitutional, that should not invalidate those provisions of the act found to be constitutional.

The constitutionality of the act was challenged in a suit which reminds us of the one which led to the invalidation of the income tax law. James W. Carter, president of the Carter Coal Company, believed that the law was invalid and called upon his company not to comply with it. The rebellious company disagreed with him and said that it would comply with it. Despite his high office and large holdings, Mr. Carter apparently had no other means to persuade the company to his way of thinking, and therefore regretfully went to court to get an injunction against it. So certain was the company that it was right, that it fought the case all the way up to the Supreme Court, where to its dismay it found that it was wrong and that Mr. Carter was right all the time. The law, said a majority of the nine Justices in *Carter* v. *Carter Coal Company* was unconstitutional.

Sutherland, speaking for the majority, denounced the act as an infringement of the rights of the states. The states themselves did not seem to think so; seven of them, including the major coal producing states of Pennsylvania, Kentucky and Ohio, filed briefs with the Court urging it to uphold the law, and not a single state filed a contrary brief.

But Sutherland knew what was good for the states better than they did themselves.

Mining is not commerce, no more than manufacturing or agriculture is. If fixing hours for miners affects interstate commerce, it does so indirectly, and that is not enough. Therefore, the labor provisions of the act are unconstitutional and therefore the whole act is unconstitutional, even though Congress specifically stated that any unconstitutional provisions could be amputated without killing the patient.

Even Hughes could not accept the last point. He agreed with Sutherland that the labor provisions were unconstitutional but asserted that the rest of the law should not be declared invalid. Cardozo, in an opinion joined by Brandeis and Stone, dissented completely. The only issues before the Court, he said, were the provisions fixing the price of coal sold in interstate commerce. There was no need to pass on the labor provisions because these were not yet in effect. As to these, he said, "the complainants have been crying before they are really hurt." As to the other provisions, Congress was not "condemned to inaction in the face of price wars . . . so pregnant with disaster."

Hard upon the Carter case came *Ashton* v. *Cameron County Water District*, in which by another five to four vote the Court held unconstitutional the Municipal Bankruptcy Act. This law, enacted in 1934, authorized insolvent municipalities and municipal corporations to resort to the federal bankruptcy courts for readjustment of their obligations. Plans scaling down or compromising debts could be enforced by the federal courts if approved by two-third of the creditors and if authorized by the laws of the state in which the municipality was located. The act was declared unconstitutional as an invasion of the rights of the states. Cardoza wrote a sharp dissenting opinion in which Brandeis, Stone and Hughes joined.

The Court ended its term on June 1, 1936 with the case of *Morehead* v. *Tipaldo* which invalidated New York's carefully drafted minimum wage law for women. The law prohibited the employment of women in certain industries at wages "both less than the fair and reasonable value of the services rendered and less than sufficient to meet the minimum cost of living necessary to health." It had been so drawn to avoid the grounds on which the Court, in the case of *Adkins* v. *Children's Hospital*, had declared unconstitutional the District of Columbia minimum wage law for women. The reference to living wages was made to bring the law within the state's police power. The provision that the fixed wage must not be less than the fair and reasonable value of the services was inserted to prevent invalidation on the ground that the employers were being deprived of their property without due process of law by being made to pay more for the women's services than they were worth.

All to no avail. Butler, speaking for the majority of five, declared the law unconstitutional as an interference with freedom of contract. "In making contracts of employment," said Butler, "generally speaking, the parties have equal right to obtain from each other the best terms they can by private bargaining," and "the state is without power by any form of legislation to prohibit, change or nullify contracts between employers and adult women workers as to the amount of wages to be paid." There was no difference between the District of Columbia law and the New York law, and if the former was unconstitutional so too was the latter. Even if the Adkins decision was incorrect, the Court could not overrule it because counsel for New York State had not asked it to do so but had relied on the erroneous theory that the two laws were different.

Hughes filed a dissenting opinion for himself in which he disagreed with the majority's claim that the two laws could not be distinguished. He would not overrule the Adkins decision but would nevertheless hold the New York law constitutional.

In a dissenting opinion as blistering as that in the AAA case, Stone, with the concurrence of Brandeis and Cardozo, demanded that the Adkins case be overruled. He could, he said, "find nothing in the Federal Constitution which denies to the states the power to protect women from being exploited by overreaching employers through the refusal of a fair wage. . . . There is grim irony in speaking of the freedom of contract of those who, because of their economic necessities, give their service for less than is needful to keep body and soul together."

It was not recognized at the time, but the Tipaldo case marked the end of the Court that Marshall had created. When the Justices left for their summer vacation in June of 1936 they almost certainly did not anticipate that never again (at least until 1965, the time of the present writing) would the Court employ the Constitution to interfere in any substantial extent with government regulation of economic affairs. The era of judicial nullification of social welfare laws had come to an end.

It was, however, recognized universally that something had to happen. The Court had employed concepts of federalism or states' rights to keep Congress out of the field of economic regulation in the interests of public welfare and then employed due process and freedom of contract to keep states out. Stone did not overstate the situation in a letter he wrote to his sister on June 2:

> We finished the term of the Court yesterday, I think in many ways one of the most disastrous in its history. At any rate it seems to me that the Court had been needlessly narrow and obscurantic in its outlook. I suppose no intelligent person likes very well the way the New Deal does things, but that ought not to make us forget that ours is a nation which should have the powers ordinarily possessed by governments, and that the framers of the Constitution intended that it should have. Our latest exploit was a holding by a divided vote that there was no power in a state to regulate minimum wages for women. Since the Court last week said that this could not be done by the national government, as the matter was local, and now it is said that it cannot be done by local governments, even though it is local, we seem to have tied Uncle Sam up in a hard knot.

One thing was certain: Uncle Sam was not going to permit himself to remain tied up in a hard knot. McReynolds, Van Devanter, Sutherland and Butler may have been too far gone to see it; but Roberts could not be blind to it. The Tipaldo decision alienated many of the Court's most ardent defenders. It seemed to condemn America to a sweatshop economy. Even the Republican party could not accept it. In its national platform for the 1936 Presidential campaign it almost expressly repudiated the Tipaldo decision. It pledged the party to "support the adoption of state laws and interstate compacts to abolish sweatshops and child labor, and to protect women and children with respect to maximum hours, minimum wages and working conditions. We believe that this can be done within the Constitution as it now stands."

It could, perhaps, be done within the Constitution as it then stood. But not within the Supreme Court as it then stood. A revolution was needed to accomplish that, and unless all American history was false, one would be forthcoming. The only question was whether it would be (symbolically) a bloody revolution or a bloodless one. McReynolds–Van Devanter–Sutherland–Butler were beyond hope. The choice had to be made by Roberts.

ATTACK

After the Supreme Court adjourned, the 1936 Presidential campaign got under way. The Court may or may not have been a major issue in the campaign, but there was no doubt that the New Deal was, and the people's choice was clear. Roosevelt was re-elected by the largest electoral vote in the history of the nation since Monroe's Era of Good Feeling. In a sense this may have been unfortunate, for not only did Roosevelt interpret it as a mandate to proceed with his program notwithstanding the opposition of the Court (which it probably was), but it gave him a feeling of overconfidence. He saw well his own victory; but it was so brilliant that it blinded him to the status and prestige that the Court had achieved since Marshall took office. The Court had been the victim of what Hughes called in his book "self-inflicted wounds," but no single one of them was mortal. With less cause for self-confidence Roosevelt might have prepared his campaign with greater care. In the end he won anyway, decisively and (as of now) permanently; but not in the way he planned or expected.

In view of Roosevelt's personality and his smashing victory at the polls, some measure of effective action to overcome the Court's refusal to recognize the twentieth century was inevitable. Roosevelt would, in fact, have been less than faithful to his obligation to the people as expressed in the election returns if he had accepted the judicial veto as the final word. A counterattack was called for; all that remained to be decided was its nature.

There were two alternatives: either the Constitution or the Court could be reformed. Reformation of the Constitution could be accomplished by adopting an amendment or amendments specifically authorizing the states to enact minimum wage laws for women or Congress to regulate the coal industry or to meet the problem of depressed farm prices. That was the method which was tried to overcome the income tax and child labor decisions, but it had proved successful only in the first case. Almost twenty years had elapsed since *Hammer* v. *Dagenhart*, and the proposed amendment authorizing Congress to ban child labor still had ten states to go. And if an amendment were at long last adopted, the Supreme Court would still have the last word as to its meaning and application, and its record in respect, not only to the Income Tax Amendment but even more in respect to the Fourteenth Amendment, was far from encouraging. Finally, even the Republican party in its 1936 platform had agreed that amendment of the Constitution was not necessary to abolish sweatshops, child labor and the exploitation of women.

The only reliable way, Roosevelt and his advisers were convinced, was by reforming the Court. This, too, could be done either by amending the Constitution or by an act of Congress. Most of the liberals and progressives both in Congress and among Roosevelt's advisers favored the former method. Burton K. Wheeler, Democratic senator from Montana, who was to assume the leadership of the fight against the method that Roosevelt chose, himself introduced a resolution for a Constitutional amendment allowing Congress by a two-thirds vote to overrule Supreme Court decisions on constitutional issues. Senator Joseph C. O'Mahoney, another liberal Democrat who joined the opposition to the Roosevelt plan, proposed an amendment requiring a two-thirds vote of the Court in order to declare any law unconstitutional. Both proposals involved the long, drawn-out and never certain means of Constitutional amendment, and Roosevelt was in no mood to wait. Another possibility was to seek to accomplish the same result by Congressional action, such as a law requiring a two-thirds or seven-ninths vote of the Court to declare an act of Congress or of the states to be unconstitutional. The difficulty with this was that such a law itself would probably be declared unconstitutional by the Court.

Despite a general impression to the contrary, the proposal that Roosevelt did make to Congress in his judiciary reorganization message of February 5, 1937, was not an impulsive, spur-of-the-moment idea. For more than a year the brain trust had been wrestling with the problem. As early as December, 1935, according to Harold Ickes' *Diary*, Roosevelt told his cabinet that he expected the Court to declare unconstitutional all the major measures of the New Deal and suggested three ways of meeting the eventuality: "(1) by packing the Supreme Court, which was a distasteful idea; (2) by trying to put through a number of amendments to the Constitution to meet the various situations; and (3) by a method that he asked us to consider very carefully"—a Constitutional amendment empowering Congress to re-enact at its next succeeding session, a law declared unconstitutional by the Court. The Reorganization Bill of 1937 was decided upon after all other proposals were eliminated as impracticable or unattainable.

Congress, said Roosevelt in his message proposing the bill, must take action to quiet the complaints of the citizens over "the complexities, the delays, and the expense of litigation in United States courts." The overcrowded dockets proved "the need for additional judges" in all ranks of the Judiciary. "A part of the problem of obtaining a sufficient number of judges to dispose of cases is the capacity of the judges themselves.

This brings forward the question of aged and infirm judges—a subject of delicacy and yet one which requires frank discussion." A law enacted in 1869 allowed judges who had served for ten years to retire at full pay at the age of seventy, but many judges, both in the lower federal courts and in the Supreme Court, refused to retire. "Life tenure of judges, assured by the Constitution, was designed to place the courts beyond temptations or influence which might impair their judgments; it was not intended to create a static judiciary. A constant and systematic addition of younger blood will vitalize the courts and better equip them to recognize and apply essential concepts of justice in the light of the needs and the facts of an ever-changing world."

To achieve this infusion of new blood, Roosevelt submitted to Congress, along with the message, a judiciary reorganization bill, prepared by, or under the direction of, Attorney-General Homer Cummings. The bill provided that when any federal judge attained the age of seventy and had served for ten years and then failed to resign or retire within six months, the President would be empowered to appoint an additional judge to the same court. Not more than fifty new judges would be permitted under the bill, and at no time would the Supreme Court exceed fifteen Justices in its membership. (In 1937, six of the nine Justices were over the age of seventy; only Stone, Cardozo and Roberts were not. Enactment of the bill, therefore, would have allowed Roosevelt, who had not yet had the opportunity of naming a single member to the Court, to appoint six Justices.)

The message and the bill fell like a bombshell upon the nation; and the reaction was violent and widespread. Overwhelmingly the press condemned it with unrestrained fury. It was immediately termed a court-packing plan—which indeed it was, though hardly the first one in the history of the country. Even the Democratic party was badly split over it. Generalship of the campaign in Congress fell to the party floor leader in the Senate, Joseph T. Robinson of Arkansas, and as reward Roosevelt promised him the first available vacancy on the bench. But Robinson could not enlist the unanimous support even of his own fellow Democrats. The opposition of the conservative wing of the party, Carter Glass and Harry F. Byrd of Virginia, Walter F. George of Georgia and others, was expected; but the leadership of the opposition was taken by the liberal, western Democrat, Wheeler of Montana.

Even Roosevelt partisans are agreed that the President blundered in his approach. His proposal, it is said, was at the very least disingenuous. It was not the physical but the political age of the Justices that was the problem. The oldest member of the Court in terms of years was Brandeis, the intellectual godfather of the New Deal, and had there been nine, or even five Brandeises on the bench, Roosevelt would have had no occasion to complain. It was not the delay in the Court calendar that was the cause of the New Deal's difficulties. This pretense was pretty thoroughly demolished by a letter which Wheeler obtained from Hughes and read at the Senate committee hearing. (Wheeler had wanted Hughes to testify in person, but Brandeis strongly opposed this, and suggested instead that Hughes send a letter. Hughes's letter was seen in advance only by Van Devanter and Brandeis, and Stone resented the Chief Justice's failure to consult the entire Court before sending it.) "The Supreme Court," the letter stated, "is fully abreast of its work." There was no congestion of cases upon its calendar, all appeals that were granted were argued and decided promptly, and that condition had existed for several years.

This, too, according to critics of the Court, was somewhat disingenuous. The Court, they said, kept abreast of its work by refusing to accept many important cases. But this was a technical explanation, not readily understandable by the general public. As far as could be seen by non-lawyers, Roosevelt's complaint that the Court was behind in its work was completely false.

Roosevelt, himself, later conceded that he had blundered. "I made one major mistake when I presented the plan," he commented. "I did not place enough emphasis upon the real mischief—the kind of decisions which, as a studied and continued policy, had been coming down from the Supreme Court. I soon corrected that mistake—in the speeches which I later made about the plan."

Many did not agree that he "corrected the mistake," although they agreed that he tried to. A month after he delivered the message to Congress he took to the air in a fireside chat to explain "the real mischief." He threw back at Hughes the oft-repeated statement which, probably more than anything else in his life, the latter regretted having made: "We are under a Constitution but the Constitution is what the Judges say it is." He cited the Chief Justice's dissenting opinion in the Railroad Retirement case, and Stone's in the AAA and Minimum Wage Law cases to show that "there is no basis for the claim made by some members of the Court that something in the Constitution has compelled them regretfully to thwart the will of the people." He was not seeking to pack the Court but only to unpack it. There was nothing sacred in the number nine; the number of Justices had changed several times in American history. Nor was there anything unprecedented in retiring judges at seventy or adding judges if septuagenarians refused to retire; such a proposal had passed the House of Representatives as long ago as 1869.

Supreme Court historians and students sympathetic to liberalism and progressivism and writing close to the event seemed to agree that the initial blunder was irremediable. Roosevelt should have chosen a less devious approach, and should have been more frank in stating his purpose at the very outset. He had overestimated his own popularity and underestimated the Court's tarnished but still unshaken prestige. By appearing to attack the Court simply because of the old age of the Justices he had aroused the sympathy of Americans for the elderly while at the same time slapping in the face his best friend on the bench. For once, Roosevelt's uncanny political sense had left him. The result was defeat.

Time has made possible a different appraisal. In the first place, it is likely that no matter what plan Roosevelt would have proposed or how well written had been the message accompanying it, the wrath of the press and radio would have descended upon him. If the battle cry had not been "court-packing," it would have been something else. The emotional frenzy whipped up by the bitterly anti-Roosevelt press was not motivated by the details of the President's plan, nor by his method of presenting it. Any plan proposed by him in any way would have suffered the same fate.

Nor is it by any means certain that the people were against Roosevelt's proposal. The election of 1936 showed, as that of 1948 was likewise to show, that press reaction is not always an accurate barometer of the political atmosphere. Had the judiciary reorganization bill been brought to a vote promptly it might well have passed, though by a narrow margin. It is more than probable that had there been another AAA, Railroad Retirement or Minimum Wage decision, had the Court invalidated the National Labor Relations Act, the Social Security Law or the Wage and Hour Law, then the judiciary reorganization bill or something considerably more radical would have been passed. In fact, Roosevelt himself expressed the hope that this would happen. The truth of the matter is that he won, and won a far greater victory than he anticipated or had any reason to hope for. The remark of the late Edmond Cahn of New

York University Law School that Roosevelt "lost the battle but won the war" has become almost a cliche in legal circles. He sought a reformation; he won a revolution. By adding six new members to the bench he hoped to get a more progressive "third House of the Legislature"; instead he achieved the abolition of the Third House altogether insofar as social welfare legislation was concerned. The revolution did not come all at once; revolutions rarely do. First there was to be a period of retreat, in which the Court would seriously consider various social welfare laws of the type so frequently invalidated before 1937, and would find that after all they did not violate the Constitution. Then would come surrender—the present era, when the Court, for all practical purposes, no longer passes on such legislation.

RETREAT

On February 5, 1937, Roosevelt sent his message to Congress. On March 9th, he delivered his "fireside chat" explaining and defending his proposal. On March 29, the Court handed down its decision in the case of *West Coast Hotel* v. *Parrish*. Involved was a minimum wage law of the state of Washington substantially identical with the New York law thrown out less than a year earlier in the Tipaldo case. Again the case was decided by a vote of five to four—but this time it was five to four in favor of constitutionality. Roberts had deserted the conservatives and joined the liberals. The opinion was written by Hughes, and it appeared that he too had signed up. It was not a half-way measure, saying that the Washington law was different from the District of Columbia statute invalidated in the Adkins case; it went all the way and expressly overruled the Adkins decision. The opinion rediscovered the police power, and in effect told the states that henceforth they could adopt not only minimum wage laws for women, but anti-sweatshop legislation and anti-child labor laws as well—and all this without amending the Constitution.

Wags quickly coined the famous aphorism "A switch in time saves nine." Both Hughes and Roberts bitterly resented the insinuation that the President's reorganization proposal in any way affected this or any other of their decisions in 1937 and later. "The President's proposal," Hughes said in his Biographical Notes which he made available to Merlo Pusey, "had not the slightest effect on our decision." Roberts, too, felt a burning need to vindicate himself in the eyes of posterity. In 1945, after he resigned from the Court, he left a memorandum with Frankfurter explaining his votes in the Tipaldo and Parrish cases; he authorized Frankfurter to publish the memorandum whenever he felt it appropriate, and the latter did so after Roberts' death.

Roberts' explanation is interesting. When the Tipaldo case came to the Court he implies (though he does not expressly say so) that he was ready to overrule the Adkins case and uphold the New York law. But counsel for New York state did not ask the Court to overrule the Adkins decision, urging instead that the New York law was different and could be upheld without overruling the earlier decision. "I could," wrote Roberts, "find nothing in the record to substantiate the alleged distinction. At conference [of the Justices after the argument] I so stated, and stated further that I was for taking the State of New York at its word." As it turned out, when Butler wrote the majority opinion he did not content himself with saying that the two cases were indistinguishable and that the Court had not been asked to overrule the earlier one, but said also that the Adkins case was correctly decided and should not be overruled even if the Court were asked to do so. Roberts admits, rather lamely, that perhaps he should have written a special concurring opinion indicating that he did not agree with Butler on the second point, but he did not do so. At all events, when the Washington law came to the Court in the Parrish case, counsel for that state did not, as counsel for New York had done, adopt an argument which was "disingenuous and born of timidity." He honestly and courageously asked the Court to overrule the Tipaldo holding, and Roberts was ready to reward such honesty and courage, and accordingly did vote to sustain the Washintgon law. "No action taken by the President in the interim," he writes as definitely and unqualifiedly as Hughes, "had any causal relation to my action in the Parrish case."

Samuel J. Konefsky, an astute student of the Supreme Court, comments on the Hughes disclaimer contained in the latter's Biographical Notes: "In the history of social forces, even as in the life of an individual, there are times when conduct speaks for itself, particularly when the course that is pursued represents a crucial choice in the presence of reasonable alternatives. Just as hindsight is no substitute for insight, so the backward glance even by an honest man may turn out to be a kind of ex post facto rationalization."

What Konefsky says of Hughes is applicable as well to Roberts. But even if Roberts were not engaging in *ex post facto* rationalization, to persons not privileged to share in the esoteric mysteries of the legal profession his explanation would seem more astounding than what it seeks to explain. Apparently, Roberts was prepared to allow millions of women workers to continue to be exploited for an indefinite period (since there was no way of knowing when the Court would get another opportunity to overrule the Adkins decision) merely because the attorney for New York in the Tipaldo case chose one theory of approach rather than another, or even because he was "disingenuous" and "timid." This is judicial irresponsibility run riot. (Even to a lawyer the explanation seems puzzling. The only issue before the Court in the Tipaldo case was not whether the New York law was similar to or different from the District of Columbia law, but only whether the New York law was constitutional. If Roberts believed it was, it would seem to have been his duty to vote to uphold it, adding, if he wished, an admonition to the attorney for not suggesting the correct theory for upholding it. While courts often say that they will not declare a law unconstitutional on a ground not urged by counsel, they are unanimous in holding that a constitutional law will be upheld on any valid ground, whether or not argued by counsel or considered by the lower courts.)

In one respect there is merit to Roberts' claim. The Justices voted on the Parrish case on December 19, 1936, almost seven weeks before Roosevelt's message, and Roberts voted to uphold the law. Stone, however, was ill at the time and the case was therefore set down for further consideration so as to avoid a four to four vote. Stone returned on February 1, 1937 and thereafter the Justices voted once more, and again Roberts voted to uphold the law. Thus it is undeniable that the Roberts switch took place before the judiciary reorganization bill became public.

Actually, whether or not Roberts knew of the bill when he changed his vote is of little significance. Unless he read nothing but law briefs and heard nothing but arguments of counsel in Court, Roberts could not have been unaware that some move by Roosevelt toward Court reform or reorganization was impending. Roosevelt's smashing victory at the polls, the Republican party platform plank, and countless other factors all pointed in that direction. A Justice of the Supreme Court in Washington could hardly have failed to get some inkling of the deliberations that had gone on for almost a year within the cabinet and the brain trust on appropriate means to overcome the judicial barrier. It is of little moment whether the switch in time that saved nine was made in December of 1936 or February of 1937. In either case, its explanation lies in political rather than judicial terms.

On the same Monday, March 29, 1937 (White Monday, Robert Jackson called it in his book, *The Struggle for Judicial Supremacy*) that the Parrish decision was announced, the Court, in *Virginia Railway* v. *Federation*, sustained the constitutionality of the amended Railway Labor Act, which provided for collective bargaining, mediation and arbitration in the railroad industry. On the same day, too, it upheld (in *Wright* v. *Mountain Trust Company*) a revised Frazier–Lemke Act for the protection of mortgaged farm lands.

Stone exulted; yet he was still somewhat fearful. What effect, he wrote in a letter to his sons, "all this will have on the President's pending proposal remains to be seen. I am fearful, though, that the dissent of the four so-called conservatives, expounding their views of a rigid and changeless Constitution . . . will stimulate criticism of the Court and give emphasis to the demand that it be reformed."

ROUT

Stone had no cause to be fearful. The retreat soon turned into a rout. Two weeks after White Monday, the Court, in *National Labor Relations Board* v. *Jones & Laughlin Steel Corporation*, upheld the National Labor Relations Act and threw out all the laboriously built up niceties regarding direct and indirect effects on interstate commerce, declaring that Congress may regulate activities which affect interstate commerce, whether directly or indirectly. For the almost pathetically unyielding conservatives, McReynolds wrote a dissenting opinion in which he protested that under the majority opinion "almost anything—marriage, births, death—may in some fashion affect commerce." But what really happened was that in the Jones & Laughlin case the Court for the first time held the twentieth century to be constitutional.

Quickly thereafter the Court (in *Senn* v. *Tile Layers Union*) upheld state laws banning injunctions on picketing. Then, in *Carmichael* v. *Southern Coal Company*, it sustained a state social security law, and in *Steward Machine Company* v. *Davis* and *Helvering* v. *Davis* it upheld the federal Social Security Law with its provision for compulsory taxation to protect workers against inpecunious old age and unemployment. Later decisions were to uphold an Agricultural Administration Act (*Mulford* v. *Smith*) and the Fair Labor Standards Act, with its ban on child labor (*United States* v. *Darby*), thus finally and conclusively overruling *Hammer* v. *Dagenhart*.

There were a host of other similar decisions. The upshot of them was that the Court recognized that America at midcentury had graduated from the era of unrestrained and government-encouraged capitalist expansion and was becoming a modified welfare state, and that no matter how much the Justices might deplore the development, they could not, even by invoking the Constitution, stop it. It recognized, too, although Hughes and Roberts vigorously denied it, that if the Court persisted in sitting on the shore and commanding the tides to recede, it would be the Court that would be engulfed. The Court at the last moment wisely decided to retreat and let the sea have its way.

During all this many judicial landmarks were overthrown and many decisions of the Fuller, White and Hughes Court overruled. Hughes himself made a desperate effort to pretend that the Court was not really overruling precedents, but only that the earlier decisions had been misunderstood. The pretense may have been effective as a conscience-easing device for Hughes and Roberts, but it fooled few others. As time went on, this pretense was dropped, and earlier decisions were unabashedly overruled by name.

In view of these developments, there was hardly any further need for the judiciary reorganization bill. By midsummer of 1937 it had become quite clear to the nation which way the wind was blowing, and the bill was permanently shelved by the Senate.

REVOLUTION

The nation assumed that there was no longer any need to reform the Court because the Court had reformed itself, or at least indicated its repentance and intent to reform itself. Actually the change was far more radical than that, although it would take the passage of years to reveal it. It was not a reformation but a revolution that the Court experienced.

It was a bloodless revolution because Roberts, walking in darkness, had seen a great light; but it was a revolution none the less.

The revolution consisted in the Court's withdrawal entirely from the arena of social welfare legislation. Ever since Marshall took over the Chief Justiceship, the Court deemed its mission to be the protection of property against depredations by the people and their legislatures. After 1937 it gave up this mission. In 1963 it was invited to re-assume it, but it firmly refused. The case was *Ferguson* v. *Skrupa*, and it merits summarization here.

In *Adams* v. *Tanner* the White Court in 1917 had ruled unconstitutional a state law which forbade employment agencies to charge fees to workers for whom it found jobs. The Court held that while the state could regulate the business of employment agencies, it could not prohibit a business which is useful and not inherently immoral or dangerous to the public welfare. In *Ferguson* v. *Skrupa*, a lower federal court, on the basis of *Adams* v. *Tanner*, declared unconstitutional a Kansas law which sought to outlaw the business of debt adjustment, under which credit companies, for a fee, undertook to adjust the debts of small businessmen among their creditors so that they could be paid off in small amounts over a long period of time.

The Supreme Court reversed the lower court's decision, and, in an opinion by Black, said:

> There was a time when the Due Process Clause was used by this Court to strike down laws which were thought unreasonable, that is, unwise or incompatible with some particular economic or social philosophy. In this manner the Due Process Clause was used, for example, to nullify laws prescribing maximum hours for work in bakeries (Lochner v. New York), outlawing "yellow dog" contracts (Coppage v. Kansas), setting minimum wages for women (Adkins v. Children's Hospital), and fixing the weight of loaves of bread (Burns Baking Co. v. Bryan). This intrusion by the judiciary into the realm of legislative value judgments was strongly objected to at the time, particularly by Mr. Justice Holmes and Mr. Justice Brandeis.
>
> . . . .
>
> The doctrine that prevailed in Lochner, Coppage, Adkins, Burns and like cases—that due process authorizes courts to hold laws unconstitutional when they believe the legislature has acted unwisely—has long since been discarded. We have returned to the original constitutional proposition that courts do not substitute their social and economic beliefs for the judgment of legislative bodies, who are elected to pass laws.
>
> . . . .
>
> We refuse to sit as a superlegislature to weigh the wisdom of legislation, and we

emphatically refuse to go back to the time when courts used the Due Process Clause to strike down state laws, regulatory of business and industrial conditions, because they may be unwise, improvident, or out of harmony with a particular school of thought. Nor are we able or willing to draw lines by calling a law "prohibitory" or "regulatory." Whether the legislature takes for its textbook Adam Smith, Herbert Spencer, Lord Keynes, or some other is no concern of ours.

Despite this, even today the Court still assumes it has the right to intervene where an act of the legislature, federal or state, constitutes a particularly horrendous instance of expropriation of property or wealth. This is largely meaningless, for so committed are the American people to capitalism that it is highly unlikely that they would normally sanction any such action by a federal or state legislature. If the time ever comes that by reason of an economic or social upheaval such as the depression of the 1930's (although even greater severity would be required) the people would permit such expropriation of wealth and the legislature would be willing to carry it out, it can reasonably be predicted that the Supreme Court would not be able to stand in the way.

This does not mean that the Supreme Court no longer has any influence on the economic affairs of the nation. Of course it has; every court has, and the Supreme Court, as the highest judicial interpreter of national legislation, has more than any other court. But its power and hence influence are severely limited. It can construe economic laws liberally or narrowly, but it no longer vetoes them. It can arbitrate competing claims between states and offer some modest protection to interstate commerce against undue harassment by some state legislature. But even in these cases it can act only when Congress authorizes it to, or when Congress remains silent. When Congress speaks, it must obey. It has become a court, and is no longer a branch of the legislature.

Symbolic of the revolution of 1937 is the 1938 decision of *Erie Railroad* v. *Tompkins*, although this did not effect economic legislation. It is symbolic because it shows how the Court gave up a vast field of civil law in which it had exercised sovereignty for a century. In *Swift* v. *Tyson* the Taney Court had asserted the right to create a whole federal civil law system. If a resident of New York driving in New Jersey collided with a resident of that state and sued or was sued in the federal courts, which could be done by reason of the diversity of citizenship, the federal court was not bound to apply the law of negligence either of New York or of New Jersey, but could apply its own notions of the law of negligence. The result was the building up of a federal common law of negligence—and of contracts, sales, negotiable instruments, personal property, etc.

In *Erie Railroad* v. *Tompkins* the Court suddenly and dramatically overruled *Swift* v. *Tyson*, and did so on the ground that the almost century old decision had been unconstitutional. Thereafter, if an accident occurred in New Jersey, the decisions of the courts of that state on the law of accidents would be applied in the federal courts. In one decision, the Court repealed a whole system of federal law.

Particularly interesting and somewhat amusing about the Tompkins case is the fact that the result was completely unexpected. Counsel for the railroad (which won the case) expressly told the Court on the argument that he was *not* challenging *Swift* v. *Tyson*, nor asking the Court to overrule it. Yet the Court did just that. The opinion was written by Brandeis, but Roberts concurred in it. Completely forgotten was the position he took but a bare year earlier that the Court would not overrule a decision unless expressly asked to do so by counsel.

Erie Railroad v. *Tompkins* symbolized a revolution in which the Court abdicated almost a century and a half of supreme authority in the field of economic legislation. But a revolution does not merely bring an end to the old; it also ushers in the new. Death had taken place; transfiguration was due. Revolution was to be followed by rebirth.

chapter thirteen

Stone and the Reborn Court

BLACK ENTERS THE COURT

Congress did not enact the judiciary reorganization bill, but it did adopt a measure assuring full salaries for life to Supreme Court Justices who retired at the age of seventy and had served for ten years or more. (The 1869 act did not fully guarantee this privilege; after Holmes retired, Congress reduced his salary, which angered the Justices and may have contributed to the refusal of some of the aged Justices to retire.) In June of 1937, after the measure became law, Van Devanter, reportedly at the urging of Hughes, became the first Justice to take advantage of its provisions and retired from the Court. (Perhaps more important even than the guarantee of continued full salary in the retirement act was the prop it afforded to the morale of the Justices in its provision that even after retirement they could be called upon by the Court to sit in circuit when needed to ease calendar congestion.) Roosevelt had promised Senator Robinson the first available seat on the Court as reward for his leadership in the reorganization bill battle, but Robinson had died of a heart attack in the midst of the campaign. Instead, Roosevelt named Senator Black of Alabama.

In their book on the Court fight, *The 168 Days*, Joseph Alsop and Turner Catledge suggest that the President chose the extremely liberal Black in order to get back at the conservative members of the Senate who fought his reorganization bill but who would nevertheless be compelled by the unwritten yet potent tradition of senatorial courtesy to confirm the appointment of their fellow member. Stone himself suspected that Roosevelt appointed Black "in a fit of pique." John P. Frank, Black's biographer, implies that the speculation on the part of Alsop and Catledge may have been a shrewd analysis of the working of Roosevelt's mind and personality, although the exact reasons for the nomination are not a matter of record. If that was the President's motive he was as eminently successful in this respect as he was not in obtaining passage of the reorganization bill, for the right wing senatorial opponents of that bill were furious at the nomination of Black and even more so in their frustration in not being able to defeat confirmation.

Hugo L. Black was the son of a fairly prosperous small-town Alabama storekeeper and landlord-farmer. After attending college, Black enrolled in medical school because his brother was a doctor and his mother wanted him to be one too. After one year, however, he decided that medicine was not for him and switched to law. A year after admission to the bar he moved to Birmingham and there became in turn police court judge and county prosecutor. He also became a rather successful poor man's lawyer, specializing in personal injuries cases, in which he was able to obtain substantial verdicts from juries. After service in the Army during the First World War, he was discharged as a captain and he resumed his law practice and his interest in politics. In 1926 he ran for United States senator against three far better known but considerably older opponents. He campaigned vigorously as the "poor man's candidate" and his major qualification, as stated in the handbills distributed by his campaign headquarters, was that "If Elected Will Take Office at Age 41 Years—Can Give to State Best Years of His Life if Elected." To the surprise of most everybody, he nosed out his three rivals, and in 1932 was re-elected.

In the Senate Black immediately aligned himself with the liberal Democrat-Progressive wing and established a particularly warm relationship with Senator Norris. He gained national fame in his conduct first of the air mail subsidy investigation and then of the even more dramatic utility holding company investigation. He was co-author of the Black-Connery Bill to limit the hours of labor, and although the bill did not pass, it became the basis of the Wage and Hour Law that was later enacted. He voted against the confirmation of both Hughes and Parker, and strove valiantly with Robinson to push through the judiciary reorganization bill. On August 12, 1937, Roosevelt sent his name to the Senate to fill the vacancy left by Van Devanter's retirement.

As Frank describes it, when the nomination was announced, "The resultant silence was stupendous. The conservative Democrats and Republicans could not have been more horrified to learn that Satan himself had been appointed to the High Court. . . . The stunned victors of the Court fight slowly realized that F. D. R. was having his revenge." Black had one decisive advantage that Satan lacked; he was a member of the club, and so after a hearing and two days debate, Black was confirmed by a vote of 63 to 16, with ten Republicans and six conservative Democrats feeling sufficiently strong to break with tradition and vote against confirmation.

It turned out that it was Black's membership in the club that saved him. Had he been an ordinary citizen, the Senate would have probably taken longer to pass upon his appointment, with the result that Ray Springle's disclosure would have become public before confirmation. Had this happened, it is quite likely that Roosevelt would have withdrawn the nomination. As it was, Black had already received his commission, taken his oath of office and left for a vacation in Europe when the skies fell.

On September 13, 1937, Springle's articles began to appear in the Pittsburgh *Post Gazette* and through it in the entire press of the nation. They revealed that from 1923 to 1924 Black had been a dues-paying member of the Birmingham chapter of the Ku Klux Klan. He had formally resigned from it upon his entry into the senatorial campaign, but in 1926, after he had won the Democratic nomination for senator (which, in Alabama, was tantamout to election), he was awarded a Grand Passport by the chapter and delivered a speech of acceptance. This series of six articles won for Springle the Pulitzer Prize, although it was hardly a revolutionary discovery. The incident was well known throughout Alabama, having been made an issue by Black's opponents in the 1932 senatorial campaign in which he won re-election.

It was now the turn of the anti-New Deal forces to be jubilant. Almost the entire press had opposed the appointment and naturally now condemned it all the more. The demand that Black resign appeared, if one judged by the newspapers, to be universal. If he would not resign, the press declared, he should be impeached. To labor and the liberal Democratic-Progressive wing in the Senate, the outcry appeared hypocritical. Senator Norris expressed their feeling in his statement that "Actually, Justice Black is being subjected to all this criticism because he is a liberal, because he wants to bring the Supreme Court closer to the people—not because he is a Klansman."

Although beseiged by reporters while in Europe, Black refused to talk about the matter. Upon his return he took to the radio and made his only statement on the subject:

My words and acts are a matter of public record. I believe that my record as a Senator refutes every implication of racial or religious intolerance. It shows that

I was of the group of liberal Senators who have consistently fought for the civil, economic and religious rights of all Americans, without regard to race or creed. . . . I did join the Klan. I later resigned. I never rejoined. I never have considered and I do not now consider the unsolicited card given to me shortly after my nomination to the Senate as a membership of any kind in the Ku Klux Klan. I never used it. I did not even keep it. Before becoming a senator I dropped the Klan. I have had nothing whatever to do with it since that time.

On October 4, three days after the radio address, the Court opened its 1937-1938 term, with Black taking the seat on the extreme left—the one reserved for the most junior member of the Court. Two lawyers appeared and made motions to unseat him. With Black not participating, the Court without comment denied both motions and settled down to business. The incident was ended.

But not Black's troubles. In the fall of 1937, Marquis Childs, Washington correspondent of the St. Louis *Post-Dispatch*, began taking daily walks with Stone, and the latter spoke freely about his concern for the Court as an institution, citing Black as an example of the sort of Justice Roosevelt might continue to appoint. On January 22, 1938, the *Post-Dispatch* printed Childs' article relating the substance and tenor of the conversations, although he did not mention Stone by name. Stone highly approved of the article and suggested that Childs "publish something of the sort in a magazine having national publication." Childs took the suggestion, and in May *Harper's* published an article by him entitled, "The Supreme Court Today." In it Childs spoke on behalf of "those Justices [meaning Stone] who are just now gravely concerned for the future of the institution in which they are a part." He wrote of Black's "lack of legal knowledge and experience, deficiencies in background and training" that led him "into blunders which have shocked his colleagues." To make matters worse, Black was "unable to carry his share" of the Court's work, and "several opinions he has written have been rephrased by other members of the Court."

The purpose of the article and of Stone's comments to Childs was not to attack Black but to stress the importance of judicial self-restraint on the left as well as on the right. But whatever its purpose, its effect was again to bring down the wrath of the press on Roosevelt, Black and the whole New Deal. Stone had hardly anticipated the angry backwash, and both Childs and Stone's secretary denied that he was the source, although the denial fooled few people. ("I always told the Judge," Stone's secretary complained to Childs, "he talks too much.")

Black had his defenders. They pointed out that during this first term as a member of the Court, Black had written twenty-six opinions, the exact amount written during the same period by Stone after twelve years on the bench. The difference was that twenty-three of Stone's opinions were for the majority and only three were dissenting opinions, while in only fifteen cases did Black write for the majority. Professor Walton Hamilton of Yale Law School wrote in the *New Republic* that "Justice Black has had legal training enough. What he needs is a course in hallowed platitudes."

What probably really troubled Stone, although he was of course not consciously aware of it, was that Black's first term on the bench indicated that what had occurred in 1937 was not a reformation, which was all that Stone bargained for, but a revolution. Stone expected a more enlightened and more liberal third branch of the legislature; Black's appointment was the harbinger of the virtual abolition of the third branch. Revolutionaries bring with them their own language, literature and behavior patterns; they do not use, and certainly do not pay homage to, the ancient mysteries and shibboleths. Stone was no more bothered by precedents than was Black; but there were accepted ways of getting around them, and Black did not use those ways. As a revolutionary, he wasted no time in carefully wrapping the idols in cotton and placing them away out of use and also out of harm; he would simply sweep them all out of the door. (Stone, not to mention Hughes, McReynolds and Butler, was most shocked by Black's dissent in *Connecticut General Life Insurance Company* v. *Johnson*, where, shortly after he took his oath of office, he calmly, but in splendid solitude, proposed to overrule a mountain of precedents and hold that a corporation was not a "person" within the meaning of the Fourteenth Amendment. This was like a newly qualified young priest of Ancient Israel telling his horrified colleagues that there really was nothing inside the Holy of Holies, so why not pull the curtain down and let the people see.) The irony of the whole controversy was that, as will be seen later in this chapter, it was to be Stone and not Black who, probably without realizing it, supplied the revolution with its intellectual rationale in a manifesto contained in a footnote.

REED, FRANKFURTER AND DOUGLAS

Roosevelt had to wait a long time before he could name anybody to the bench, but once vacancies came, they came fast. Sutherland, too, had decided to step down after the Retirement Act was passed, but rather than leave two vacancies at the same time, he waited until the Van Devanter vacancy was filled. To succeed Sutherland Roosevelt appointed Stanley F. Reed, who had served under Hoover and Roosevelt, first as general counsel of the Federal Farm Board, then of the Reconstruction Finance Corporation, and then as Solicitor-General of the United States. In the latter capacity he defended many of the New Deal measures in arguments before the Supreme Court and was fully at home with all the mysteries of constitutional law. The fact that he had originally been brought into government service by Hoover indicated that he was no left winger. But he had loyally defended Roosevelt's New Deal in the Court, including those parts of it with which he did not agree, and he received his reward. On the bench, he proved to be able, steady, centrist, and unspectacular.

Cardozo died in July of 1938 and as his successor Roosevelt named Felix Frankfurter. Frankfurter was a disciple of Brandeis and a warm friend of Stone, who strongly urged Roosevelt to appoint him. He had been born in Vienna, had received his liberal arts education at the College of the City of New York where he came under the influence of the legal philosopher, Morris Raphael Cohen. His law degree was obtained at Harvard. He became assistant United States attorney in New York in 1906, and five years later became legal officer in the Bureau of Insular Affairs. In 1914 he returned to Harvard as professor of law, a post which he held for twenty-five years until his appointment to the Supreme Court. While at Harvard he acted as counsel in a number of important social welfare legislation cases, wrote several books, including one (as co-author) critical of the labor injunction, enlisted in the unsuccessful struggle to free Sacco and Vanzetti, turned down an offer of appointment to the Massachusetts supreme judicial court, acted as intellectual mentor of the New Deal, and supplied from among his students and colleagues a goodly proportion of the men who made up Roosevelt's brain trust. It was quite natural that the scholar Frankfurter should succeed to the seat occupied in turn by Gray, Holmes and Cardozo.

Frankfurter remained the professor on the bench. He questioned lawyers arguing before him as if they were students reciting in a classroom. A master of the technical aspects of law, he seemed to many at times to elevate federalism, or the proper relationship between the state and Federal governments to an end in itself, rather than a means to secure freedom and civil rights.

In 1939 Brandeis retired. Protocol requires that when a Justice retires from the Court the other members prepare a letter which they all sign and in which they say whatever nice things they can about him and express their appreciation for his services and their best wishes for a happy future off the bench. The letter is usually read by the Chief Justice at the opening of the term in which the retirement becomes effective, and is published in the Court's official reports for that term. When Brandeis retired such a letter was prepared, but McReynolds, unrepentant anti-Semite to the end, refused to sign it. Hughes might have signed the letter alone, in his capacity as Chief Justice, on behalf of the Court generally, but he had no intention of sparing McReynolds from public knowledge of his bigotry. He calmly read the letter and the names of the seven signers, and the letter was so published and is thus to be found in the official reports.

To succeed Brandeis, Roosevelt named William O. Douglas. As Frankfurter's appointment delighted Stone, so Douglas' delighted Black. The two were kindred spirits, socially and politically. At the age of four, Douglas had had infantile paralysis and to overcome its effects he had become a passionate hiker and mountain climber. When he was a boy of twelve, he was shocked to see a local sheriff drag a union organizer out of town behind a motorcycle. As an impecunious worker he labored in the western wheat fields alongside of IWW members. He lived in a tent while attending college in Washington state and traveled to Columbia Law School in New York as custodian of a train load of sheep. He joined the law faculty at Columbia but resigned after his first year when Nicholas Murray Butler appointed a successor to Dean Harlan Stone without consulting the faculty. He then became professor at Yale Law School. In 1934 Roosevelt appointed him a member of the Securities and Exchange Commission, and in 1937 he became its chairman, serving in that capacity until his elevation to the Supreme Court two years later. In a way, just as it was appropriate that Cardozo should be succeeded by Frankfurter, so too was it that Douglas should succeed Brandeis, for in the Vinson Court a decade later, the phrase "Black and Douglas, dissenting" was to become as familiar as the term "Holmes and Brandeis dissenting" had been in the White and Taft Courts two decades earlier.

THE OLYMPIAN AND THE PROPHET

Holmes had served on the Court for thirty years, Brandeis for twenty-three. For sixteen years they had served together. During that period there was a warm and close friendship between them, and almost always they found themselves together in concurrence or dissent. Yet they were entirely different personalities, politically, spiritually and intellectually.

Holmes almost lost his appointment by reason of a speech he made expressing some skepticism in respect to the basis of the legend the Federalists had made of John Marshall. Holmes, too, has been made a legend, by the liberals, but legend-making is pretty much the same whether the makers be conservatives or liberals. The method is to emphasize the virtues and, if impracticable to eliminate the faults, then to minimize or explain them away. Take, for example, Max Lerner's explanation of Holmes's dissent in the Northern Securities anti-trust case, in which, with the concurrence of Fuller, White and Peckham, Holmes denied the constitutional power of Congress to "reconstruct society" under the "pretense" of "a regulation of commerce." Holmes, says Lerner, had reason to suspect that Theodore Roosevelt expected him to uphold trust busting, and this may have caused him to "lean backward."

Professor Fred Rodell of Yale is even more adept at making a legend. "Only a handful of men in all United States history," he says, "have made with their minds so manifest a mark on their own age and on ages still to come as did Justice Holmes. Benjamin Franklin probably, Thomas Jefferson surely, John Marshall possibly, and after him Abraham Lincoln—and the list is closed." Just about the only opinion of Holmes that Rodell finds questionable (only questionable, because it was not an "important" infringement of a "clear-cut" civil liberty) is his dissent from McReynolds' opinion in *Meyer* v. *Nebraska* invalidating a law barring the teaching of foreign languages. Rodell does not mention, for example, Holmes's mischievous aphorism that although one may have "a constitutional right to talk politics, . . . he has no constitutional right to be a policeman"; his opinion permitting the barring of political speakers from public parks; his upholding of the governmental kidnapping of Moyer and Pettibone; his concurrence (notwithstanding dissents by Brandeis and Clarke) in the Van Devanter decision in *New York Central* v. *Winfield* forbidding states to provide through employers' liability for thousands of railroad workers injured or killed on their jobs; his dissent in the Bailey anti-peonage decision; or his opinion in *Pennsylvania Coal Company* v. *Mahou*, where, over Brandeis' dissent, he held that a state's police power did not justify a ban on mining coal in such a way as to threaten the cave-in of buildings in which human beings live; his refusal, in *McCabe* v. *Atchison, Topeka and Sante Fe Railway*, to agree with Hughes that the Fourteenth Amendment's guarantee of equality was not satisfied by providing railroad sleepers for whites while Negroes sat up all night in a waiting room until there were enough of them to make a "black sleeping car" pay; or his concurrence (over Brandeis' dissent) in *Gilbert* v. *Minnesota*, affirming a conviction under a state law prohibiting pacifist speeches.

Even Holmes's greatest contribution to constitutional law, the clear and present danger test, was a retreat from the libertarian philosophy of Jefferson and no longer satisfies Black and many other defenders of freedom of expression. In fact, during the six years between 1910 and 1916 when Hughes and Holmes were on the bench together, the former had a more consistent liberal record than did the latter. Holmes's record improved after 1916, but that must be in some measure attributed to the influence of Brandeis. Even Holmes conceded that Brandeis exercised a profound influence upon him, and Taft later complained that Brandeis cast two votes, his own and Holmes's.

I do not mean to imply that Holmes was not a liberal; he was indeed, and a great one too. He was not, however, the legend that liberals have made of him. (I do not think it necessary to define "liberal"; I use the term in the general sense used by those who call Holmes a great liberal.)

Holmes was an Olympian. He was above the battle and little concerned with its moralities. He spoke contemptuously of "the stinking sense of justice" which hampered the proper administration of law. He had little faith in social reform by legislation. He was a child of Darwin and Herbert Spencer and believed that the natural law of survival of the fittest applied in the social and economic world as it did in the animal kingdom. Spencer had opposed legislative interference with the operation of natural law in economics and in the Lochner dissent Holmes said that the Constitution did not embody Spencer's *Social Statics*, with its opposition to governmental interference with the evolutionary process. Yet Holmes's economic philosophy, if he can be said to have had any, was probably closely akin to Spencer's. He would allow the legislatures to interfere undoubtedly in large part because of his usually great sense of judicial tolerance, but also in part because he considered the interference futile, and perhaps too, because as an Olympian god he was amused by the battle going on so far below him. His great admiration and respect for Brandeis somewhat mitigated his Olympian aloofness, perhaps because he must have felt that if Brandeis was a crusading reformer, crusading reformers could not be all bad.

As Holmes was a god out of Olympus, so Brandeis was a prophet out of Israel. One can almost picture him as an ancient Isaiah (Roosevelt addressed him by that name in his letters) declaiming against the monopolists of Judah; "Woe unto them that join house to house, that lay field to field, till there be no place!" Or, "Woe unto them that decree unrighteous decrees!" As Holmes was above the struggle, so Brandeis, once he entered, never left it. He was consumed by a burning passion for social justice and to him the law had to be used to further and not obstruct the never ending struggle for justice.

Yet, in a sense he was outdated almost as soon as he entered the fray. Paul Freund of Harvard, who was Brandeis' law clerk in 1932, said of him that he had one of the finest minds of the nineteenth century. He was completely out of harmony with mass movements, separation of ownership from control in corporations and above all bigness, all characteristic of the twentieth century. He had, in the words of Charles Beard, "a holy fear of bigness," and bigness is the key to American economy in the present century. When Brandeis ascended the bench, his ideal of regulated competition of small or moderate entrepreneurs was rapidly becoming as romantically archaic as Jefferson's ideal of agrarian democracy. American prosperity is predicated on mass production and distribution, and both require not only bigness but substantial monopoly, informal if not formal. Brandeis never fully recognized this, and never accepted it.

It was Holmes and not Brandeis who proved to be finally right about the role of the Supreme Court in the struggle of economic forces. Brandeis implicitly accepted the Supreme Court as a super-legislature in the economic arena. With the missionary zeal so characteristic of everything he undertook, he sought to educate the Court to be an enlightened super-legislature and to permit the United States to undertake the social welfare reforms which all civilized countries had undertaken. This was the rationale of both the Brandeis brief and the Brandeis opinion, the primary purpose of both of which was educational. Holmes, on the other hand, took the position (except when he faltered) that the Court simply had no business in the arena altogether; that while all Brandeis' sociological and economic facts might be interesting (they weren't to Holmes), they were relevant only to a legislature deciding whether to enact a law, and not to a Supreme Court passing on the law after it was enacted. If the legislature, duly elected by the people and subject to be thrown out by them, wishes to enact foolish and even dangerous laws, it is their constitutional right to do so, and it is not the business of the Court to save the people from themselves or from their legislatures. Holmes stated this imperially, as befitted an Olympian, but this turned out to be the ultimate outcome of the revolution sparked by Roosevelt's judiciary reorganization bill.

In the area of civil liberties Brandeis' record was superior to Holmes's. Brandeis lacked the latter's grand style and his opinions in this field are neither as eloquent nor as quotable as Holmes's—although his concurring opinion in *Whitney* v. *California* (a conviction under the California Criminal Syndicalism Law which for technical reasons Brandeis and Holmes felt the Supreme Court could not upset) stands on a par with Holmes's dissent in the Abrams case as a great document in the history of American liberties. Only in Prohibition cases is the record of Brandeis in civil liberties cases sullied. His opposition to the liquor trade as a social evil was so intense that it blinded him to the violation of civil liberties attendant upon enforcement of the Volstead Act. (Here, too, one can picture the Biblical Isaiah: "Woe unto them that rise up early in the morning that they may follow strong drink; that they continue until night, till wine inflame them!") Elsewhere his record as a judicial defender of personal freedoms is almost impeccable.

The conventional assumption is that the great contribution of Holmes to constitutional law was in the field of civil liberties, and of Brandeis in the field of economic jurisprudence. It is by no means impossible that the converse is closer to the truth.

FROM PROPERTY RIGHTS TO PERSONAL LIBERTIES

Abdication of supremacy in the realm of economic legislation was only one-half of the revolution of 1937. The Supreme Court did not merely end its almost century-and-a-half role of protector of property rights; it also assumed a new role as protector of personal freedoms. In the long run, this new aspect of the revolution will probably prove to be the more important one. Even in its best days the Court could never halt the progress of America towards a welfare-modified capitalism, nor permanently frustrate the will of the people and their legislature. At most it could act like the British House of Lords; that is, it could delay, but not defeat. It could, for example, delay the introduction of revenue raising through taxes measured by ability to pay; but it could not prevent it. Even if there had been no revolution in 1937, ultimately child labor would have been abolished, wage and hour laws established, old age and unemployment insurance provided, etc., just as in the end legal tender and income tax laws were accepted.

In the field of personal freedoms, too, the power of the Court is limited to delay. But here delay is of vital importance. America has a strong commitment to freedom that only fear is sufficiently potent to overcome. Our history shows that the really grave violations of personal freedom occur during periods of great fear, and when they pass we return to our senses and to our devotion to liberty. Hence, where delay in the domain of economic legislation is of secondary importance, it is of primary importance where personal freedoms are endangered, and the great contribution of the post-1937 Court has been in providing delay until fear passes and courage returns, bringing freedom with it.

The Supreme Court's activism in protecting personal freedoms began during Taft's Chief Justiceship. The Hughes Court took up where the Taft Court left off. The White Court would not interfere with judicial lynching in the case of Leo Frank. The Taft Court would not allow it in *Moore* v. *Dempsey*, nor the Hughes Court in the Scottsboro cases.

The first Scottsboro case, *Powell* v. *Alabama*, reached the Supreme Court in 1932. Seven young, uneducated, derelict Negro boys were accused of raping two white girls aboard a freight train in Alabama. All were indicted, arraigned, tried, found guilty, and sentenced to death. They were not advised of their right to counsel, nor were they offered court-appointed counsel or the opportunity to communicate with their relatives to obtain counsel. Before the morning of the trial the trial judge had generously "appointed all the members of the bar" for the limited "purpose of arraigning the defendants," but this was hardly more than an expansive gesture. At the morning of the trial two attorneys stepped forward and volunteered to assist the defendants. The trial then proceeded without any preparation or opportunity to prepare for it by the two attorneys. It was only after the defendants' conviction that they first obtained the benefit of adequate legal assistance.

The Supreme Court reversed the conviction. The Fourteenth Amendment's guarantee that no person shall be deprived by a state of his life or liberty without due process of law, the Court held, means that he shall have a fair trial, and, at least in a case where the penalty is death, this means that he must be provided with counsel who must be afforded an adequate opportunity to prepare for trial.

Three years later, the Scottsboro case again came to the Supreme Court in the case of *Norris* v. *Alabama* and once more the conviction was reversed. This time the ground was that Negroes had been excluded from the grand jury which had indicted the boys. In the interim national public opinion was increasing in intensity and began making itself felt. Ultimately all the boys but one were freed. The Supreme Court had made its contribution; it had provided delay until the good sense and conscience of America could make itself effective.

In 1937 the Hughes Court again exercised its powers for the protection of personal freedom, and in doing so revived the "clear and present danger" doctrine that had lain dormant from the day Holmes announced it in the Schenck case. In *Herndon* v. *Lowry*, a five to four decision, the Court set aside the conviction under a Georgia anti-insurrection statute of a Negro organizer for the Communist party (then a legal party) who had in his room Communist literature calling on whites and Negroes to overthrow class rule in the Black Belt by violent revolution, had addressed three public meetings, and had possessed a Communist party membership book. The Georgia court had upheld the conviction on the ground that under the statute the test was the defendant's evil intent and that it was not necessary to show that his intent was likely to be carried out at any time in the immediate or even foreseeable future. In reversing the conviction, the Supreme Court held that speech could not be penalized merely because of the speaker's evil intent; there must be a reasonable apprehension of danger to organized government. The evil tendency of the words was also not sufficient, nor the possibility that in the distant future they might lead to violence and revolution; there must be a clear and present danger of unlawful force and violence.

Also during 1937 the Court upheld civil liberties in the case of *De Jonge* v. *Oregon.* Kirk De Jonge, an organizer for the Communist party, was convicted under a state criminal-syndicalism law for helping to organize and for speaking at a public meeting in Portland held under the auspices of the Communist party, which, the state charged, was an organization advocating violent or unlawful change in government or industry. The evidence showed that some one hundred fifty to two hundred persons were present at the meeting, which was open to the public without charge. Its purpose was to protest against illegal raids on workers' halls and houses and against the shooting of striking longshoremen by the police. The meeting was peaceful and orderly; it was raided by the police and De Jonge was arrested, convicted and sentenced to prison for seven years.

The Supreme Court set aside the conviction on the ground that an assembly otherwise lawful may not be held unlawful merely by reason of the auspices under which it is conducted. If it is conducted peaceably for a lawful purpose, it does not become unlawful merely because it is sponsored by the Communist party.

In 1939 the Hughes Court once more acted in defense of civil liberties, but this time, instead of reviving and following a principle announced by Holmes, it overruled one. The case, *Hague* v. *CIO*, represented the culmination of the long series of incidents involving public assemblies for political and economic purposes in New Jersey. Meetings called to organize workers and induce them to join labor unions were frequently suppressed, as were meetings called to protest the suppressions. Roger Baldwin, director of the American Civil Liberties Union, was arrested when he started to read the Declaration of Independence in front of the city hall in Paterson and was convicted of conducting an unlawful assembly.

Restrictions on public assemblies were most severe in Jersey City, whose mayor, Frank Hague, achieved a short-time immortality with his proclamation, "I am the law." Hague resisted the unionization of Jersey City workers with all his energy and ingenuity. Speakers seeking to protest were promptly relieved of their literature, escorted to the wharf, placed on ferry boats, and "deported" to New York. The editor of the *Catholic Worker* was refused permission to explain the papal encyclicals at a public meeting. Even a United States senator, William Borah, was not allowed to speak. Organizers for the AF of L and CIO were invariably denied permits to hold meetings in streets and parks.

The permits were denied under a city ordinance forbidding all public assemblies in the streets or parks without a permit, which might be refused by the director of public safety "for the purpose of preventing riots, disturbances or disorderly assemblage." Counsel for the Jersey City officials contended before the Supreme Court that if the proposed meetings were held riots were likely to follow. They showed that protests against the meetings had been received from the Chamber of Commerce, two veterans' organizations, and the Ladies of the Grand Army of the Republic. A group of veterans had announced that if the CIO were allowed to hold an open-air meeting they would take matters in their own hands and see to it that the meeting was broken up. (It was also shown by opposing counsel that at least some of the protests were inspired by Mayor Hague and his associates. As the federal circuit court remarked: "Reversing the usual procedure, Mayor Hague troubled the waters in order to fish in them.")

In *Hague* v. *CIO* the Supreme Court held the ordinance unconstitutional. Holmes, when he was on the Massachusetts supreme court, had held that a city has the same rights as any owner of private property; just as the latter may forbid political meetings and speeches in his house, so may the former in the public parks that it owns. In *Davis* v. *Massachusetts*, the Supreme Court had affirmed this decision, but in *Hague* v. *CIO* it overruled it. While political and religious meetings can be regulated in public places in the interests of traffic and safety, they cannot, the Court said, be absolutely forbidden.

MANIFESTO IN A FOOTNOTE

By 1938 the revolution was in full swing. While the Court was refusing, in case after case, to interfere with federal and state social welfare legislation, it was busily engaged in intervening for the protection of civil liberties and personal freedoms. But every revolution needs a rationale and a manifesto. It was Stone who supplied both, tentatively, briefly, and so unobtrusively that it might seem as if he were trying to sneak it into constitutional law, or perhaps as if it had come to him as an afterthought.

The case was *United States* v. *Carolene Products Company*. This was simply one of the many cases in which the revolutionary Court refused to interfere with government regulation of business (here the manufacture and distribution of filled milk). It apparently occurred to Stone that some rationale was needed to justify the Court's giving carte blanche to legislatures in economic affairs while at the same time exercising ever increasing censorial control over them where personal freedoms were concerned. Ever since the Supreme Court, even before Marshall, had asserted its power to declare laws unconstitutional, it had repeated the principle that there is a presumption that a law is constitutional and will not be invalidated unless the presumption is overcome by clear proof that the legislature acted arbitrarily or otherwise beyond its powers. Just as a defendant in a criminal case was presumed to be innocent and may not be convicted unless his guilt was proved beyond a reasonable doubt, so a statute may not be condemned unless its unconstitutionality was established by the same strict standard of reasonable doubt.

Nowhere had it been suggested that this presumption of constitutionality was operative only in respect to laws regulating business and not to laws governed by the Bill of Rights or aimed against racial or religious minorities. So, in what has since become famous among constitutional lawyers as "Footnote 4," Stone suggested timidly and tentatively that:

> There may be narrower scope for operation of the presumption of constitutionality when legislation appears on its face to be within a specific prohibition of the Constitution, such as those of the first ten amendments, which are deemed equally specific when held to be embraced within the Fourteenth. It is unnecessary to consider whether legislation which restricts political processes which can ordinarily be expected to bring about repeal of undesirable legislation, is to be subjected to a more exacting judicial scrutiny under the general prohibitions of the Four-

teenth Amendment than are most other types of legislation. Nor do we enquire whether similar considerations enter into the review of statutes directed at particular religious, national or racial minorities, whether prejudice against discrete and insular minorities may be a special condition which tends seriously to curtail the operation of those political processes ordinarily to be relied upon to protect minorities and which may call for a correspondingly more searching judicial inquiry.

Before putting this into less legalistic and more understandable language, a comment should be made at the modest way in which so revolutionary a doctrine is proposed. Aside from the fact that it was placed in an easily overlooked footnote, the language itself is almost timorous. "It may be," "It is unnecessary to consider," "Nor need we enquire." It is as if Stone were saying, "I'm only asking." Indeed, he does not even go that far, saying in effect, "I am not asking, but some day I may have to." This is in stark contrast with the magisterial manner in which Marshall announced new doctrines.

Yet, this is not unprecedented. In the Gitlow case, the Taft Court had brought into constitutional law a radical new principle, one on which the second part of the 1937 revolution is based, the principle that the guarantee against state deprivation of liberty without due process of law means that the state cannot deprive one of freedom of speech, press, religion or assembly. It did this almost as timidly and tentatively as Stone did in Footnote 4. The Court in effect said there that "We're not saying it's so; just let's assume it for argument's sake." By 1938, however, the principle was firmly established. Kirk De Jonge went free and the CIO could hold public meetings in Jersey City.

What Footnote 4 says is that there may be (meaning, really, there is) a basic difference between laws restricting business and those restricting the exercise of personal freedoms. If the former are unwise, we can rely on the legislature to repeal them, and if it does not, then we can rely on the people to elect a legislature that will. But when a law restricts freedom of speech or press, or freedom of the ballot, we cannot have the same reliance because the law itself operates to hamper the election of a new legislature. We cannot, for example, expect the legislature easily to be voted out of office if it makes it a crime for anyone publicly to criticize its activities. Similarly, where a law operates oppressively on a minority, Negro, Japanese, Puerto Rican, Catholic or Jewish, we cannot rely exclusively on the ballot box, because by the nature of things the oppressed minority is not likely to succeed at the ballot box. In these cases, therefore, it may be proper that the Court should examine the legislation with care and be more liberal in declaring it unconstitutional than in cases where only business interests are affected.

This was the manifesto in a footnote. Later, during Stone's Chief Justiceship, it was elaborated and expanded until it became a full blown rationale and rationalization for the 1937 revolution. In substance it embodied two interrelated concepts: first, the freedoms guaranteed by the Bill of Rights (including the right of equality under the Fourteenth Amendment) stand in a preferred position; second, therefore, while a law restricting business interests is presumed to be constitutional until the contrary is shown, a law restricting personal freedoms may almost be said to be presumed unconstitutional until the contrary is shown.

Not all the Justices have accepted this "preferred position" principle. Frankfurter, for example, waged an unyielding war against it, and left the bench without ever having accepted it. Yet it probably does represent the philosophy of the Court ever since the 1937 revolution, with the possible qualification that it was not applied to political liberties during the three or four years that McCarthy dominated the American political scene.

HUGHES AND STONE

Butler died late in 1939 and as Roosevelt had named a Jew to succeed Cardozo, so he named a Catholic to succeed Butler. For the post he chose Frank Murphy of Michigan. Murphy had been, in order, assistant United States Attorney in Detroit, a member of the faculty of the law school at the Jesuit University of Detroit, judge of a Michigan lower court, mayor of Detroit, governor-general of the Philippines and then its High Commissioner. He was elected governor of Michigan in 1936, and his settlement of the automobile strike made him a national figure. He was defeated for re-election in 1938 but soon after was named United States Attorney-General, a position he held for about a year, until his appointment to the Supreme Court. He had been an ardent New Dealer and on the bench he aligned himself with Black and Douglas as a steadfast champion of civil liberties. He died in 1949, after serving for a period of only nine years, interrupted briefly in 1942 for a short term of service as a lieutenant-colonel in the army.

In 1941 Hughes retired from the Court at the age of seventy-nine, having served eleven years as Chief Justice and earlier six years as Associate Justice.

Hughes, according to Irving Brant, wanted above all to be known as a liberal, even though often his heart belonged to the conservatives. In the conferences of the Justices, if Stone's report to Brant is correct, Hughes frequently argued on the "reactionary" side but voted with the liberals if they had a majority without him—which they more often had after 1938 than before. If Hughes found himself with the conservative side in a majority, he assigned the writing of the majority opinion to another Justice; when he was with the majority on the liberal side, he would write the majority opinion himself.

This was the evaluation of Stone and Brant. It contrasts sharply with Pusey's. Somewhere in between is the appraisal by Samuel Hendel, whose biography of Hughes is more objective than Pusey's. "When the pressure for innovation became great," writes Hendel, "and the risks to the nation and to the Court itself apparent, reluctantly at first, but increasingly Hughes went along with change. Having sedulously sought to protect the precedents of the Court, sometimes at the risk of offending logic, he witnessed and often participated in the shattering of one precedent after another. He stood thus as a kind of heroic and, in a sense, tragic figure, torn between the old and the new, seeking at first to stem the tide but then relentlessly caught up and moving with it."

Actually, Hughes's overriding passion was the preservation of the Court. Whatever might have been his economic predilections either in his early crusader-reformer days or in his later corporation-lawyer career, when he became Chief Justice they were in either case subordinated to his devotion to the protection of the Court and its prestige. His economic conservatism was never as intellectually steadfast as Sutherland's, nor his progressivism as Brandeis'. If he could have saved the Court by declaring unconstitutional every New Deal measure, he would have done that. If he could have saved it by upholding every one, he would have done that too. The real tragedy of Hughes is that he delayed too long in recognizing the course of twentieth-century America, and thus was tardy in the utilization of his unquestionably powerful personality and intellectual excellence. In the end it was not Hughes but the far less gifted Roberts who really saved the Court.

Roosevelt's personal inclination was to appoint his Attorney-General,

Robert H. Jackson, as Hughes's successor, but both Hughes and Frankfurter urged the appointment of Stone. Moreover the nation was on the verge of entering the war, and the interests of national unity made advisable the naming of a Republican to the post of Chief Justice. Considering these and other factors, Roosevelt sent Stone's name to the Senate, the nation unanimously endorsed the nomination and confirmation was practically automatic. (Before Roosevelt announced his choice, several papers reported that Stone had been responsible for Roosevelt's flunking out of Columbia Law School. Stone asked the dean to consult the ancient records, and to his relief, learned that the report was unfounded and that the President-to-be had not taken any courses under the Chief-Justice-to-be.)

Stone was sixty-nine on his elevation, and served only five years until his death in 1946. His brief administration contrasted sharply with that of his predecessor. Hughes kept a firm control over the Justices' conferences. When he felt that there had been enough discussion on a case, he halted further talk and called for a vote. He sought to keep the Justices to the point in their discussions and exercised freely the prerogatives of a presiding officer. Stone was far more easy going. He let the Justices talk themselves out. When Hughes was Chief Justice, the Court would get through its Saturday conferences, in which it considered cases argued in the preceding week, in four hours; under Stone the conferences sometimes continued for four days. Nor did Stone employ what many considered the high pressure tactics of Taft and Hughes in an effort to discourage dissenting opinions. He made no effort to gloss over differences to create an impression of unity where there was none. Stone never did what Hughes is believed by many to have done on more than one occasion—switch his own vote in order to give an appearance of larger agreement to a position with which in fact he did not agree.

On the other hand, Stone shared much of Hughes's passion for preserving the appearance of continuity in respect to precedents. He would generally not let a precedent stand in the way of a necessary change in the law, but he had a strong aversion to the direct method of Black and Douglas, the frank and express overruling of the precedent. Appearance of unity was not of major importance, but appearance of continuity was. He used all of his legal skills in an effort to show that a particular decision was not really contrary to the earlier one, but that the two cases could be distinguished if they were examined carefully enough. In 1940, in the case of *Apex Hosiery Company* v. *Leader*, he wrote an opinion in which he strove mightily to show that in throwing out a suit by a company for damages against a striking union, the Court was not really overruling the holding in the Duplex Deering and Journeyman Stone Cutters cases that labor unions are subject to the Sherman Anti-Trust Law, although for all practical purposes that was the effect of the decision.

Perhaps most symbolic of Stone's attitude toward the sanctity of precedents is the last opinion he ever read from the bench. In 1929, in the case of *United States* v. *Schwimmer*, the Taft Court had held that Rosika Schwimmer, international pacifist and woman suffragist, was properly denied naturalization because, in answer to a question on the printed form of petition for citizenship, she said she would not take up arms in defense of this country. Two years later, in *United States* v. *Macintosh*, the Hughes Court reaffirmed this decision and upheld the denial of citizenship to a pacifist professor of divinity at Yale. On decision day (Monday), April 22, 1946, Douglas read for the majority the opinion in *Girouard* v. *United States*, in which both the Schwimmer and the Macintosh decisions were expressly overruled. Then Chief Justice Stone read a dissenting opinion in which he stated that although he had dissented in the earlier cases, the rule of *stare decisis* required him to follow precedents, and therefore he was required to dissent in this one. A few minutes after he finished reading his dissent, he slumped forward, unconscious, in his chair. Black, senior Associate Justice, picked up the gavel and banged it, declaring the Court in recess. A few hours later Stone was dead of a cerebral hemorrhage.

Roosevelt had chosen Robert H. Jackson to fill the post made vacant by Hughes' retirement and Stone's elevation. Jackson had been a lawyer in a small city in upstate New York, had become general counsel of the Bureau of Internal Revenue, and then Assistant Attorney-General in charge of the anti-trust division. A strong advocate of the New Deal, he took a leading part in the judiciary reorganization struggle, later writing a book on it, *The Struggle for Judicial Supremacy*, which was published in 1941 shortly before he was named to the Court. He succeeded Reed as Solicitor-General and then Murphy as Attorney-General. In 1945 he took a leave of absence from the Court for a year to serve as chief prosecutor at the Nuremberg war crime trials against the Nazi leaders, a step that Stone opposed vigorously, as he had opposed Murphy's entering the army.

Jackson and Frankfurter had been close friends before the former's appointment to the Court; when Roosevelt asked Frankfurter's advice as to a successor to Hughes, Frankfurter told him that personal considerations would have dictated the recommendation of Jackson. On the bench, the friendship between the two became even closer, and so too did their approach to most issues that came before the Court for determination. Jackson was gifted with a brilliant pen, which could be vitriolic or eloquent as occasion demanded. His opinions are a delight to read, and their avoidance of legalistic jargon make them as readable for the nonlawyer as they are for the lawyer.

In 1941, too, the aged but unreformed McReynolds retired from the bench. He was succeeded by James F. Byrnes, United States senator from South Carolina. After serving about a year, Byrnes resigned to accept the new post of chairman of the Economic Stabilization Board, and later to become one of the Court's most bitter critics. In his place Roosevelt named Wiley B. Rutledge who had taught law at the University of Colorado, Washington University and Iowa University, serving as dean in the latter two institutions, and had been appointed by Roosevelt to be a judge of the United States court of appeals for the District of Columbia. On the bench Rutledge aligned himself with Black, Douglas and Murphy as a staunch champion of civil liberties and of the 1937 revolution.

RELIGION AND THE REVOLUTION

It was appropriate that the revolution of 1937 should reach its first full bloom during the Chief Justiceship of Stone, the author of the Footnote 4 manifesto. It is, however, a little surprising that it should come about not in the political but in the religious arena. During the first century and a half of its existence, the Supreme Court had little occasion to pass on religious issues. In 1872, in *Watson* v. *Jones*, it had decided that it would not involve itself in ecclesiastical controversies and therefore would leave it to the Presbyterians themselves to decide whether the northern (antislavery) or the southern (pro-slavery) Presbyterian Church represented the true faith. In 1878, in *Reynolds* v. *United States*, it held that the federal government could constitutionally prohibit bigamy in the territories notwithstanding the Mormons' claim that it was required by the doctrines of their church and that the prohibition therefore interfered with their religious liberty. During the First World War it held, in *Arver* v. *United States*, that religious objection to war was not a constitutionally recognized excuse for failure to register in the draft and serve if selected, and in 1934, the Hughes Court, in *Hamilton* v. *Regents of the University of California*, held that a state university had the right to expel religiously motivated pacifists who refused to participate in compulsory military training.

These and one or two cases of lesser significance were the sum of all religion cases that had reached the Supreme Court before 1937. In the next ten years the Court was to decide more religion cases than during the entire one hundred fifty preceding years. Largely, but by no means exclusively, these cases arose out of the activities of the sect known as Jehovah's Witnesses. Like all religious sects that manage to survive, the Witnesses have acquired a degree of respectability, but in the decade following 1937 they were a despised group, principally because of the aggressiveness of their missionary activities and the violence of their verbal attacks upon other religions, particularly Catholicism. Their refusal to salute the flag or to serve in the armed forces also contributed substantially to their unpopularity.

When the Witnesses swept down upon a community in a mass-conversion campaign, acrimonious and violent reactions were almost inevitable. In many instances the outraged citizenry took the law into its own hands and resorted to force. In others the Witnesses were met by the legal arm of the community and were arrested for disturbing the peace, or for violating anti-peddling ordinances, laws against the use of sound trucks, traffic regulations or revenue laws. Often these cases reached the Supreme Court, and out of its decisions came much of the American constitutional law not only of religious liberty, but of freedom of speech, press and assembly as well.

One case, *Cantwell* v. *Connecticut* (1940), arose out of the action of a Witness, Jesse Cantwell, who accosted two pedestrians upon the streets of New Haven, and with their permission played for them a record on a portable phonograph he carried with him. The record contained an attack on organized religions generally and particularly on Catholicism, which was described as an instrument of Satan that for fifteen hundred years had brought untold sorrow and suffering upon mankind by means of fraud and deception. No violence occurred, but Cantwell was arrested and convicted of inciting a breach of the peace.

Cantwell appealed all the way to the United States Supreme Court, which reversed the conviction as an unconstitutional violation of his right to the free exercise of religion and speech. While there can be no doubt, the Court said, that the state has the right to prevent breaches of the peace and to punish those who incite such breaches even out of religious considerations, the fact that a person resorts to exaggeration or vilification in his missionary endeavors and thereby arouses public animosity may not render him subject to punishment in the absence of a clear and present menace to public peace. In the case at issue there was no assault or threat of bodily harm, no truculent bearing, no intentional discourtesy, no personal abuse—and therefore no clear and present danger to the public peace.

In other cases the Court upheld the right of Jehovah's Witnesses to distribute their literature on the public streets, hold religious meetings in public parks, engage in religious parades subject to regulation in the interests of safety and traffic control, be free of license taxation for engaging in their activities, use sound trucks in their missionary endeavors and ring doorbells to offer their pamphlets to householders. But the most famous and dramatic of the Jehovah's Witnesses decisions were in the flag salute cases.

These cases arose out of the refusal of Jehovah's Witnesses' children in the public schools to participate in the usual assembly ceremony of saluting the flag and pledging allegiance to it. Their refusal was based upon the belief that saluting the flag would constitute an act of idolatry in violation of the Biblical commandment. In most schools sensible authorities worked out some practical solution of the difficulty; but in a number the authorities insisted that the children comply, and upon their refusal expelled them from the school system.

The Jehovah's Witnesses organization brought many legal suits to prevent expulsion or to compel re-admittance of the children. Beginning in 1937, they appealed to the Supreme Court from unsuccessful suits in lower courts. In each case the Court dismissed their appeal on the basis of the University of California military-training decision. In 1940 the Court finally agreed to consider their appeal but then handed down a decision—from which only Stone dissented—rejecting their claims.

Frankfurter's opinion stated that "national unity is the basis of national security" and that the states have the constitutional power to take such measures as they deem appropriate to achieve national unity. If state authorities decide that the way to achieve it is to have all children participate in a symbolic act of unity, such as saluting or pledging allegiance to the flag, then, said Frankfurter, the Court will not interfere with their judgment even if it disagrees with them as to the effectiveness of the means chosen by them to accomplish their purpose.

The announcement of this decision, *Minersville School District* v. *Gobitis*, loosed upon the Jehovah's Witnesses throughout the country a torrent of abuse, physical as well as verbal. In a period of only one week hundreds of physical attacks upon Jehovah's Witnesses were reported to the federal Department of Justice, and hundreds more probably went unreported. Their meeting places were burned, their assemblies dispersed, and their leaders driven out of town. In one town the chief of police and the deputy sheriff forced a group of them to drink large doses of castor oil and then paraded them through the streets tied together with police-department rope. In another, a local judge warned a group of Witnesses that unless they compelled their children to salute the flag he would take the children away from them and place them in an institution where they would be taught to understand what Americanism really is.

These incidents shocked the American conscience. The Court's decision that had evoked them was subjected to almost unanimous adverse criticism among enlightened leaders of community opinion. The dissatisfaction of responsible Americans with the Court's decision was evidenced by the fact that one of the most nationalistic of all organizations, the American Legion, sponsored a bill enacted by Congress in 1942 providing that "civilians will show full respect to the flag when the pledge is given by merely standing at attention, men removing the headdress," conduct with which the Jehovah's Witnesses always expressed their willingness to comply. The controversy again came before the Supreme Court in 1943 in a suit by Witness Walter Barnette to restrain the West Virginia State Board of Education from enforcing a compulsory flag-salute regulation.

In *West Virginia State Board of Education* v. *Barnette*, the Court by a six to three vote overruled the Gobitis decision and held that the First Amendment prohibited governmental agencies from using compulsion to achieve national unity through participation in a symbolic ceremony. Of the eight Justices who had joined in the Gobitis decision, Hughes and McReynolds were no longer on the bench; their successors, Jackson and Rutledge, disagreed with them. So, too, now did Black, Douglas and Murphy, all of whom changed their minds and now agreed with Stone. Only Frankfurter, Roberts and Reed maintained the position they had taken originally. What had happened was that shocked American opinion made its influence felt on the Supreme Court. The Court follows not only the election returns, but also the enlightened conscience of the community.

The opinion in the Barnette case was written by Jackson, by far his greatest opinion, and undoubtedly one of the great opinions in the history of the Supreme Court. It merits inclusion along with Holmes's dissent in the Abrams case and Brandeis' concurring opinion in the Whitney case in any collection of documents in the history of American freedoms. "If there is any fixed star in our constitutional constellation," his eloquent opinion concludes, "it is that no official, high or petty, can prescribe what shall be orthodox in politics, nationalism, religion, or other matters of opinion, or force citizens to confess by word or act their faith therein."

Two cases decided in the decade after 1937 illustrate sharply how the revolution converted the Court from a protector of property rights to a protector of personal freedoms. In *Schneider* v. *Irvington,* the Court, in 1939, held unconstitutional a municipal ordinance, enforced against some Jehovah's Witnesses, that forbade the distribution of religious handbills or other religious literature to pedestrians. The purpose of the ordinance, the town counsel argued, was to prevent the littering of the streets. This, the Court held, was not sufficiently important to justify interference with freedom of religion and of the press. The constitutional way to prevent littering is to arrest litterers, not to prohibit the dissemination of *religious* or *political* pamphlets and handbills. Three years later, in *Valentine* v. *Chrestenson,* the Court held that a municipality could constitutionally enforce such an ordinance against the distribution of *commercial* (advertising) handbills. Twenty years earlier, the decisions might well have been exactly reversed; then the Court protected business interests against undue state regulation and restraints, but left freedom of political and religious expression pretty much to the states' uncontrolled discretion. By 1942 the Court had left the field of controlling state regulation of business, but maintained a suspicious eye over any attempt to regulate religion or speech, particularly against unpopular minorities. Here was Footnote 4 in full force.

PERSONAL FREEDOMS AND THE PEARL HARBOR PANIC

The gravest threats to civil liberties occur in periods of great national fear. Such a period followed the Japanese attack on Pearl Harbor, and the victims of the consequent restrictions on personal freedoms, not only in Hawaii, but in continental America as well, were American citizens of Japanese descent. A few of the resultant cases reached the Supreme Court.

In *Hirabayashi* v. *United States*, the Supreme Court unanimously upheld the conviction of an American-born college student of Japanese ancestry who was found outside his apartment after 8 P.M. one evening, in violation of a curfew on Japanese Americans imposed by General De Witt, West Coast military commander.

In *Korematsu* v. *United States* the Court upheld an order by General De Witt issued five months after Pearl Harbor, giving all Americans of Japanese ancestry, citizens as well as aliens, five days to get out of the West Coast and the inland states of Idaho, Montana, Nevada and Utah. Because of pressing public necessity and the gravest imminent danger to the public safety, the majority of the Court held, some restrictions upon the liberties of a particular racial group, motivated not by racial prejudice but by military necessity, must be tolerated.

On the same day in 1944 that the Korematsu case was decided, the Court called a halt in *Ex parte Endo*. Curfew and evacuation it could with difficulty accept; internment of loyal American citizens in concentration camps solely because of the accident of racial descent was too closely akin to what the Nazis were doing for the Court to acquiesce in, even under the claim of military necessity. Once the military authorities determined that a particular Japanese-American citizen was loyal, they were not authorized, the Court held, to detain him any further, although they could, according to the Korematsu decision, prohibit him from returning to his home on the West Coast or in the Rocky Mountain states.

The record of the Supreme Court in respect to civil liberties was better in the second World War than it had been in the first, particularly in view of the fact that the earlier cases reached the Court after fighting had ceased, while the Second World War was still going on in full force when the Court passed on the related cases. Nevertheless, the record was not one which reflects any glory upon a Court considered by many to have been the most liberal in the entire history of the nation. That a Court whose majority consisted of Stone, Black, Douglas, Murphy and Rutledge could sanction the Japanese evacuation program indicates strongly that in periods of great national fear, only modest reliance can be placed on the Supreme Court. The Court may keep its head when most have lost theirs, but it cannot single-handedly preserve the civil liberties that every other dominant part of our nation seeks to suppress. The experience of the Vinson Court during the McCarthy era testifies to that.

chapter fourteen

Vinson in the Shadow of McCarthy

In July, 1945, some three months after Roosevelt's death, Roberts retired from the Court and Truman made his first appointment to it. This was the honeymoon period between Truman and the Republicans, while the shock of Roosevelt's death was still fresh. As an earnest of Truman's desire to continue the era of good feeling (it turned out to be the shortest era in American history), he decided to name a Republican to succeed the Republican Roberts. Moreover, he was going to choose him from among his old colleagues and companions in the Senate. Truman had not been a particularly outstanding senator and chose for the post someone whose career in the Senate was even less distinguished than his own.

The fortunate recipient of Truman's offer of harmony to the Republican party was Harold H. Burton of Ohio. Burton had been a prosperous utilities and corporation lawyer in Cleveland, law teacher at Western Reserve, Congressman, "reform" mayor of Cleveland, and then senator from Ohio since 1941. He was a close friend of and had been co-member with Truman on the War Investigating Committee.

When Roosevelt passed over Jackson for Stone in naming a successor to Hughes, he indicated to his Attorney-General that the latter was not quite ready for the top post but that his turn would come. Had Roosevelt been still living at Stone's death it may be assumed that the post of Chief Justice would have gone to Jackson. Jackson was in Nuremberg when word of Stone's sudden death arrived, and he undoubtedly expected that Truman would fulfill the promise Roosevelt had implicitly made. There were the usual rumors and newspaper guesses as to whom Truman would name, and among these rumors was one that Black had told Truman he would resign if Jackson were named.

It is doubtful that there was any substance to this rumor, but it was no secret that Black would have preferred practically anyone else on the bench for the elevation; and it is probably true that the friends of Black and Douglas, when it became clear that the appointment would not come from the left wing, threw their influence behind the genial Reed as the person most likely to bring harmony back to what seemed to the public to be a continually squabbling Court. Truman, however, apparently came to the conclusion—and probably with justification—that peace was more likely to return to the troubled tribunal if its new chief came from outside its ranks. For whatever reason, he passed over Jackson, Reed and all other members of the bench and named his Secretary of Treasury, Fred M. Vinson of Kentucky.

Jackson was convinced that Black was responsible for his failure to receive the appointment. His fury caused him to lose his head, and again bring Black into the center of public controversy. From Nuremberg he wrote a letter to the Judiciary Committees of both Houses of Congress. In it he stated that the "feud" among the Justices had been so well advertised that Congress had "a right to know the facts." According to the reports that he had been getting, one of his colleagues "made public threats to the President," thereby giving the appearance that "offensive behavior" on Jackson's part was responsible for the feud.

The feud had started about a year earlier. It grew out of a case which interpreted the Wage-Hour law and involved the application of the "portal-to-portal" doctrine to the mining of coal. The Court, in an opinion from which Jackson dissented, held the doctrine applicable and thus decided in favor of the miners. Then counsel for the companies made a motion to rehear the case on several grounds, one of which was that Black had not disqualified himself even though the attorney arguing the case for the United Mine Workers was Crampton Harris, who had been Black's law partner in Birmingham twenty years earlier. The petition for rehearing was denied, but Jackson and Frankfurter felt it necessary to read a short memorandum noting that they did not consider it within their province to express any view on the merits of the disqualification question. This was damnation by neutrality; it was unusual, if not unprecedented, for Justices to comment on motions relating to disqualification.

At the time the incident went unnoticed by any but a small coterie of lawyers who follow the Court's activities as part of their professional or avocational pursuits. However, during the vacancy in the Chief Justiceship, newspaper columnist Doris Fleeson revived the story and stated that the special opinion had caused Black to react "with fiery scorn" to what he deemed a "slur upon his personal and judicial honor"; Truman, she reported further, had been told of the dispute and this was one of the reasons why Jackson was not likely to be appointed.

Jackson considered the Fleeson story to be a "direct specific attack" on him, and he felt it necessary to reply. He had filed his special opinion, he wrote in his letter, because he did not want to "lend blind and unqualified approval" to Black's conduct. "I told Justice Black," he continued, "in language that was sharp but no different than I would use again that I would not stand for any more of his bullying." Black might deny that he had made "threats" to the President in opposing Jackson, but it was "equally sinister that a fabrication about a Justice should be so assiduously advertised without denial from any source."

Black did not reply to the charge. During the five years preceding the controversial case he had seen Crampton Harris socially but once, and then only for a few minutes. Whether many Justices in similar circumstances would have disqualified themselves is disputable. Stone, Brandeis and Cardozo, to mention but Justices contemporary with Black and Jackson, had not disqualified themselves in similar situations. A judge generally does not participate in any case which was in the office while the partnership was still undissolved, but it is not usual for him to disqualify himself in a case which arose twenty years after he had severed all relationships with the attorney arguing the case. The members of the Judiciary Committee, usually all lawyers, apparently did not deem that Black's conduct warranted further consideration, for they took no action at all on Jackson's letter.

Press reaction, as was to be expected, varied with the political geography of the commenter. An extreme rightist, such as David Lawrence, praised Jackson and condemned Black. More moderate rightists took the opportunity to say "a plague on both your houses." Centrists felt that Jackson had made a rather evil smelling mountain out of a rather meaningless molehill. Leftists thought that Jackson was either trying to wreak personal vengeance against the man he held responsible for his failure to get the Chief Justiceship or, more charitably, that the explanation was to be sought in the enormous mental strain of the Nuremberg trial. The moral of the entire unhappy incident is perhaps that, as Lincoln pointed out after the Dred Scott decision, Supreme Court Justices are like all other mortals and that the donning of a black robe is not sufficiently potent to alter the course of human nature.

VINSON, MINTON AND CLARK

Vinson had served in Congress for some thirteen years until his appointment by Roosevelt in 1938 to be a judge of the court of appeals for the District of Columbia, and later chief justice of the emergency court of appeals. From 1943 to 1945 he served as director of the Office of Economic Stabilization, succeeding Byrnes in that post. He then served briefly as federal loan administrator and as director of the Office of War Mobilization before becoming Truman's Secretary of the Treasury. Even during his service in Congress his chief interest was in financial affairs, gaining for him a reputation of being something of a fiscal expert, with, however, a strong pro-labor record. Except for the period that he was a member of the court of appeals, his offices were all in the field of public finance. Vinson could not be said to have the type of background that would particularly fit him to carry forward the revolution of 1937, assuming that the times were propitious for such a mission—which they decidedly were not.

Even a less likely candidate for the role of champion of civil liberties was Truman's third appointee to the bench, Tom C. Clark of Texas, appointed in 1949 on the death of Murphy. Clark had risen in government service as a protege of the powerful Texas Senator Tom Connally. In 1937 he was appointed special assistant to the Attorney-General and in 1942 was given the responsibility of relocating the Japanese-Americans banished from the West Coast. The next year he was made head of the anti-trust division of the Department of Justice and two years later head of the Criminal Division. In 1945 Truman appointed him Attorney-General and in the ensuing four years Clark's interest shuttled between the prosecution of big corporations violating the anti-trust laws and little radicals violating the anti-subversive laws. Practically Clark's entire pre-judicial public career had been spent as a prosecutor, hardly appropriate training for service on a Court now committed to the protection of personal liberties.

The background of Truman's last appointee gave better promise of accord with the new role of the Court as protector of personal freedoms. Like Truman, Sherman Minton had served as a captain in the First World War. Later he became counsel to the Indiana public service commission and in 1934 was elected Democratic senator from Indiana. In the

Senate he joined the New Deal contingent and remained a loyal adherent of Roosevelt's policies, including the ill-fated judiciary reorganization bill. After Minton was defeated for re-election in 1940, Roosevelt appointed him his administrative assistant, and the next year named him a judge of the federal circuit court of appeals. On Rutledge's death in 1949, Truman promoted him to the Supreme Court. Minton's service as a New Deal senator for six years and as administrative assistant to Roosevelt for a year would seem to indicate a sympathetic approach toward civil liberties, but his seven years on the Supreme Court disappointed those who expected it. Perhaps in less trying times his record in civil liberties cases would have been more in harmony with that of his fellow New Deal senator, Hugo Black; but, whatever may have been his private sympathies, Minton lacked the fortitude or foolhardiness of Black in quixotically trying to hold back the surging tide of McCarthyism.

This was the bench over which Vinson presided during what was probably the darkest period in the history of American freedoms. The solid libertarian phalanx of Black, Douglas, Murphy and Rutledge had been halved by the almost simultaneous deaths in 1949 of Murphy and Rutledge. It was replaced by an equally solid conservative phalanx of Vinson, Burton, Clark and Minton. Reed, Jackson and Frankfurter for a short time maintained a centrist position, but Reed quickly joined the right-wing group, and so too did Jackson in most cases involving Communists.

Frankfurter maintained a special position of his own, one that he called judicial self-restraint but might also be called judicial laissez faire. He always opposed the rationale set forth in Footnote 4 that there was a hierarchy of democratic values in which personal freedoms occupied a higher constitutional level than property rights. He believed that the Court should equally avoid overruling the decisions of the democratically elected legislators and executives in both fields. The result was that only in cases involving the fairness of trials in federal criminal courts was he to be consistently found on the libertarian side with Black and Douglas. Here, the Supreme Court as the head of the federal judiciary system had both the right and duty to make sure that the lower courts and the federal prosecuting officials adhered strictly to constitutional and statutory requirements designed for the protection of persons accused of crime. In respect to other matters, he was fond of invoking Stone's reminder in the AAA case dissent, that the Court is not the only agency of government that should be presumed capable of governing and that the forum for the removal of unwise laws is the ballot box, not the courtroom. The practical result of this philosophy was that during the serious civil liberty crisis of 1949 to 1953, Frankfurter was generally to be found with the Vinson group, almost always writing a special opinion stating why he concurred with the majority decision, leaving Black and Douglas in splendid libertarian isolation.

TRUMAN AND THE JUSTICES

It is often an amusing and generally harmless diversion to speculate what would have happened had what at the time seemed to be a particularly minor incident not occurred. Confining ourselves to the subject of this book, we could speculate on what would have happened had John Jay accepted reappointment as Chief Justice in 1800 so that Adams would not have been required to turn to John Marshall as a second choice, or had Mrs. John Schofield learned to wear shoes so that Cleveland would not have found it necessary to name Melville Fuller to the Chief Justiceship. Similarly, it is interesting to speculate on what would have happened had not some alert reporter learned in advance of Truman's plan to send Vinson to Moscow.

During the 1948 campaign the Wallace Progressives' principal issue was the claimed "warmongering" of the Truman administration. The Dixiecrats had already split off from the Democratic party and named their own candidate. If, in addition, the Progressives would draw off a substantial number of Democrats from the left flank, the Truman prospects, already bleak, would become even darker. Sensitive to this, Truman decided that he must make some dramatic move to prevent the alienation of those Democrats and independents who were concerned about the apparent drift to war. Accordingly, he conceived the idea of sending Chief Justice Vinson to the Kremlin to sound out Stalin on the possibilities of easing tensions between East and West and resuming negotiations with the Russians.

When Truman put the request to Vinson the latter pointed out that he had but recently requested the Associate Justices to confine themselves to their judicial duties and stay out of all side activities, particularly in an election year. It would therefore be improper for him to be the first to violate his own rule. As Chief Justice, therefore, he "must decline," but, he added, "if you make it as a Presidential request, I shall have a clear duty to comply." Truman took the hint and made it as a Presidential request (there was ample precedent for it) and Vinson replied promptly, "I'll be ready in a few days."

It is conceivable that had Truman been able to carry out his plan, some modus vivendi might have been worked out with Stalin and the Cold War might have been averted. Had this happened, it is almost certain that the nation would not have reached the nadir in the protection of civil liberties as it did in the ensuing five years. Unfortunately for the mission, however, some reporter learned of the plans before they were formally announced and the details worked out. Immediately, the press, hostile as it in any event was to Truman and the Democratic party, broke out almost spontaneously with one big cry of "appeasement." The opposition grew so heated that Truman felt that he had no choice but to abandon the entire project.

One can also speculate that this incident had a traumatic effect on the Democratic party. During the next five or six years, the party strove mightily to live down any possible charge that it was "soft on Communism." In 1954 even the most articulate anti-McCarthy Democrats in the Senate were shouting and voting for the enactment of a bill to outlaw Communists, a bill so Draconian that the Republicans feared for its constitutionality.

Had Vinson been allowed to proceed on his mission and had he come back even moderately successful, the ensuing persecution of Communists, alleged Communists, pro-Communists and Communist dupes would not have occurred, or at least not with the severity that it did. Conversely, had Vinson gone and been treated as Marshall had been in France, the reaction here would have been the same as that against the French in 1798. But what actually happened was that Vinson did not go at all, yet the domestic reaction was the same as if he had gone and had received the treatment that Marshall and his associates had received at the hands of the French.

The effect of the failure of the mission on Vinson's handling of civil liberties cases can, of course, be only speculative. Yet, it is reasonable to suppose that just as the Democratic party feared to be labeled as soft on Communism, so too did Vinson, and his decisions reflect that fear. Nor, if this speculation is correct, did the consequences end with Vinson.

By the time a person reaches the position of Supreme Court Justice he is generally mature, sophisticated and quite independent. Supreme Court Justices are not easily dominated by other men, even Chief Justices. Nevertheless, there have been in the history of the Supreme Court, Justices who have exerted a more than ordinary influence on all or some of their associates. Marshall certainly did, and so too did Vinson in respect to Burton, Clark and Minton. Had Vinson cast his weight in the direction of Black and Douglas in the numerous civil liberties cases that came to the Court during his administration, it is likely that Burton, Clark and Minton would have gone along with him, and the Supreme Court would have been spared what is probably the least defensible series of decisions in its history.

As the abortive mission to Moscow may have had a traumatic effect on Vinson so the Hiss trial may have had a similar effect on Frankfurter and Reed. Alger Hiss was technically charged with perjury; but in the eyes of the American public he was on trial for treason, in turning over secret documents to Whittaker Chambers for transmission to the Russians. At the trial both Frankfurter and Reed testified on behalf of Hiss as character witnesses. (Hiss had been one of Holmes's brilliant law clerks.) Nevertheless, Hiss was found guilty and sentenced to the federal penitentiary. Although a few die-hards continued to believe him innocent, the press and the nation at large judged him guilty of treason. The consequent public impression that Frankfurter and Reed had testified in favor of a traitor may well have had some psychological effect on the two Justices and motivated their leaning backward on the side of security in cases involving alleged subversives.

If we want to continue the harmless diversion, we can speculate on the effect Jackson's expreiences at Nuremberg may have had on his decisions as a Supreme Court Justice. Throughout all his opinions regarding Communists from the time of his return from Nuremberg until his death in 1954 one finds a consistent theme: the Communist party is not a political party at all, not even a radical political party as the syndicalists and anarchists were, but an international conspiracy whose purpose it is to totalitarianize the world. To meet such a danger few measures taken by the American government can be deemed too extreme or unjustified. Is it not reasonable to suppose that this attitude toward Communism was in substantial measure the result of his dealings with the Soviet judges, prosecutors, and military political officials at Nuremberg? It is probable that by the time he returned to his judicial duties in Washington he may have reached the conclusion that as between totalitarianism of the Nazi and Soviet varieties there was little to choose.

All this is speculation. It is equally and perhaps more probable that even if these experiences did have psychological consequences in respect to the individual Justices, the resultant effect on the course of Supreme Court decisions during the Presidency of Truman and the Chief Justiceship of Vinson was slight. The course of American History during that period could not have been stayed by any Supreme Court. The cold war and the fear were too great for any small group of human beings, even those possessing the prestige of Supreme Court Justices, substantially to prevent the American people from releasing their hysteria in the way they did. At the depth of the dementia, just before the execution of Julius and Ethel Rosenberg, the intervention of the Pope himself was not able to mitigate the cry for vengeance, even among Roman Catholics.

America's obsession about the dangers of domestic Communism had been growing gradually ever since the disillusionment caused by the Ribbentrop-Litvinov agreement, following as it did hard upon the honeymoon between American Communists and the New Deal in Roosevelt's first administration. During the period when the United States and Soviet Russia were allies in a world conflict against a common enemy there was a temporary abatement in the crusade against Communism. With the return of peace, the inevitable disagreement between the erstwhile allies as to the political consequences of the victory, and the hardening of Stalinism, the crusade resumed with ever increasing vigor. Loyalty was rapidly becoming the number one issue in the nation.

Martin Dies and J. Parnell Thomas, respectively Democratic and Republican chairmen of the House Committee on Un-American Activities, had found political pay dirt in hunting subversives. In 1947 the pressure of events and public opinion compelled Truman to order a loyalty check on all government employees and dismissal of those found to have subversive affiliations. The labor unions, particularly the CIO, undertook their own cleansing, by expelling a number of unions found to be Communist infiltrated and purging others.

Other events contributed to the heightening of the fever. In June, 1949, Judith Coplon, an employee of the Justice Department, was convicted of taking secret documents with the intention of passing them on to a Soviet agent. The fact that the conviction was later set aside because the Department of Justice had used illegal wiretap evidence only served to intensify the growing fear-hatred. The conviction of Alger Hiss, the prototype of young, intellectual New Deal idealism, had a yet more profound effect, for it dismayed and disillusioned many of the liberals who otherwise could be expected to have striven to stem the tide. As in all crusades, the converted were to be found in the van, and confessions by repentant ex-Communists, some of whom discovered capitalism and religion simultaneously, were legion.

Whatever hope there might have been for averting the plunge disappeared when the North Koreans crossed the thirty-eighth parallel and the Chinese Communists crossed the Yalu River. What had been a "cold war" had become a hot one. America was at war and acted accordingly. The fact that the war was a limited one and sometimes euphemistically called a police action was hardly material. The intensity of internal fear is not necessarily related to the extent of external danger. Fear and the concomitant repression of civil liberties were far less serious during the Second World War than during the considerably less perilous First.

The public demand for anti-Communist legislation became irrepressible. In 1940, in the wake of the Nazi-Soviet pact, Congress had passed the Smith Act, aimed at subversives, but this was now deemed to be inadequate. In 1950 Congress passed the McCarran Internal Security Law, which required registration with the Attorney-General of all Communist and Communist-front organizations and all individual members of such groups. Members were forbidden to receive passports or to work for the government or in defense industries. Communists could not enter the country as aliens and those who were already here and were still aliens were made subject to deportation. Finally, the law empowered the government in case of war to establish detention (in Germany, called concentration) camps, in which Communists and other potential saboteurs could be held in custody. Truman quixotically vetoed the bill as a violation of the Constitution and antagonistic to American traditions of freedom, but the veto was overriden by large majorities.

THE MC CARTHY ERA

The times were ripe for Joseph R. McCarthy, although it took him some three years to discover it, and then he did so almost by accident.

He had been elected to the Senate during the Republican sweep of 1946, ironically after winning the primary against Robert M. La Follette, Jr. with the blessing, if not active assistance, of the Communists, who hated La Follette. For three years he remained an inconspicuous, mediocre senator with a reputation for having a somewhat unsavory personal character. Primaries and election would be coming about again in two years, and McCarthy was not too confident of victory. He needed, he felt, a dramatic issue, one that would excite the people. He asked advice of Father Edmund Walsh of Georgetown University, and the latter suggested Communism. McCarthy instantly accepted the suggestion and shortly thereafter made a speech before the Women's Republican Club in Wheeling, West Virginia, in which he asserted that he held in his hands a list of the names of two hundred and five (or eighty-one or fifty-seven) card-carrying Communists in the State Department.

This was the beginning of a period in American history which, fortunately short as it was, McCarthy dominated as perhaps no single individual in American history had previously done. The years between 1950 and 1954 have already been marked in history as the McCarthy Era, and the word "McCarthyism," probably coined by Herbert Block (Herblock) of the Washington *Post*, is an accepted addition to the American language.

Everything of any political significance that happened in the United States during this period is understandable only against the background of McCarthy. His influence reached every segment of government, federal, state and municipal, and included private industry. He could and did destroy the political lives of long-known and respected conservative leaders, such as Senator Millard Tydings of Maryland, and the economic and social lives of completely unknown workers in private industry. He held two Presidents of the United States in practical captivity and compelled one of them, when a candidate, publicly to snub the man most responsible for his own rise to fame. Individually, he straddled all three departments of government, acting as a one-man legislature, an Executive Department making its own foreign relations, and a combination judiciary and prosecuting agency.

The four years after 1950 were in some ways the most tragic in the history of our nation. The American people were sick with a great sickness. For the first time in our national life we had lost rationality, and with it almost all sense of decency, fairness, mercy or even justice whenever Communism was in any way involved. In 1952, two social psychologists, Marie Jahoda and Stuart W. Cook, published in the *Yale Law Journal* the results of a pilot study they had made on the social and psychological effects of the crusade against Communism on government employees. Typical of the responses they received to their inquiries was the statement of one employee: "Why lead with your chin? If Communists like apple pie and I do, I see no reason why I should stop eating it. But I would." A number of the respondents recommended that federal employees should keep out of all discussion of controversial subjects, such as religion, equal rights for Negroes, atomic energy, etc. Another suggested that federal employees should join no organization other than the "Knights of Columbus, and perhaps the Masons." Others felt it wise to avoid association with Jews, Negroes, foreign-born persons or persons having foreign-sounding names, union members, persons who join organizations and intellectuals.

This was the background of the civil liberties decisions of the Vinson Court during that period. Without an awareness of that background these decisions cannot be understood nor can a fair evaluation be made of the extent to which the Court carried out its function as protector of American liberties.

COMMUNISTS IN LABOR UNIONS

The first major encounter with the problems of civil liberties and internal security experienced by the Vinson Court concerned the labor union movement. This was in the case of *American Communications Association* v. *Douds*, decided in 1950. Involved was the so-called "non-Communist oath" requirement of the Taft-Hartley Act. This disqualified from the benefits of the Labor Relations Act any union whose officers failed to sign an affidavit stating that they were not members of the Communist party or any other organization advocating the forcible overthrow of the government and that they themselves did not believe in forcible overthrow.

Of the nine Justices, three, Douglas, Clark and Minton, for one reason or another did not participate in the case. Of the remaining six, five believed the law constitutional insofar as it required an oath of non-membership in a subversive organization; but only three, Vinson, Reed and Burton, believed it constitutional insofar as it required an oath of non-belief. Frankfurter and Jackson considered the non-belief oath unconstitutional. Black considered both parts violative of the Bill of Rights and would have thrown the entire section out.

Vinson's opinion held that it was within the constitutional power of Congress to discourage labor unions from choosing as officers persons who were members of the Communist party; Congress had acted on the basis of evidence that Communist leaders of labor unions had in the past and would continue in the future to subordinate legitimate trade-union objectives to obstructive strikes, often in support of a foreign government. There was considerable evidence concerning a strike at the Milwaukee plant of the Allis-Chalmers Manufacturing Company, which was producing vital materials for the national defense program. The strike, according to the testimony presented to Congress, had been called in 1941 (before the Nazi invasion of Russia changed the Communist party line in respect to the nature of the war) solely in obedience to party orders for the purpose of starting the "snowballing of strikes" in defense plants.

Jackson's concurring opinion set forth for the first time the thesis on which he based his later concurrence in other cases involving anti-Communist statutes and which was to pervade most legislative and much judicial thinking—that behind its political-party facade the Communist party is a conspiratorial and revolutionary junta, organized to reach ends and to use means incompatible with our constitutional system. In many ways the Communist party is basically different from real political parties, including radical parties. The goal of the Communist party, he said, is to seize powers of government by and for a minority rather than to acquire power through the vote of a free electorate. Alone among American parties, past and present, it is dominated by a foreign government. Violent and undemocratic methods are the calculated and indispensable means to attain its goal. It has sought to gain its leverage and hold on the American people by acquiring control of the labor movement. Finally, every member of the Communist party is an agent to execute the Communist program.

Since the Communist party is not a political party in the traditionally understood sense, but a criminal conspiracy, constitutional concepts of freedom of speech and of association are irrelevant, and membership in the party may validly subject the member to such sanctions as disqualification from holding labor-union office.

Black's dissent was based on the directly contrary thesis—that the

Communist party is not fundamentally different from the other hated, radical, and dangerous political groups for whose protection in the interest of democracy the constitutional guarantees of the First Amendment and the rest of the Bill of Rights have been developed.

LOYALTY OATHS AND GOVERNMENT SERVICE

In 1951, following the Douds decision, the Supreme Court in *Gerende* v. *Board of Supervisors* upheld a Maryland statute that barred from a place on the ballot any candidate who refused to take an oath that he was not knowingly a member of an organization engaged in an attempt to overthrow the government by force or violence. During the same year, in *Garner* v. *Los Angeles Board,* the Court sustained an ordinance of the city of Los Angeles requiring all civil service employees to file affidavits stating whether they were or ever had been members of the Communist party. The Court (with Black and Douglas dissenting) upheld the requirement on the ground that past conduct may well relate to present fitness, and past loyalty may have a reasonable relationship to present and future trust.

The next year the Court (Black and Douglas dissenting) in *Adler* v. *Board of Education,* sustained a New York statute barring from employment as a public school teacher any member of an organization advocating the overthrow of government by force, violence, or unlawful means. A teacher, said the Court, works in a sensitive area where he shapes the attitude of young minds toward the society in which they live. In this the state has a vital concern, for it must preserve the integrity of the schools, and school authorities therefore have the right and duty to screen teachers as to their fitness. To the claim that the effect of the statute is to infringe teachers' freedom of association, the Court replied that one's associates, past and present, may properly be considered in determining fitness and loyalty. From time immemorial one's reputation has been determined in part by the company one keeps. There is, therefore, concluded the Court, no constitutional rule that prevents a state, in determining the fitness and loyalty of public school teachers, from considering the organizations and persons with whom they associate.

The Vinson Court never did have the occasion to write an opinion on the federal government's extensive program to weed out subversives from its employ. The issue was involved in the case of *Bailey* v. *Richardson,* where the Court was called upon to consider the validity of the discharge of Dorothy Bailey, a government employee alleged to have been a Communist or active in Communist-front organizations. The charge was based on reports by anonymous informers whose identities were not disclosed to her nor, for that matter, to the Loyalty Review Board which passed upon the charges. The government took the position that it would be prejudicial to the national interest to reveal the identities of the informers or even to give such specific details of the charges as might enable the employee to infer who they were. Miss Bailey vigorously denied the accusations, but the Board upheld her dismissal.

Conviction in a criminal court under such circumstances would have been in flagrant violation of the due process clauses of the Constitution. But the federal circuit court of appeals held that discharge from government employment was not a criminal conviction. No one, it held, had a right to work for the government; government employment was a privilege which could be withdrawn at any time for any reason or no reason at all. Therefore, Miss Bailey could have been summarily dismissed without any hearing, and she accordingly cannot complain because the hearing that was voluntarily given to her did not measure up to her standards of fairness.

When the case reached the Supreme Court, Clark did not participate. The other eight Justices split four to four: Vinson, Reed, Burton and Minton would have upheld the procedure; Black, Douglas, Frankfurter and Jackson would have declared it invalid. Since there was an even division, the lower court's decision was deemed affirmed, but no opinions were written. It remained for the Warren Court to pass upon the validity of dismissals for disloyalty on evidence supplied by what came to be called "faceless informers."

On the other hand, in *Joint Anti-Fascist Refugee Committee* v. *McGrath* the Court held that the Attorney-General had acted unlawfully in promulgating his list of subversive organizations without giving the organizations listed an opportunity to present evidence at a hearing that they were in fact not subversive. Condemning an organization without a trial, the Court held, deprived it of its good name without due process of law.

And in *Wieman* v. *Updegraff* the Vinson Court invalidated a loyalty oath prescribed by Oklahoma of all officers and employees of the state. They were required to swear that they were not affiliated with any organization on the Attorney-General's list. The Court held that the oath went too far, for it condemned equally persons who joined a subversive organization with knowledge of its purposes and those who may have joined innocently without such knowledge. Joining, of itself, the Court held, is not sufficient to impute disloyalty.

THE CASE OF THE COMMUNIST TEN

Next to the Rosenberg trial, the case that attracted most interest and drama during the cold war was the case of the ten top Communist leaders in the United States. (Eleven were indicted, but one was too ill to stand trial.) The indictment charged them with conspiring to organize the Communist party and to advocate and teach the necessity of overthrowing the government of the United States by force and violence.

The difficulty with the theory of the indictment was that for years the Communist party had been considered to be not a criminal conspiracy but a legal political party not fundamentally different from other political parties. It had been on the ballot in many states and had presented to the electorate its candidates for public office. In fact, one of the defendants had been elected to the city council of New York on the Communist party ticket.

The prosecution overcame this difficulty by asserting that in April, 1945 a change took place in the character of the Communist party. At that time, on orders from Moscow, the leaders of the Communist party abandoned their previous goal of peaceful coexistence and of working within the framework of democracy to achieve peace and prosperity in the postwar period, and instead reorganized the party and established as its goal the initiation of a violent revolution to capture the government of the United States. The Communist party then exhibited its true character as a highly disciplined conspiratorial organization, adept at infiltration into strategic positions, use of aliases and of Aesopian or double-meaning language, rigidly controlled and tolerating no dissent.

The trial took place in New York City; it extended over a period of nine months, and was front-page news for most of the period. It was as thrilling as a television drama, with the forces of good arrayed against the forces of evil. As in all acceptable television drama, in the end the good triumphed over the evil. The defendants were convicted and received long prison sentences. Their lawyers were imprisoned for contempt of court and disbarred. On the other side, the judge who presided over the trial and sentenced the defendants and their attorneys was elevated to a higher court, and the prosecuting attorney received a judgeship.

The evidence shows that the defendants taught and advocated the Marxist-Leninist doctrine contained chiefly in four books: Stalin's *Foundation of Leninism*, *The Communist Manifesto* of Marx and Engels, Lenin's *State and Revolution*, and his *History of the Communist Party of the Soviet Union.* These works preached the necessity of overthrowing the government by force and violence, and the trial judge (Harold Medina, prominent corporation lawyer and professor at Columbia Law School) instructed the jury that, if the defendants advocated these doctrines with the intent to overthrow the government by force and violence as speedily as circumstances would permit, they should be found guilty.

In *Dennis* v. *United States*, the Vinson Court upheld the conviction, Black and Douglas dissenting. These two Justices were of the view that the "clear and present danger" test was applicable to Communists as to anyone else, that the test should not be impaired, qualified or compromised, and that under that test the indictment should have been dismissed since there was no substantial danger that the handful of known, discredited, and detested Communists in the country could successfully overthrow the government of the United States by force or violence.

Jackson concurred in the conviction on the ground that the clear and present danger test was devised for the American type of individualistic, native radicalism, such as IWW syndicalism, but was not applicable to an international conspiracy. Frankfurter concurred on the ground of judicial restraint—the Smith Act, under which the Communists were indicted, was not clearly and unarguably irrational; hence, it should not be set aside by the Supreme Court any more than a similar statute affecting economic interests or regulating business.

Vinson, writing for himself, Reed, Burton and Minton (Clark, as former Attorney-General in whose administration the prosecution was begun, did not participate in the decision) held that the clear and present danger, while applicable, must be understood. It is not an absolute standard that can be applied like a yardstick equally in all circumstances. It is a relative concept to be applied in the light of the particular circumstances in which it is invoked. A danger that is clear in one set of circumstances may not be clear in another set, and what is present in one instance may not be in another. In any case in which the "clear and present danger" test is involved the courts must decide whether the gravity of the evil, discounted by its improbability, justifies such invasion of free speech as is necessary to avoid the danger.

This means that in determining whether the requisite clarity and immediacy is present to justify a restriction on speech, due consideration must be given to the degree of gravity of the evil sought to be presented. If it is a comparatively minor evil, such as littered streets, the evil must be extremely clear and close to justify the restriction on speech. If, however, the evil is a serious one, such as the loss of life and property attendant upon an even unsuccessful attempt to overthrow the government by force or violence, much wider scope must be given to the discretion of the government in seeking to avert the evil, and the courts must accept a much lower standard of clarity and immediacy. The "clear and present danger" test, properly understood, does not require the government to wait until the *putsch* is about to be executed, the plans have been laid, and the signal is awaited. In view of the nature of the Communist conspiracy, highly organized with rigidly disciplined members subject to the immediate and unquestioned call of their leaders, and in view of the inflammable nature of world conditions, the Chief Justice held that the danger was sufficiently clear and present to justify punishing the defendants for conspiracy to advocate the overthrow of the government by force and violence.

DEPORTATION AND DUE PROCESS

One of the cruelest aspects of the cold war was the treatment accorded by the government to non-citizens suspected of possible disloyalty or subversive affiliation. In respect to at least one alien, Harry Bridges, the radical West Coast labor leader, the campaign long antedated the cold war. For some twenty years, through Franklin Roosevelt's New Deal, Harry Truman's Fair Deal and the first term of

Dwight Eisenhower's Republican administration, the government of the United States was engaged in a persistent campaign to deport Bridges. In 1945, about halfway through the history of the war of the United States against Harry Bridges, Justice Murphy, concurring in the decision of a majority of the Supreme Court in *Bridges* v. *Wixon* that Bridges' alleged affiliation with the Communist party had not been proved, stated: "The record in this case will stand forever as a monument to man's intolerance of man. Seldom if ever in the history of this nation has there been such a concentrated and relentless crusade to deport an individual because he dared to exercise the freedom that belongs to him as a human being and that is guaranteed to him by the Constitution."

Undeterred by this strong condemnation, the government resumed the campaign. After the third attempt to deport him had failed, Bridges became a naturalized citizen, and a citizen is not subject to deportation. But this fact did not halt the government's efforts. It claimed that Bridges had committed perjury in denying in his application for citizenship that he had ever been a member of the Communist party, and that his naturalization should therefore be revoked for fraud, preparatory to deportation. In 1955, a Federal judge refused to accept the testimony of several bitter ex-Communists and dismissed the proceeding to denaturalize Bridges. Thereafter, the campaign was dropped, apparently for good.

Bridges was fortunate; rarely does an alien have a loyal and financially strong union behind him to help in the exceedingly costly struggle to prevent deportation sought by a determined government. And deportation proceedings against suspect aliens were one of the major weapons in the arsenal of defense against internal subversion during the dark years of midcentury.

The Alien Registration Act of 1940 and the Internal Security Act of 1950 directed the deportation of any alien who during his stay in the United States was, for no matter how short a period, a member of the Communist party or any other organization that advocated the violent overthrow of the government. The validity of these provisions came to the Vinson Court for determination in 1952 in the cases of *Harisiades* v. *Shaughnessy* and *Carlson* v. *Landon*.

In these cases the Court refused to interfere with the deportation of an Italian, father of an American-born child, who had come to the

United States in 1920, joined the Communist party in 1923 when he was nineteen years old, and resigned from it in 1929; nor with the deportation of a mother of three American-born children, who between 1919 and 1936 had on three separate occasions signed up for membership in the party and paid dues (but taken no other part in its activities) for a total of four or five years. It was immaterial, the Court held, that both these aliens had resigned from the party long before the Alien Registration Act was adopted and at a time when the Communist party was still a legal party entitled to be on the ballot and elect its members to public office.

Deportation, the Supreme Court has consistently held, is not a criminal proceeding even though the consequences to the alien may be far more drastic than fine or imprisonment. Therefore, as the decision in *Calder* v. *Bull* had held during the Ellsworth Chief Justiceship, the constitutional ban on *ex post facto* laws is inapplicable. These decisions, the Vinson Court held, are too well fixed in our constitutional law to be overruled, no matter how harsh and arbitrary they might seem. Black and Douglas dissented.

The Vinson Court went even further. It upheld the power of the government to deport an alien to a country where his return might spell his death. Moreover, he could be compelled to cooperate in his own deportation, that is, in effect be compelled to sign his own death warrant. International law just does not sanction sailing up to the shores of a foreign nation and dropping an unwanted alien there; protocol requires that the foreign country agree to accept the deportee. For this to happen, the deportee must ask the country to receive him. In the case of *United States* v. *Spector*, the Vinson Court in 1952 upheld the validity of a federal law making it a felony for a deportable alien to fail to make application for travel documents necessary for his own departure. Under the Spector case, the alien has a choice. He can sign the application to his own native country asking that it allow him to be deported there. Or he can refuse to sign and thus remain in the United States. But if he does the latter, he is guilty of a felony and will remain in the United States in a federal penitentiary. At the end of his term, of course, the whole thing starts over again (his stay in the penitentiary certainly did not purge him of his deportability), and again he has the alternative; and so on, for the rest of his natural life.

THE ROSENBERG CASE

The most dramatic case, and the one which by far received most attention throughout the world during the entire cold war era was the Rosenberg case. On January 31, 1951 a grand jury indicted Julius Rosenberg, his wife Ethel, her brother David Greenglass, Morton Sobell and Anatoli Yakolev of conspiring to communicate to the Soviet Union documents, writings, sketches and notes relating to the national defense of the United States. The events on which the indictment was based occurred principally during the years 1944 to 1946, at a time when the United States and Russia were allies against a common enemy. However, the law under which they were indicted made no difference between transmission to friendly nations or to enemies; in either case, the penalty could be death.

Yakolev, a Russian diplomat, had returned to Russia and could not be tried. On March 6, the trial against the others began in the United States district court in New York City. It ended three weeks later with a verdict of guilty against all the defendants. Judge Irving Kaufman sentenced Julius and Ethel Rosenberg to death, Sobell to thirty years imprisonment, and Greenglass, who had cooperated with the authorities and testified against his sister and her husband, to fifteen years imprisonment.

It was without doubt the imposition of the death sentence during peace time that chiefly aroused world-wide excitement, and pleas for clemency came pouring in from every corner of the world. Contributing elements were the fact that the verdict of guilty was based on the practically uncorroborated testimony of David Greenglass and his wife Ruth, testimony which was in every respect denied by Julius and Ethel Rosenberg, and the fact that all the characters in the drama—the defendants, the judge, the prosecuting attorney and the defendants' attorneys—were Jewish, and it was felt by many that the death penalty was inflicted by the Jewish judge to still anti-Semitic charges identifying Jews with Communists. Before imposing the sentences Judge Kaufman went to his synagogue and prayed long and hard. He concluded that the death sentence was warranted because, as he told the Rosenbergs when he imposed it, they were guilty of "putting into the hands of the Russians the A-bomb years before our best scientists predicted Russia would perfect the bomb," and this "has already caused the Communist aggression in Korea, with the resultant casualties exceeding 50,-000." Their crime, consequently, was "worse than murder," and the death sentence was the least that could be imposed. (Klaus Fuchs, who had transmitted far more valuable information to the Russians, had been sentenced in England to imprisonment for fourteen years.)

The Rosenbergs appealed to the federal circuit court of appeals, but that court affirmed the decision. They then sought to appeal to the Supreme Court, which refused to accept the appeal. (As indicated in the first chapter, the Court does not deem its function to be the correcting of incorrect decisions by lower courts or even the prevention of a miscarriage of justice. Unless there is an important issue of federal law presented, the Court will refuse to accept an appeal, even if the Justices individually might believe that the lower court was wrong in its decision.) Only Black expressed a dissent from the refusal to accept the appeal. Later, another effort was made to get the Supreme Court to review the case, but again without success, although this time Douglas joined Black in dissenting. On June 15, 1953, a further effort was made and the attorneys asked to be permitted at least to argue to the Court why it should review the case. Black, Douglas, Frankfurter and Jackson agreed that the attorneys should be permitted to present their oral arguments on this point, but the other five Justices said they saw no reason for listening, and so the motion for oral argument was turned down. Immediately after Vinson announced that the motion had been denied, he declared the Court adjourned until October, and the Justices began to leave Washington or to pack for leaving. The execution of the Rosenbergs was now scheduled for June 19, 1953.

The next day a most unusual, if not unprecedented, thing happened. Two attorneys, having no relation to the case other than as interested newspaper readers, suddenly came to the conclusion that the death sentence was unwarranted. The Espionage Act of 1917, under which Judge Kaufman issued sentence, permitted the imposition of the death sentence at the discretion of the judge. But the Atomic Energy Act of 1946 allowed the death sentence only if recommended by the jury, and the jury had not recommended death for the Rosenbergs. This point had not been presented by the Rosenbergs' attorneys, and moreover it was just the type of legal question that the Supreme Court does generally consider.

Accordingly, the two lawyers rushed over to Douglas and presented him with a petition asking that he issue a stay of the execution of the Rosenbergs until the full Court had an opportunity to consider this new point. (Obviously, if a stay of the execution were not granted, there would be no point to considering the question, for in four days the Rosenbergs would be dead.)

On June 17, 1953, Douglas signed an order staying the execution until the Court could consider the question. But the last thing the government wanted was any further drawn-out agitation; it wanted no repetition of the Sacco-Vanzetti case where seven years intervened between conviction and execution. Immediately, Attorney-General Herbert Brownell rushed to Vinson and requested him to convene a special session of the Court to consider Douglas' action. Vinson was still in Washington, and so too were Jackson, Clark, Burton and Black, while Reed was nearby, so that a quorum could be gotten together. Vinson was accommodating. He immediately issued a call to all the Justices to appear at the courthouse the next day for a special session. Douglas, who was motoring somewhere in Pennsylvania, heard about it on his car radio and headed back to Washington at once.

In the meantime, other repercussions of Douglas' action appeared. In Congress, Representative W. W. Wheeler of Georgia introduced a resolution "That William O. Douglas, Associate Justice of the Supreme Court of the United States, be impeached of high crimes and misdemeanors in office." The chairman of the House Judiciary Committee immediately announced that a prompt hearing would be held on the Wheeler resolution. Telegrams and telephone calls poured into Washington from all over the country condemning Douglas, many of them charging him with being a pro-Communist, a Communist or a Soviet espionage agent himself. So serious did the situation appear, that, when the Court met the next day, Vinson felt impelled to announce, and assert in the Court's decision, that Douglas was entirely within his rights in issuing the stay.

The Justices, with the exception of Black, also agreed that Vinson was justified in calling the special session to consider the correctness of Douglas' action. They then listened to arguments on the new point.

The next morning, June 19, they announced their decision holding the point invalid. They thereupon set aside Douglas' stay, refused to allow any further stay and ordered the execution to proceed. Black, Douglas and Frankfurter dissented, asserting that the point raised had sufficient validity to justify a more deliberate consideration by the Court. After hearing the decision, the attorneys for the Rosenbergs rushed to the White House for a decision on their (second) petition to the President for clemency. There, too, they were met with disappointment; Eisenhower again refused to grant clemency.

June 19th fell on a Friday. The execution by electrocution was scheduled for eleven o'clock that night. Since the Jewish Sabbath begins at nightfall on Friday, and ends at nightfall on Saturday, a request was made that the execution be postponed for twenty-four hours. But the federal government would countenance no delay. Instead of postponement, the execution was hastened. At about eight o'clock, shortly before nightfall, Julius and Ethel Rosenberg were electrocuted at Sing Sing prison in New York in time to avoid desecration of the Sabbath.

It is difficult to escape the conclusion that over the entire Rosenberg case falls the shadow of McCarthy. The trial, the death sentence, the affirmances by the federal court of appeals, the refusals of review by the Supreme Court, the haste in which Attorney-General Brownell sought and Vinson granted a special session of the Court and in which the Court handed down a decision snuffing out two human lives, the refusal of Eisenhower to commute the sentences or otherwise exercise clemency—all these make no sense except with a realization that in the United States during the period of 1950 to 1953 rationality had completely given way to McCarthyism. The spectre of McCarthy haunted the velvet draped chamber in the Supreme Court building no less than it did the Capitol across the park or the White House further up on Pennsylvania Avenue.

CIVIL LIBERTIES AND THE VINSON COURT

Under the Chief Justiceship of Vinson, the Supreme Court brought to a halt the steady progress toward full judicial protection of personal freedoms in the political area instituted after the 1937 revolution. Not since the pre-1937 days was the Court subjected to such intense criticism and condemnation by liberals. The hopes that the Court would stand steadfast as a wall against the surge of McCarthyism proved vain. Disillusionment and despair were universal in liberal circles. Fred Rodell's reference (in his book, *Nine Men*) to the "mass attack on civil liberties by the 1949-1953 Truman-Vinson Court" sounds rather emotional and extreme, but it undoubtedly reflected the feelings of many liberals. Only Black and Douglas were exempted from the universal condemnation and inherited the halo of reverence earlier ascribed to Holmes and Brandeis.

This condemnation of the Vinson Court is less than fair. In the first place, the Court compares favorably with the post-World War I Court. Then, not a single lower court decision impairing civil liberties was set aside or mitigated. The Vinson Court did set aside the Oklahoma loyalty oath in *Wieman* v. *Updegraff*. More important, in the Joint Anti-Fascist Refugee Committee case it effectively demolished the Attorney-General's listing of subversive organizations. Even in the Dennis case, although the Court affirmed the conviction, it refused to discard completely the clear and present danger test, which it could well have done. While it modified the principle, it maintained it, whereas the post World War I Court, after announcing the principle, discarded it and returned to the common law of sedition, under which the evil mind of the speaker and the evil tendency of his words were sufficient to nullify the guarantee of free speech.

In the second place, this condemnation by liberals of the Vinson Court ignores the truism that no agency of government, not even the Supreme Court, can protect the people from themselves. The brave and eloquent dissenting opinions of Black and Douglas were a luxury made possible only by the fact that they were dissenting opinions and that Vinson's opinions represented the effective decisions of the Court. Had Black and Douglas each possessed three votes so that their opinions would constitute the decisions of the Court they would have either spoken differently or the Court would not have survived. During the years from 1949 to 1954 the people of the United States would not have let anything stand in the way of their obsessive, bloody crusade against domestic Communism. For the Court to attempt to speak reason to an irrational people would not have been merely quixotic, it would probably have been suicidal. Had the Court attempted to free the Communist Ten or Julius and Ethel Rosenberg or to bar the federal or state governments from dismissing suspected Communists or pro-Communists, the consequences would have probably proved disastrous to the Court without in any substantial way ameliorating the underlying conditions that gave rise to infringements on personal freedoms.

The liberals were expecting the impossible of the Court. The liberals in Congress did not dare to put any restraints upon McCarthy, the Senate or House Committees investigating subversion, or the Attorney-General in his prosecutions of alleged subversives. When the Republicans introduced a bill in 1952 to tighten the anti-subversion laws, the liberal Democrats in Congress sought to improve it by making the penalties even harsher. Neither Truman nor Eisenhower, and certainly not any significant number of congressmen (Senator Herbert Lehman of New York was an exception) dared openly to challenge McCarthy or oppose increased appropriations for loyalty investigating committees during the period that Vinson was Chief Justice of the Supreme Court. Every popular election held during this period indicated an almost universal demand for the intensification of the crusade against Communism. It was neither fair nor realistic to expect the Court to do what every other liberal agency in the nation failed dismally to do—to bring reason to a people plagued with a psychopathic fear and hatred.

The unfairness of the liberals' condemnation of the Vinson Court becomes clear when one considers its decisions in the areas in which it did enjoy some freedom of choice. In cases that did not directly affect subversives its record as a protector of personal freedoms was outstanding. In cases concerning religious freedom and separation of church and state, censorship, discrimination against Japanese, and, above all, the rights of Negroes, its achievements were more than merely creditable. (Its record in cases involving civil liberties in criminal trials, such as use of wiretap testimony, double jeopardy, "third degree" confessions, etc. was considerably less so.) In its other lives the Vinson Court was faithful to the spirit of the 1937 revolution.

STEEL STRIKE AND SEIZURE

On November 1, 1951, in the middle of the Korean War, the United Steelworkers of America announced that on the expiration of its contract at the end of the year it would strike unless it received a new contract providing for increased wages and improved working conditions. The steel industry countered by refusing to consider the demands and the union directed its members not to report for work after December 31, 1951. Truman sought to avert the strike by seeking mediation and was able to obtain postponements that extended until April, 1952. On the last day of the last period of postponement, upon being informed that there would be no further postponements of the strike, Truman issued an order declaring that the government had seized all the steel mills of the nation. The seizure was symbolic rather than physical. The American flag was hoisted over the plants, a government notice was posted in each factory to the effect that the plant was now controlled by the government, and everything else continued as theretofore.

The union accepted the symbol and promptly called off its strike. But the industry was not so accommodating. It went into court and sought an injunction compelling the government to remove the flag and notices and get out of the plants. It contended that the President had no authority to seize private property simply because labor and management could not get together on a mutually acceptable contract.

The case promptly reached the Supreme Court and in *Youngstown Sheet and Tube Company* v. *Sawyer* it held by a six to three vote that the steel industry was right and the President was wrong. Vinson, Reed and Minton were of the opinion that the President acted within his authority. He had, they said, inherent power as President to act in an emergency situation. The other six Justices disagreed, but did so for different reasons. However, the crux of the matter was that they deemed the power to seize the mills to belong exclusively to Congress, and while Congress might have authorized the President to seize the mills, it did not do so, and without such authorization his action was invalid. Truman accepted the decision and returned the mills to their owners. The strike took place and went on as strikes do until finally settled.

Here was a case of the Supreme Court intervening for the protection of property rights against the federal government. Was this a retreat from the revolution of 1937? Probably not. In the first place, the Court never renounced its right to step in to prevent a particularly egregious violation of the rights of property, and an outright seizure of private property might well be considered to be within that class.

Second, and more important, even the majority of the Court did not dispute the power of the government to seize the mills in the emergency situation facing the nation. Had Congress authorized the President to seize the mills, the seizure would have been upheld. What, therefore, was involved in the decision was not a conflict between the government and property rights, but a question of the constitutional separation of powers between the President and Congress.

The principal significance of the decision lies in the national reaction to it. Not only did the President accept the decision and comply with it, but the nation uniformly commended him for his acceptance and compliance. The Supreme Court too was the recipient of widespread praise for upholding the rule of law even against the President of the United States. There may be irony in the thought that had personal freedoms rather than property rights been at stake in the case, a similar decision by the Supreme Court at that time would have brought upon it the wrath of the nation.

CHURCH AND STATE

The opening words of the Bill of Rights provide that "Congress shall make no law respecting an establishment of religion or prohibiting the free exercise thereof." The Hughes Court in its post-1937 years and the Stone Court after it were called upon frequently to decide cases under the "free exercise" aspect of the amendment; it fell to the Vinson Court to be the first in American history to be required to pass on the meaning of the "no establishment" aspect. Not the least of the contributions of the Vinson Court was its definitive interpretation of the meaning and implications of the principle of the separation of church and state.

The occasion arose in 1947 in the case of *Everson* v. *Board of Education.* Involved was the constitutionality of a state law providing that parents who sent their children to parochial schools could obtain bus transportation to the schools at public expense. A resident of the state brought a suit to stop the payments on the ground that by providing bus transportation the state was supporting church schools in violation of the principle of separation of church and state.

The Supreme Court, in a five to four decision, upheld the statute.

It did not, said Black speaking for the majority, provide for an expenditure of state funds for religious education or for church schools; if it did, it would be unconstitutional. Its purpose and effect was simply to insure the safety of children going to school and protect them from the traffic hazards of modern day road travel. Rutledge, Jackson, Frankfurter and Burton dissented on the ground that it was really the parochial schools and not the children that were the beneficiaries of the state expenditure of tax-raised funds.

The real importance of the decision was not the specific holding allowing public paid transportation to parochial schools. It lay in the Court's interpretation of the meaning of separation of church and state and the consequences of that interpretation. In this respect all nine Justices agreed. They held that while the First Amendment says only that Congress shall make no law respecting an establishment of religion, this prohibition—which, in modern day language means maintenance of the separation of church and state—is equally applicable against the states by reason of the Fourteenth Amendment. (The Hughes Court had so held in respect to the "free exercise" aspect of the First Amendment; the Vinson Court extended the holding to the "no establishment" clause.) They then spelled out definitively what separation of church and state entails in the American democratic system.

It means, said the Court, that neither a state nor the federal government can set up a church. Neither can pass laws which aid one religion, aid all religions, or prefer one religion over another. Neither can force or influence a person to go to or remain away from church against his will, or force him to profess a belief or disbelief in any religion. No person can constitutionally be punished for entertaining religious beliefs or disbeliefs, for church attendance or non-attendance; no tax in any amount, large or small, may be levied to support any religious activities or institutions, whatever they may be called, or whatever form they may adopt to teach or practice religion. Neither a state nor the federal government may, openly or secretly, participate in the affairs of any religious organizations or groups and vice versa. It means, in short, not only that government must be neutral as among competing religious sects, but that it must be neutral as between religious belief and disbelief.

This was the first time the meaning of separation of church and state had been spelled out by the Supreme Court, and it was this fact that was the most significant aspect of the Everson decision. But that was not generally recognized at the time. All that the public could see was that the Court had upheld the use of taxpayers' money to transport Catholic children to parochial schools, and this caused a storm of protest among Protestants. They considered the decision a severe defeat for them. An organization, entitled Protestants and Other Americans United for Separation of Church and State, was established to defend the public treasury against raids by the Catholic Church. Conversely, Catholic circles hailed the decision as a victory for religious freedom and a recognition of the equal status of public schools and Catholic parochial schools. Both Protestants and Catholics were oblivious to the broader implications of the decision.

A year later the Catholic Church suddenly realized that it should have more carefully examined the mouth of the gift horse. For in *McCollum* v. *Board of Education of Champaign, Ill.*, decided in 1948, the Court showed what separation of church and state entails practically. In that case it held, with only Reed dissenting, that religious instruction may not be conducted in the public school, even if all faiths are permitted to teach the children adhering to them and even if the salaries of the religious teachers are paid out of private funds. The opinion, again written by Black, repeated the definitive interpretation of the "no establishment" clause set forth in the Everson case and ruled that under this interpretation the public schools, being tax supported, must be secular schools.

Now it was the turn of the Catholics to protest long and loud. The Court was condemned as an agent of secularism indifferent to the cause of religion. It was charged with being completely ignorant of the history of the First Amendment, which, the Catholic spokesmen contended, was meant only to bar preferential treatment of one sect or denomination over others, but not to prohibit equal, non-preferential government aid to all religions. The Catholic bishops of the United States joined in a statement bitterly attacking the decision and the Court and calling upon "all who believe in God and are devoted to freedom under God to avert the impending danger of a judicial 'establishment of secularism' that would ban God from public life."

To those committed to the principle of the separation of church and state, the McCollum decision is one of the greatest decisions of the Supreme Court. It may truly be called the Magna Carta of the secular public school system. It will be remembered long after the cold war decisions of *Dennis* v. *United States* and *American Communications Association* v. *Douds* will have been forgotten. It accords constitutional and judicial protection to a uniquely American contribution to civilization—religious freedom and the mutual independence of religion and government. Everson-McCollum constitute truly creative constitutional law, and it is perhaps amusing that the author should be the same Hugo Black of whom Stone was so critical.

Nevertheless, the effects of McCarthy and the cold war were felt here too. For four years sectarian sources, led by the Catholic Church, waged a bitter and continuous attack on the McCollum decision and the Court which had announced it. Perhaps the principal motif of the attack was that the decision helped Communistic atheistic godlessness at the expense of patriotic American godliness. The years 1948 to 1952 were not hospitable to anything that might be considered in harmony with any aspect of Communism, and a secular state and public school system was within this category.

The effect of the four-year attack on the McCollum decision and the Vinson Court showed itself in the 1952 decision of *Zorach* v. *Clauson*. This involved the constitutionality of the New York City program of released time for religious education. The difference between the Champaign and New York systems was that in the former the public school authorities were deeply involved in the religious education program; not only was the instruction given within the public school buildings during school hours, but the school authorities undertook a general supervision of the program. In New York, on the other hand, public school involvement was minimal. All the school authorities did, according to the Court, was to release from their regular secular studies for one hour a week those children who, without urging or pressure by the school authorities, wished to partake of religious instruction in churches or church schools off the public school premises. The school authorities assumed no further responsibility in respect to the program.

This, said the majority of the Court (Black, Frankfurter and Jackson dissenting) is distinguishable from the Champaign program. Here all that is involved is no more than an adjustment of the public school schedule to accommodate the religious needs of the children. While the principle of the McCollum case—that government may not finance religious groups or undertake religious instruction or blend secular and sectarian education—was reaffirmed, it was not to be extended to the present situation.

What happened to the McCollum decision illustrates vividly the truth that the Court cannot be expected alone to uphold American liberties or to be too far in advance of articulated public opinion. The Zorach decision represented a retreat from the broad Everson-McCollum principle. The retreat was not so much in the specific holding of the Zorach case, which was quite narrow and limited, but in some of the language used by Douglas in his opinion for the majority of the Court. "We are," he said, "a religious people whose institutions presuppose a Supreme Being." The First Amendment "does not say that in every and all respects there shall be a separation of church and state." It requires only that "there shall be no concert or union or dependency one on the other."

Despite this language, the Zorach case does not affect the basic validity of the Everson-McCollum principle. Douglas was careful to point out that the Zorach decision did not overrule the McCollum decision, but on the contrary affirmed and followed it. As later cases were to show, the Everson-McCollum principle of separation of church and state is still the law of the land, and in the long run of history this may well be the greatest contribution made to the cause of freedom by the Vinson Court.

This principle was carried forward by the Vinson Court in 1952 in *Kedroff* v. *St. Nicholas Cathedral*, known as the Russian Orthodox Church case. After the Bolshevik Revolution in Russia, most of the Russian Orthodox churchmen in the United States, asserting that the Moscow patriarchate was under the domination of the Soviet state, declared themselves independent of the patriarchate in respect to the administration of church affairs in America. In New York the state legislature enacted a statute that this "Russian Church in America" was the true Russian Orthodox Church and therefore entitled to obtain possession of St. Nicholas Cathedral, the seat of the Church in New York City, from the Metropolitan Benjamin, who had been designated by the Moscow patriarchate as Archbishop of North America.

When the case reached the Supreme Court, the Court held the statute unconstitutional. A state, no less than the federal government, may not enact a law impairing the separation of church and state or infringing upon religious freedom. Separation of church and state and religious freedom mean that government has no capacity to intervene in ecclesiastical controversies or to determine which faith is true and which is false or which faction in a church schism represents the orthodox faith and which is heretical. Under the Constitution such determinations can be made only by ecclesiastical tribunals, and the determination of the highest ecclesiastical authority of the particular religion (in this case the Moscow patriarchate) must be accepted by secular government.

One of the most significant aspects of the Kedroff case was that the Court (with Jackson dissenting) in 1952 decided in favor of the Moscow patriarchate against an American branch of the church which had broken off from the mother church because the latter was a tool of Stalin. It required no little courage to issue such a decision at the height of McCarthy's power.

CENSORSHIP

A broad libertarian anti-censorship decision handed down by the Vinson Court was *Burstyn* v. *Wilson*, decided in 1952. The case involved the motion picture entitled *The Miracle*. This was a forty-minute, Italian-language film relating the tale of a simple peasant girl who is seduced by a bearded stranger she imagines to be St. Joseph and later gives birth to a baby she believes to have been divinely conceived.

New York has a law requiring that all commercially exhibited films receive a license from the state department of education. The law further provides that licenses shall be denied to films that are obscene, immoral, crime-inciting or "sacrilegious." *The Miracle* had been duly granted a license, but after a furor against the film was raised by the Catholic Church under the leadership of Cardinal Spellman, the department of education reversed itself and revoked the license on the ground that the film was sacrilegious, presumably because it cast doubt on the authenticity of the Biblical account of the conception and birth of Jesus.

When the case reached the Supreme Court, that tribunal was faced with a decision, *Mutual Film Corporation* v. *Industrial Commission of Ohio*, handed down in 1915, in which it had held that the exhibition of a motion picture is "a business, pure and simple," and is neither speech nor press within the protection of the First Amendment. In *Burstyn v. Wilson,* the Vinson Court overruled the Mutual Film decision and held that the First Amendment did protect motion pictures. Moreover, it held, the state cannot censor films merely because they are derogatory to religion or treat religious subjects with ridicule. This would be an unconstitutional abridgement of the freedom of speech and press.

RACIAL DISCRIMINATION AND SEGREGATION

The record of the Vinson Court in cases involving racial discrimination and segregation was undoubtedly far superior to that of any Court that preceded it. It can hardly be denied that in substantial measure this was because the times were ripe for progress in this area as they were not for progress in the area of political freedoms. The major victims of racial discrimination in the United States have been the Negroes and, particularly on the West Coast, the Chinese and Japanese. In respect to the Chinese and Japanese, one of the by-products of the cold war was a rapprochement between the United States and Japan. The development of a friendlier and more hospitable attitude to Americans of Japanese ancestry in our own midst harmonized with America's political objectives. The McCarran-Walter Immigration Act of 1952 finally removed from our immigration law the clause excluding Japanese and Chinese. In respect to Negroes, the fact that large numbers of them served in the armed forces and worked in defense plants alongside whites during World War II served to instill in them a sense of equality and encourage them to resort to political and legal action to secure that equality. It is difficult to dispute either the logic or the morality of the proposition that if a Negro is good enough to die alongside a white, he is good enough to live alongside him.

That the times were conducive for progress in the struggle for racial equality should not detract from the contribution made by the Vinson Court. During the years that followed the close of the Second World War, the major credit for effective contribution to the struggle on the part of the federal government to secure equality to the Negro belongs overwhelmingly to the Supreme Court. Compared to what was accomplished as a result of the decisions of the Supreme Court, the accomplishments of the President and of Congress at least until the enactment of the Civil Rights Act of 1964, are slight. The Hayes-Tilden settlement in 1876 brought a halt in the march toward racial equality on the part of all branches of the federal government. During World War II both Roosevelt and Truman made some efforts to achieve equality for the Negro in the armed services, but it was the Vinson Court that really resumed the march forward.

Some modest steps had been taken earlier. In 1938 the Hughes Court, in the case of *Missouri ex rel Gaines* v. *Canada*, held that while a state could constitutionally provide separate college and university education for whites and Negroes, the education had to be really equal; and it was not equal if the whites could attend the state university while Negroes were sent out of the state to attend a Negro college or university (there being none in the state) at the state's expense. And in 1944 the Stone Court held in the case of *Smith* v. *Allwright* that a Democratic primary election in the south from which Negroes were barred was unconstitutional. In the same year the Stone Court also held, in the case of *Steele* v. *Louisville Railroad*, that a labor union enjoying the right of collective bargaining under the National Labor Relations Act could not legally discriminate against Negro workers and favor whites in its bargaining with the employer. All were important cases, but it was the Vinson Court which returned to the mission abandoned three-quarters of a century earlier.

Before we relate the achievements of the Vinson Court in fighting discrimination against Negroes, mention should be made of two decisions concerning discrimination against Japanese and Chinese Americans. In 1948 the Court, in *Takahashi* v. *Fish and Game Commission*, invalidated a California law that in effect barred Japanese and Chinese non-citizens from fishing the state's waters. And in the same year, in the case of *Oyama* v. *California*, the Court held in effect that a state law barring Japanese and Chinese non-citizens from owning land was unconstitutional.

In 1948, in the case of *Shelley* v. *Kraemer*, the Vinson Court struck a blow at one of the legal devices widely used to exclude Negroes from buying homes in white neighborhoods. It ruled that a racial restrictive covenant, that is an agreement by a group of owners in a particular neighborhood that none of them will sell his house to a Negro, could not constitutionally be enforced in either a federal or a state court. In this decision the Vinson Court made a truly creative advance in constitutional law, just as it did in the Everson-McCollum, Miracle and Russian Orthodox Church cases. It said, in effect, that while whites may, if they wish to, enter into a gentlemen's agreement to keep their neighborhood lily white, they would have to rely on a gentleman's word for the enforcement of the agreement. If one of the house owners turns out to be no gentleman and does decide to sell to a Negro, it would violate the Fourteenth Amendment's guarantee of the equal protection of the laws for a court of law to try to stop him. In reaching this decision, the Vinson Court was compelled to and did overrule a contrary decision handed down by the Taft Court in 1926 in the case of *Corrigan* v. *Buckley*. The practical effect of the Shelley decision was to open up to occupancy by Negroes many neighborhoods previously closed to them.

After permitting the South to live with the Gaines decision for a decade, the Court in 1948 resumed the attack on segregation in education with its decision in *Sipuel* v. *Board of Regents*. There a Negro sought admission to the law school at the state university. He was told that under the state's compulsory racial-segregation law he could not be admitted, but that he should be patient since a separate law school for Negroes was in the process of formation. The Supreme Court held that the Fourteenth Amendment did not impose an obligation of patience upon Negro youths seeking a legal education. To open the doors of the law school to whites while Negroes were required to wait was to deny Negroes the equal protection of the laws. The state of Oklahoma, the Court held in the sequel case of *Fisher* v. *Hurst*, decided in the same year, had the choice of admitting Negroes to the law school or closing the school to white applicants until the school for Negroes was ready to open.

Two years later in *Sweatt* v. *Painter* the Supreme Court interpreted the equality obligation in such a way as to make separate professional schools legally impossible. Under the pressure of lawsuits, the state of Texas had established a law school for its Negro residents. It had a student body of twenty-three (the white law school had eight hundred and fifty), five faculty members (the white school had nineteen), and a library of sixteen thousand volumes (the white school had sixty-five thousand).

The Supreme Court unanimously held that this did not constitute equality. Far more important, the Court also held that a law school which excludes members of the (white) racial group that numbers 85 per cent of the state's population—including most of the lawyers, judges, witnesses, jurymen, and court officials with whom the Negro law student will deal when he becomes a lawyer—does not and cannot accord to the Negro students the advantages and benefits accorded to students attending the white school. Put simply, the Court held that racial segregation in law schools is by its very nature inequality.

Clearly, the reasoning applicable to law schools is no less applicable to all professional schools. The legal effect of the Sweatt case, therefore, was to outlaw racial segregation at the level of university professional schools.

On the same day that the Sweatt decision was announced, the Court handed down its decision in *McLaurin* v. *Oklahoma State Regents*. The decision held in effect that Negroes admitted to white universities may not be segregated within the school. McLaurin, a Negro candidate for a doctorate in education, succeeded in gaining admission to the University of Oklahoma, but then his troubles began. First he was required to sit at a designated desk in an anteroom, adjoining the classroom, from which he could hear though not see the professor. He was not permitted to use the regular desks in the reading room, or to eat in the school cafeteria at the same time as the other students. Then, as he started a lawsuit to remove these restrictions, the university officials altered them. He was allowed to sit in the classroom, but a rail and low curtain were placed around his seat, and a sign was hung on it, reading: "Reserved for Colored."

McLaurin's white fellow students, becoming somewhat exasperated with both the university officials and the Oklahoma segregation laws, took matters in their own hands and forcibly removed the railing, curtain, and sign. Thereupon the university officials, no doubt embarrassed but feeling bound by the state's segregation laws, required McLaurin to sit in a row specified for colored students and at specified tables in the library and cafeteria.

Even this nominal and purely symbolic separation was unacceptable to the Supreme Court. The conditions under which McLaurin was required to receive his education, it held, deprived him of the equal protection of the laws. Having been admitted to a state-supported graduate school, he must receive the same treatment at the hands of the state as students of other races. Equal protection means equality, not something less.

The Sipuel, Sweatt, and McLaurin decisions raised little more than a ripple of discontent in the South. Within two years over a thousand Negroes were attending southern graduate and professional schools with no visible ill effects. On the contrary, campus newspapers in a number of white colleges openly called for integration. The stage was set for outright invalidation of racial segregation in its most prevalent form, segregated elementary school education, and abrogation of the "separate but equal" doctrine of *Plessy* v. *Ferguson*.

It is hardly open to doubt that the Vinson Court was prepared to take this step too. In 1950, in the case of *Henderson* v. *United States*, the Court held in effect that segregation of whites and Negroes on railroads and buses traveling between states was as illegal as segregation in universities and professional schools. Everything pointed to a similar decision in respect to segregation in elementary and secondary public schools. In 1953 the Vinson Court indicated that it was ready for this. It issued orders agreeing to review a number of state and federal lower court decisions in which the issue of the constitutionality of public school segregation was squarely raised. Unfortunately, before the Court had the chance to hear and decide these cases, Vinson died (but a short time after the Rosenbergs were executed) and it remained for his successor to have the honor of heading the Court which after a half-century brought an end to the "separate but equal" principle of *Plessy* v. *Ferguson*, against which Harlan had so vigorously dissented.

chapter fifteen

Warren and the Return of Reason

THE WARREN COURT

To succeed Vinson as Chief Justice, Eisenhower named Earl Warren of California. Warren had been successively district attorney, state attorney-general and governor of California. In 1948 he had run for Vice-President of the United States but was defeated in the surprise victory of Truman over Thomas E. Dewey. Warren was nominated on September 30, 1953 and was promptly confirmed by the Senate, so that he was able to take his oath of office and preside at the opening of the Court on October 5, less than a week after he was named.

Late in 1954, Jackson died and Eisenhower appointed as his successor John Marshall Harlan of New York, grandson and namesake of the great dissenter of the Waite, Fuller and White Courts. The second Harlan had been Assistant United States Attorney, and a member of one of the top Wall Street law firms. In 1954 Eisenhower had appointed him to be a judge of the federal circuit court of appeals in New York. After serving in that capacity for a year, he was elevated to the Supreme Court.

In October of 1956, Minton retired from the bench and his seat was taken by William J. Brennan, Jr., of New Jersey. Brennan had been a member of a prominent Newark law firm, a colonel in the United States Army, and then in quick succession judge of the New Jersey superior court, the appellate division and the supreme court of the state. Brennan's appointment brought a Roman Catholic back to the bench for the first time since Murphy's death seven years earlier.

Reed's retirement in February, 1957 brought to the bench Charles Evan Whittaker of Missouri, the first Missourian in history to be named to the Supreme Court. Whittaker had been a member of a Kansas City law firm, then a judge of the federal district court, and then a judge of the federal circuit court of appeals. (After five years on the bench, Whittaker retired because of ill health, and President Kennedy appointed as his successor Byron R. White of Colorado, Deputy Attorney-General and former Rhodes scholar.)

Potter Stewart of Ohio was appointed in October, 1958, to succeed Burton, who had retired the previous day. Stewart had graduated from Yale Law School and had practiced law in New York and Cincinnati until named by Eisenhower in 1954 to be a judge of the circuit court of appeals. He served in this capacity for four years, until his elevation to the Supreme Court.

It is interesting to note that with the exception of Warren, all Eisenhower's appointees had some judicial experience before being named to the Supreme Court, although Harlan's judicial experience amounted only to one year on the federal circuit court of appeals. On several occasions Eisenhower expressed the view that only persons having judicial experience should be appointed to the Supreme Court. This expression was in response to criticism from sources whose dissatisfaction was in reality with the Court's decisions rather than with its personnel.

An examination of the history of the Supreme Court indicates that there is no necessary correlation between prior judicial experience and excellence of performance on the Supreme Court. If one took a consensus among those familiar with the history of the Supreme Court as to the greatest and most competent Justices, one would be amazed to note how few of them—Holmes and Cardozo are the most notable exceptions—had any judicial experience before serving on the Supreme Court. Marshall, Story, Taney, Miller, the first Harlan, Hughes, Brandeis, Stone, Black and Frankfurter, to mention but a few, would never have been Justices of the United States Supreme Court had all the Presidents followed the announced policy of Eisenhower that no person not having previous judicial experience should be appointed to the Court. The truth of the matter is that the Supreme Court of the United States is so different from any other court that experience in a conventional court is of comparatively secondary importance as a qualification for excellence of service on the Supreme Court. (Kennedy did not share Eisenhower's view; neither of his two appointees, White and Arthur Goldberg, had any prior judicial experience.)

This was the Warren Court that presided over the rather anticlimactic end of McCarthyism and over the first giant strides of the turbulent social revolution leading towards full equality for all human beings.

THE END OF MC CARTHYISM

Two or three years before McCarthy died McCarthyism expired. A consideration of the causes is not within the purview of this volume; our concern is with its relationship to the Supreme Court. Even a cursory examination of the decisions of the Court during the first five or six years of Warren's Chief Justiceship reveals an almost radical return to libertarianism in political decisions. Was this in any way the cause or merely one of the effects of the death of McCarthyism?

No certain answer is of course possible. Probably both are true. McCarthyism ended because it was a sickness and, as in individuals so in nations, sicknesses generally come to an end sometime. Because American commitment to freedom is so traditional and solid, the end came with a whimper rather than, as in Nazi Germany, with a great bang. Had there been no Supreme Court, the American people would still have recovered and the disease would in any event have come to an end. Nevertheless, it is hardly deniable that the courage and libertarianism of the Warren Court accelerated the return to sanity. Here again, although in an undreamed of way, the work of Marshall has borne fruit. The prestige which he endowed upon the Court had proved of great value in securing public acceptance of judicially protected capitalist expansion. In the late 1950's it similarly proved valuable in securing acceptance of retreat from the obsession with security.

Under Warren the Court reasserted its responsibility for the protection of all American liberties, a responsibility assumed in the 1937 revolution. For four or five years it had, in large measure, to suspend its activities in the area of political liberties because substantial intervention would have been not merely futile, but might well have destroyed the Court. Beginning in 1955, it was again able to be the nation's most effective force in the protection of political liberties.

THE FIFTH AMENDMENT

One of the most significant achievements of the Warren Court has been its giving practical meaningfulness to the Fifth Amendment's guarantee against compulsory self-incrimination. During the McCarthy period an assertion of the guarantee was universally equated with a confession of guilt, and brought with it the political, social and economic consequences of such a confession. The decisions of the Warren Court reduced in some measure the universal obloquy that formerly attended "taking the Fifth." In addition, of course, the Court's decision in much more substantial measure mitigated the legal consequences of asserting the guarantee.

The first step had actually been taken by the Vinson Court, another of the few but significant contributions which that Court was able to make in defense of political freedoms. In the case of *Blau* v. *United States*, the Vinson Court held in 1950 that a witness who was asked whether he is a member of the Communist party could assert the Fifth Amendment and refuse to answer, this although mere membership in the party was not of itself a criminal offense. In *Quinn* v. *United States* and in *Emspack* v. *United States*, the Warren Court held in 1955 that a witness before a Congressional committee may assert the privilege. Moreover, since such a witness is rarely a lawyer and often does not have a lawyer to advise him, he will not be required to recite any particular legalistic formula, but will be protected if he makes reasonably clear to the investigating committee that he is relying on the guarantee against self-incrimination.

The next year, in *Slochower* v. *Board of Higher Education*, the Court gave practical effect to a principle stated in the Quinn case—that assertion of a constitutional right may not be penalized and that pleading the Fifth Amendment does not constitute an admission of guilt and may not be so interpreted. New York has a law providing for the dismissal of all state and municipal employees who assert the Fifth Amendment. Slochower, an instructor in a municipal college, pleaded the amendment when questioned by the Senate Internal Security Committee. The law, the Supreme Court held, is unconstitutional at least in respect to one who asserts the privilege before a federal investigating body, since it in effect seeks to penalize a person for asserting a constitutional right.

LEGISLATIVE INVESTIGATIONS

The Quinn case had been decided purely on the ground that Quinn had effectively asserted his privilege against self-incrimination.

But as an indication of its revived libertarianism, the Court went out of its way to express constitutional limitations on what McCarthy and others had considered Congress' limitless power of investigation. The power to investigate, the Court said, broad as it may be, is subject to recognized limitations. It may not be used to inquire into private affairs unrelated to a valid legislative purpose. Nor does it extend to an area in which Congress is forbidden to legislate, by reason of the first Amendment's guarantee of freedom of expression. Similarly, the power to investigate must not be confused with any powers of law enforcement; those powers are assigned under our Constitution to the Executive and the judiciary.

It was during the following year that the practical implications of these statements became clear. A number of far-reaching decisions were handed down relating to the power of the federal government and the states to investigate subversion. The most significant of these cases involved John T. Watkins, a former labor union leader, who refused to answer questions asked of him by the House Committee on Un-American activities. Watkins' conviction for contempt of Congress was reversed by the Supreme Court in the case of *Watkins* v. *United States* because the pertinency of the question which he refused to answer was not made clear to him. Warren, writing the majority opinion, in which he was joined by Douglas, Black, Harlan and Brennan, recognized that the power to investigate is inherent in the legislative process. He warned, however, that the power is not unlimited. He said that "there is no Congressional power to expose for the sake of exposure" and added that investigations conducted solely for the "personal aggrandizement" of the investigators or to "punish" those investigated are "indefensible." He also stated that legislative investigations are subject to the restraints of the First Amendment, which secures freedom of speech, press and association.

The Warren Court also reversed the contempt conviction of Professor Paul Sweezy, which arose out of a state investigation. Sweezy refused to answer questions put to him by the attorney-general of New Hampshire regarding a lecture he had delivered at the state's university and his connection with the Progressive Party and the Progressive Citizens of America. Warren's opinion in *Sweezy* v. *New Hampshire* stated that the legislature had not authorized the state attorney-general to obtain the information which he attempted to elicit from Sweezy. In addition, it pointed out, the questioning of Sweezy "unquestionably was an invasion of petitioner's liberties in the area of academic freedom and political expression."

THE CRIME OF BEING A COMMUNIST

One of the most startling achievements of the Warren Court was its use of the Smith Act (under which the Communist party leaders had been convicted and imprisoned) for the *protection* of civil liberties. Practically every state in the Union has on its books some law making it a crime to advocate the violent overthrow of the government. Many of these laws, commonly called anti-sedition statutes, criminal anarchy laws, criminal syndicalist laws, etc., antedate the cold war period, some (as the New York statute under which Ben Gitlow was convicted) going back to the assassination of President McKinley at the beginning of the century. In *Pennsylvania* v. *Nelson* the Warren Court held that in enacting the Smith Act in 1940 Congress intended to preempt the entire field of anti-subversive legislation and supersede all similar state laws. The Court therefore held that Steve Nelson, a Pennsylvania Communist, could not be prosecuted under the laws of that state for conspiring to advocate the forcible overthrow of the United States government. Probably no decision of the Warren Court in the area of political liberties was subjected to more strident condemnation and criticism than the Nelson decision. It should be noted, however, that in this case the Supreme Court simply affirmed the decision of the Pennsylvania supreme court, which had independently arrived at the same conclusion.

In the Dennis case, the Vinson Court had upheld the constitutionality of the Smith Act and sustained the conviction under it of ten leaders of the Communist party in America. In *Yates* v. *United States*, the Warren Court, in 1957, while not overruling the Dennis decision, went far towards nullifying its effectiveness. It did this by narrowly interpreting the Smith Act and thereby upsetting the conviction of fourteen California Communists.

The fourteen defendants were convicted of advocating and teaching the overthrow of the United States government by force and violence and of "organizing" the Communist party, which advocates and teaches such overthrow. The sections of the Smith Act that make this conduct unlawful were held constitutional by a divided Supreme Court in 1951 in the Dennis case.

The Warren Court, with Harlan writing the majority opinion, held that the Smith Act did not prohibit advocacy and teaching of forcible overthrow of government *as an abstract principle*. The Smith Act, the Court said, "was aimed at the advocacy and teaching of *concrete action* for the forcible overthrow of the government, and not of principles divorced from action." The Court did not disturb Vinson's holding of the Dennis case that "advocacy of violent action to be taken at some future time was enough." However, it emphasized that there must be advocacy of *action* in order to hold the defendants guilty.

The practical effect of the Yates and Nelson decisions was to halt, at least temporarily, prosecutions of Communists for being Communists. Because of the strict test imposed by the Yates decision, the federal Department of Justice came to the conclusion that it would not be able to obtain convictions under the Smith Act and consented to the dismissal of many of the still outstanding cases. In others, the federal courts decided that the test set down in the Yates decision could not be met, and ordered the defendants acquitted. The Nelson decision had the same effect in respect to the prosecutions under state anti-sedition laws. Thus, although the Warren Court did not expressly overrule the Vinson Court's Dennis decision, its practical effect was the same. While the Yates decision was the subject of considerable criticism, it was universally accepted. What was impossible in 1951 when the Dennis case was decided, was realizable in 1957, for in the intervening period sanity had returned to the United States.

LOYALTY PROGRAMS

The federal government's loyalty program first reached the Warren Court in 1956 in the case of *Cole* v. *Young*. In *Bailey* v. *Richardson*, the Vinson Court had affirmed by a four to four vote a lower court decision that a federal government employee could be discharged as a security risk without any hearing at all and without even knowing the specific charges that had been made against him. In 1950, Congress authorized the suspension or dismissal of federal employees by department heads "in the interests of national security." Under this statute, and executive orders issued by both Truman and Eisenhower, numerous employees were suspended and dismissed as "security risks" without a hearing. In *Cole* v. *Young*, the Warren Court, in a decision by Harlan, held that the statute applied only to "sensitive positions," that a food and drug inspector did not occupy a sensitive position, and being a civil service employee, he could not be discharged except for misconduct and only after a hearing on charges filed against him.

The federal government's loyalty program again came up for examination by the Warren Court in 1957 in the case of *Service* v. *Dulles*. John Stewart Service won a six-year fight for reinstatement to his position as a foreign service officer in the State Department when the Court held unanimously that his discharge for security reasons by Secretary of State Dean Acheson had been illegal. The Court, with Harlan again writing the opinion, held that although the Secretary of State had been given authority by Congress to discharge any employee within his absolute discretion and without the necessity of any hearing or other administrative procedures, nevertheless, since the Secretary had prescribed procedures for discharge, he was required to follow them, and this he did not do in Service's case.

A year later, the Court ruled invalid the government's refusal to grant security clearance to an employee of a defense contractor. It held, in the case of *Greene* v. *McElroy*, that there was no authority for the aspect of the Industrial Security Program which allowed clearance to be denied on the basis of secret evidence and without the right of confrontation and cross-examination.

On two occasions in 1957 the Court reversed rulings by state courts refusing to admit applicants to the bar because of questionable loyalty. In both cases the Court held that past membership in the Communist party was not in itself sufficient to bar a person from practicing law. In neither of the cases (*Konigsberg* v. *State Bar of California* and *Schware* v. *Board of Bar Examiners of New Mexico*) did the Court pass on the effect of present membership in the Communist party.

THE ARMED FORCES

A number of significant decisions handed down by the Warren Court emphasized the American commitment to the principle that the military must be subordinate to the civil powers. Of these, the most important were *United States ex rel Toth* v. *Quarles*, decided in 1955, and *Harmon* v. *Brucker*, decided in 1958.

In 1866 the Supreme Court had held in the Milligan case that civilians may not be tried by military tribunals if civil courts were open and functioning. This precedent was followed in *Duncan* v. *Karanomoku*, where, two years after the Pearl Harbor attack, a military court in Honolulu tried and sentenced a civilian employee in the navy yard who had engaged in a brawl with two armed Marine sentries. The Stone Court, in upsetting the conviction and sentence, held that Congress had not authorized the trial of civilians by military tribunals where the civil courts were open and unobstructed. While the Court's opinion did not find it necessary to discuss the question of constitutionality, the tenor of the opinion indicated that even if Congress were to authorize military trials for civilians where the civil courts are functioning, the Milligan holding would be followed and the authorization held unconstitutional.

This was borne out in the Toth case. Here the Court not only held military trials of civilians to be unconstitutional but went even further and voided a federal statute authorizing military trial after discharge from the armed forces for crimes committed before discharge. Under our Constitution, the Court held, a civilian may not be tried by court martial even for crimes committed while he was in military service. (In *Reid* v. *Covert*, decided two years after the Toth case, the Court extended the ruling of that case to bar military trials of two wives, living with their soldier husbands on army bases overseas, who were charged with having murdered their husbands.)

Although not stated, the explanation for the Army's action in *Harmon* v. *Brucker* was to be found in McCarthy's war against the Army, a war whose battle cry was "Who promoted Peress?"—the reference being to Irving Peress, a dentist and alleged Communist who had been promoted from captain to major.

In the Harmon case, the Court held that the Army had no authority to give a soldier a less than honorable discharge because of alleged subversive activities which took place before his induction. Harmon's conduct while he was in the armed forces, the Army admitted, was exemplary and ordinarily he would have received an honorable discharge. The Justice Department, representing the Army before the Supreme Court, went further and conceded that the Army's refusal to grant Harmon an honorable discharge was unlawful. The Department, however, contended that no civil court, not even the Supreme Court, could interfere with the Army's management of its own affairs, including the nature of the discharge it grants to its soldiers.

Following in the spirit of the Milligan, Duncan and Toth decisions, the Court refused to accept this claim. Judicial relief, it said, is available to any person who is injured by government officials when they act in excess of their power, and the armed services are government officials within this principle.

TRAVEL—VOLUNTARY AND FORCED

In an important decision (*Kent v. Dulles*) decided in 1958, the Warren Court held that the Secretary of State was not authorized to withhold passports from citizens because of their political beliefs and associations. The case involved Rockwell Kent, prominent artist, and Walter Briehl, a psychiatrist from California. Kent was refused a passport because he allegedly was a Communist and had consistently adhered to the "Communist party line." As to Briehl, the State Department asserted that it had evidence of his association with various Communist groups. Both applicants refused to submit affidavits regarding past or present membership in the Communist party, which the Department demanded of them before it would further consider their cases.

The majority of the Court, in an opinion written by Douglas, held that the passport laws did not authorize the Secretary to refuse passports because of a person's political beliefs and associations. "The right to travel," Douglas held, "is a part of the 'liberty' of which the citizen cannot be deprived without the due process of law of the Fifth Amendment." In view of this constitutional guarantee, "we will not readily infer that Congress gave the Secretary of State unbridled discretion to grant or withhold it." Serious constitutional questions would be raised if the Secretary were held to have authority "to withhold passports to citizens because of their beliefs or associations. Congress has made no such provision in explicit terms; and absent one, the Secretary may not employ that standard to restrict the citizens' right of free movement."

Among the decisions of the Supreme Court most difficult to justify in terms of fairness and humaneness are those which upheld the deportation of a non-citizen because he was once a member of the Communist party, although his membership in the party may have occurred many years before and at a time when it was legal. The Supreme Court, during the Vinson Chief Justiceship, felt itself unable to overrule long-standing decisions holding deportation to be a civil and not a criminal matter, and thus not within the constitutional prohibition against retroactive or *ex post facto* laws. In the Konigsberg and Schware cases, the Warren Court refused to allow an otherwise eligible candidate for admission to the bar to be denied a license to practice law merely because a long time ago he was a member of the Communist party when such membership was entirely legal. Clearly, the spirit of these cases is diametrically opposed to the deportation decisions, and it was inevitable that the libertarianism of the Warren Court would not continue to accept the deportation rulings.

To Black and Douglas, and probably Warren and Brennan, the shortest way with bad precedents is to overrule them. It is probable that they would have preferred simply to overrule expressly *Harisiades* v. *Shaughnessy* and *Galvan* v. *Press*, the 1954 decisions in which the Court held an alien party member to be deportable even if he was an innocent dupe without knowledge of the illegal purposes and aims of the Communist party. But, it may be surmised that Frankfurter, to whom *stare decisis* was a major mandate of constitutional law, was not prepared to do that, although he was now willing to use some other means to ameliorate the harshness and unfairness of the deportation decisions.

This he was able to do in 1958 in the case of *Rowoldt* v. *Perfetto*, in which he wrote the opinion for the majority of the Warren Court. The case involved the interpretation of a section of the Internal Security Act of 1950 which requires the deportation of aliens who "at any time" were members of the Communist party. Rowoldt had entered the country in 1915. According to his undisputed testimony, he was a member of the Communist party for less than a year in 1935, primarily because of the "fight for bread" and not because of dissatisfaction with democracy. Frankfurter concluded that Rowoldt, although concededly a "member" of the Communist party, did not meet the test laid down in an earlier case, which interpreted the law to authorize deportation only if the alien "joined the party aware that he was joining an organization known as the Communist party which operates as a distinct and active political organization, and that he did so of his own free will." Rowoldt's membership, the Court held, was not the "meaningful association" which this test must be held to require. Particularly in view of harsh consequences of deportation, it must be concluded that his membership may have been "devoid of any 'political' implications," and therefore he was not deportable under the law.

FAIR TRIAL

In one of its most controversial decisions, *Jencks* v. *United States*, the Warren Court upheld the right of a defendant in a federal criminal trial to inspect the confidential reports made by witnesses to the FBI which related to their testimony at the trial.

This case involved Clinton E. Jencks, official of the Union of Mine, Mill and Smelter Workers, who was prosecuted for perjury in filing an allegedly false non-Communist affidavit under the Taft-Hartley Act. At Jencks's trial, Harvey Matusow and J. W. Ford, two government undercover agents, testified regarding Jencks's alleged Communist activities. Counsel for Jencks requested the lower court to direct the government attorney to bring into court for examination the reports that Matusow and Ford had made to the FBI about the meetings they described. The argument of Jencks's lawyers was that they were entitled to try to show that the witnesses had told different stories in their original reports than they had told at the trial. This would weaken their testimony and strengthen the defendant's case. The trial judge refused this request.

The Supreme Court, with Brennan writing the opinion, held that Jencks was entitled to see the witnesses' reports. The Court rejected the argument that these reports should be kept confidential because of national security. The government, Brennan said, may choose not to reveal the reports but can do so "only at the price of letting the defendant go free."

Clark alone voted to affirm the conviction. "Those intelligence agencies of our government engaged in law enforcement," he said, "may well close up shop, for the Court has opened their files to the criminal and thus afforded him a Roman holiday for rummaging through confidential information as well as vital national secrets."

Few Supreme Court decisions have been so grossly misunderstood or misrepresented in the press as this one was during the succeeding months. Clark's dissent provided some plausibility for the conclusion that the decision opened all FBI files to any person charged with a crime, even a Soviet espionage agent. In fact, the Court did no more than require production of reports given by those witnesses whom the government put on the stand to testify against the accused, and only those reports relating to "the events and activities as to which they testified at the trial."

The Jencks decision did have important practical consequences. In quite a number of prosecutions under the Smith Act the Department of Justice was very reluctant to reveal to defense attorneys statements made to the FBI by some of the prize witnesses in subversion cases. A number of these witnesses had already become thoroughly discredited, and there was grave danger that others would suffer the same fate if their statements to the FBI were disclosed. This fact, together with the Court's decision in the Yates case, explains the dramatic discontinuance of prosecutions under the Smith Act.

THE ASSAULT UPON THE WARREN COURT

These were the major decisions of the Warren Court in the area of civil liberties during its first four or five years. (Almost all were split decisions, with Clark and Whittaker the chief dissenters.) With rare exceptions, they breathe a spirit of liberalism and a return to the commitment to personal freedoms which characterized the 1937 revolution. Coming as they did while the cold war had still not completely thawed and McCarthyism was still more than merely a nightmarish memory, it was to be expected that they would arouse considerable controversy. Criticism and condemnation, both of the Court and its decisions, came from a variety of sources. Some of the more strident and extreme illustrations were recounted in the first chapter of this book. Only slightly less extreme attacks came from such rightist groups as the American Legion, the Veterans of Foreign Wars and the Daughters of the American Revolution. The Committee on Communist Tactics, Strategy and Objectives of the American Bar Association joined the assault, declaring that the Court had paralyzed our internal security program and had left us defenseless in the face of our enemies. On a more dignified level was the "Declaration" signed by the chief justices of the supreme courts of thirty-six of the states at their annual conference in August, 1958, in which they took exception to a number of the decisions of the Warren Court.

The principal complaint against the Court was that it had dangerously weakened our nation's defenses against the threat of Communism, internal subversion and espionage. It had done this by means which themselves merited condemnation, even were their consequences to national security not so grave. One of these was the unprecedented invasion of states' rights, as, for example, its decision in the Nelson case outlawing state anti-subversion statutes; or its decisions in the Konigsberg and Schware cases, dictating to the states who shall be permitted to practice law in the courts of the states; or the Slochower decision, forbidding the states from discharging teachers and other state employees considered to be Communists and subversives.

Another unjustifiable means, it was often charged, that the Warren Court employed to hinder the successful prosecution of our never-ending war on subversion was its blatant disregard of the clearly expressed intention of Congress, as, for example, in the Yates case, where it interpreted away the whole effectiveness of the Smith Act; or in *Cole v. Young*, where it accorded the same treatment to the government's employee security and loyalty program. A third complaint against the Warren Court was that it disregarded its own prior precedents and thus nullified the principle of *stare decisis*. A fourth was that it unduly hampered the enforcement of criminal laws, particularly by the FBI, by allowing Communists and other criminals to examine the confidential reports of the FBI. A fifth was that it interfered with the proper conduct of our foreign affairs by the State Department and gave carte blanche to Communists and espionage agents to travel all over the world and plot against our nation, for it prohibited the Department from refusing passports to them.

Other illustrations can be cited, but these are enough to give the flavor of the assault upon the Court. It must not be assumed that the Court did not have its defenders. The faculties of law schools, particularly Harvard and Yale, the American Civil Liberties Union, the American Jewish Congress, the Association of the Bar of the City of New York, to mention but a few, could be heard in defense of the Court and its decisions. Even the American Bar Association was of two minds. In February of 1959, its Committee on Communist Tactics, Strategy and Objectives issued a report strongly critical of the Warren Court and its decisions, but six months later the Committee on the Bill of Rights of the same American Bar Association issued a report strongly critical of the first committee's report and concluded that: "on balance, this committee is unable to see any indication that the security of the nation or of the states had been impaired by the Supreme Court of the United States."

The assault on the Court was neither the first nor the last such experience. What is particularly significant about it, however, is its source. For the first time in the history of the Court an attack upon it came from the right, and defense of it from the left. Only the revolution of 1937 can explain this; the Supreme Court before that date was a different institution than thereafter. Previously it had been a protector of property, and as such was defended by those to whom protection of property was the highest objective of government, while it was criticized by those who accorded this status to the protection of personal freedoms. After 1937 the situation was reversed, and the critics and defenders naturally changed roles.

As in previous assaults, the critics did not limit themselves to expressions of dissatisfaction. Standard operating procedure calls for demands upon and in Congress for corrective legislation. The first major effort along these lines was a bill introduced in 1957 by Senator William Jenner of Indiana to bar appeal to the Supreme Court in five types of cases: those involving acts of Congressional committees (Watkins decision); the federal employees loyalty program (*Cole* v. *Young*); state anti-subversion laws (Nelson case); action by state school boards relating to subversive activities (Slochower); and action by a state denying a person admission to the bar (Konigsberg). However, even those critical of the Court's decisions were in the main unsympathetic to the Jenner bill, for it was a direct attack on the Court's powers and jurisdiction, and the prestige with which Marshall had endowed the Court was still a potent factor.

Instead, the defenders of national security turned to separate bills aimed at expressly nullifying the rulings of specific decisions but not otherwise limiting the jurisdiction of the Supreme Court. Thus, bills were introduced to declare that every position in the federal government was a "sensitive" position; to permit the states to enact anti-subversion laws; to allow the Department of State to withhold passports in the national interest; to amend the Smith Act so as to define "organize" to include any ongoing activities by the Communist party and to define "advocate" to include all types of advocacy even without direct incitement to action. Further illustrations need not be given; it is sufficient to indicate that probably at least one bill was introduced in one or the other House of Congress to overrule every one of the decisions recounted in this chapter.

Surprisingly, however, these numerous bills achieved a singular lack of success. At the present writing (1965) only two bills have been enacted into law by Congress to deal with libertarian decisions of the Warren Court, the Jencks decision in which defense attorneys were allowed to examine a report given by a prosecution witness to the FBI, and a part of the Yates decision which related to the statute of limitations. The remarkable thing about these laws is that one of them, instead of nullifying the Court's decision (in the Jencks case), affirmed it (with but a slight modification) and made it applicable to all federal criminal trials, and the other was of negligible practical significance. Such an outcome would have been inconceivable when McCarthy dominated Congress.

TACTICAL WITHDRAWALS

The history of the Supreme Court presents considerable evidence in support of the inference that widespread and sustained public criticism of particular decisions is reflected in the later decisions of the Court. If it is an oversimplification to say—as it undoubtedly is—that the Court follows the election returns, it is nevertheless true that the Court has developed a sensitivity to prevailing public opinion. Disaster is the inevitable consequence of the Court's allowing itself to get too far out of line with the strongly expressed feelings of the American public. In the past, public opinion has generally been ahead of the Court; but it is equally dangerous for the Court to get too far ahead of public opinion. It was this caution that explains the disparity between what are generally considered the anti-libertarian decisions of the Vinson Court in the field of political freedoms and its great pro-libertarian decisions in defense of other freedoms and of racial equality.

A similar caution began to take hold within the Warren Court. In

1958, 1959 and 1960 a number of its decisions in the political area indicated some withdrawals from positions too forward for general public acceptance. Warren himself, probably Brennan, certainly Black and Douglas, did not share this caution. Clark and Whittaker, on the other extreme, never approved the taking of the forward positions in the first place. But the other Justices—Frankfurter, Harlan and Stewart—may well have been affected by it, consciously or not. In any event, the decisions of the Court in those years manifested a trend towards a more conservative approach to civil liberties.

The trend began in 1958, with two five to four decisions which in practical effect withdrew much if not all of the protection accorded to state employees by the Slochower decision.

In *Lerner* v. *Casey*, a subway motorman was discharged under the New York Security Risk Law after he had pleaded the Fifth Amendment in refusing to answer a question put to him by the city's commissioner of investigation as to whether he was then a member of the Communist party. The Security Risk Law provided for the discharge of state employees whose employment "would endanger the security or defense of the nation and the state."

Harlan, writing the majority opinion, upheld the dismissal. Distinguishing the Slochower decision, he said that Lerner was dismissed not because he had invoked the Fifth Amendment but "because of the doubt created as to his 'reliability' by his refusal to answer a relevant question put by his employer."

In *Beilan* v. *Board of Education*, Beilan, a teacher in the Philadelphia public school system for twenty-two years, was twice interrogated by the superintendent of schools about his past Communist affiliations. He refused to answer these questions but he did not assert the Fifth Amendment. Subsequent to the second interview, he asserted the privilege against self-incrimination when he was interrogated at a hearing of the House Un-American Activities Committee. Proceedings were afterwards brought against him under the Pennsylvania public school code and he was discharged for "incompetency."

The majority opinion in the Beilan case was written by Burton, who followed the same general argument made by Harlan in the Lerner case. Noting that Beilan was dismissed because he lacked "frankness and candor" and not because of his disloyalty, he concluded that the federal Constitution does not prevent Pennsylvania from dismissing a teacher for "incompetency" for refusing to answer relevant questions regarding his fitness to be a teacher.

The effect of the Lerner and Beilan decisions was simply this: If a state or city employee was called before a Congressional investigating committee and asserted the Fifth Amendment when he was questioned regarding possible Communist affiliation, he could not be discharged by his employer. But the latter could then put the same question and if the employee again refused to answer, he could now be dismissed for lack of "reliability" or for "incompetency," both of which were indicated by his "lack of candor and frankness" in not answering questions put to him by his employer. Not surprisingly, Warren, Black, Douglas and Brennan dissented on the ground that a faithful following of the Slochower decision would have required a contrary result. The Lerner and Beilan decisions gave back to the states pretty much everything that had been taken from them in the Slochower case.

In 1959, the Court, with the same four Justices dissenting, accorded similar treatment to the Watkins decisions and gave back to Congressional investigating committees most of what had been taken from them in that case. In *Barenblatt* v. *United States*, the majority upheld the conviction of Lloyd Barenblatt, a teaching fellow at the University of Michigan, for contempt of Congress in refusing to answer questions concerning his alleged Communist affiliations put to him by the House Un-American Activities Committee.

Harlan, speaking for the majority, stressed the power of Congress to conduct investigations, saying that the scope of this power is as broad as the power to legislate and this power "in the field of Communist activity . . . is hardly debatable." Turning to the field of education, he said that, while the Court would always be alert to protect "academic teaching-freedom and its corollary learning-freedom . . . this does not mean that Congress is precluded from interrogating a witness merely because he is a teacher." Finally, answering the defendant's argument that the investigation was not conducted for a legislative purpose but was designed only for "exposure," Harlan said that, in condemning exposure "for the sake of exposure" in the Watkins case, the Court had also observed that "motives alone would not vitiate an investigation" for a legitimate legislative purpose.

In *Uphaus* v. *Wyman*, also handed in 1959, the same five-man majority held that the New Hampshire attorney-general, acting as an investigating agency for the state legislature, could punish the executive director of World Fellowship, Inc., for refusing to produce a guest list of a summer camp operated by it. In an opinion by Clark, the majority held that the Nelson decision had barred only state laws aimed at efforts to overthrow the *federal* government. The states retained jurisdiction to prohibit overthrow of *state* governments and therefore still had power to investigate such efforts.

On the constitutional claim under the First Amendment, Clark weighed the "public interests" against the "private ones." He found that the evidence before the attorney-general, even though of a kind that could not be introduced in court, was enough to justify his belief that guests at World Fellowship "might be subversive persons within the meaning of the New Hampshire act." The state's interest in "self-preservation" justified attempts by the legislature "to learn if subversive persons were in the state."

These and some other similar decisions, the Court was soon to show, did not manifest a broad retreat, but rather a temporary tactical withdrawal. Decisions handed down in 1962 and later showed clearly that the Court was far from ready to abandon its function as chief guardian of American liberties or to halt the forward march of American freedoms. However, before this is recounted the climax of the struggle against racial segregation should first be related.

THE END OF "SEPARATE BUT EQUAL"

The Warren Court's earlier decisions in political liberty cases were a radical departure from those of the Vinson Court, but its decisions in cases involving racial discrimination and segregation followed naturally those of the Vinson Court. The whole trend of decisions from the close of World War II until Vinson's death pointed in one direction: the ultimate achievement of full equality for the Negro, and the immediate elimination of the fifty-year-old "separate but equal" principle announced by the Fuller Court in *Plessy* v. *Ferguson.* The first major step was achieved in 1954 in the case of *Brown* v. *Board of Education of Topeka, Kansas.*

In a unanimous decision written by Warren, the Court brushed aside all questions as to the relative physical superiority or inferiority of schools attended by colored children. The court hit at the heart of the problem; in effect it adopted the "badge of slavery" concept rejected by all but Harlan in *Plessy* v. *Ferguson.*

Segregation of white and colored children in the public schools, Warren said, has a detrimental effect upon the colored children. The impact is greater when it has the sanction of law, for the policy of separating the races is usually interpreted as denoting the inferiority of the Negro group. A sense of inferiority affects the motivation of a Negro child to learn. Segregation with the sanction of law, therefore, has a tendency to retard the educational and mental development of Negro children and to deprive them of some of the benefits they would receive in a racially integrated school system. In support of this assertion, Warren cited a number of studies made by educators, psychologists and sociologists on the effects of racial segregation on Negro children.

In the field of public education, he concluded, the doctrine of "separate but equal" has no place. Separate educational facilities are inherently unequal and are therefore unconstitutional as a denial of the equal protection of the laws.

RACIAL IRRATIONALITY

Now that McCarthyism is a matter of history, the most critical issue in civil liberties today is that of racial segregation in the South. The Supreme Court's decision in the Brown case outlawing racial segregation in public elementary schools marked a milestone in the history of Negro-white relations in the United States. The decision itself was clearly foreshadowed by the Vinson Court's previous decisions invalidating segregation at the university level, and the school decision came as no great surprise even in the South. For that reason the immediate repercussions were almost unbelievably mild—so mild, in fact, that for a short time it appeared that integration at the elementary and secondary school level might proceed almost as smoothly as had been going on in many southern states at the university and professional school level.

When the southern reaction did manifest itself more than a year after the decision itself, it was as vigorous as it was delayed. There were renewed outbreaks of violence against individual Negroes, particularly those affiliated with the National Association for the Advancement of Colored People. The association itself became the subject of attack, with its members often barred from public teaching positions or other public employment. Legislatures in the South revived the "interposition" movement of pre-Civil War days and cast about for means to frustrate the Court's decision. Laws were passed authorizing the abolition of the public school system if implementation of the decision should be attempted, or cutting off public funds from schools not practicing racial segregation.

Cries of defiance could be heard all through the South. In Washington, ninety-six southern senators and representatives issued a declaration attacking the Supreme Court and pledging themselves "to use all lawful means to bring about a reversal" of its decision, which, they asserted, was "contrary to the Constitution," and "to prevent the use of force in its implementation."

An example of the extremes to which the attack on the Supreme Court could go is found in the following editorial that appeared in the Augusta (Georgia) *Courier* on October 13, 1958.

> No man knows today what his rights are in this country. No man today has any liberties left. His rights and his liberties are in the laps of the nine crazy men who sit on the Supreme Court bench. And the Lord only knows what these crazy men will do next. . . . Today, they are the most dangerous tyrants that ever existed. Like Hitler, Mussolini, and the other modern-day tyrants, they are mentally deranged. They are crazed with a desire to serve a minority for political purposes. Their insanity has made them unscrupulous in the methods they have employed to do the bidding of this minority. They are mentally deranged tyrants ruling as unscrupulously as any tyrant in all of history. The members of this court must be curbed or they must be removed from the bench.

This is typical of the irrational attacks on the Court in the South. Others were somewhat more dignified, but no less bitter. Not surprisingly at all, they echoed in many instances the grievances asserted by those dissatisfied with the Warren Court's decisions in the field of political liberties. Even the charge that the Court was aiding Communism and subversion was frequently made, the logic being that "race-mixing" was a well-known objective of the Communist conspiracy. Other grievances were that the Court had wantonly nullified the principle of *stare decisis* in overruling a precedent of a half-century (*Plessy* v. *Ferguson*); that it had invaded states' rights and thus destroyed the system of federalism fashioned by the fathers of the Constitution and (this often appeared to be its most serious offense) had decided the Brown case not on law but on the findings of pseudo-social scientists.

The most serious challenge to the Court's decision came in Little Rock, Arkansas. Pursuant to the Supreme Court decision, various school boards prepared plans for orderly integration. One of these communities was Little Rock, and all the indications were that integration there would be peaceful and orderly. Suddenly, however, Governor Orval Faubus announced that the danger of riot and bloodshed required him to order state troopers to keep out all Negro students from Central High School. Since this was defiance of a federal court order, President Eisenhower found it necessary to dispatch federal troops to Little Rock to prevent interference with the carrying out of the order.

In June, 1958, a federal district judge, on petition of the Little Rock school board, ordered that integration of Central High School be suspended until January, 1961, because of "intolerable conditions" resulting from attendance of Negroes at the school. The parents of the eight Negro children who had been admitted to the school pursuant to the original order appealed to the federal circuit court of appeals. That court reversed the order postponing integration and declared that "the time has not yet come in these United States when an order of a Federal court must be whittled away, watered down, or shamefully withdrawn in the face of violent and unlawful acts of individual citizens in opposition thereto." This decision was then appealed to the Supreme Court, which, in the case of *Cooper* v. *Aaron*, handed down its unanimous decision in a special session held in September, 1958, upholding the ruling of the circuit court.

The usual practice is for one Justice to write and sign an opinion and the others to concur or dissent. In *Cooper* v. *Aaron*, however, the decision was signed individually by each of the nine Justices. The purpose of this procedure was to show that although there had been some changes in the personnel of the Court since the Brown decision had been handed down in 1954, every one of the present Justices agreed with that decision and was committed to its effectuation and implementation. The Brown decision had its antecedents, going back at least to 1938 when the Court ruled the requirement that separate educational facilities be equal was not satisfied when the state paid the tuition for Negro law students in an out-of-state law school because the law school at the state university was all white. Other decisions, primarily in the post-World War II years, continued the chipping process until the decisive blow at the separate-but-equal doctrine was struck in 1954 in the Brown case. That decision inaugurated a new era in civil rights, an era whose conclusion is not yet in sight.

Undoubtedly, during the major part of the decade after Brown the principal role in civil rights was played by the Supreme Court. In a sense, this was no more than just, for it was the Court which, by striking down the Reconstruction Civil Rights Acts and promulgating the separate-but-equal doctrine, was principally responsible for the substantial nullification of the Fourteenth Amendment and the frustration of the purpose for which the Civil War was fought. If the life of the Fourteenth Amendment was taken by the Supreme Court, so a new one was given by the Court.

The Court's role during this past decade consisted of preserving the integrity of the Brown decision. In *Cooper* v. *Aaron*, it showed in terms unmistakable even to the most die-hard southern officials that it was not prepared to retreat in the face of massive resistance and even defiance accompanied by violence. In the 1964 Prince Edward County case (*Griffin* v. *Prince Edward County School Board*) it showed that the requirement of desegregation "with all deliberate speed" was not a license to deliberate forever, that ten years was long enough a period of grace, and that further delays would not be countenanced. In other decisions it extended the principle of the Brown case from public schools to all facilities and operations of the state, ruling unconstitutional, for example, segregated seating in state courtrooms. In still other cases, it gave liberal interpretations and broad scope to the word "state" in the Fourteenth Amendment, thus preventing evasion by such devices as a state's leasing publicly owned facilities to private operators or abolishing a public school system and paying for the tuition of children attending privately operated segregated schools.

In *Heart of Atlanta Motel* v. *United States* it upheld the constitutionality of the public accommodations section of the Civil Rights Act of 1964. It did this by a broad interpretation of the power of Congress to regulate commerce, rather than under the Fourteenth Amendment. But the practical effect was the same—overruling the 1883 Civil Rights Cases decision as it had ten years earlier overruled *Pressy* v. *Ferguson.*

A maxim in the Talmud commands that "in the place where there is no man, try to be a man." The Court appeared to be following this maxim. It seemed to have stepped into the vacuum created by the default of Congress in discharging the responsibilities imposed on it by the Constitution. Each of the three post-Civil War amendments enacted to insure full equality for the Negro, the Thirteenth, Fourteenth and Fifteenth, provides that Congress shall have power to enforce its provisions by appropriate legislation. It was undoubtedly contemplated and intended thereby that the primary responsibility for according equality to the Negro would lie with Congress. The Reconstruction Congress so interpreted the mandate of the amendments and enacted a number of laws which, though in large measure nullified by decisions of the pre-1937 Supreme Court, nevertheless still supply the legal bases for much of the litigation in the federal courts aimed at racially discriminatory practices. However, for more than three-quarters of a century after 1875, when Congress enacted the last of the postwar civil rights statutes, not a single law was adopted by it to help make real the promise of equality expressed in the amendments. The two minor civil rights laws enacted by Congress in 1957 and 1960 hardly came close to fulfilling Congressional responsibility.

The existence of this vacuum, and the demand not merely by the Negro but by the overall American conscience that it be filled, resulted in activities on the part of the other two arms of the federal government, the executive and the judiciary, to an extent undoubtedly much greater than contemplated by the generation that added the Thirteenth, Fourteenth and Fifteenth Amendments to the Constitution. Of these two arms, the postwar generation undoubtedly contemplated that the responsibility of the executive would be greater than that of the judiciary. However, history refused to agree with that decision. The contribution of the Supreme Court to the struggle for racial equality was much greater than that of the Presidents (Roosevelt, Truman, Eisenhower, Kennedy and Johnson), and of course immeasurably greater than that of Congress, at least until enactment of the Civil Rights Act of 1964.

In 1964 the Court refused to upset a decision handed down in Indiana which declared that there is no constitutional obligation on the part of a state to eliminate public school segregation resulting not from laws or regulations adopted by the state, but by reason of the fact that children usually go to neighborhood schools and Negro children generally live in Negro neighborhoods. The Court's refusal to require states to eliminate such *de facto* segregation may indicate that it feels that it has done about as much as it can in seeking to assure full equality for the Negro, and that under our system of government there are some things that the Court simply cannot do.

If this is the message the Court sought to convey, it may well be succeeding. In many northern states efforts are being made to eliminate *de facto* segregation or at least ameliorate its damaging consequences. President Johnson has spoken out on the moral issue in racial discrimination and segregation more vigorously than his predecessors and has manifested an intent to use the powers of his office to meet it. Most important, in 1964 the Congress enacted the most sweeping civil rights bill since the Reconstruction period and seems to have indicated a willingness to re-assume the responsibility assigned to it by the Fourteenth Amendment in securing full equality for the Negro. The future may well see a substantially diminished role on the part of the Supreme Court in the area of discrimination against Negroes.

THE FORWARD MARCH RESUMED

The Court's effort to secure equality for the Negro after the Second World War was in no way affected by the McCarthy interlude. The Warren Court's decisions in this area were the natural development of the Vinson Court's decisions. In respect to other American freedoms, particularly political freedoms, the Court, early in 1962, made it clear that it was ready to resume the march it had temporarily halted after the reaction from the post-McCarthy decisions. Its progress was aided by a change in Court personnel which occurred in that year. Whittaker retired from the bench and Kennedy appointed as his replacement Arthur J. Goldberg of Illinois, long-time general counsel of the CIO and then Kennedy's Secretary of Labor. Goldberg quickly associated himself with the quartet of Black, Douglas, Warren and Brennan to make up a strong liberal majority.

Most conservative on this Court has been Harlan, who, in the two years that at this writing have followed the Goldberg appointment, has found himself in the role of chief dissenter. Justices Clark, Stewart and White have occupied the center position, with White, a Kennedy appointee, perhaps most often voting with the Black majority. Nevertheless, using the terms of liberalism and conservatism as convenient generalizations, the conservatism of Harlan is hardly to be equated with that of the McReynolds-Van Devanter-Sutherland-Butler quartet of the 1920's and early 1930's. Harlan was not their heir but the heir of Frankfurter and inherited from him a commitment to judicial restraint, a concept completely alien to the quartet in the Taft and Hughes Courts. Harlan, like Frankfurter, would refrain equally from declaring unconstitutional laws restricting civil liberties and economic expansion; the four would uphold the former laws but invalidate the latter.

As we have seen in the discussion of the Negro civil rights cases, the Court has taken the lead because the other branches of government had defaulted in fulfilling the responsibility initially imposed upon them by the Fourteenth Amendment. Harlan concurred in these decisions, but when the same philosophy was employed in respect to constitutional rights other than those of the Negro, he rebelled. Dissenting in the reapportionment cases, shortly to be discussed, he said:

> These decisions give support to a current mistaken view of the Constitution and the constitutional function of this Court. This view, in a nutshell, is that every major social ill in this country can find its cure in some constitutional "principle," and that this Court should "take the lead" in promoting reform when other branches of government fail to act. The Constitution is not a panacea for every blot upon the public welfare, nor should this Court, ordained as a judicial body, be thought of as a general haven for reform movements. This Court, limited in function, does not serve its high purpose when it exceeds its authority, even to satisfy justified impatience with the slow workings of the political process.

The two terms of the Court following Whittaker's replacement by Goldberg were probably the most liberal two-year period in its history. In a sense it constituted the vindication of Hugo Black. As Anthony Lewis of the New York *Times* noted, "It can now be said that Justice Black has seen more of his dissents become the law than any man who ever served on the Supreme Court." During the same period, the Court disregarded the principle of *stare decisis* perhaps more than ever before; on one single decision day it refused to follow five previous decisions. Among the numerous libertarian decisions of the Court, the following merit mention.

In *Yellin* v. *United States* the Court returned to its role of reining the activities of legislative committees investigating subversion, this time the House Un-American Activities Committee. It held that if the Committee does not strictly follow its own rules for the protection of witnesses it cannot get the courts to punish a witness for contempt because he refuses to answer questions put to him by the Committee. (In this case, the staff director rather than the Committee itself, as its rules provided, denied the request of the witness to testify in executive session before testifying in public sessions.)

In *Baggett* v. *Bullitt* it struck down a Washington state law requiring all public employees to take a loyalty oath that they were not "subversive persons." In *Aptheker* v. *Secretary of State* it held that the right to travel was constitutionally protected and that the State Department could not deny a passport to a person simply because he was a Communist. And in the Communist party registration case it upheld a lower court decision the practical effect of which was to render ineffective the law requiring the Communist party and other subversive organizations to register.

In *Gideon* v. *Wainright* it held that when a poor person is charged with a felony and cannot afford to hire a lawyer, the state must provide him with one without cost. (Previously the Court had held that this was required only if the defendant was charged with a crime punishable by death or if because of immaturity of age or mental deficiencies he could not handle his own defense.) If the state fails to do this, the conviction will be set aside by the Supreme Court no matter how clear the guilt of the defendant may be. Of course, this does not mean that the accused will go free; a new trial may be ordered in which he will have state-appointed counsel.

Three important decisions strengthened the privilege against self-incrimination. In *Escobedo* v. *Illinois* the Court held that when the police question a criminal suspect they must allow him to see his lawyer and if they fail to do this, any self-incriminating statements he makes may not be used at the trial. In *Malloy* v. *Hogan* it overruled precedents going back for some sixty years and held that the provision in the Fifth Amendment that no person may be compelled to incriminate himself is applicable to state as well as federal proceedings; and in *Murphy* v. *New York Harbor Waterfront Commission*, again overruling many precedents, it held that if a witness is granted immunity and compelled to testify before a state body, that testimony may not be used against him if he is later tried in a federal court, and vice versa.

These are typical of the many libertarian decisions handed down in 1963 and 1964. But, as indicated previously, the most revolutionary decisions concerned the right to vote and the secularity of public education.

ONE PERSON, ONE VOTE

Theoretically, perhaps, every citizen's vote should be the equal of every other's. This, however, has never been the case. Since a senator from a sparsely populated state has exactly the same powers as one from a heavily populated state, the vote of a citizen in a small state is obviously more valuable than that of a citizen in a large state. Even in the House of Representatives, where representation is based upon population, the growth of cities through migrations from farm areas and immigration from abroad, combined with the use of antiquated population estimates and districting laws, deliberate gerrymandering and a variety of other devices, all have resulted in larger populations in urban Congressional districts than in rural districts. The same is true of state legislative districts. The consequence is that the vote of a city dweller is less valuable, less effective, than that of a farm dweller. There are many instances when a single rural vote is the equivalent of as many as forty or fifty urban votes.

In 1946, in the case of *Colegrove* v. *Green*, the Court refused to set aside an Illinois apportionment law which created Congressional districts of glaring inequality. For example, one of these districts, entitled to one congressman, had some 112,000 inhabitants, while another, also entitled to one congressman, had 914,000. The basis for the Court's decision was that the question of legislative representation was a "political" rather than a judicial one, and therefore not proper for court interference.

Judicial intervention came only after the legislative branch of government had more than adequate opportunity to discharge the responsibility initially given it by the Constitution. The philosophy of the Court's decision in *Colegrove* v. *Green* was that primary if not exclusive responsibility for eliminating the inequalities rested with the legislative bodies, federal and state. The passage of fifteen years showed clearly that those bodies were either unwilling or unable to act. Accordingly, in 1962, in *Baker* v. *Carr*, the Court announced that it was prepared to intervene to discharge a duty that had been abandoned by the organ of government to which it had initially been entrusted by the Constitution.

In *Baker* v. *Carr* the Court in effect overruled *Colegrove* v. *Green.* It held (with only Frankfurter and Harlan dissenting), that the federal courts can and should take jurisdiction to remedy an obvious denial of the equal protection of the laws guaranteed by the Fourteenth Amendment. If the state legislatures, given reasonable opportunities to do so, did not reapportion election districts so as to provide for more equal representation among urban and rural voters, the courts themselves would undertake to do so.

The practical implications of *Baker* v. *Carr* became evident in *Wesberry* v. *Sanders* and *Reynolds* v. *Simms,* both decided in 1964. In the former case the Court held that in fixing Congressional districts the states must seek to achieve the principle of one person, one vote. This means that as far as practicable each Congressional district should have the same amount of voters as every other district. In *Reynolds* v. *Simms* the Court extended this principle to apply to state legislatures as well, and refused to distinguish between lower and upper houses. It is true that in the federal government representation in the Senate is not based upon population, and that the smallest state has the same number of Senators as does the most populous state. This, however, was the result of the compromise which made adoption of the Constitution possible, and does not apply to subdivisions of a state. The Court declared that "the fundamental principle of representative government in this country is one of equal representation for equal numbers of people, without regard to race, sex, economic status, or place of residence within a state."

Baker v. *Carr* and its successors are landmark cases in the history of American democracy, and must be understood and appreciated in the light of that evolutionary history. A century ago Abraham Lincoln declared in his Gettysburg Address that this nation was dedicated to the proposition that all men are created equal. Ever since the Declaration of Independence was written the United States has been engaged in a tortuous march toward the goal of equality expressed in that proposition. In the area of exercise of the elective franchise there has from the beginning been an unending if halting effort to remove inequalities.

The first step was the removal of inequalities based upon religious differences. In Colonial times the right to participate in the election of government officials was limited to Protestants. Vestiges of this continued after the Constitution was adopted. It was not until the opening of the nineteenth century that New York removed from its books a requirement that all applicants for citizenship disavow allegiance to any foreign potentate, religious as well as secular, thus effectively disenfranchising conscientious Roman Catholics. At about the same time, the states began to remove inequality in voting based on wealth. They did this by repealing the numerous provisions limiting the franchise to those owning substantial property, real or personal. The enactment of the Fifteenth Amendment after the Civil War was an effort to remove inequality in the exercise of the franchise based upon difference in race, and of the Nineteenth Amendment after the First World War to remove inequality based upon difference of sex. The decision in *Baker* v. *Carr* and its successors represent another step forward in this march—an attempt to remove in part inequality in the franchise based upon differences in place of residence. As the Court stated in one of these decisions: "The conception of political equality from the Declaration of Independence to Lincoln's Gettysburg Address, to the Fifteenth, Seventeenth and Nineteenth Amendments can mean only one thing—one person, one vote."

It is too early to anticipate all the consequences of the apportionment decisions. It was quickly recognized by many that readjustment of vote weighting in accordance with the decisions would aid Democrats at the expense of Republicans, liberals at the expense of conservatives, and city-centered ethnic minorities, such as Catholics and Jews, as against white Protestants. Above all, perhaps, the decisions were expected to increase the political influence of Negroes. In the North the Negroes are city-centered, and accordingly would benefit along with other city-centered ethnic minorities. In the South, Negroes have and exercise much greater freedom of franchise in the cities than in the rural areas. The increased importance of the Negro's vote as a result of the decisions would not only lead to increased representation in state legislatures but would also make political parties more responsive to his demand for equality.

THE PRAYER-BIBLE DECISIONS

Notwithstanding the tremendous significance of *Baker* v. *Carr* and its successors, the public reaction to them was mild. The reaction to the Prayer-Bible decisions handed down in 1962 and 1963 was not. The first of these decisions was *Engel* v. *Vitale*, issued in 1962. In that case the Court, with only Stewart dissenting, ruled unconstitutional the practice in some New York public schools of daily recitation of a so-called non-denominational prayer which had been formulated by the state educational authorities. The prayer consisted of only twenty-two words and seemed quite innocuous. ("Almighty God, we acknowledge our dependence upon Thee, and we beg Thy blessings upon us, our parents, our teachers and our country.") Nevertheless, its formulation aroused considerable controversy in New York and only about one-tenth of the school districts adopted it as part of their daily schedule. One of the districts that did was the village of New Hyde Park on Long Island, and a group of parents living there brought suit in the state courts to declare the program unconstitutional as a violation of the principle of the separation of church and state. Unsuccessful in the state courts, they appealed to the Supreme Court and won.

Among constitutional lawyers the decision was not unexpected. The principles upon which it was based had been well established in earlier cases and had been restated by the Court but a year earlier in two cases—one (*McGowan* v. *Maryland*) upholding as social welfare (rather than religious) laws statutes requiring businesses to close on Sundays, and the other (*Torcaso* v. *Watkins*) holding that a state could not exclude non-believers in God from holding public office. Nevertheless, announcement of the decision aroused a storm of fury as intense as any evoked by other controversial Supreme Court decisions in the past few years. So intense was it that Justice Clark felt it necessary to defend the decision in a public address.

Cardinal Spellman of New York declared that he was "shocked and frightened" at the decision which, he said, struck "at the very heart of the Godly tradition in which America's children have so long been raised." The evangelist Billy Graham called it "another step toward the secularization of the United States." Senator Robert C. Byrd of West Viriginia asked, "Can it be that we, too, are ready to embrace the foul concept of atheism? Is this not in fact the first step on the road to promoting atheistic and agnostic beliefs? Somebody is tampering with America's soul. I leave it to you who that somebody is." Representative George W. Andrews of Alabama asserted that "They put the Negroes in the schools, and now they've driven God out." And Representative

L. Mendel Rivers of South Carolina said: "The Court has now officially declared its disbelief in God."

Just about the time the decision was announced, the governors of the states were holding their annual Governors' Conference. With but Governor Nelson Rockefeller of New York abstaining and no one voting nay, they adopted a resolution deploring the decision and calling for a constitutional amendment to nullify it.

Such amendments were introduced in both Houses of Congress and Senator James O. Eastland of Mississippi, chairman of the Senate Judiciary Committee, conducted public hearings on them. While support was expressed by a number of senators and congressmen as well as from some religious sources—particularly Roman Catholic and Fundamentalist Protestant—a delayed but nevertheless quite vigorous opposing voice was heard, from Protestant, Jewish, Negro (both the National Association for the Advancement of Colored People and the revered Negro leader Rev. Martin Luther King expressed their approval of the Court's decision and opposition to any amendment to overrule it), and other secular sources. In view of this opposition, Senator Eastland quietly dropped his efforts to amend the Constitution, only to see them resumed with increased energy a year later, after the second of the Prayer-Bible decisions, *School District of Abington Township* v. *Schempp* and *Murray* v. *Curlett*, known as the Schempp-Murray decision, was handed down. In these cases the Court in a single decision ruled, again with only Stewart dissenting, that it is unconstitutional for the public schools to conduct Bible reading or recitation of the Lord's Prayer as part of the school program. As in *Engel* v. *Vitale*, the Court held that it was immaterial what prayer was recited or which version of the Bible was used, and that children who did not wish to participate could be excused. The crux of the decision, following the principle laid down in the McCollum case, was that the public schools are a secular institution and the Court would keep them so.

Compared to the reaction evoked by the Engel decision, the response that greeted Schempp-Murray was moderate. Unlike the former decision, which affected a practice that existed only in 10 per cent of the schools of but one state, the Schempp-Murray decision affected practices in perhaps half the schools of the nation. Nevertheless, the critical reaction evoked by Schempp-Murray was remarkably subdued, characterized more by sorrowful resignation than outraged defiance. It seemed that the nation was prepared to accept a Bible-less and prayerless public school system.

One Congressman, however, Frank Becker of New York, undertook a one-man crusade to nullify the decision and restore God to the public school classroom. First he prevailed upon the ninety-odd congressmen who had introduced separate measures to amend the Constitution to join on one single bill. After this new measure was referred to the House Judiciary Committee, Becker began rounding up signatures to a petition for its discharge. Becker himself had before always refused to sign discharge petitions, including those for civil rights bills aimed at achieving equality for Negroes and other racial minorities. The reason for the difference, Becker explained, was that all other discharge petitions "dealt with material things and material benefits. This one deals only with the spiritual. The urgency of this matter leaves no alternative if we are to prevent the advocates of a godless society to accomplish in the United States that which the Communists have accomplished in Soviet Russia."

The proposed amendment agreed to by the various congressmen read as follows:

> Section 1. Nothing in this Constitution shall be deemed to prohibit the offering, reading from, or listening to prayers or Biblical Scriptures, if participation therein is on a voluntary basis, in any governmental or public school, institution, or place.
>
> Section 2. Nothing in this Constitution shall be deemed to prohibit making reference to belief in, reliance upon, or invoking the aid of God or a Supreme Being, in any governmental or public document, proceeding, activity, ceremony, school, institution, or place or upon any coinage, currency, or obligation of the United States.
>
> Section 3. Nothing in this Article shall constitute an establishment of religion.

At first Becker enjoyed phenomenal success. Congressmen by the score signed his petition for discharge. The Republican Policy Committee in the House adopted his measure as party policy. It was freely predicted that if the measure were brought to a vote on the floor of the House it would be overwhelmingly and perhaps even unanimously approved. Congressman Emanuel Celler of New York, chairman of the House Judiciary Committee and personally opposed to the measure, found it necessary to schedule public hearings. These hearings changed the complexion of the situation. With rare exceptions, every responsible voice of religion either appeared personally or submitted statements in opposition to the proposed amendment. So too did the leading constitutional lawyers in the country. The result was that Congress adjourned without taking any action on the Becker proposal and it too found its way in the oblivion of forgotten amendments to nullify Supreme Court decisions.

THE TRIUMPH OF JOHN MARSHALL

One final effort to curb the Court by constitutional amendment merits relating. After the decision in *Baker* v. *Carr* was announced in 1962, the Council of State Governments drafted and sponsored three amendments to the Constitution. One would have changed the method of amending the Constitution, and the second would have nullified *Baker* v. *Carr* by providing that "no provision of this Constitution, or any amendment thereto, shall restrict or limit any state in the apportionment of representatives in its legislature." It is, however, the third with which we are most interested. It was the most far-reaching. Its purpose was to set up a new "Court of the Union," consisting of the chief justices of the supreme courts of each of the fifty states of the Union. By majority vote, this "court" could set aside any judgment of the United States Supreme Court which it deemed to infringe on states' rights. (The Court of the Union could act any time up to two years after the Supreme Court hands down its decision, but the proposal made no provision for what should be the effect of the decision during this two-year period.)

The proposal provided that the Court of the Union should be the ultimate court, that no appeals from its decision could be taken to any other tribunal and that the only way its decisions would be subject to change would be by amending the Constitution. Since it is the decisions of state courts which are reviewed now by the Supreme Court, the net result might in effect well have been that after the Supreme Court reversed a state court or a number of state courts, its reversal might in turn be reversed by the same state courts acting through their chief justices in the Court of the Union.

The ancient Jewish high court, the Sanhedrin, consisted of seventy judges, but in modern times it has generally been assumed that as a practical matter membership of courts should be considerably smaller. The present Supreme Court has nine members and most state high courts have even less. Those who have participated in or observed hearings before the United States Supreme Court or a state high court know that the justices frequently interrupt the argument of counsel in order to ask him questions. One can imagine a hearing in which each of fifty judges would have the opportunity to interrupt the attorneys to ask them questions during the presentation of their arguments.

Aside from its cumbersomeness, there was another problem. State supreme court judges serve for varying terms so that the personnel of the Court of the Union would be in a state of continuous flux.

Despite all this, three states—Arkansas, Florida and Wyoming—approved the "Court of the Union" Amendment. This was accomplished within three months and with no publicity of any kind. It is quite probable that if the wall of silence surrounding the activities of the Council of State Governments had been maintained, many other state legislatures would have acted similarly. However, the proposal became public and evoked such widespread popular condemnation that it was speedily buried. It was quite clear that notwithstanding the unpopularity of some of its decisions, the American people would sanction no tampering with the Supreme Court.

John Marshall had triumphed, not in the way he had anticipated or would have wanted, but he triumphed nevertheless. He sought to make of the Court an institution which would withstand the shifts of popular passions and would shape the patterns of the nation. He had assumed that it would shape these patterns in accordance with Hamilton's economic philosophy and would stand as an unmovable guardian of the rights of property and capitalist expansion. For a century and a quarter it did just that. In 1937 it abandoned that role and instead became the nation's principal guardian of the liberties of the people. Paradoxically, the institution least democratic in its structure—consisting of nine men serving for life and responsible to no one—has become the institution most committed to and effective in the promotion and preservation of democracy. Marshall would have been unhappy had he been able to foresee this. Yet it was he who created the Court that Stone, Warren and even Vinson utilized to secure the liberties of Americans. Whether he would have liked it or not, John Marshall had triumphed.

Justices of the United States Supreme Court

Name and residence (** denotes Chief Justice*)	*Term*	*Appointed by*
*John Jay, N.Y.	1789-1795	George Washington
John Rutledge, S.C.	1789-1791	George Washington
William Cushing, Mass.	1789-1810	George Washington
James Wilson, Pa.	1789-1798	George Washington
John Blair, Va.	1789-1796	George Washington
Robert H. Harrison, Md.	1789-1790	George Washington
James Iredell, N.C.	1790-1799	George Washington
Thomas Johnson, Md.	1791-1793	George Washington
William Paterson, N.J.	1793-1806	George Washington
*John Rutledge, S.C.	1795-1795	George Washington
Samuel Chase, Md.	1796-1811	George Washington
*Oliver Ellsworth, Conn.	1796-1799	George Washington
Bushrod Washington, Va.	1798-1829	John Adams
Alfred Moore, N.C.	1799-1804	John Adams
*John Marshall, Va.	1801-1835	John Adams
William Johnson, S.C.	1804-1834	Thomas Jefferson
Brockholst Livingston, N.Y.	1806-1823	Thomas Jefferson
Thomas Todd, Ky.	1807-1826	Thomas Jefferson
Joseph Story, Mass.	1811-1845	James Madison
Gabriel Duval, Md.	1812-1835	James Madison
Smith Thompson, N.Y.	1823-1843	James Monroe
Robert Trimble, Ky.	1826-1828	John Quincy Adams
John McLean, Ohio	1829-1861	Andrew Jackson
Henry Baldwin, Pa.	1830-1844	Andrew Jackson
James M. Wayne, Ga.	1835-1867	Andrew Jackson
Philip P. Barbour, Va.	1836-1841	Andrew Jackson
*Roger B. Taney, Md.	1836-1864	Andrew Jackson
John Catron, Tenn.	1837-1865	Andrew Jackson
John McKinley, Ala.	1837-1852	Martin Van Buren
Peter V. Daniel, Va.	1841-1860	Martin Van Buren
Samuel Nelson, N.Y.	1845-1872	John Tyler
Levi Woodbury, N.H.	1845-1851	James K. Polk

Robert C. Grier, Pa.	1846-1870	James K. Polk
Benj. R. Curtis, Mass.	1851-1857	Millard Fillmore
John A. Campbell, Ala.	1853-1861	Franklin Pierce
Nathan Clifford, Me.	1858-1881	James Buchanan
Noah H. Swayne, Ohio	1862-1881	Abraham Lincoln
Samuel F. Miller, Iowa	1862-1890	Abraham Lincoln
David Davis, Ill.	1862-1877	Abraham Lincoln
Stephen J. Field, Cal.	1863-1897	Abraham Lincoln
*Salmon P. Chase, Ohio	1864-1873	Abraham Lincoln
William Strong, Pa.	1870-1880	Ulysses S. Grant
Joseph P. Bradley, N.J.	1870-1892	Ulysses S. Grant
Ward Hunt, N.Y.	1873-1882	Ulysses S. Grant
*Morrison R. Waite, Ohio	1874-1888	Ulysses S. Grant
John M. Harlan, Ky.	1877-1911	Rutherford B. Hayes
William B. Woods, Ga.	1881-1887	Rutherford B. Hayes
Stanley Matthews, Ohio	1881-1889	James A. Garfield
Horace Gray, Mass.	1882-1902	Chester A. Arthur
Samuel Blatchford, N.Y.	1882-1893	Chester A. Arthur
Lucius Q. C. Lamar, Miss.	1888-1893	Grover Cleveland
*Melville W. Fuller, Ill.	1888-1910	Grover Cleveland
David J. Brewer, Kan.	1890-1910	Benjamin Harrison
Henry B. Brown, Mich.	1891-1906	Benjamin Harrison
George Shiras, Jr., Pa.	1892-1903	Benjamin Harrison
Howell E. Jackson, Tenn.	1893-1895	Benjamin Harrison
Edward D. White, La.	1894-1910	Grover Cleveland
Rufus W. Peckham, N.Y.	1896-1909	Grover Cleveland
Joseph McKenna, Cal.	1898-1925	William McKinley
Oliver W. Holmes, Mass.	1902-1932	Theodore Roosevelt
William R. Day, Ohio	1903-1922	Theodore Roosevelt
William H. Moody, Mass.	1906-1910	Theodore Roosevelt
Horace H. Lurton, Tenn.	1910-1914	William H. Taft
Charles E. Hughes, N.Y.	1910-1916	William H. Taft
Willis Van Devanter, Wy.	1911-1937	William H. Taft
Joseph R. Lamar, Ga.	1911-1916	William H. Taft
*Edward D. White, La.	1910-1921	William H. Taft
Mahlon Pitney, N.J.	1912-1922	William H. Taft
Jas. C. McReynolds, Tenn.	1914-1941	Woodrow Wilson
Louis D. Brandeis, Mass.	1916-1939	Woodrow Wilson
John H. Clarke, Ohio	1916-1922	Woodrow Wilson
*William H. Taft, Conn.	1921-1930	Warren G. Harding
George Sutherland, Utah	1922-1938	Warren G. Harding
Pierce Butler, Minn.	1922-1939	Warren G. Harding
Edward T. Sanford, Tenn.	1923-1930	Warren G. Harding
Harlan F. Stone, N.Y.	1925-1941	Calvin Coolidge

*Charles E. Hughes, N.Y.	1930-1941	Herbert Hoover
Owen J. Roberts, Penn.	1930-1945	Herbert Hoover
Benjamin N. Cardozo, N.Y.	1932-1938	Herbert Hoover
Hugo L. Black, Ala.	1937-	Franklin D. Roosevelt
Stanley F. Reed, Ky.	1938-1957	Franklin D. Roosevelt
Felix Frankfurter, Mass.	1939-1962	Franklin D. Roosevelt
William O. Douglas, Conn.	1939-	Franklin D. Roosevelt
Frank Murphy, Mich.	1940-1949	Franklin D. Roosevelt
*Harlan F. Stone, N.Y.	1941-1946	Franklin D. Roosevelt
James F. Byrnes, S.C.	1941-1942	Franklin D. Roosevelt
Robert H. Jackson, N.Y.	1941-1954	Franklin D. Roosevelt
Wiley B. Rutledge, Iowa	1943-1949	Franklin D. Roosevelt
Harold H. Burton, Ohio	1945-1958	Harry S Truman
*Fred M. Vinson, Ky.	1946-1953	Harry S Truman
Tom C. Clark, Texas	1949-	Harry S Truman
Sherman Minton, Indiana	1949-1956	Harry S Truman
*Earl Warren, Cal.	1953-	Dwight D. Eisenhower
John Marshall Harlan, N.Y.	1955-	Dwight D. Eisenhower
William J. Brennan, Jr., N.J.	1956-	Dwight D. Eisenhower
Charles E. Whittaker, Mo.	1957-1962	Dwight D. Eisenhower
Potter Stewart, Ohio	1958-	Dwight D. Eisenhower
Byron R. White, Colo.	1962-	John F. Kennedy
Arthur J. Goldberg, Ill.	1962-	John F. Kennedy

Selected Bibliography*

Adams, Randolph, ed., *Selected Political Essays of James Wilson*, New York, Alfred A. Knopf, Inc., 1930. With an introductory essay on Wilson's thought.

Alfange, Dean, *The Supreme Court and the National Will*, Garden City, N.Y., Doubleday & Company, Inc., 1937. Written just before the 1937 Reorganization Bill, at height of popular discontent with the Court.

Alsop, Joseph, and Catledge, Turner, *The 168 Days*, Garden City, N.Y., Doubleday & Company, Inc., 1938. On the court-packing fight.

Barry, Richard, *Mr. Rutledge of South Carolina*, New York, Duell, Sloan & Pearce, Inc., 1942. A few pages on his Supreme Court career.

Bates, Ernest Sutherland, *The Story of the Supreme Court*, Indianapolis and New York, The Bobbs-Merrill Co., Inc., 1936. Popularly written, short account.

Beard, Charles A., *The Supreme Court and the Constitution*, New York, The Macmillan Company, 1912. Classic defense of the legitimacy of judicial review.

Bent, Silas, *Justice Oliver Wendell Holmes*, Garden City, N.Y., Vanguard Press, 1932. Discusses Holmes' thought as well as life.

Beth, Loren P., *Politics, the Constitution and the Supreme Court*, Evanston, Ill., Harper & Row, Publishers, 1962.

Beveridge, Albert S., *The Life of John Marshall*, Boston and New York, Houghton Mifflin Company, 1916. The classic biography. Idolizing but invaluable.

Bickel, Alexander M., *The Least Dangerous Branch: The Supreme Court at the Bar of Politics*, Indianapolis and New York, The Bobbs-Merrill Co., Inc., 1962.

Biddle, Francis, *Mr. Justice Holmes*, New York, Charles Scribner's Sons, 1942. Popular and anecdotal.

Black, Charles L., Jr., *The People and the Court: Judicial Review in a Democracy*, New York, The Macmillan Company, 1960. Defense of Supreme Court's activist role in civil liberties.

Boudin, Louis B., *Government by Judiciary*, New York, William Godwin, Inc., 1932. A two-volume attack on judicial review.

Bowen, Catherine, *Yankee from Olympus*, Boston, Little, Brown and Company, 1944. Popular biography of Justice Holmes; emphasis on personality rather than on legal career.

Brown, William G., *Life of Oliver Ellsworth*, New York, The Macmillan Company, 1905.

Butler, Charles Henry, *A Century at the Bar of the Supreme Court of the United States*, New York, G. P. Putnam's Sons, 1942. Intimate, anecdotal account by the Court's long-time official reporter.

Cahn, Edmond, ed., *Supreme Court and Supreme Law*, Bloomington, Ind., Indiana University Press, 1954. A symposium.

* I express my appreciation to my son, Alan, for his assistance in the preparation of this bibliography.

Carr, Robert K., *The Supreme Court and Judicial Review,* New York, Holt, Rinehart & Winston, Inc., 1942.

Carson, Hampton L., *The Supreme Court of the United States: Its History,* Philadelphia, John Y. Huber Company, 1891. Published in commemoration of the Centennial Anniversary of the establishment of the Supreme Court.

Clayton, James E., *The Making of Justice: The Supreme Court in Action,* New York, E. P. Dutton & Co., 1964. A non-technical account of the 1962 term of the Supreme Court.

Corwin, Edward S., *Court Over Constitution,* Princeton, Princeton University Press, 1928.

———, *John Marshall and the Constitution,* New Haven, Yale University Press, 1921. The contributions of "the greatest of the chief Justices."

Countryman, Vern, ed., *Douglas of the Supreme Court,* Garden City, N.Y., Doubleday & Company, 1959. Selection of opinions with a biographical sketch.

Craigmyle, Lord, *John Marshall in Diplomacy and Law,* New York, Charles Scribner's Sons, 1933. Englishman's highly laudatory portrait. ("Marshall's . . . constitutional judgments . . . saved the very existence of the United States")

Curtis, Charles P., Jr., *Lions Under the Throne,* Boston, Houghton, Mifflin Company, 1947. The political role of the Supreme Court.

Danelski, David J., *A Supreme Court Justice Is Appointed,* New York, Random House, Inc., 1964. How Pierce Butler was selected and confirmed. Excellent for its insight into what goes into choosing a Supreme Court Justice.

Dictionary of American Biography, 20 volumes, New York, 1928-1936. Invaluable for the lesser known Justices.

Dilliard, Irving, ed., *One Man's Stand for Freedom,* New York, Alfred A. Knopf, Inc., 1963. A collection of Justice Black's major constitutional liberties opinions, with an introductory biographical chapter.

Dunham, Allison, and Kurland, Philip B., eds., *Mr. Justice,* Chicago, University of Chicago Press, 1964. Biographical essays on eleven Justices, written by different scholars.

Ewing, Cortez A. M., *The Judges of the Supreme Court, 1789-1937,* Minneapolis, University of Minnesota Press, 1938.

Fairman, Charles, *Mr. Justice Miller and the Supreme Court, 1862-1890,* Cambridge, Harvard University Press, 1939. Biography centers on his Court career.

———, "What Makes a Great Justice?" (Bradley) In *Gasper G. Bacon Lectures on the Constitution of the United States,* Boston, Boston University Press, 1953.

Flanders, Henry, *Lives and Times of the Chief Justices of the Supreme Court of the United States,* Philadelphia, Lippincott, Grambo & Co., 1855-58 (2 volumes), Jay, Rutledge in 1st series. Cushing, Ellsworth, Marshall in 2nd. Old, but still useful.

Frank, John P., *Marble Palace,* New York, Alfred A. Knopf, Inc., 1958. A nontechnical explanation of the Court and its operations.

———, *Mr. Justice Black,* New York, Alfred A. Knopf, Inc., 1949. By a former law clerk of Justice Black.

Frank, John P., and Karsh, Yousuf, *The Warren Court,* New York, The Macmillan Company, 1964. Biographical sketches of the members of the Warren Court.

Frankfurter, Felix, ed., *Mr. Justice Brandeis,* New Haven, Yale University Press, 1932. Essays on Brandeis by Hughes, Lerner, Frankfurter and others.

———, ed., *Mr. Justice Holmes,* New York, Coward-McCann, Inc., 1931. Essays about Holmes written between 1916 and 1931 by Cardozo, Dewey, Hand, Laski, Lippmann and others.

———, *Mr. Justice Holmes and the Supreme Court,* Cambridge, Harvard University Press, 1938. Three lectures on Holmes' thought. Reissued in 1961 with Frankfurter's article from the *Dictionary of American Biography.*

———, *Of Law and Men,* New York, Harcourt, Brace & World, 1956. A collection of the Justice's papers and addresses.

Frankfurter, Felix and Landis, James, *The Business of the Supreme Court,* New York, The Macmillan Company, 1927.

Freund, Paul, *On Understanding the Supreme Court,* Boston, Little, Brown and Company, 1949. Contents incorporated into *The Supreme Court of the United States.*

Freund, Paul, *The Supreme Court of the United States, Its Business, Purposes and Performance,* Cleveland, World Publishing Co., 1961. By the nation's most respected constitutional law teacher.

Garraty, John A., *Quarrels That Have Shaped the Constitution,* New York, Harper & Row, Publishers, 1962. Non-technical accounts of sixteen major cases, from *Marbury* v. *Madison* to the School Segregation Case.

Gerhart, Eugene C., *America's Advocate,* Indianapolis, Bobbs-Merrill Co., 1958. Biography of Robert Jackson.

Gordon, Rosalie, *Nine Men Against America,* New York, Devon-Adair Co., 1958. A right-wing polemic against the Court.

Hagemann, Gerard, *Man on the Bench,* Notre Dame, Ind., Dujarie Press, 1962. Biography of Chief Justice White.

Haines, Charles G., *The American Doctrine of Judicial Review,* Berkeley, California, University of California Press, 1932.

———, *The Role of the Supreme Court in American Government and Politics, 1789-1835,* Berkeley and Los Angeles, University of California Press, 1944. First of projected two-volume work completed by Haines' student Sherwood Foster.

Haines, Charles G., and Foster, Sherwood, *The Role of the Supreme Court in American Government and Politics, 1835-1864,* Berkeley and Los Angeles, California, University of California Press, 1957. An account of the Taney Court and its consolidation of Federal judicial power.

Harris, Robert J., *Judicial Power of the United States,* Baton Rouge, Louisiana, Louisiana State University Press, 1940.

Hellman, George S., *Benjamin N. Cardozo,* New York, McGraw-Hill Book Company, 1940. Popularly written.

Hendel, Samuel, *Charles Evans Hughes and the Supreme Court,* New York, King's Crown Press, 1951. A short, critical biography.

Howe, Mark De Wolfe, *Justice Oliver Wendell Holmes,* Cambridge, Mass., Harvard University Press, 1957, 1963. Only two volumes of this authoritative and comprehensive biography by Holmes' law clerk have as yet been published, covering only the period up to 1882.

Hughes, Charles Evans, *The Supreme Court of the United States*, Garden City, N.Y., Garden City Publishing Co., 1928. Though written almost forty years ago, this still remains the classic short introduction to the Court.

Jackson, Robert H., *The Struggle for Judicial Supremacy*, New York, Alfred A. Knopf, Inc., 1941. Apologia for the Court Reform struggle.

———, *The Supreme Court in the American System of Government*, Cambridge, Mass., Harvard University Press, 1955. Three undelivered lectures published posthumously.

Jacobs, Clyde, *Justice Frankfurter and Civil Liberties*, Berkeley and Los Angeles, University of California Press, 1961.

King, Willard L., *Melville Weston Fuller*, New York, The Macmillan Company, 1950. Objective, well written.

———, *Lincoln's Manager*, Cambridge, Harvard University Press, 1960. Biography of David Davis.

Klinkhamer, Marie C., *Edward Douglas White*, Washington, D. C., Catholic University of America Press, 1943.

Konefsky, Samuel J., *Chief Justice Stone and the Supreme Court*, New York, The Macmillan Company, 1945. Stone's contributions to various phases of constitutional law.

———, *The Legacy of Holmes and Brandeis*, New York, Collier Books, 1961. Their influence on American democracy.

Lawrence, David, *Nine Honest Men*, New York, D. Appleton-Century, 1936. A conservative's defense of the pre-1937 Court.

Lerner, Max, *The Mind and Faith of Mr. Justice Holmes*, Garden City, N.Y., Halcyon House, 1948. Highly laudatory, perhaps uncritically so.

Lewis, Anthony, *Gideon's Trumpet*, New York, Random House, Inc., 1964. Dramatic story of a landmark case on right to counsel, by the nation's leading reporter on Supreme Court actions.

Lief, Alfred, *The Social and Economic Views of Mr. Justice Brandeis*, New York, Vanguard Press, 1930. Includes, in abridged form, the prototype "Brandeis Brief" submitted in *Muller* v. *Oregon*.

McCloskey, Robert J., *The American Supreme Court*, Chicago, University of Chicago Press, 1960. Interpretive account of judicial review.

McCune, Wesley, *Nine Young Men*, New York, Harper & Row, Publishers, 1947. Popular account of the Supreme Court 1937-1948 with sketches of Justices.

Magrath, C. Peter, *Morrison R. Waite*, New York, The Macmillan Company, 1963.

Mason, Alpheus Thomas, *Brandeis: A Free Man's Life*, New York, Viking Press, 1946. Only 70 of the 713 pages of this biography deal with Brandeis as Supreme Court Justice.

———, *Harlan Fiske Stone*, New York, Viking Press, 1956. Comprehensive, authorized, yet objective. Most of this large book is devoted to Stone's career in the Court.

———, *The Supreme Court from Taft to Warren*, Baton Rouge, Louisiana, Louisiana State University Press, 1958. Purpose is to "dispel superstition and promote understanding of the judicial function in American politics."

Mason, Alpheus T., and Beaney, William M., *The Supreme Court in a Free Society*, Englewood Cliffs, N.J., Prentice-Hall, Inc., 1959. Analytical and theoretical.

Mendelson, Wallace, *Capitalism, Democracy and the Supreme Court*, New York, Appleton-Century-Crofts, 1960.

Mendelson, Wallace, ed., *Felix Frankfurter: A Tribute*, New York, Reynal & Company, Inc., 1964. Essays by various contributors on the Justice's influence upon his generation.

———, *Justices Black and Frankfurter: Conflict in the Court*, Chicago, University of Chicago Press, 1961. Judicial activism vs. judicial restraint.

Monaghan, Frank, *John Jay*, New York, The Bobbs-Merrill Co., Inc., 1935.

Morgan, Donald G., *Justice William Johnson: The First Dissenter*, Columbia, S.C., University of South Carolina Press, 1954.

Murphy, Walter F., *Congress and the Court*, Chicago, University of Chicago Press, 1962.

Myers, Gustavus, *History of the Supreme Court of the United States*, Chicago, Charles H. Kerr & Co., 1918. A Marxist "debunking" history. Important, but must be read with caution because of many inaccuracies.

Oster, John E., *Political and Economic Doctrines of John Marshall*, New York, Neale Publishing Co., 1914. Collection of letters and speeches.

Palmer, Benjamin W., *Marshall and Taney*, Minneapolis, University of Minnesota Press, 1939.

Paschal, Joel F., *Mr. Justice Sutherland*, Princeton, Princeton University Press, 1951.

Pfeffer, Leo, *The Liberties of an American: The Supreme Court Speaks*, Boston, Beacon Press, 1963.

Phillips, Harlan B., *Felix Frankfurter Reminisces*, New York, Reynal & Company, Inc., 1960. Based on tape recordings.

Pollard, Joseph, *Mr. Justice Cardozo*, New York, Yorktown Press, 1935.

Pringle, Henry F., *Life and Times of William Howard Taft*, New York, Farrar & Rinehart, Inc., 1939. Standard two-volume biography.

Pritchett, C. Herman, *Civil Liberties and the Vinson Court*, Chicago, University of Chicago Press, 1954. Written contemporaneously, the author expected more of the Court than he had a right to.

———, *Congress versus the Supreme Court, 1957-1960*, Minneapolis, University of Minnesota Press, 1961.

———, *The Roosevelt Court*, New York, The Macmillan Company, 1948. An approving liberal's account.

Pritchett, C. Herman, and Westin, Alan F., eds., *The Third Branch of Government*, New York, Harcourt, Brace & World, 1963. Editors discuss Supreme Court since 1937 and then examine eight contemporary cases in depth.

Pusey, Merlo J., *Charles Evans Hughes*, New York, The Macmillan Company, 1961. Two-volume, Pulitzer Prize-winning, authorized, highly laudatory biography by journalist.

Rodell, Fred, *Nine Men*, New York, Random House, Inc., 1955. A highly critical political history of the Court.

Romaswamy, M., *Creative Role of the Supreme Court of the United States*, Stanford, Stanford University Press, 1956.

Schmidhauser, John R., *The Supreme Court as Final Arbiter in Federal-State Relations, 1789-1857*, Chapel Hill, N.C., University of North Carolina Press, 1958. Justifies Supreme Court's role as intended by Constitution's framers.

Schwartz, Bernard, *The Supreme Court: Constitutional Revolution in Retrospect*, New York, The Ronald Press Company, 1957. An analysis of 1937 revolution in the Supreme Court's jurisprudence.

Schwarz, Mortimer A., and Hogan, John C., eds., *Joseph Story*, New York, Oceana Publications, 1959. Selection of prose and poems.

Smith, Charles P., *James Wilson*, Chapel Hill, N.C., University of North Carolina Press, 1956.

Stone, Irving, *Earl Warren*, New York, Prentice-Hall, Inc., 1948. Campaign biography for 1948 election.

Story, William W., ed., *Life and Letters of Joseph Story*, Boston, C. C. Little and J. Brown, 1851. 2 volumes.

Surrency, Edwin C., ed., *A Marshall Reader*, New York, Oceana Publications, 1955. Essays on Marshall with a few selections of his own.

Swisher, Carl B., *Stephen J. Field: Craftsman of the Law*, Washington, Brookings Institute, 1930.

———, *The Supreme Court in Modern Role*, New York, New York University Press, 1958. Six analytical lectures by a political scientist.

———, *Roger B. Taney*, New York, The Macmillan Company, 1936. The standard biography.

Todd, A. L., *Justice on Trial*, New York, McGraw-Hill Book Company, 1964. Account of the struggle to confirm Brandeis.

Tompkins, Dorothy, *The Supreme Court of the United States: A Bibliography*, Berkeley, California, University of California Press, 1959. A recent comprehensive bibliography.

Tresolini, Rocco J., *Justice and the Supreme Court*, Philadelphia, J. B. Lippincott Co., 1963. A non-technical account of eight civil liberties decisions.

Warden, Robert B., *Salmon Portland Chase*, Cincinnati, Wilstach, Baldwin & Co., 1874.

Warren, Charles, *The Supreme Court in United States History*, Boston, Little, Brown & Company, 1922. Except for a meager single chapter on the administrations of Fuller and White up to 1918, this three-volume work ends for all practical purposes in 1888. For the century of the Court's life it does cover, it remains the classic history from which all students of the Court start. Undoubtedly the most important single work on the Supreme Court, though written from a strongly Federalist point of view.

Westin, Alan F., *The Anatomy of a Constitutional Law Case*, New York, The Macmillan Company, 1958. An account of the Steel Seizure Case (*Youngstown Sheet and Tube Co.* v. *Sawyer*).

———, *An Autobiography of the Supreme Court*, New York, The Macmillan Company, 1963.

———, ed., *The Supreme Court: Views from Inside*, New York, W. W. Norton & Co., 1961. Selected views of Supreme Court Justices on the Court and its operations.

Williams, Charlotte, *Hugo L. Black: A Study in the Judicial Process*, Baltimore, Johns Hopkins Press, 1950.

Umbreit, Kenneth B., *Our Eleven Chief Justices: A History of the Supreme Court in Terms of Their Personalities*, New York, Harper & Row, Publishers, 1940.

Index of Cases Cited

Index